Pentecostalism, Catholicism, and the Spirit in the World

STUDIES IN WORLD CATHOLICISM

Michael L. Budde and William T. Cavanaugh, *Series Editors*

Karen M. Kraft, *Managing Editor*

Other Titles in This Series

Beyond the Borders of Baptism: Catholicity, Allegiances, and Lived Identities. Edited by Michael L. Budde. Vol. 1, 2016. ISBN 9781498204736.

New World Pope: Pope Francis and the Future of the Church. Edited by Michael L. Budde. Vol. 2, 2017. ISBN 9781498283717.

Scattered and Gathered: Catholics in Diaspora. Edited by Michael L. Budde. Vol. 3, 2017. ISBN 9781532607097.

Fragile World: Ecology and the Church. Edited by William T. Cavanaugh. Vol. 4, 2018. ISBN 9781498283403.

A Living Tradition: The Holy See, Catholic Social Doctrine, and Global Politics 1965–2000. By A. Alexander Stummvoll. Vol. 5, 2018. ISBN 9781532605116.

Love, Joy, and Sex: African Conversation on Pope Francis's Amoris Laetitia and the Gospel of Family in a Divided World. Edited by Stan Chu Ilo. Vol. 6, 2019. ISBN 9781532618956.

The Church and Indigenous Peoples in the Americas: In Between Reconciliation and Decolonization. Edited by Michel Andraos. Vol. 7, 2019. ISBN 9781532631115.

Pentecostalism, Catholicism, and the Spirit in the World

EDITED BY
Stan Chu Ilo

CONTRIBUTORS

Candy Gunther Brown
Simon Chan
Marcelo Ayres Camurça
Zorodzai Dube
Paul Gifford
Simon C. Kim
Ben-Willie Kwaku Golo
Ludovic Lado, SJ

Laurenti Magesa
Clement Majawa
Cecília L. Mariz
Philomena Njeri Mwaura
Terry Rey
Cecil M. Robeck Jr.
Jakob Egeris Thorsen

CASCADE Books • Eugene, Oregon

PENTECOSTALISM, CATHOLICISM, AND THE SPIRIT IN THE WORLD

Studies in World Catholicism 8

Copyright © 2019 Wipf and Stock Publishers. All rights reserved. Except for brief quotations in critical publications or reviews, no part of this book may be reproduced in any manner without prior written permission from the publisher. Write: Permissions, Wipf and Stock Publishers, 199 W. 8th Ave., Suite 3, Eugene, OR 97401.

Cascade Books
An Imprint of Wipf and Stock Publishers
199 W. 8th Ave., Suite 3
Eugene, OR 97401

www.wipfandstock.com

PAPERBACK ISBN: 978-1-5326-5035-2
HARDCOVER ISBN: 978-1-5326-5036-9
EBOOK ISBN: 978-1-5326-5037-6

Cataloguing-in-Publication data:

Names: Ilo, Stan Chu, editor.

Title: Pentecostalism, Catholicism, and the Spirit in the World / edited by Stan Chu Ilo.

Description: Eugene, OR : Cascade Books, 2019. | Series: Studies in World Catholicism 8. | Includes bibliographical references and index.

Identifiers: ISBN 978-1-5326-5035-2 (paperback) | ISBN 978-1-5326-5036-9 (hardcover) | ISBN 978-1-5326-5037-6 (ebook)

Subjects: LCSH: Catholic Church—Relations—Pentecostal churches. | Catholic Church—Doctrines. | Pentecostal churches—Relations—Catholic Church. | Pentecostal churches—Doctrines.

Classification: BX8764.2 .P45 2019 (print) | BX8764.2 .P45 (ebook)

Scripture quotations marked (NIV) are from the Holy Bible, New International Version®, NIV®. Copyright © 1973, 1978, 1984, 2011 by Biblica, Inc.™ Used by permission of Zondervan. All rights reserved worldwide. www.zondervan.com The "NIV" and "New International Version" are trademarks registered in the United States Patent and Trademark Office by Biblica, Inc.™

Scripture quotations marked (NKJV) are taken from the New King James Version®. Copyright © 1982 by Thomas Nelson. Used by permission. All rights reserved.

Manufactured in the U.S.A.   10/15/19

Contents

Contributors | ix

Introduction by Stan Chu Ilo | 1

PART ONE: Theologies of the Holy Spirit

1: A Pneumatological Crossroad: Cultural Imaging of the Holy Spirit in Need of a Christological Counterpart | 17
SIMON C. KIM

2: Lived Pneumatology and Ecclesiology among Charismatic Catholics in Latin America | 31
JAKOB EGERIS THORSEN

3: The Contribution of Pentecostalism to the International Community: Opportunities for Socioreligious Transformation in Africa and Beyond | 55
CLEMENT MAJAWA

PART TWO: Spiritual Warfare and Healing

4: Spiritual Warfare and Healing in Kenyan Neo-Pentecostalism | 81
PHILOMENA NJERI MWAURA

5: Locating Exorcisms and Faith Healing in African Pentecostalism within Constructive Postmodernity | 99
ZORODZAI DUBE

6: Francis MacNutt and the Globalization of Charismatic Healing and Deliverance | 115
CANDY GUNTHER BROWN

PART THREE: Relationships between Catholics and Protestant Pentecostals

7: Catholic–Pentecostal Relations in Asia: Conflict and Cooperation | 137
SIMON CHAN

8: "Do Not Quench the Spirit": Some Thoughts on the International Roman Catholic–Pentecostal Dialogue | 153
CECIL M. ROBECK JR.

9: Perceptions of the Holy Spirit in the African Initiated Churches: Lessons for Christianity in Africa | 176
LAURENTI MAGESA

10: The Catholic Charismatic Renewal as Ecumenical and Intercultural Experiment in Africa | 192
LUDOVIC LADO, SJ

11: The Spirit in Africa | 211
PAUL GIFFORD

PART FOUR: Prosperity and Poverty

12: Poverty and Prosperity: Comparing Pentecostal Protestant and Charismatic Catholic Groups' Values and Attitudes in Brazil | 231
CECÍLIA L. MARIZ

13: The Prosperity Theology of Africa's Neo-Pentecostals: Socioeconomically Transforming or in Need of Transformation? | 247
BEN-WILLIE KWAKU GOLO

PART FIVE: Politics and Modernity

14: The Brazilian Catholic Charismatic Renewal: A Spiritual Style Between Tradition and Modernity | 271
MARCELO AYRES CAMURÇA

15: Fear and Trembling in Haiti: A Charismatic Catholic Prophecy of the 2010 Earthquake | 280
TERRY REY

Index | 301

Contributors

Candy Gunther Brown is a professor in the Department of Religious Studies at Indiana University Bloomington. A historian and ethnographer, she received her doctorate from Harvard University and is the author of numerous journal articles and book chapters, as well as several books such as *The Healing Gods: Complementary and Alternative Medicine in Christian America* (Oxford University Press, 2013) and *Testing Prayer: Science and Healing* (Harvard University Press, 2012).

Simon Chan is a retired and re-engaged part-time faculty member at Trinity Theological College (Singapore), where he previously served as the Earnest Lau Professor of Systematic Theology. He holds a PhD from the University of Cambridge. He has published a great variety of journal articles and book chapters, and his books include *Pentecostal Ecclesiology: An Essay on the Development of Doctrine* (Deo, 2011) and *Liturgical Theology: The Church as Worshipping Community* (InterVarsity, 2006).

Marcelo Ayres Camurça is a retired full professor, now serving as a guest professor in the Department of Religious Studies at the Federal University of Juiz de Fora in Minas Gerais, Brazil. He holds a PhD in social anthropology from the National Museum of Anthropology at the Federal University of Rio de Janeiro. The author of numerous journal articles and book chapters, he has also coauthored the book *Ser Jovem em Minas Gerais: Religião, Cultura, e Politica* (Argumentum, 2009).

Zorodzai Dube is a senior lecturer in New Testament Studies at the University of Pretoria in South Africa and received his PhD in New Testament Studies at the University of Oslo (Norway). His publications include variety of book chapters and journal articles; he is also the author of *Storytelling in*

Times of Violence: Hearing the Exorcism Stories in Zimbabwe and in Mark's Community (Scholars, 2013) and a contributor to *The Bible and Sociological Contours: Some African Perspectives* (Peter Lang, 2018).

Paul Gifford is professor emeritus in the Department of Religions and Philosophies at the University of London's School of Oriental and African Studies (SOAS), where he has taught since 1992. He holds an MLitt from the University of Oxford and has a diversity of publications to his name. Among his major works are *Christianity, Development, and Modernity in Africa* (Hurst, 2015); *Christianity, Politics, and Public Life in Kenya* (Hurst, 2009); and *Ghana's New Christianity: Pentecostalism in a Globalizing African Economy* (Hurst, 2004).

Simon C. Kim served as the first director of Intercultural Initiatives at Santa Clara University's Jesuit School of Theology. A Catholic priest of the Diocese of Orange, California, he holds a PhD in systematic and historical theology from The Catholic University of America. His publications include *A World Church in our Backyard: How the Spirit Moved Church and Society* (Liturgical, 2016) and *Embracing Our Inheritance: Jubilee Reflections on Korean American Catholics (1966–2016)* (Pickwick, 2016).

Ben-Willie Kwaku Golo is a senior lecturer in the Department for the Study of Religions at the University of Ghana in Legon. He received a PhD in eco-theological ethics from the Norwegian University of Science and Technology; his publications include the journal articles, "In Search of a Sustainable Society in Africa" in *Philosophia Reformata*, and "The Groaning Earth and the Greening of Neo-Pentecostalism in Twenty-First Century Ghana," in *PentecoStudies*.

Ludovic Lado, SJ, is director of the Centre for Studies and Training for Development (CEFOD) in N'Djamena, Chad. A Catholic Jesuit priest, he received his doctorate in social anthropology from the University of Oxford. His publications include *Catholic Pentecostalism and the Paradoxes of Africanization* (Brill, 2009); *Le Pluralisme Religieux en Afrique* (PUCAC, 2015); and *Towards an Anthropology of Catholicism in Africa* (forthcoming).

Laurenti Magesa is a priest of the Catholic Diocese of Musoma in Tanzania, a lecturer in theology at Hekima University College in Nairobi, and a groundbreaking scholar whose work has reshaped the study of Catholicism in Africa. He is the author of over one hundred academic articles and nine books, including *African Religion: The Moral Traditions of an Abundant Life*, considered a landmark text in the field. He holds a PhD from the University of Ottawa (Canada) and a doctorate in sacred theology (STD) from St. Paul University, also in Ottawa. He is a founding member of the Ecumenical Symposium of East Africa Theologians (ESEAT).

Clement Majawa is director of the School of Graduate Studies as well as an associate professor of theology at the Catholic University of Eastern Africa (CUEA) in Nairobi. A priest of the Archdiocese of Blantyre (Malawi), he holds a PhD in dogmatic theology from the Pontifical Urbaniana University (Rome). In addition to numerous book chapters and journal articles, he is also the author of many books including *Patristic Education* (AIC Kijabe, 2014) and *The Holy Spirit and Charismatic Renewal in Africa and Beyond* (AIC Kijabe, 2007).

Cecília L. Mariz is associate professor of sociology in the Institute for Social Sciences at Rio de Janeiro State University (Brazil), where she has taught since 1995. She received her doctorate in sociology from Boston University (Boston, MA) and conducted postdoctoral work at the School for Advanced Studies in the Social Sciences (Paris). Her publications include many journal articles as well as the book, *Coping with Poverty; Pentecostal and Base Communities in Brazil* (Temple University Press, 1994).

Philomena Njeri Mwaura is an associate professor in the Department of Philosophy and Religious Studies at Kenyatta University in Nairobi, Kenya. She holds a doctorate in religious studies from Kenyatta University, and her publications include the coauthored volumes, *Patterns of Urban Christianity in East Africa* (Acton, 2016), and *HIV/AIDS, Women, and Religion in Africa: Ethical and Theological Response* (Cluster, 2008).

Terry Rey is chair of and an associate professor in the Department of Religion at Temple University (Philadelphia, PA), where he also teaches in the Global Studies Program; previously, he taught the sociology of religions at the University of Haiti in Port-au-Prince. Recent publications include *The Priest and the Prophetess: Abbé Ouvière, Romaine Rivière, and the Revolutionary Atlantic World* (Oxford University Press, 2017) and *Crossing the Water and Keeping the Faith: Haitian Religion in Miami* (New York University Press, 2013).

Cecil M. Robeck Jr. is senior professor of church history and ecumenics, as well as special assistant to the president for ecumenical relations, at Fuller Seminary (Pasadena, CA), where he also received his MDiv and PhD. Since 1985, he has worked with the Vatican and since 1992, served as co-chair of the International Catholic-Pentecostal Dialogue. He also co-chairs the International World Communion of Reformed Churches-Pentecostal Dialogue and works with numerous other ecumenical groups. A prolific author of scholarly articles, he is also the editor and co-editor of several books, as well as the author of *The Asuza Street Mission and Revival: The Birth of the Global Pentecost Movement* (Thomas Nelson, 2006).

Jakob Egeris Thorsen is associate professor of church history and practical theology in the School of Culture and Society at Aarhus University (Copenhagen), where he earned his PhD. His publications include various articles and anthology chapters, as well as a book based on his fieldwork in Latin America: *Charismatic Practice and Catholic Parish Life: The Incipient Pentecostalization of the Church in Guatemala and Latin America* (Brill, 2015). Additionally, he serves on various commissions in the Catholic Diocese of Copenhagen.

Introduction: What We Have Seen and Heard (1 John 1:3)

STAN CHU ILO

"The Catholic charismatic movement is one of the many fruits of the Second Vatican Council, which, like a new Pentecost, led to an extraordinary flourishing in the Church's life of groups and movements particularly sensitive to the action of the Spirit. How can we not give thanks for the precious spiritual fruits that the Renewal has produced in the life of the Church and in the lives of so many people? How many lay faithful—men, women, young people, adults, and elderly—have been able to experience in their own lives the amazing power of the Spirit and his gifts! How many people have rediscovered faith, the joy of prayer, the power and beauty of the Word of God, translating all this into generous service in the Church's mission! How many lives have been profoundly changed!"

—ST. POPE JOHN PAUL II

When Pope John XXIII prayed for a "new Pentecost" in the Church in preparation for the Second Vatican Council, it was an invitation to all Christians to embark on the path of renewal and reform. This renewal and reform, it was hoped, would have profound effects on the lives of Christians and their witnessing to the faith in the world. It was also expected to touch the entire life of the Church and her structures, pastoral life, liturgies, teachings, and social commitments. It was an invitation to a renewal in the spirit and a healthy dialogue and engagement with the world through reading the signs of the times and following the movement of the spirit in history. Vatican II and its subsequent and ongoing reception is still seen by many as the greatest gift of the Holy Spirit to modern Catholicism.

More than fifty years after this prayer was said, one can say that God has indeed listened to the prayers of God's people through the manifestation and renewed recognition and appropriation of the gifts of the Holy Spirit in the Roman Catholic Church. This is particularly evident in the birth and presence of the Catholic Charismatic Renewal movement as one of the gifts of the Church's openness to a new Pentecost since Vatican II. There are also many flourishing lay groups and sodalities in the Catholic Church which could be called new Spirit movements within the Catholic Church. They are all reviving the life of the church and her members especially in small communities and parish groups, in small Christian communities, among migrants and refugees, in prisons, and in slums in many big cities throughout the world. They provide, even in imperfect ways, new points of light from many marginal sites of human existence where faith in the shadows of life offers new hope and new grace.

When one looks at this irruption of the Spirit in the Catholic Church vis-à-vis what is happening in world Christianity today, one can say that Pentecostalism has become the new face of Christian expansion. There are certainly revival movements which make appeals to traditional Catholic spirituality—Eucharistic adoration, Marian devotions, cult of the saints as expressed through Toca de Assis in Brazil; however, all these forms of spirituality seem to coalesce in a unique way in the life of the Spirit. The momentum of Christian expansion in world Christianity today, especially in the global South, cannot be accounted for theologically without understanding the features of the Pentecostalizing thrust of evangelization and mission, as well as the new identities and faces that these new movements give to contemporary Christianity.

Indeed, the words of 1 John 1:3 about "what we have seen and heard" is, for me, a critical juncture in the narrative of the Christian mission in the world today. The Pentecostal story is not an add-on to the Christian mission, nor is it a new story in the history of the Church. The present shape and texture of Pentecostalism may carry within it the cultural currents of present history, but the continuing work of the Holy Spirit has been identified as central to the birth, life, and witness of the churches and her members from the early beginnings of the Christian movement. However, there are some questions that emerge in the present context of Christian mission: Are we as Christians, scholars, and leaders of God's people paying attention to what God is doing in our world and in our churches? Are we allowing ourselves to be led into deeper mysteries through a humble openness to learning from these stories of the spontaneous irruptions of the work of God in the Pentecostalizing of the Christian mission in every corner of the globe? Do we see ourselves in these stories as scholars and church leaders, since these stories are the warp and weft of the narrative identity of faith communities in our neighborhoods, parishes, and church traditions?

How can we account for what we have seen and heard in world Christianity today? My proposal is that, in the Christian academy, there is the need to develop new navigational tools for following these emerging Pentecostal and Charismatic stories. These tools can help scholars to understand the cultural and spiritual currents driving the Pentecostalizing momentum in today's Christianity. It will also offer some hermeneutical and historical tools which can help scholars to look at some of the commonalities and differences between these groups across different church traditions and across different cultural and regional groups. There is the need to dig deeper into these diverse stories, to understand and critically engage the stories emerging from the frontiers of faith driven by Pentecostal and Charismatic currents with a hermeneutic of humility, of hope, and an openness to following these narratives as pathways to finding the footprints of God in history. Particularly for the Catholic Church, openness is needed to stretch our gaze beyond our limited ecclesial horizon, to enable us to walk outside the road well-traveled and step into the arena of the Spirit with other churches. This, no doubt, would help the Roman Church to find, through these new movements, some helpful practices for ecumenical relations in the search for greater Christian unity through the Spirit who is the principle of unity (Eph 4:2–3).

The essays which we have assembled here represent the finest collection of the best scholars and leading practitioners in the Pentecostal and Charismatic movements from all four corners of the world. It is an ecumenical ensemble of scholars who, in their contributions, have brought together diverse denominational perspectives and dialogue to understanding the present momentum of Pentecostal and Charismatic drive in the World Church. They demonstrate diverse methodologies which transverse the latest and emerging approaches to studying Pentecostal and Charismatic movements in world Christianity.

This volume is unique, because these contributors are not simply theorists. Rather, they are very active as leaders in their communities, and some have been involved in intercultural and interdenominational conversations and dialogue about the place and future of these movements in world Christianity. Their essays are not only descriptive but also illustrative, giving readers an adequate portrait of the range and depth of beliefs and practices of these movements as well as their appeal and legitimization through and outside of the traditional canons of Christian orthodoxy. These authors also move from illustration to giving explanatory account of these movements. They point the way forward for studying these movements and show some of the lessons learned not only for the academy but also for pastoral life, education, and social ministries in the World Church. In doing so, they show us new ways of understanding, interpreting, and judging the context of diverse Christian communities and how they construct ideas and practices for the future. The topics they address in this volume include questions of salvation and eschatology, health and healing, prosperity and poverty, suffering and death, fear and faith, despair and hope, as well as the conflict between charism and institution, and the tension between cultic clericalism and the affirmation and use of the gifts and talents of lay members of Christ's faithful in the Church.

The contributors here ask the following questions in different ways: How does one validate the kind of religious claims which Pentecostals and Charismatics make? How is this kind of Christian faith consistent with or different from contemporary and past Christian traditions that represent fidelity to the faith, beliefs, and practices which have defined the movement of the Church from the time of Jesus guided by the Holy Spirit? Some contributors point to the lack of form and firm structure in these movements—their ecclesial status—particularly for those communities of faith gathered around charismatic leaders and founders who claim a pneumatic vocation to form a church or ministry. Some, on the other hand, see these irruptions of new movements as expressing the emergence of an unrestricted experience of the Lordship of Christ and the power of the Holy Spirit.

What becomes obvious from this volume is that Pentecostal and Charismatic movements in the World Church are here to stay. They can no longer be simply dismissed as new Christian fads that are doling out Christian tranquilizers which have an expiration date. Indeed, these new movements are attempts on the part of many Christians to use the resources of the Christian heritage—especially biblical and cultural narratives—to address the challenging social context of suffering, poverty, political instability, disease, war, and death which have characterized the histories of many marginalized people in the world. In many cases, they are also some form of protest against a too-rigid and predictable clerical church where there is often no room for creativity and use of the gifts of the whole people of God. These groups, then, are developing new hermeneutics and exegesis which have never been applied elsewhere. They thus present, in many cases, new typologies of belief and practices which may not be properly and fully accounted for through theological traditions developed in the West. To borrow Zygmunt Bauman's characterization of contemporary societies, these groups, therefore, represent a "liquid modernity," because they are transgressing traditional norms and canons of faith while, at the same time, reinforcing the claims of traditional faith.[1] In doing this, they are retrieving old traditions in new ways, while reinventing Christianity as something that possesses a genuine newness which cannot be contained in one cultural or ecclesial vessel or fossilized in time. Pentecostalism, therefore, represents a unique version of modernity which cannot be simply identified with any particular contemporary dominant discourse. Rather, it presents us with a "liquid modernity" that cannot be housed in the ideological world of either the liberal or conservative wing of the traditional churches, because it exudes multiple shapes in its teaching and practices which lead to many directions. Thus, for many Pentecostals and Catholic Charismatics in Ghana, Brazil, the Philippines, or Ukraine, the Spirit may lead them in different directions, but there is a unity of gifts which, when used to serve God and society, all lead to a new reality and the realization of God's promises. This liquid modernity that is shaping a new culture within churches cannot be defined by Western epistemology but rather through narratives of dominion, conquest, victory, and restoration which Pentecostals and Catholic Charismatics hope will bring about a new heaven and a new earth.

Summaries of Chapters

The essays here are organized into four groups. The first section is on theologies of the Spirit where contributors explore particularly how to ground Pentecostalism through some theological foundations. In chapter 1, Simon Kim uses the christological and pneumatological images developed in the theology of the earlier councils as an exemplary portrait of how a theology of Charismatism can be born through an adequate Trinitarian and cultural foundation. As a result, he argues strongly for a theology of the Spirit which is deeply linked to cultural imaginings and representations not only of the Spirit but also of Christology. Drawing from the lived experience of Korean

---

1. Bauman, "Education in Liquid Modernity." Bauman defines liquid modernity as a social state "in which all social forms melt faster than new ones can be cast." According to Carlo Bordoni, through the term "liquid modernity," Bauman wants to depict our present society as one caught between shifting modern structures and the relativism of postmodernity, a society constantly in flux because of the limitless appetite for consumption rather than the stability of production. To put it as bluntly as Carlo Bordoni wrote in relation to Bauman, liquid modernity is similar to Gramsci's portrayal of the morbid symptoms of modern life and the interregnum experienced in social change, where the old is not yet dead and the new is not yet born. This tension is what I find in present-day Pentecostalism and Charismatism: they are neither old nor new; they reflect old patterns yet they exude a breathtaking newness which often defies characterization. See also Bauman, *Chronicle of Crisis*, ix.

Catholics exemplified in the *yeondo*, forty-nine days of prayer for the dead, he shows the limit of folk and Charismatic spiritualities when they fail to develop a christological counterpart. This challenge is clearly manifest in the present spiritual experience of Korean-American migrants in the US whose spirituality and wholehearted embrace of the movement of the Spirit often face the limitations of incompletion without adequate christological cultural imaginations. Simon Kim shows the need for a more holistic and integrated, lived faith in the Charismatic groups, a faith that is grounded in an adequate Trinitarian theology and mediated through cultural images and symbols from the everyday experiences of people.

Like Simon Kim's essay, Jakob Egeris Thorsen's lifetime research and fieldwork on Latin American Catholic Charismatic Renewal (CCR) pays special attention to "lived pneumatology" with stories of actual faith of Catholic Charismatics in Guatemala. In his chapter, Thorsen shows that the activities and ministries of CCR members have become very significant on the new Latin American map of Catholicism and Christianity in general. While these groups have made possible the unhinging of institutional control over the charismata, helped the baptismal priesthood to flower, and contributed to developing new tools for the New Evangelization in Latin America, there are some fundamental challenges which need to be addressed both pastorally and theologically. One such challenge is that of parallel ecclesiologies between the institutional church and the charismatic groups which sometimes have led to division and schism. Other challenges include the polarization and pluralization of religious practices in the Church which may give the impression of superior and inferior spiritual traditions in the Church and the failure to fully integrate CCR practices into both the liturgical life of the Church and her social mission.

Clement Majawa, in his essay, looks at Pentecostalism's possible contributions to the transformation of human values and social justice. Majawa develops the African concept of *Ubuntu* which highlights the interconnectedness of all things and all humans in promoting the conditions for human and cosmic flourishing. He uses this concept to develop a road map for local and global transformation through global Pentecostalism. He sees the global nature of Pentecostalism as a sign of the positive values that can bring about a world where there is love, peace, and transformation. This can happen, he hopes, when people pay more attention to the movement of the Spirit in history and the Ubuntu spirit, which he identifies as the pulsating motion that moves the world to greater convergence around the practices and priorities of Jesus of Nazareth.

The volume's second section explores the theme of spiritual warfare and healing which is very prominent in Pentecostal and Charismatic groups.

Philomena Mwaura begins this section with an exceptional essay that brings together her research in psychology, theology, missiology, and cultural studies to help us understand spiritual warfare and healing in East Africa. Her essay asks the following questions: How do Pentecostals understand healing, deliverance, and spiritual warfare? What mechanisms do they employ to mediate healing? What is the meaning of healing, deliverance, and spiritual warfare in the self-understanding of the individual and churches? Concentrating on selected neo-Pentecostal churches in Kenya, Mwaura shows that, in many instances, these groups help people make sense of their condition through faith healing and bring greater integration to the community, restoring relationships with God, self, community, and nature. She warns, however, of the danger of over-spiritualization, amidst some other excesses which could arise where forms of healing, deliverance, and spiritual warfare are promoted that exploit people's vulnerability.

In his chapter, Zorodzai Dube asks a fundamental question: Besides providing coded protest language, how does African Pentecostalism mediate alternative survival strategies, ethical instructions as a strategy for good citizenship, and a personal sense of agency? Dube locates African Pentecostalism's exorcisms and faith healing within constructive postmodernism, which traces the creativity of postmodernity subjects dealing with oppressive local and global structures. He argues that these movements do not operate in a vacuum. Rather, they are responses to multiple issues, particularly within postcolonial African states. Using Zimbabwe as a good example of a postcolonial state that gradually slipped from economic glory into political and economic chaos, Dube shows that the nature of Pentecostal movements in such a country bears the marks of the socioeconomic and political miasma that plague the people of God.

In the next chapter, Candy Gunther Brown examines Francis MacNutt's impact on universalizing healing ministries in both Pentecostal Protestant groups as well as Catholic Charismatic groups. She shows how MacNutt, in his global healing ministries, brought together different biblical, pastoral, and missiological dimensions of healing as integral to the work of evangelization. She also demonstrates how healing ministries take on the shape and context of diverse human experiences as the faith crosses different cultural and spiritual frontiers. Through the pioneering work of Francis MacNutt, Brown explains how aspects of healing and deliverance, spiritual warfare, and social justice all overlap in the Pentecostal experience and how the common spiritual quest and hunger of all people are being met through the globalization of Pentecostalism and Catholic Charismatic movements beyond any denominational claims or institutional priority.

The third section of the volume looks at the complex but hopeful relations between the Catholic Church and Protestant Pentecostals. Simon Chan begins this section with a descriptive and hopeful analysis of the different ways in which Catholics and Pentecostals in Asia could develop strong ecumenical relationships. The strength of his essay is the historical range of his analysis of the diversity and features of the movement of the Spirit in the Asian church today from Manila to Singapore, and from Seoul to Malaysia. He lays out the limitations of the partnership but points at some positive developments in terms of the shared concerns and advocacy of all Christian groups in Asia for some visibility on a continent where Christianity is a minority religion. Whereas the Catholic Church's focus in Asia has been on dialogue with religions, cultures, and the poor, Chan shows that the positive grassroots relations among the churches should serve as a guide and inspiration to institutionalize these efforts in order to remove the obstacles to ecumenical relations.

In his contribution to this volume, Cecil M. Robeck Jr. takes the reader on a historical, theological, and missional journey of the six rounds of the International Roman Catholic-Pentecostal Dialogue. He illustrates how greater understanding of key divisive issues—in doctrine, charism, liturgical practice, spirituality, authority, and the use of the gifts between Catholics and Pentecostals—have continued to improve through dialogue and closer encounters. He explains that there are extensive theological and missiological studies on all dimensions of this dialogue and from different regions of the world, all of which help make clear the horizons of differences but also the points of convergence in Catholic-Pentecostal relations. As one who not only studies these relations as a theologian but is also a key player at the highest level of institutional discussion, practice, and advocacy, Robeck's voice is an optimistic one.

Laurenti Magesa takes up this discussion through an in-depth study of the African Initiatives in Christianity (AICs). He demonstrates how these groups mine the depths of African religio-cultural traditions and spirituality, especially ancestral worldviews and traditions. As he illustrates, mainline Christian traditions like the Catholic Church fail to understand and inculturate the rich African religious worldview, spirituality, and exuberant liturgies into their beliefs and practices as they cross different spiritual and cultural frontiers in Africa. Rather than dismiss the AICs and African spirit movements, Magesa proposes that the Catholic Church can learn from them, to help it to develop African contextual theologies, pastoral practices, and liturgies.

Ludovic Lado's chapter is based on his ethnographic study of fifteen Charismatic Renewal groups in Cameroon in Central Africa. He sees

Charismatic and Pentecostal movements in Africa as spaces for spiritual transits, as they straddle the multiple worlds of African traditional religious beliefs, worldviews, and practices, as well as Christian traditions in the instituted churches and modernity's cultural tensions and social changes. He explores the spiritual, structural, and social forces that are driving the momentum of Pentecostal and Charismatic movements in Africa. Contrary to many other voices in African theology, he concludes that the impact of Catholic Charismatic movements in the Catholic Church is waning. However, he proposes that these movements can offer the churches in Africa some loci for interreligious and intercultural experimentations. These movements are capable of bringing about greater integration of the faith and life of people in Africa; they can hopefully help to mine the riches of African spirituality without resulting in the kind of schism that was experienced in Zambia in the pioneering Charismatic ministry of Lusaka's former archbishop, Milingo.

Paul Gifford proposes moving toward functional reality and away from an enchanted religious imagination in Africa. Drawing on his ethnographic study and five years of living in Senegal, he describes the pervasiveness of enchantment in African religions and why it should be an important area of study for African theologians. It is significant that his data are drawn from Muslims, because it demonstrates how pervasive the narratives and counter narratives of spirit are in Africa and how they cut across Christian, Islamic, and traditional religions. Thus, they provide a valid and irreplaceable site for deeper understanding of the African map of the universe, beyond what is being done by African theologians of inculturation in the Catholic tradition. Gifford argues that theological engagement with this enchanted universe and other areas of study, especially development studies, will be helpful in transitioning Africa to modernity.

The volume's fourth section engages the voices of scholars who have researched the ways that Pentecostals construct narratives of prosperity and poverty, particularly the so-called "prosperity gospel." In her chapter, Cecília L. Mariz seeks to help us understand the Pentecostal Charismatic relationship to prosperity and poverty. She achieves this through an analysis of the attitudes and values of the Universal Church of the Kingdom of God (UCKG) and the Toca de Assis, each having emerged from the Pentecostal spirituality movement in very different but related contexts in Brazil. She argues that the predominant narrative—that Pentecostals and Charismatics are, for the most part, preachers of prosperity gospel—does not always apply to all groups within these movements. By comparing the social work programs of these two groups and a few others in Brazil, she helps us understand their inner logic and their dominion theologies vis-à-vis their commitment to an evangelical poverty and social justice. Besides illustrating the diversity among Pentecostal-Charismatics, Mariz's comparative analysis of these different groups reveals some shared similarities to conversion. It also reveals a shared spirituality, one that aims to follow Jesus Christ and, in some cases, models itself after the examples of saints like Francis of Assisi. It is obvious from her study that Pentecostal Charismatic spirituality recognizes that human beings can individually relate to God, and that through this relationship, they can be free of all social, natural, and supernatural forces that work against their movement toward God.

Using data mainly from Nigeria and his homeland of Ghana, Ben-Willie Kwaku Golo continues this discussion with a critical theological study of the logic and narratives of the prosperity gospel in Africa. While he admits the positive impact and the burgeoning number of neo-Pentecostals in Africa, he explores why and how the prosperity gospel that they preach fails to meet the challenges of socioeconomic transformation on the continent.

In his chapter, Marcelo Ayres Camurça asserts that the Catholic Charismatic Renewal in Brazil is an attempt to engage modernity with traditional Catholicism. In this regard, he proposes interpreting Pentecostalism, not as a distortion of beliefs and practices, but as an effort to renew and recover aspects of traditional Catholicism. One should see its inner logic, features, and practices within the bigger picture of the cultural and social changes Catholicism faces in the modern world. He argues that the shared spiritual spaces of Catholic Charismatics and Pentecostals have become sites of competition and contestation that require a deeper and more relevant theological account, beyond generalizations and dismissive institutional judgments.

Terry Rey, in his chapter, explores the tension in Haiti between different prophetic traditions with regard to the earthquake that occurred there in 2010. His is a breathtaking historical and theological account of Haiti's convoluted history. He describes how Haiti's persistent national tragedies, going back to the earthquake of 1842 and the political crisis, turned *Tilegliz* from a street protest and religious movement into a political force. All of these, he proposes, point to the convoluted and complex nature of religious narratives in modern Haiti. Using the ministry of Fr. Jules Campion as a test case, he raises important questions about how Pentecostals, Charismatics, and Evangelicals interpret misfortune, sin, the movement of history, and eschatology. He also raises important questions about multiple and opposing interpretations of traditional voodoo religious beliefs and practices vis-à-vis traditional Catholic beliefs and inculturation. What is obvious is that the suffering of Haitians and the post-earthquake recovery will require greater openness and engagement in dialogue between the different religious accounts that are contending for space in the country.

Rey shows the need for a critical reading of religious narratives to understand how they are helping or hurting the evolution toward a new and transformed Haitian society. The challenges Haiti faces are matters of life and death. Like people everywhere, especially those who have experienced cycles of tragedy and socioeconomic deprivation, Haitians long for a new heaven and a new earth, which they seek in their enthusiastic embrace of charismatic and Pentecostal Christianity.

Conclusion

What will Pentecostalism and Charismatism in the World Church look like in the future? Some advice from Pope Francis is germane for concluding this introductory essay. Francis calls on the Church today to adopt a pastoral discernment in embracing the broader context of people's lives and faith *through a culture of deep encounter*. I propose three such practices here.

First, the Church, through her ministers, must *enter into the depths and dumps with the people of God, especially those who suffer,* in order to be present to their pain and tears. This is the only way pastoral agents can come to understand that, sometimes, it may be a symbolic beast or demon that is "sucking the blood of people" when they claim that a witch is after them or that they need a voodoo priest to take away the power of Satan. Such a "beast" might present itself as poverty, failed religious or political leadership, deep emotional abuses and traumas, fears and worries, failed health care and social service systems, religious exploitation, and false religious narratives and interpretations that hunt people by day and torment them by night. Most of the time, through their way of life, message, and outreach, church leaders have promoted a version of the Christian message that enslaves rather than liberates God's people.

The liberative power of the gospel must be brought to bear on the actual faith and daily context of the people. However, it must begin with meeting people where they are, rather than projecting an idealized notion of faith and life that is removed from their lived faith experiences. In order to encounter God's people in these new sites of faith and life, church scholars and pastors must leave the protected precincts of their churches and cathedrals to meet God's people in the Payatas dump site of Quezon City, Philippines; the favelas of Brazil's Rio de Janeiro; the slums of Kenya's Kibera; and the many shrines and healing and herbal centers where they are searching for God and for help. Theological and pastoral reflection on Pentecostalism and Catholic Charismatic renewal movements will be richer and most helpful if it emerges from the dumps of history and many marginal sites—where God's people are acutely feeling the impact and pain of social, spiritual, economic, and political forces which, in a metaphoric sense, are "sucking their blood."

A second practice I propose is *to suspend quick, uninformed, and unscientific judgment* about Pentecostal and Charismatic healing and phenomena. In order to evaluate "what we have seen and heard," scholars and pastors must be prepared to suspend hasty judgments of realities that they do not fully understand or have not fully encountered. In many instances in my own work, I see these groups as having good intentions: to purify the Church and the world of evil; to harvest fully the powers and graces of God; and to unify the diverse and tensile points within their sociocultural, political, economic, and religious contexts. God's people are searching for integration and unity of experience so that they can make sense of life's challenges. However, pastors and theologians can only help them realize their desires for integration—symbolically indicated in prayers and preaching among these groups as the search for solutions to problems—through the right forms of worship and relationships with God, nature, and their fellow humans.

Pastors and theologians can achieve this by being with God's people and making a judgment, by being present with the people they serve through what Pope Francis calls "the art of accompaniment." In many dioceses and parishes, Charismatic groups are still seen as marginal or "strange" and are often left on their own without the guidance and presence of their pastors and religious educators. In some contexts, as shown by some of this volume's contributors, the Catholic clergy and hierarchy look down on Pentecostal ministers as some sort of lower-grade Christians—because in many cases, they have less education than the Catholic clergy—and will not associate with them.

The same abandonment is experienced by migrants, those suffering in the slums, etc.—marginal people left to make it on their own and who sometimes find in Pentecostal and Charismatic groups their only hope for a positive message and a helping hand. How are our churches and pastors accompanying people in their places of pain and sorrow? What kind of teaching do the Catholic faithful receive in homilies to stimulate a critical and mature faith in their lives so that they can enter more deeply into the mysteries of God? What kind of faith formation is available to Catholics today to challenge them to cultivate a strong faith, one that can withstand trials and tribulations without looking for quick fixes to permanent everyday experiences or even limit situations? What theological aesthetics are we proposing to lead people from *theodrama* (the experience of suffering as necessary for Christian life) to the glory and triumph that comes from enduring suffering like the Lord with hope and courage to face and fight evils through active agency, virtues, and values rooted in a spiritual habit and daily praxis? How can we bring the many suffering people down from the cross of suffering? What alternate Christian praxis is out there in world Christianity to offer a viable riposte against or complement to the Pentecostal ideals? Why can't all Christians who are led by the Spirit work together as equal children of God in the search for the footprints of God in history? So, rather than simply dismiss these movements or question the faith of those Christians who are led by the Spirit in these groups, it might be helpful to ask: Why are they leaving our churches? Why are they unsatisfied with our traditional beliefs and practices? What is that "more" that they seek and don't find in our churches?

The third practice that I propose is a *deeper theological study of Pentecostalism and Charismatism grounded in sociocultural and historical methods* in our seminaries, church schools, and universities. We cannot condemn what we have not fully understood. In the same way, we cannot sheepishly embrace what others are doing, simply because it is profitable in the short run. The Catholic Church has always been a leader in the fields of Christian education and cultural formation and evolution. Candidates for the priesthood and pastors must deepen their understanding of Pentecostal and Charismatic Christian beliefs and practices and acquire an in-depth knowledge about religion, among other competences needed to meet the challenges and opportunities of social change. The specific nature of the manifestation of these Pentecostal and Charismatic experiences in different cultures and regions must spur our churches to develop tools for basic and advanced ethnographic survey as well as sophisticated historical tools for pastoral situation analysis; our churches must then transmit these tools to our seminarians, bishops, priests, religious, and pastoral workers. Simply put, churches must think outside the box, experimenting with new theological methods beyond the traditional approaches to systematics and pastoral theology. This can help them give an account to God of what is going on in our communities as well as help them to guide and serve God's people. Adopting a disciplinary and legislative approach, rather than a pastoral and dialogic one to meet these challenges has proven unworkable and has created schism and divisions in many churches around the world.

Ultimately, Pentecostalism and Charismatic movements call on us to get back to the basic grassroots evangelization and deepening of the faith of God's people. This is particularly important in an anonymized world, worsened sometimes by the alienating and impersonal tendencies of social media. This requires a greater closeness and tenderness to build bonds of friendship, love, and outreach in faith communities where people are relating at a deeper level. It is also an invitation to reflect deeply, as this volume's contributors have done, on what defines the mission of God in the life of Christians and in our churches and how we can become part of it. Some of the challenges that will require further consideration by scholars are the instrumentalization of religion, the quest for power and dominion, and the projection of Christianity as a problem-solving religion. As I read through these essays, one fundamental question kept popping up in my head, and I leave that to readers as a point for further reflection: What kind of power should Christians seek in today's world as followers of the Lord Jesus who rejected all power and dominion except the victory which came through the vulnerable path of love, sacrifice, poverty, service, and death on the cross?

Bibliography

Bauman, Zygmunt. *A Chronicle of Crisis: 2011–2016*. London: Social Europe, 2017.
———. "Education in Liquid Modernity." *Review of Education, Pedagogy, and Cultural Studies* 27 (2005) 303–17.

PART ONE

Theologies of the Holy Spirit

1

A Pneumatological Crossroad: Cultural Imaging of the Holy Spirit in Need of a Christological Counterpart

SIMON C. KIM

Lex orandi, lex credendi has been the ancient mantra for theological investigations especially when reflections crossed into uncharted waters. Religious practices in the form of communal prayers and popular devotions often paved the way for formal declarations of the faith when needed. Therefore, the order of faith emerged from the order of prayer. In particular, the Eucharistic prayer of the early church is a prime illustration, balancing the relationship between the second and third persons of the Trinity. The Eucharistic celebration provides a framework for not only a cultural imaging of the Holy Spirit in our theological reflection but also a christological one. The two are necessary as shown in the differing theologies on how Christ is made present at the table of the Lord. For the West, *anamnesis* is central as the words of institution make Christ real by the community remembering what Jesus has done. In the East, the focus is on the *epiclesis* or the calling down of the Holy Spirit, for the Spirit allows for the presence of Christ to occur in the midst of the believers. The theological difference between the East and the West illustrates the intricate connection between the Son and the Spirit found in the communal prayer of a Eucharistic people. This intimate connection is also found in the scriptural understanding of the early church as well as theological developments afterwards.

Biblical Understanding to Theological Reflection

In the incarnation, the Spirit's role is evident as the angel Gabriel announces to Mary the nature of her conception. The Spirit is present by coming upon the virgin as well as being active in "overshadowing" her (Luke 1:35). In Catholic circles, Mary's *fiat* is often highlighted in allowing for the humanity of Jesus. Without taking away from the virgin's courageous faith, the Spirit also needs deeper appreciation in the incarnation, for the second and third persons of the Trinity are intimately connected in the divine mission. Building upon Raymond Brown's, *The Birth of the Messiah*, Kilian McDonnell emphasizes this dynamic by drawing upon the Lucan and Pauline understanding for "[b]oth go back to the common theological tradition which ascribed the conception of the Son of God in Mary's womb to the creative act of God's Spirit."[1] Once again, a careful theological reflection of the Spirit must always take into consideration a christological counterpart since revelation was communicated in such a manner especially in the incarnation.

Early Christian theologians also intimated the connection between the Son and the Spirit. St. Augustine, in particular, connected the earthly Jesus for all humanity with the outpouring of the Holy Spirit to all believers.

> [Augustine] distinguished between the visible (incarnation and Pentecost) and invisible missions of the Son and the Holy Spirit. With remarkable insight, he recognized that the missions reveal the processions; in other words, the missions are the processions revealed in time. He distinguished between mission and procession, in terms of temporal and eternal, *ad extra* and *ad intra*. He distinguished between substantial and relational categories (categories relating to substance and categories relating to the relations), and this distinction provided a coherent framework within which to accommodate both the distinction among the Three (in terms of relational categories) and unity of the one God (in terms of substantial categories). He recognized that the unity of the one God requires that all the works of the Trinity *ad extra* are indivisible, as from one principle. He maintained, however, that each of the divine persons possesses the divine nature in a particular manner and, thus, in the operation of the Godhead *ad extra*, it is proper to attribute to teach of the Three a role that is appropriate to the particular divine person, by virtue of the Trinitarian origin of that person.[2]

---

1. McDonnell, "Trinitarian Theology," 205.
2. Hunt, *Trinity*, 18.

Augustine's understanding of the procession *ad extra* is still important for our pneumatological reflections today. In Augustinian thought, the Father sends the Son who in turn sends the Spirit. Thus, the encounter with the Spirit should naturally lead us to the encounter with the Son and eventually completes the encounter with the Godhead in the Father.

A proper Trinitarian outlook is thus necessary especially since the economic Trinity allows us to better understand the relational aspect of the Godhead. While the temptation to displace "pneumatology from its Trinitarian context has been evident throughout the centuries," McDonnell emphasizes the need to overcome such thought as "[t]o do pneumatology is to do Trinitarian doctrine, more especially the doctrine of the economic threeness."[3] Therefore, in order to regain a proper understanding of the Spirit today, an equally developed christological understanding is also needed. Just as the *epiclesis* brings about Christ in the Eucharistic celebration, the Holy Spirit still continues the work of bringing about Christ today by "coming upon us" and "overshadowing us." Thus, contemporary theological investigations regarding the Spirit are also a contemporary inquiry about Christ:

> In pneumatology, the theological orientation must be Christological and Trinitarian . . . If Jesus is the "what," the Spirit is the "how." Because the invisible mission of the Son and that of the Spirit are coextensive and simultaneous, the Spirit is central, but not as displacing Christ from the center. Each occupies the center, each according to a proper function, even while the doctrine of Christ remains the content object of theological reflection. Such a framework is a guarantee against a contextless pneumatology and other strained misplace nets.[4]

Creedal Developments

> The New Testament does not contain a doctrine per se of the Trinity, in the sense of an understanding of three distinct coequal subjects within the one Godhead; indeed, it leaves open the issue of the relation of the Son and Spirit to the Father, as later controversies amply demonstrate. What the New Testament does is to attest strongly to a profound sense in the early Christian community of the threeness of God, with references that are admittedly probably more liturgical than confessional and certainly not creedal. Threading resonances and an abundance

---

3. McDonnell, "Trinitarian Theology," 227.
4. McDonnell, "Trinitarian Theology," 214–15.

of fragmentary arcs and intimations throughout the New Testament combine to reinforce the threefold pattern that emerges there. While the Scriptures do not give an explicit *doctrine* of the Trinity, however, they do more than simply pave the way for it: they attest to the vibrant lived experience in the early Christian community of the threefold structure of God's self-revelation; they witness to the threefoldness of God as expressed in liturgical and sacramental practice; they provide clear intimations of a Trinitarian pattern; they establish a rhetoric for the expression of Trinitarian faith; and they provide the basis for later development of Trinitarian doctrine.[5]

Thus, through a creedal statement, the council fathers at Nicaea were able to proclaim the humanity and divinity of Jesus as the solution against Arius and his followers who claimed Christ as the highest of creatures. By professing Christ as both fully human and divine, the council fathers differentiated what was distinct of the Son in relation to the Father, while maintaining the *homoousia* or consubstantiality between the two, thereby setting the stage for the life of the Trinity. However, the council fathers did not continue to provide a similar distinction with an acceptable relational framework to the Holy Spirit other than the inclusion to the divine life with a primitive Trinitarian statement by concluding, "We believe in the Holy Spirit."

Such an abrupt ending to the creedal solution at Nicaea has been cautiously explained over the centuries. Explanations for an underdeveloped pneumatology range from the primary reason for calling the council to combat Arius and his followers; running out of time as this was the first ecumenical council; or the idea that the understanding of the Holy Spirit in the early church was just in the infancy stages of development and the council fathers were not equipped for such matters. However, had the Spirit been a similar concern threatening the unity of the faith, would the council fathers have continued to apply Greek thought to the third person of the Trinity as well? Even though the council fathers took a non-biblical term, *homoousia*, to discredit Arius's position, they did not take the same Greek thought beyond this application and apply it to the third person of the Trinity. Given the storm of controversy over the introduction of a foreign term in the development of a christological formula, the council fathers' cautious and abbreviated approach to the Holy Spirit is understandable. Nevertheless, the unintentional shortcomings of not formulating the Trinitarian life of the divine would eventually emerge as the central topic for gathering church leaders once again.

5. Hunt, *Trinity*, 10–11.

The christological controversies at the Council of Constantinople surrounding the understanding of how the divinity and humanity of Christ exist in a single person continued to challenge the church's dogmatic formulation at Nicaea. In addition, the unfinished business of the Spirit also came to the forefront as a result of the ongoing discussion of the second person of the Trinity as well as problematic theological positions raised by those denying the divinity of third. "As the Trinitarian controversy continued on its weary way the Church was being buffeted by two new dangers—errors in the theology of Christ and of the Holy Spirit."[6] The former controversy was spearheaded by Apollonaris who could not reconcile two natures in the one God-man, while the latter controversy had similar theological overtones incited by pneumatomachians, also known as the "fighters against the Spirit" who preferred:

> . . . to say the Son is like the Father in substance or in all things. But they agreed that the Holy Spirit is neither God nor a mere creature. They argued that the Scripture seems to indicate the inferiority of the Spirit to the Father and the Son and says nothing explicit of His divinity. Further, there is no other relationship possible in the Godhead but that of the Father and Son. Therefore, the Spirit is not God.[7]

Thus, the twofold challenge leading up to the Council of Constantinople was not necessarily a new question but a familiar one emerging due to the incomplete treatise of the Trinity in the prior christological declaration. This time, the *ousia* in question was not with the Son but with the Spirit.

> The challenge in Trinitarian theology is how to talk coherently and intelligibly about the reality of God as both three and one. Clearly, precision in terminology and clarity in conceptuality is required. Conceptual clarity demanded terminological clarity. Two terms in the fourth-century Greek emerged in Christian theological usage in the East, *ousia* and *hypostasis*, both of which refer to something that subsists. However, the terms were effectively synonymous at that time.[8]

Just as the divinity of Christ was called into question at Nicaea, the understanding of the Spirit was perhaps even more complex since christological language could not be simply applied to the Spirit now that a more detailed understanding was needed regarding unity and distinction. While

---

6. Davis, *First Seven Ecumenical Councils*, 103.
7. Davis, *First Seven Ecumenical Councils*, 107.
8. Hunt, *Trinity*, 14–15.

the Father had no origin or generation, the Son was said to be generated from the Father. The same could not be said of the Spirit. Thus, rather than generation, procession was eventually embraced for the internal dynamics of the Godhead. However, *ousia* alone could not capture the complexity of this Trinitarian thought. Therefore, another culturally-charged term from Greek thought was needed to maintain distinction within the unity of the Godhead. With the use of *hypostasis*, which at prior times was being used interchangeably with *ousia*, the Cappadocian Fathers were able to emphasize unity (*ousia*) while maintaining distinction (*hypostasis*).

There are at least two lessons to glean from the church's Trinitarian development for our inquiry today in imaging a cultural understanding of the Holy Spirit. A cultural christological understanding is needed in addition to a cultural imaging of the Spirit. Both enterprises entail a similar methodology, a complementarity that highlights unity and distinction. The council fathers attempted to explain the distinction and unity of the third person of the Trinity as a direct reflection of the distinction and unity from the discussions of the second. Therefore, without the cultural understanding of Christ illustrated at Nicaea through the embrace of *homoousia*, further developments of the Trinitarian life would not have been realized given the limitations of the initial Christian mindset emerging out of the Jewish milieu. The challenge or task for a deeper understanding of the Spirit for today follows a similar path. In order to understand the Spirit in our own cultural traditions, a cultural incarnation is also needed. Without Christ appearing in a humanity that resonates with our reality, a cultural distinction highlighting the Sonship's generation of the Father, the cultural imaging of the Spirit highlighting the spiration from the Father and the Son is also incomplete as the distinction of the Spirit's procession remains solely within the life of the immanent Trinity.

Although the following ecumenical council at Chalcedon set out to settle the christological formula once and for all, the final declarations of Christ's humanity and divinity still need unfolding throughout salvation history for deeper comprehension in every generation. "The Definition ended, 'it is unlawful for anyone to produce another faith, whether by writing, or composing, or holding, or teaching others,' and provided suitable penalties for those who would attempt to do so."[9] Thus, the Council of Chalcedon settled the christological formulation for generations to come. However, the encounter of each generation with the humanity and divinity of Christ in its own lived reality further deepens the understanding of the early council fathers without betraying their intentions. In order to do so,

9. Davis, *First Seven Ecumenical Councils*, 187.

the methodology of cultural infusion for clarification set forth by the early christological councils needs to be realized once again. Since the process of arriving at a christological "definition" in the early church was also a process of developing a dogmatic statement through a cultural imaging for both the Son and the Spirit, a similar methodology is needed for the church to realize the fullness of the council declarations in every generation.

Fears about aberrations or novelties from following or repeating this christological process often hinder contemporary cultural incarnation. However, without a proper understanding of how to incarnate Christ in the language of each culture, a deepening of the Chalcedonian definition without alteration of the dogmatic statements made over a century and half ago will have limited bearings on our lives. In addition, the lack of a cultural imaging further complicates our understanding of the Spirit since the language and formation of theological concepts was initially derived from the struggles to formulate Christ in cultural terms of the divine as well as the human.

This is not to say that a cultural understanding of the Holy Spirit is impossible. In many instances, the cultural view of the spiritual realm and acknowledging the workings of the Spirit are much more attainable than the incarnation itself, especially since the basis of most indigenous cultures contain elements or explanations of the world beyond our own. However, without the christological context complementing a particular spiritual understanding, the foundation for a proper and creative imaging of the Holy Spirit within one's reality is often absent. By this, I mean that the vantage point that many cultures possess regarding the spiritual dimension do not adequately contribute to our understanding of the economic Trinity, which in turn affects our ability to fully comprehend the immanent Trinity since a complementary christological outlook has not been properly investigated. One of the key experiences of the early church is the complementary formulation for both the second and third persons of the Trinity—a universal understanding of unity (*ousia*) with distinction (*hypostasis*) as the relational Godhead of the Father, Son, and Spirit.

> There are a number of reasons why theologians have failed to deal adequately with pneumatology. Beyond the elusiveness, there is the fear of the Spirit . . . But the basic reason is broader and deeper, and that is the want of a bold Trinitarian theology. In the economic Trinity the difficulty, which arises out of fear of economic tritheism, is the reluctance to recognize any work as functionally proper to the Spirit. In the immanent Trinity, the difficulty is the predisposition to think of the manner or mode of the Spirit's existence too exclusively according to the mode of the Father and the Son, rather than understanding the Spirit according to the His

own proper mode, as the Spirit of the Father and the Son. Within Trinitarian doctrine, whether economic or immanent, it is a lack, in one way or another, of a sense of *proprium*.[10]

Cultural Infusion in Korean Prayer

One of the attractive aspects of the Catholic Church in Korea has been attributed to cultural expressions incorporated into the Christian faith. In particular, *yeondo,* or the prayer for the dead, utilizes the litany of saints and psalm prayers with rhythmic chanting reflective of a shamanic heritage. This unique adaptation allows prayers and prayer styles from the Catholic tradition within the framework of familiar sounding cultural invocations. Therefore, the religious and cultural overtones are attractive elements to Koreans contemplating the afterlife. The cultural and religious manner of their earthly departure reassures those preparing for the afterlife and ensures their continued remembrance in this life through communal prayer.

The coming together of cultural and religious elements in this ritual appears less complicated on the surface as the marriage of two different traditions come to truly represent the Korean people of faith. However, the theological underpinnings from such a merger are problematic when the cultural understanding of the spirit world attempts to explain boundaries beyond the faith tradition. For Korean Catholics, *yeondo* is repeated continually for the deceased. It is a consoling way of praying for family and friends of the recently departed or on the anniversary of the deceased. Chanting the litany of saints and psalm prayers together allows for group participation through a call-and-response format. Thus, the communal nature of *yeondo* allows families and friends to gather and share in a spiritual experience that is unique to Korean Catholicism.

The challenge that *yeondo* presents is that it pushes the Christian boundaries of the spiritual realm as prayers are offered for the recently deceased for forty-nine days. This length of time is not arbitrary but comes from a shamanic background. In shamanism, the spirits of the deceased wander for forty-nine days before being released into their more permanent state in the afterlife. The forty-nine-day Korean Catholic prayer for the dead is derived from this cultural heritage without reconciling such cultural beliefs of the afterlife with the Christian understanding of eternal life.

What *yeondo* represents is not just an isolated example of the cultural adaptation of a religious practice. Rather, the Korean way of praying for the

---

10. McDonnell, "Trinitarian Theology," 214.

dead illustrates the tension between our human encounters and transferring them onto the spiritual realm and vice versa. Although the Holy Spirit is never equated with the spirit of the dead, we still need to ask ourselves if the cultural imaging of the spiritual realm affects the way we come to understand the third person of the Trinity. The short answer is yes, indeed it does, as the spiritual concepts held within our cultural beliefs shape what is hidden from our reality. Just as the shamanic understanding of the afterlife is a culturally created imaging of the spiritual realm, the Holy Spirit is also tied into that imaging. After all, the *Imago Dei* is not simply limited to the first person of the Trinity but must also resonate within the totality of the divine. The question then becomes: how do we reconcile what we are able to project from our cultural experiences upon the Holy Spirit, and what are the protocols for such applications? In the end, isn't this what the council fathers did at the early ecumenical councils?

The influence of shamanic spirit world is not isolated to Catholicism, nor is it a new innovation in overall Korean society. Rather, shamanic understanding of the spirit world is evident from the beginnings of the Korean people. From folkloric tales of how the Korean people began when heaven and earth came together or how the seventh daughter went to the spiritual realm to obtain medicinal objects for her parents' recovery, Koreans have utilized cultural imaging of the spirit world as a way of explaining the metaphysical realities of their origins. In addition to the direct impact on Korean society, past and present, shamanism also indirectly impacts the population through its encounter with other religions. Unlike other Asian countries where shamanic practices were absorbed by other religious practices such as Taoism or Buddhism, the Korean variation remained resolute, persisting either as an independent cultural practice or merging with other religious practices, but still retaining its own positions.[11] Through these mergers, it is evident that both religious and cultural practices allowed shamanic thought to pervade the general mindset of the Korean people in very subtle but impactful ways.

The pervasive influence of shamanic thought on many religious and cultural practices is not without its critics. Since the historical longevity of shamanic practices on the Korean peninsula is evident in all aspects of life, Christianity was not immune to this influence when first introduced by the Catholic laity themselves and, later, through Protestant missionary activities. In both instances, the Christian faith eventually incorporated certain elements of the existing religious practices of the local inhabitants. Today, some of the faithful may deny or ignore these direct or indirect influences;

---

11. Cho, "Cultural Interbreeding," 50, n.1.

however, consequences of such encounters are present as illustrated in the Korean Catholic prayer, *yeondo*, and in the Evangelical movements of the Protestant faith. The lack of attention given to shamanism's influence on Korean Christian thought has raised concerns as membership has risen rapidly in recent decades. In relation to this phenomenon, the academic and journalistic worlds have also voiced their concerns about the shamanization of Korean Christianity. In particular, the movement of the Holy Spirit within the Protestant churches has been particularly questioned with its infusion of shamanic notions of blessings. The frequency of revival services, prayer meetings at dawn, all-night prayer meetings, and enthusiastic services that often result in cries and shouts are associated with many of the churches' claims of healing power and glossolalia, which in turn also bring about a sense of the worship of wealth and material well-being.[12]

The lack of a cultural christological image complementing these movements of the Spirit makes it difficult to discern the appropriateness of cultural elements in understanding the divine, and it naturally leads to criticisms of cultural infusion, jeopardizing the authentic expressions of the faith. Without a complementary christological image, the cultural imaging of the Holy Spirit is problematic, because it is left to interpretations that do not necessarily resonate within the faith tradition. A complementary cultural imaging of the Son is a difficult challenge since it involves political, cultural, and religious willingness to expound on the Chalcedonian christological definition in relevant cultural terms. In turn, such inquiries would allow for better theological rationale for the cultural experiences of the Holy Spirit by being faithful to the unity and, at the same time, acknowledging the distinction as it was applied to the Godhead by the council fathers.

Cultural Rationale in the Korean-American Charismatic Renewal

Korean Americans who arrived in the US during the 1970s and 1980s have openly embraced Catholic movements such as the Charismatic Renewal, *Cursillo*, Marriage Encounter, *Legio Mariae*, etc. These gatherings afforded the immigrant generation both a religious and social dimension missing from their everyday lives. The isolation of living as a minority in a new homeland was offset by the welcoming aspect found in the communal nature of these movements' prayers. Such factors were crucial in the initial generation's embrace of the faith but are not as much a part of the next

---

12. Cho, "Cultural Interbreeding," 58.

generation's experience, and that may partly explain why these communal prayers have not transmitted well to the next generation.

Because the Charismatic Renewal was similar to many ministries in their local faith communities, Korean-American Catholics embraced it for both the social and religious dimensions this gathering afforded them. Prayer meetings involving praise and worship, healing Masses, and verbal or physical expressions of the faith life appealed to the immigrant situation. Beyond the religious and social similarities of the various communal prayers, the Charismatic Renewal offered another dimension that was socially absent for Korean immigrants. The charismatic element of prayer allowed for the emotional response of a people who did not express themselves in such a manner otherwise. For the immigrant faithful, the charismatic actions of raising voices, crying out loud, and shedding tears while not worrying about others around them created a new and refreshing atmosphere. Without this charismatic opportunity, such emotional outpourings and displays of personal vulnerability would not be acceptable in Korean social circles.

Being able to open up their lives or release years of pent-up emotion were rare and welcomed opportunities. Many times, immigrants were not even aware of their closed-off situation that stemmed from their inability to express themselves due to linguistic barriers as well as their difficulties navigating, often times poorly, the cultural hurdles of Korean social norms in a new host country. Thus, the Charismatic Renewal's appeal for Korean-American Catholics went beyond the traditional understanding of the Spirit's manifestations such as speaking in tongues and resting in the Spirit. Within these manifestations of the holy, the ability to express oneself in an acceptable manner not found anywhere else differentiated those who embraced the charismatic way of prayer. While everyone participating in the Charismatic Renewal, regardless of ethnicity, searches for these types of spiritual encounters, the Korean immigrant experience held these same prayers in a slightly different regard. In contrast, those who were not comfortable going beyond the cultural and social norms of personal expression were not drawn to such prayer styles. While many elements of the Charismatic Renewal were attractive to the faithful during the 1970s and 1980s regardless of their cultural background, the immigrant attraction to such movements involved the cultural struggles of trying to maintain one's heritage while navigating a new environment.

The absence of many of these struggles in the next generation explains some of the loss of interest in the charismatic movement within the Korean-American Catholic communities today. However, this decline has simply paralleled the waning numbers within the mainstream charismatic movement. Although one may explain this decline citing the opportunities of the next generation to express themselves better and find other avenues to release their struggles, a theological discussion has been absent between shifting generational needs. Within every culture, popular piety and devotionals are important, especially in maintaining an identity in the immigrant process of displacement and resettlement. While subsequent generations fulfill their life needs differently than did the previous generation, they often fail to comprehend that these cultural religious expressions help the immigrant identity evolve into one that they themselves can embrace.

As Catholics, the natural progression of the Charismatic Renewal is to align the spontaneous prayers found within charismatic encounters with the church's pinnacle liturgy of the Mass. The coming together of communal prayer may seem like an easy task since the faithful are praying in both instances. However, the extremes of both liturgical styles pose quite a challenge. While the charismatic way of prayer emphasizes spontaneity with the manifestation of the Spirit both in an individual and communal manner, the Eucharistic liturgy has its prescribed rubrics that cannot always accommodate the former. In addition, the movement of the Spirit has not been properly understood within the liturgy for the Catholic Church, as noted in the earlier mention of the differences between the Eucharistic theologies of the East and the West. Without such theological reflection, efforts to align spontaneous charismatic expressions centered at the Eucharistic table have not always benefitted the wider community.

How to smooth out sometimes awkward and disjointed liturgical combinations is not simply a matter of finding a better way to integrate or accommodate. A theological understanding is necessary to allow the spontaneity of the Spirit-led charismatic prayer to complement the traditional liturgical prayers the faithful have come to know and to allow for the practical or prayerful to emerge. Both the cultural imaging of the Son and the Spirit are lacking for Korean-American Catholics as well as in the overall Charismatic Renewal in the US Church. While cultural considerations can be taken for granted back in the homeland, the US religious experience demonstrates that intentional efforts are needed for both a cultural christological and pneumatological imaging. We must always remember that a complementary theological understanding underlies the liturgical aspect that resonates with the lived experience, especially as immigrants.

Conclusion

Through the christological developments of the early church, a theology of the Spirit emerged to solidify the life of the Trinity. While the distinctions of persons is evident in the revelation of the economic Trinity, the unity of the immanent Trinity needed to emerge through the use of unfamiliar cultural expressions. Through newfound ways of imaging the Trinity, the unity and distinction of the Son and the Spirit with the Father revealed an intimate relationship between the second and third persons of the Trinity.

> [T]he link between Jesus and the Spirit remains crucial. Western theology has tended to stress the unsurpassable character of the Christ-event. True as this is, there lies in this theology the danger of christomonism. There also lurks in this theology the danger of a new bondage under the law. The Spirit is certainly bound forever to the Christ-event. The Spirit has the noetic role of recalling to our minds all that Christ said.[13]

Thus, the early church's christological developments allowed for the theology of the Spirit to emerge in a complementary manner. In a similar light, a complementary imaging of both persons of the Trinity is necessary, as the Spirit was intimately connected with the humanity of Jesus two thousand years ago, and the Spirit is needed today to continue the saving work of Christ for all generations.

The Korean and Korean-American encounters of the Spirit today illustrate a theological awkwardness or incompleteness without a complementary cultural imaging of Christ, especially since the former is to make present the latter. This revealing of the unity of the Trinity through their distinctions is not just for the past events of Jesus as recorded in Scripture, but as the ecumenical councils have shown, the life of the Trinity is continually being deepened through our ongoing human encounters with both the Son and the Spirit.

> To be sure, he will not lead us to deny Jesus Christ. But in each epoch, how he will interpret the Christ-event remains a matter of his unpredictable creativity . . . Thus, the Spirit's role is not only a noetic one, the task of recalling the past, but also an ontological one, the task of creating the future.[14]

Bibliography

Cho, Hung-youn. "Cultural Interbreeding between Korean Shamanism and Imported Religions." *Diogenes* 47 (1999) 50–61.

---

13. O'Donnell, "Theology of the Holy Spirit," 63.
14. O'Donnell, "Theology of the Holy Spirit," 63.

Congar, Yves. *I Believe in the Holy Spirit*. Translated by David Smith. Reprint. New York: Crossroad, 2013.

Davis, Leo. *The First Seven Ecumenical Councils (325-787): Their History and Theology*. Collegeville, MN: Michael Glazier, 1988.

Hunt, Anne. *Trinity: Nexus of the Mysteries of Christian Faith*. Maryknoll, NY: Orbis, 2005.

McDonnell, Kilian. "A Trinitarian Theology of the Holy Spirit?" *Theological Studies* 46 (1985) 191–227.

O'Donnell, John. "Theological Trends: Theology of the Holy Spirit, I: Jesus and the Spirit." *The Way* 23 (1983) 48–64.

2

Lived Pneumatology and Ecclesiology among Charismatic Catholics in Latin America

JAKOB EGERIS THORSEN

Introduction

The Catholic Charismatic Renewal (CCR) is by far the largest ecclesial movement within the Roman Catholic Church in Latin America today. Though figures are uncertain, more than one hundred million Catholics may be involved in the movement or categorized as "Charismatics."[1] In the first years after the movement's birth in 1967, Charismatic Catholics called themselves "Catholic Pentecostals," and like their Protestant counterparts, they have a strong emphasis on the Holy Spirit and the charismatic gifts described in the New Testament (i.e., Spirit baptism, healing, glossolalia, and prophecy). These gifts are open to all and freely bestowed on individual believers. Since Pentecostalism is associated with the antihierarchical and egalitarian free church tradition, it has been interesting to follow how the Pentecostal awakening unfolded within a Catholic ecclesial context, where charisma is traditionally institutionalized and where there is a clear distinction between clergy and laity.

After conflicts with the Church hierarchy, split-offs, and fierce disputes in its first decade, the CCR in Latin America (and elsewhere) has become a stout supporter of Catholic doctrine and Church hierarchy. At the same time, the CCR created new roles for the laity as preachers and healers and developed organizational structures that operate with a high degree of independence in some places. While the CCR adheres to the official Catholic

---

1. See discussion of numbers below.

dogmatic understanding of the Holy Spirit and of the Church, the life of Charismatic prayer groups seems to embody doctrine differently than do traditional groups associated with Catholicism in Latin America.

These apparent paradoxes are the topic of this chapter, which will take a closer look at the lived—and often implicit—pneumatalogies and ecclesiologies among Charismatic Catholics in Latin America. The chapter is divided into three parts. First, I will provide a very brief introduction to the CCR in Latin America, addressing the diversity and extension of Charismatic Catholicism in this region. Second, I will examine the lived and expressed understandings of the Holy Spirit and the Church found among Catholic Charismatics in Latin America. Since there is often a discrepancy between the implicit pneumatology and ecclesiology found among common Charismatic Catholics as expressed in religious practice and discourse, and the academic theological writings on these topics by (the relatively few) Charismatic theologians, I will concentrate on the former. I draw on various ethnographic studies, but unless otherwise mentioned, the empirical examples described are from my own studies in Guatemala from 2009 and 2014.[2] While the Charismatic Renewal has proven compatible with Catholic dogma and institution, there is an ongoing effort on the part of both the movement and the institution to prevent them from drifting apart from each other and creating parallel ecclesial structures. Lastly, I will analyze the empirical findings in the context of the Catholic Church's ongoing New Evangelization in Latin America and explore the impact of the Charismatic Renewal on Catholicism in the region.

The CCR in Latin America

As is well known, the Charismatic Revival was officially born in February 1967 during a retreat for students and staff of Duquesne University in Pittsburgh, Pennsylvania. From here, the movement spread rapidly throughout the US and beyond the borders to other parts of the world. In Latin America, the movement was often introduced by North American priests or religious sisters, of whom there were thousands serving in Latin America in the 1970s. The movement rapidly gained popularity among the laity—first, mainly among the urban middle classes. Later, it spread into both the lower and upper classes and, geographically speaking, into rural areas. Since most academics working in religion in Latin America were interested in the questions regarding liberation theology (and later, the increasing growth of Protestantism), it was not until the late 1990s

2. See Thorsen, *Charismatic Practice*.

that research began paying any attention to the CCR, which by then had grown to around seventy million adherents.[3] According to the late Edward Cleary, OP—one of the pioneers in the study of the CCR in Latin America—the CCR was, for decades, the "invisible giant" in the religious landscape of the region.[4] As Cleary demonstrates in his last book, during the more than four decades since its arrival, Charismatic Catholicism has effectively adapted to various different ecclesial and social settings. Despite its easily recognizable, enthusiastic characteristics and uniform expressions, it has a high degree of plasticity and could adapt itself to different cultural and social contexts throughout the Latin American countries.[5] For example, in some places, like in various Mexican states, the CCR combined with traditional folk Catholic practices such as praying the rosary, novenas, pilgrimages, and devotions to the Virgin of Guadalupe.[6] On the other hand, an example from Colombia tells how Charismatics would furiously blame fellow Catholics for idolatry because of their legitimate veneration of the saints, and adopt a general criticism of popular Catholic devotions which was almost indistinguishable from evangelical anti-Catholic propaganda.[7] In the fieldwork I conducted in Guatemala, I encountered a variety of attitudes towards both traditional Catholic piety and the ecclesial authorities.[8] In countries such as Mexico and Colombia, where the institutional Church is relatively robust, priests appear to play a more central role. In regions where the institution has been weaker and is suffering from a priest shortage, the CCR has been almost exclusively a lay movement.

Whereas other ecclesial movements are sometimes used to emphasize a particular local identity, CCR adherents connect to a translocal and transnational global Catholic public, deliberately downplaying local Catholic customs, language, and theology.[9] The plasticity of the movement, its explosive growth, and the subsequent widespread Charismatic practices in the Latin American Church present a challenge when attempting to clearly define who and what is Charismatic—and who, and how many, actually belong to the Charismatic Renewal. We tend to identify Catholic Charismatism within the umbrella organization of CCR, but in Latin America,

3. Barrett et al., *World Christian Trends*, 275–78.
4. Cleary, *How Latin America*, 66.
5. Cleary, *Rise of the Charismatic Renewal*.
6. Várguez, "Constructing and Reconstructing," 190.
7. Ospina, "Satanás se 'desregula,'" 152.
8. Thorsen, *Charismatic Practice*.
9. Mariz and de Theije, "Localizing and Globalizing," 51.

the Charismatic awakening is no longer contained solely within that organization. Charismatic practices have spread to other prayer groups, and a variety of relatively independent Charismatic lay ministries, healing ministries, and covenant communities have emerged in many countries. Likewise, private Catholic Charismatic associations own TV and radio stations. All Catholic Charismatic groups and organizations are supposed to have an institutional anchoring, a priest supervisor or the like, but many do so only formally and not de facto. My personal experiences are from Guatemala, which has a particularly complex religious landscape, but comparing very divergent numbers on adherence to Charismatic Catholicism across Latin America leads me to think that this is a common phenomenon, although varying from country to country.

In terms of classification, it is often hard to define where the Charismatic Renewal starts and where it ends. Elsewhere, I have argued that we need to distinguish between "full-scale" and "soft" Charismatic Catholics.[10] Full-scale Charismatics have a strong identity as Charismatics, and they practice the full range of charismata: speaking in tongues, praying for healing, resting in the Spirit, and receiving and uttering words of prophecy. They are often attached to the CCR, but some have created independent groups. The "soft" Charismatics are all those who have adopted most of the less spectacular Charismatic elements: the Charismatic Holy Spirit-centered songs of praise *(alabanza),* combined with the characteristic swaying of the arms and body *(danza);* the use of vivid, Bible-based lay preaching aimed at personal conversion and moral restoration; and the use of personal testimonies and an intense style of prayer. Many of these groups are parish-based and are, in some cases, remnants of the famous Ecclesial Base Communities associated with liberation theology. As a result of the above, it is difficult to get an accurate number of Charismatic Catholics in Latin America. Here is a table listing existing data for the ten most populous countries:

---

10. Thorsen, *Charismatic Practice*, 82.

Country (percentage of Catholics who are Charismatic)	Barrett et al. (2001)[1] (CCR census)	Pew Forum (2006)[2] (Charismatic practices)	Pew Forum (2014)[3] (self-identify as Charismatic)
Latin America (total)	16 percent	No data	No data
Brazil	22 percent	57 percent	58 percent
Mexico	10 percent	No data	27 percent
Colombia	28 percent	No data	24 percent
Argentina	14 percent	No data	20 percent
Peru	10 percent	No data	32 percent
Venezuela	14 percent	No data	38 percent
Chile	14 percent	26 percent	23 percent
Ecuador	10 percent	No data	40 percent
Guatemala	9 percent	62 percent	38 percent
Bolivia	12 percent	No data	30 percent

The strength of the 2001 numbers is based on local census of participants in CCR groups in the different countries, whereas the 2006 and 2014 numbers are based on surveys. The 2001 numbers nevertheless seem inflated to some observers, since they are very inclusive regarding people who seldom participate.[14] Another weakness of the 2001 census is that it only includes those Charismatic Catholics who have participated in CCR-organized groups and events and not those outside who have adopted Charismatic practices. The 2001 numbers mainly include "full-scale Charismatics," while the 2006 and 2014 numbers include both "full-scale" and "soft" Charismatics. Nevertheless, all of the numbers are impressive and show to what degree Charismatic practices have permeated the religious lives of Catholics in Latin America.

11. Barrett et al., *World Christian Trends*, 275–78.
12. Pew Forum, *Spirit and Power*, 76–80.
13. Pew Forum, *Religion in Latin America*, 64.
14. 14 See, for example, Gooren, "CCR in Latin America," 200.

Lived Pneumatology and Ecclesiology among Charismatics

How does this huge Charismatic awakening affect Catholic life and faith in Latin America? In order to address this question, this chapter concentrates on two central and related aspects: the understanding of the Holy Spirit and the understanding of the Church among Catholic Charismatics. Since a new experience of the Holy Spirit is central to the Pentecostal and Charismatic, it is interesting to see how this unfolds within a Catholic context and to examine whether the new experiences also entail new pneumatological understandings. Likewise, we shall see whether the Charismatic experiences and practices lead to a new or different understanding of the Church among Charismatic Catholics. I am not so much interested in whether there is a formal dogmatic challenge of doctrine as I am in how the de facto understanding and ideal of the Church is expressed among Charismatics.

Pneumatology

In classical Pentecostalism, a renewed emphasis on the third person of the Trinity would become a cornerstone in theology and worship. Baptism in the Holy Spirit, along with glossolalia and prayer for healing and prophecy, are the hallmarks of this branch of the Christian family. Here, Spirit Baptism and glossolalia were traditionally understood as *sine qua non* signs of the faith that would distinguish the true believers from the lukewarm Christians in the traditional denominations. In Charismatic Catholicism, Baptism in the Holy Spirit also plays a central role, although it does not have the touchstone character of defining authentic Christianity. It must be admitted that, in Latin America, academic theological reflection played a minor role in Charismatic Catholicism. Nevertheless, due to the new, enthusiastic—in the eyes of some—controversial expressions at the start of the Renewal, theologians sympathetic to the movement formulated apologetic theological defenses of the CCR orthodoxy. Among other things, they reflected on the character of reception of the Holy Spirit in Spirit Baptism when compared to the Spirit reception in the sacraments of Baptism and Confirmation.[15]

According to Catholic (Charismatic) theologians then and now, the Baptism in the Holy Spirit is not the actual reception of something new but rather a re-vitalization, an effusion, or a "stirring up" of the graces and the same Holy Spirit already received in the sacraments of Baptism and Confirmation.[16] Whereas the Spirit reception in Baptism is connected to the

---

15. See, for example, McDonnell and Bittlinger, *Baptism in the Holy Spirit*.
16. ICCRS, *Baptism in the Holy Spirit*, 61–76.

initiation of the Christian life, in Confirmation, the Spirit equips the confirmed for the universal priesthood of all believers: for bearing witness and for fighting against sin and evil. Thus, Baptism in the Holy Spirit is understood as the experiential realization of the graces received sacramentally. In classical Pentecostalism, conversion, sanctification, and Spirit Baptism were linked in sequence, although the exact order was a topic of discussion.[17] Spirit Baptism is part of the experience of "being born again" and "being saved." For theological reasons, Charismatic Catholics deliberately have avoided the terms "being saved" or "being born again" on this side of death.[18] Nevertheless, is it very much the same enthusiastic—or even ecstatic—experience of being embraced, loved, healed, and empowered that characterizes Catholics' descriptions of Baptism in the Holy Spirit, as we shall see below. That said, due to the less central role of the phenomenon, there is considerably more variation in the perception of Spirit Baptism, its necessity, and its place in conversion narratives among Catholic Charismatics than what seems to be the norm among classical Pentecostals.

Both in my own research and in the studies of others, Spirit Baptism is understood as a single event apart from conversion and subsequent episodes of "resting in the Spirit." It is not a universal phenomenon among Charismatic Catholics, despite its central role as a defining hallmark in CCR literature and self-understanding.[19] Many participants in Charismatic or semi-Charismatic groups have not experienced Spirit Baptism as a single event and are unfamiliar with the term, doubting whether their enthusiastic conversion or healing experiences should be labeled "Baptism in the Holy Spirit." When speaking in a Guatemala City parish with prayer group participants who did claim to have experienced Spirit Baptism, their descriptions of Spirit experience were very similar to testimonies from the Pentecostal tradition. My informants described the phenomenon as "a warm burning feeling inside you," "like being covered by a warm, soft blanket." The result is an urge to cry (mostly) or to laugh. Some describe visions of Jesus and Jerusalem during their initial Spirit Baptism or their subsequent experiences of "resting in the Spirit."[20] I also read similar descriptions of marked and emotional conversions in María Ospina's ethnographic work, for example, among Charismatic Catholics in Colombia as well as in conversion narratives cited in Henri Gooren's work.[21] One example is that of Doña María,

---

17. Kärkkäinen, *Pneumatology*, 96.
18. Cleary, *Rise of Charismatic*, 24.
19. See, for example, ICCRS, *Baptism in the Holy Spirit*.
20. Thorsen, *Charismatic Practice*, 108–12.
21. See, for example, Ospina, "Satanás se "desregula,"" 150–51, and Gooren, "Conversion Careers," 59.

a fifty-eight-year-old lady in Guatemala City who told me about her Spirit Baptism, which she experienced twenty years *after* she began participating in Catholic Charismatic and semi-Charismatic prayer groups:

> I did not fall before; it's two years ago now that I fell [for the first time]. You have to give yourself totally over to God. [Before] I said "no! no!," because we [humans] are rebellious. Then, I let myself flow with the Holy Spirit. It feels as if they take a burden from you. From your childhood, you are carrying burdens, thoughts, experiences, and things like that. You suddenly feel free. You feel like you're in the air, sleeping while awake in the air. I think that is what they call "Baptism in the Spirit." Then, you give thanks to God afterwards.[22]

I find Doña María's example illustrative of the variation in how and when Spirit Baptism is experienced and addressed among Charismatic Catholics. It is noteworthy that she had participated—with varying intensity—in Charismatic prayer groups for two decades. Some of these groups had been under the umbrella of the CCR, some not. She had not followed the course laid out in CCR literature of participating in an initiatory "life in the Spirit" retreat weekend, where Spirit Baptism would normally take place. She acknowledged her personal ("rebellious") resistance to "giving herself over" in Spirit Baptism or "resting in the Spirit," which she had regularly witnessed during her years of participation in the prayer groups. Finally, after having let herself "flow with the Spirit," she still wondered whether her experience was what they call "Baptism in the Spirit." This is consistent with the fact that "Spirit Baptism" was not a term widely used nor a phenomenon addressed thematically in the full-scale, parish-based prayer group where I met Doña María, even though people would regularly speak in tongues and fall into resting in the Spirit as part of tumultuous healing sessions.

In Charismatic groups directed by Charismatic priests or well-educated lay people, there is, most properly, a more systematic application of a theology of Spirit Baptism (and a clear distinction between Spirit Baptism and other Spirit phenomena, such as "resting in" the Spirit). Nevertheless, this lack of uniformity and the lack of importance that many worshipers attribute to the phenomenon indicate that Spirit Baptism does play a less central role in Charismatic Catholicism in Latin America.

---

22. Thorsen, *Charismatic Practice*, 110.

The Sacraments and Spirit Baptism

From a doctrinal point of view, Spirit Baptism, as mentioned, is the experiential effusion of the Spirit received sacramentally. Even though the ICCRS's Doctrinal Commission acknowledges the possibility of reception prior to that of Baptism (and Confirmation), the commission discourages asking for it in prayer, at least before Baptism.[23] In many Latin American places, and certainly in Guatemala, a good part of the faithful never receives the sacrament of Confirmation, or they receive it later in life. Therefore, many Charismatic Catholics will experience Baptism in the Holy Spirit or ecstatic Spirit experiences in connection with healing before receiving the sacrament, which Spirit Baptism is meant to revitalize. With regard to Communion, I personally experienced how those excluded from receiving communion because they were living in irregular relationships would experience Spirit Baptism and resting in the Spirit. Likewise, recovering alcoholics, who would occasionally lapse, would also rest in the Spirit during prayers of healing.

The reason that I draw attention to this is to indicate that there is no clearly defined *ordo salutis* of Baptism and resting in the Spirit. This is the case in classical Pentecostalism, in which conversion should be either followed (or preceded) by complete sanctification and in which Spirit Baptism and glossolalia are expected to occur in a certain order.[24] While a thorough change of life and habits is the norm among Charismatic Catholics who have experienced Spirit Baptism, this is not always the case. Furthermore, Spirit experiences occur independently from the believers' status vis-à-vis the Church's institutional regulations of access to the sacraments. So, while Spirit Baptism would normally lead believers to sort out their irregular life situations, this was not always the case. As we saw in the example of Doña María, Charismatic Spirit experiences are often directly connected with rituals of liberation from evil spirits and the healing of physical or psychological suffering. Conversion and Spirit Baptism often take place as part of prayer sessions for healing, which is often the first time newcomers encounter the Charismatic groups. The importance of healing and liberation for the growth and popularity of Charismatic Catholicism in Latin America cannot be overestimated.[25] Prayer for healing and resting in the Spirit often take place in lay settings, prayer group meetings, or retreats where clergy are only present for a limited time, if at all.

23. ICCRS, *Baptism in the Holy Spirit*, 75.
24. Kärkkäinen, *Pneumatology*, 96.
25. See, for example, Chesnut, *Competitive Spirits*, 67, and Cleary, *Rise of Charismatic*, 21–24.

There are surely priests associated with the Charismatic Renewal, and Charismatic mega events will most often have a priest present, but in the everyday life of the thousands of Charismatic prayer groups, it is lay people who are leading. The formal communication of the Holy Spirit in the sacraments is thus the task of the ordained priesthood, while facilitating and communicating the experiential outpouring of the Holy Spirit in its Charismatic form have de facto become a task for gifted lay individuals. While this need be neither a theological nor pastoral problem, it nevertheless entails the possibility that the two forms of Spirit communication could become disconnected from each other in both understanding and practice; this is an issue I will address below.

He or It?

To uncover the understanding of the Holy Spirit and its place in the religious cosmology of Charismatic Catholics, healing experiences, together with Spirit Baptism, are a good point of departure. What happens in these rituals is an invocation of the Holy Spirit which helps establish a close personal relation to Jesus, who is the healer, comforter, and exorcist. Coming to faith through Charismatic Renewal means to establish a personal relationship with Jesus. Most "converts" are nominal Catholics who usually have not practiced their faith frequently or with much personal dedication prior to their conversion.[26] The Holy Spirit is more often described as an "it" than as a "he"; it is described as a medium and as a force which establishes the personal relationship, heals wounds, and empowers the person in the battle against sin. "[T]he Spirit is understood less as a *person* in the Trinity, but primarily as a *force*."[27] These words by German theologian Peter Zimmerling describe the understanding of the Spirit among classical Pentecostals, but they seem to apply to Charismatics as well. There is a tendency towards an instrumental view of the Spirit force as equipping the faithful with a range of "tools," prayers, and practices that they can apply individually or as a group—for example, prayers of healing from illness and of liberation from evil spirits, songs of praise, and empowerment. Always striking is the epicletical form in which the Holy Spirit is called upon, both in song and prayer. There are songs and prayers calling for the Holy Spirit, and there are songs that establish that it/he has now arrived; one of the songs has the refrain: *Ya llegó; ya llegó; el Espiritu Santo ya llegó* (in English: "Now it has arrived; now it has arrived; the Holy Spirit has arrived").

26. Gooren, "CCR in Latin America," 205–7, and Chesnut, *Competitive Spirits*, 98.
27. Zimmerling, *Die charismatischen Bewegungen*, 77 (my translation).

Once it has been established that it/he is there, the ecstatic atmosphere of singing in tongues, crying, and praying unfolds; this is followed by preaching, prayers of healing, "liberations" from evil spirits, or prayers for Spirit Baptism. Therefore, there seems to be a danger of "instrumentalizing" the force of the Spirit, whenever its manifestations are required, despite the fact that Charismatic Catholics often cite John 3:8 (*Spiritus ubi vult spirat*). This suspicion is further substantiated when considering the important role of self-development within the movement, where themes of how to be the best version of yourself, a good spouse or parent, or a successful businessman are frequent both during prayer meetings and on retreats.

Worldview

The calling upon of the Spirit, its eventual "arrival," and its workings happen within a certain worldview, a Charismatic Catholic cosmology of which one can draw the contours by listening to sermons, testimonies, and to Charismatic informants. This worldview can be compared to classical and neo-Pentecostal cosmologies as well as to "classical" Catholic and "popular" Catholic ones. A detailed and systematic comparison lies outside the scope of this chapter, but the most important characteristics should be mentioned. Catholic Charismatics inhabit a world where spiritual forces (angels and demons) are an experiential reality. Becoming aware of the reality is often part of the "conversion" to Charismatism. One of my main informants, who was already a practicing Catholic before she became Charismatic, described her process of becoming aware of the experiential existence of the Devil; she said that the depression she suffered was "not a normal illness" but rather, was "sent by the enemy."[28] She had to go through a long period of healing and eventually became a powerful healer herself.

Likewise, María Ospina gives voice to two of her main informants in Bogotá, the sisters Carmela (age 37) and Dolores (age 44), whose conversions took place when they were attending a healing congress organized by the Charismatic organization, "Minuto de Dios." Here, they witnessed a priest conducting a tumultuous exorcism in which a demon spoke with the priest through the mouth of a twenty-one-year-old woman before being cast out. The sisters realized that their sufferings might be due to demonic oppressions caused by their illegitimate romantic relationships with married men and their flirting with fortune witchcraft, so they began a process of conversion and healing where evil—in the case of one of the sisters—was

---

28. Thorsen, *Charismatic Practice*, 127.

physically "drawn out" (in the form of a deep "burp") under the guidance of a priest and fellow Charismatics.[29]

Charismatics inhabit an enchanted, holistic worldview where the immanent and transcendent spheres are deeply interconnected and interwoven. There is, thus, a continuity between the popular Catholic, Latin American perception of the visible and invisible world in the traditional sense of "magical realism," and the Catholic Charismatic's perception. This stands in contrast to liberation theology, which was essentially modern and did not take seriously traditional beliefs in spiritual entities.[30] The discovery, described above, of the devil's power nevertheless suggests a remodeling of the traditional enchanted worldview among Charismatics. In the old static cosmos, a distant and exalted Father God was influenced by the intercession of his saints with the help of promises and offerings, and health, luck, and fortune could also be enhanced through manipulative but relatively innocent witchcraft. This is replaced by a more dualistic understanding, where a close and intimate Triune God fights Satan and his cohorts of demons, whose perceived power and influence have increased substantially compared to the traditional, static view. The Catholic Charismatics' adoption of the neo-Pentecostal notion of "spiritual warfare" in the 1980s and 1990s has contributed to this development. The result is that, across the Americas, there now exists a "militarized" religious language with "battle cries," "weaponries" of prayers, and powerful mass rallies, etc., to expel the devil.[31]

Although "spiritual combat" or "warfare of prayer" holds a legitimate place within the Catholic tradition, there is a preoccupying shift of attention and emphasis from the reconciliation with God through Christ to God's victory over the devil in an ongoing battle, where the believers are fighting on God's side.[32] Far too much power is attributed to Satan and evil. Faithful believers sometimes become excessively preoccupied with the Enemy and his seeking "entrances" into their lives: "God always knocks at your door; the Evil one doesn't ask for permission [before he enters]," as one of Ospina's informants said.[33] Evil is externalized, rather than localized in one's own sinful nature, and the atonement achieved by Christ becomes less central.[34] Latin American Catholicism is said to focus traditionally on the suffering of

---

29. Ospina, "Satanás se "desregula,"" 147.

30. Mariz and Theije, "Localizing and Globalizing," 51; Boff, *Church, Charism, and Power*, 132.

31. Várguez, "Constructing and Re-constructing," 191; Ospina, "Satanás se desregula," 150; Thorsen, *Charismatic Practice*, 99.

32. See, for example, *Catechism of the Catholic Church*, §2725.

33. Ospina, "Satanás se desregula," 136.

34. Zimmerling, *Die charismatischen Bewegungen*, 379.

Christ (the humiliation, pain, and wounds), with whom the downtrodden could and can identify. In most Latin American countries, Good Friday is much more significant than Resurrection Sunday. However, in the spirituality of the Charismatic Renewal, this is not so. While acknowledging the constant fear of generalization, I think it is fair to say that the risen Christ of Glory and the powerful Holy Spirit are in focus.

In their 1986 pastoral letter on the CCR, which I will address below, the Guatemalan bishops warn that the CCR "almost never makes it clear that the effusion of the Holy Spirit proceeds from Christ's sacrifice on the cross."[35] The bishops point to a relevant preoccupation: there is a downplaying of the theology of the cross and, subsequently, a downplaying of possible cross-experiences, God's absence, and St. John of the Cross's "long dark night of the soul," within the spirituality of Charismatic Catholics. A little-researched theme in the Latin American context is the introduction of "health and wealth theology" through Charismatic Catholicism. There are indications of its presence in Ospina's work, and I have likewise found prosperity theology (more or less explicit) in Guatemalan Charismatic groups, even though Charismatic leaders ensured me that the movement did proactively try to prevent it from gaining foothold.[36] This also has consequences for the ecclesiology. Pneumatology and ecclesiology are closely linked, and we have already touched upon the ecclesiological questions, which I want to address now.

Ecclesiology

The institutionally unmediated and personal, experienced relationship with Christ through the Holy Spirit is the nerve of Charismatic Christianity. In a Catholic context, this makes the question of the Church a central one. How does becoming a Charismatic influence the understanding of and way of being Church among Catholics in Latin America? The personalized and enthusiastic God relation is the empowering strength of the CCR, but it is also its potential weakness, since it could bypass the institutional church and foster individualism and emotionalism. As I examine here the lived understandings of the Church among Charismatic Catholics, I will focus on three themes: the universal priesthood of all believers, which plays a central role in the CCR; the ecclesiological ideals envisioned by Charismatics; and finally, the relationship between movement and

---

35. Conferencia Episcopal de Guatemala (CEG), *Renovados en el Espíritu*, §7.2.4.
36. Ospina, "Sátanas de desregula," 156; Thorsen, *Charismatic Practice*, 55.

institution, as well as the delicate question of whether the rise of the CCR does result in parallel ecclesial structures.

Universal Priesthood

One of the most remarkable changes within the Latin American Catholic Church in the second half of the twentieth century is the flowering and empowering of the "universal priesthood of all believers." It is not, of course, only a result of the CCR. The groundwork was laid by the establishment of Catholic Action, the education of *catequistas*, Vatican II, Medellín, the establishment of Base Communities, "delegates of the word," etc. In a region that had a shortage of priests and was highly dependent on an influx of foreign clergy, this new organization of the laity led to a revival of Catholicism. It laid the foundation for today's strong Catholic Church, which is much more independent economically and has an increasing number of vocations.[37]

When the Charismatic movement began to grow in Latin America in the early 1970s, it made use of all these new possibilities and spaces of lay activity. It took the "universal priesthood" to new, promising—and sometimes problematic—levels of independence. Charismatic Catholics enact many different aspects of the "universal priesthood of all believers." First and foremost, they often have an extroverted way of expressing and witnessing their faith. It is very common in Charismatic circles to speak about the different gifts of service one can fulfill in the Church: singing, cleaning, preaching, participating in intercessory prayer, and practicing charity, preaching, and healing, etc. Every believer is supposed to find his or her vocation. Many Charismatic Catholics are often active members of their parishes fulfilling roles as catechists, ministers of the word (*delegados de la palabra*), and extraordinary ministers of communion.

Nevertheless, the rise of the CCR has given birth to a new figure who has become prominent and visible in the Catholic landscape of Latin America: the lay preacher. Preaching at weekly prayer meetings and mass rallies, the lay preacher is most often a man, but not exclusively; I have also witnessed many women preaching as well. Gifted preachers also preach on private Catholic radio and television channels, engaging mostly in so-called "biblical preaching" (*predicación bíblica*), which is a dynamic and emotional moral application of the biblical material to the everyday life of the listeners. For talented preachers, fulfilling their vocation entails economic win as well. Being a Catholic lay preacher can be a part- or full-time job. Part of the offerings collected

---

37. See, for example, Cleary, *How Latin America*.

during prayer meetings would be given to the invited preacher, and CDs and DVDs with sermons and praise music are sold as an additional source of income. Preachers often belong to so-called ministries that include preachers and a musical band, which can provide full service (preaching and music) to a prayer group. During my studies, I met many young men who expected lay preaching to be part of their professional career and studied theology at Catholic universities in order to enhance their skills.

The universal priesthood in its special Charismatic form—lay preaching and lay healing—unfolds in a variety of forms which are tied to the institutional Church (supervision, permission, etc.). Some prayer groups, ministries, preachers, and healers nevertheless operate de facto with an almost complete lack of institutional control and thereby threaten to develop parallel ecclesial structures. An extreme but illustrative example is that of the archbishop of Guatemala City, Monseñor Julio Vian (appointed in October 2010), who tried to regulate the Charismatic sectors of the Church in his diocese. It was his intention to obligate all lay preachers to take a series of rudimentary theology courses before being allowed to preach in prayer group meetings. Having no exact idea of the number of self-declared lay preachers, he called in all preachers for a meeting in mid-October 2011. To the astonishment of both the archbishop and the priests accompanying him, between two and three thousand lay preachers showed up at the meeting, coming from a whole range of small, self-founded lay ministries, unheard of in wider Catholic circles. Having expected no more than five hundred preachers, the priests in charge had a hard time planning and implementing the archdiocesan initiative. And one of the involved priests laughingly mentioned to me that Catholic lay ministries were mushrooming in the same anarchic fashion as (neo-)Pentecostal storefront churches.[38]

Ecclesiological Ideals

Charismatic Catholics are—or are supposed to be—fervent and active believers. Prayer meetings are always full of appeals not to be half-hearted, *mediocre*, etc., but to be instead dedicated, faithful, and *radicál* in church commitment. Likewise, Charismatics often deplore their nominal, low-practicing, popular religious, fellow Catholics for having an immature faith.[39] During my fieldwork, I learned that Charismatics regard themselves as vanguard Catholics—i.e., with the experience, openness, engagement,

---

38. Thorsen, *Charismatic Practice*, 40.
39. Thorsen, *Charismatic Practice*, 143; Ospina, "Satanás se desregula," 150–52.

and zeal) that ought to characterize all Catholics.⁴⁰ They do not identify themselves primarily as "Charismatics" but as "truly Catholic" (*verdaderamente católico*). They also used the term *cristiano católico* ("Christian Catholic"), which transcends the popular distinction between *católicos* and *cristianos* (i.e., Evangelicals). As we shall see below, this elitist attitude is both in tandem with many New Evangelization initiatives in Latin America and in tension with the status of the Catholic Church as a church of the masses, with many different forms and levels of engagement. Charismatics envision a Church of dedicated, morally restored, Spirit-radiant, and prayerful members who stand out clearly from "the world," which is generally perceived as corrupt and immoral. Personal relationships are also far more close-knit within Charismatic prayer groups than among Catholic parishioners in general. While this may not differ radically from other lay groups who meet regularly, it is nevertheless noteworthy and manifests itself in various ways—e.g., in the custom of addressing and speaking about each other as "brother" and "sister"—as also practiced among Evangelical Protestants in Latin America.

This is sometimes combined with slightly condescending attitudes towards non-Charismatic and less practicing fellow parishioners—or towards more popular Catholic practices—which has created tensions. Ospina describes how her informants look down upon the *novena* prayer traditions and upon saint devotions: "We should overcome traditions," and "[w]e have a direct relationship with God," as her informants say.⁴¹ In my own studies, I heard traditional Catholicism derogatively described as *una fe de abuelitos* ("a faith for grandparents") and less devoted Catholics as being hypocrites.⁴² This clash between ecclesial idealism and the compound nature of a "church of the masses" has also led many bishops' conferences to warn the CCR against elitism. The Guatemala Bishops' Conference, for example, pointed to the "grave problems" of "exaggerated exclusivism" and contempt for "valid forms of prayer."⁴³ This leads to the third theme, which addresses the relationship between the renewal movement and the institutional church and asks whether the CCR is developing parallel ecclesial structures.

---

40. Thorsen, *Charismatic Practice*, 139.
41. Ospina, "Satanás se desregula," 152 (my translation).
42. Thorsen, *Charismatic Practice*, 143.
43. CEG, *Renovados en el Espíritu*, §7.2.2.

Parallel Ecclesial Structures?

As brilliantly described in Francesco Alberoni's sociological classic, *Movement and Institution*, the Catholic Church has a long history of accommodating and institutionalizing renewal movements. In order for mutual accommodation to succeed, both movement and institution must be flexible and bow towards the other. The institutional Church must acknowledge and create a space for the renewal movement's special charisma, while the renewalists must acknowledge that most representatives of the institution (i.e., priests)—fewer still, the baptized masses of their fellow Catholics—will not share their vision and experience. In many ways, the CCR's history is a prime example of the process of gradual institutionalization that Alberoni describes.[44] Whereas in the 1970s, the CCR would sometimes foster split-off formations of new neo-Pentecostal communities or function as a stepping-stone for Catholics to Evangelical churches, today, the CCR has become—at least in its own self-understanding—a bulwark against Protestant proselytism.[45] During my fieldwork, I encountered many Charismatic preachers who would, again and again, emphasize the Charismatic spirituality's need for a sacramental anchoring. Likewise, CCR publications mostly overflow with papal citations and expressions of loyalty to the hierarchy. One example I would like to mention is that of the March 2011 ICCRS colloquium on "Baptism in the Holy Spirit," held in Rome. Here, it was striking how American and European Charismatics understood the Catholic Charismatic movement as part of an interdenominational, ecumenical Charismatic awakening, while Latin American participants continually stressed that the CCR was a *Catholic* movement for the benefit of the *Catholic* Church. In her status report about the CCR in Latin America, María E. de Góngora concluded with the words: "The Catholic Charismatic Renewal in Latin America can be summed up with these words: It is Catholic! It is Apostolic! It is Eucharistic! And it is Marian!"[46]

A friendly and confident hermeneutic would interpret the above as proof that Catholic Charismatism is in total sync with its ecclesial institution. A hermeneutic of suspicion, however, would see these constant affirmations, in combination with the cautious acceptance by the bishops' conferences and their numerous warnings against aspects of Charismatic

---

44. Alberoni, *Movement and Institution*, 286.

45. During my fieldwork, I have met many older, middle-class, Evangelical converts, who passed through the CCR before becoming Evangelical. Allegedly, the infamous Evangelical dictator Ríos Montt (1982–83) also pursued that conversion career; see Freston, *Evangelicals and Politics*, 273.

46. Personal recording, March 19, 2011.

practice, as incantations of how things ought to be, rather than how they are. Since schisms are rare today (though I have witnessed one Catholic Charismatic covenant community recreating itself as a neo-Pentecostal church[47]), this sincere pronouncement of orthodoxy and institutional loyalty seems to be less about avoiding Protestant split-offs and more about something else. One reason for this might be the well-intentioned attempt to reassure skeptical bishops and parish priests about the orthodoxy of the movement. I believe there is another more hidden, implicit, and even unconscious reason that both Catholic Charismatic leaders and preachers stress the Renewal's need for a sacramental and institutional anchoring and urge their members to participate in the regular Mass. I believe this is because Charismatism and traditional Catholicism represent two very different forms of piety, spirituality, and organization, which can easily drift apart if not held together. When combined, they enrich and reinforce each other, but since they share no immediate affinity, keeping them together is a continual effort for both the renewal movement and the institutional Church. Consider the table below:

Institutional Church	Charismatic groups
Ordained priest (institutional authority)	lay preacher / healer (charismatic authority)
Sacrament of Baptism and	Conversion and
Sacrament of Confirmation	Baptism in the Spirit
Sacrament of Anointing of the Sick	Prayer for healing
Exorcism (rare)	Prayer for liberation

Like their neo-Pentecostal cousins, Charismatic prayer groups and covenant communities have an almost fully-fledged ecclesial infrastructure—complete with personnel, economy, and social media—that is potentially self-propelling and autonomous from the institutional Church. In some ways, one could say that the Charismatic groups basically have at their disposal all the pastoral and spiritual elements needed to be a "complete" Christian community, and the link with the sacramental tradition of the institutional Church is "just" a wonderful "extra" to the Charismatic experience (communal and personal), which lies at the heart of these communities.

47. The *Comunidad Católica Siloé* in Guatemala City, which I studied in 2009 became the neo-Pentecostal *Iglesia Cristiana Siloé* in 2014, then and now under the leadership of the Charismatic lay preacher (now pastor) Juan Carlos Rivera; see http://comunidadsiloe.com/.

Surely, the leading CCR people would never describe it in that way but would rather vehemently emphasize their dependence on the hierarchy. In real life, Charismatic structures and those of the institutional Church are held closely together de facto by the intentional goodwill of both the movement and the institution. Thus, it is not the point that Charismatics have created parallel ecclesial structures in order to secede from the institution. The points are rather the following: First, with these structures in place, Catholic Charismatics are perfectly able to uphold their Charismatic religious life in disagreements with bishops and priests. In Guatemala, there are various examples of covenant communities (e.g., San Pablo Community in Guatemala City)[48] or tens of thousands of Charismatic Catholics of a whole diocese (Huehuetenango) that have been living in schism for more than a decade, without access to the Mass and sacraments.[49] Second, and more importantly, in light of Catholic Charismatics, the institutional Church seems to lose its inevitable and indispensable character. Priests and bishops no longer have the monopoly of speaking on behalf of the Church. There are new, self-confident voices (e.g., lay preachers and private Catholic broadcasting) who are now representing Catholicism in the public sphere and speaking with an authority based on charisma. On a pastoral level, the Charismatic laity lives a significant part of its religious and ritual life outside the gaze of parish priests and other religious authorities who influence their habits through preaching and counseling. While bishops and bishops' conferences do very much to guide their faithful Charismatics, it is beyond doubt that bishops are in no position to fully control the Charismatic Renewal. For better or worse, the rise of the Catholic Charismatism in Latin America represents a loss of institutional power and an emancipation of the laity.

Concluding Perspectives

In this last concluding reflection, I want to address two things. First, I want to briefly examine the contemporary ecclesial context of the New Evangelization in Latin America, the context in which the Charismatic Renewal is

---

48. See this community's website at http://comusanpablo.org/inicio.

49. Another, though different, example is that of the schismatic priest Eduardo Aguirre Oestmann, who was excommunicated by the Roman Catholic Church in Guatemala and founded a Charismatic Catholic church in 2003. Instead of forming a neo-Pentecostal community, Aguirre later became a member of the Syriac Orthodox Church of Antioch (via its Brazilian branch), in which he was ordained bishop in 2007. In March 2013, Aguirre was named archbishop of Central America by Patriarch Ignatius Zakka I Iwas. At least three hundred thousand people (predominantly indigenous Maya) belong to this Charismatic church community throughout Guatemala.

unfolding. Second, I want to re-examine the questions of pneumatology and ecclesiology in order to see how the Charismatic influence in these fields might affect the future life of the Latin American Catholic Church and the possible challenges that may result.

The CCR in the Context of the New Evangelization

The gradual rise of the CCR has coincided with the launching and implementation of the so-called "New Evangelization" in Latin America. The term New Evangelization (from Pope Paul VI's 1975 *Evangelii Nuntiandi*) appears in the last three conclusive documents of the General Conferences of the Latin American Bishops (known in Latin America as CELAM): the Puebla Document (1979); the Santo Domingo Document (1992); and the Aparecida Document (2007), which re-launched the New Evangelization as the "New Continental Mission." In Latin America, the New Evangelization is understood as the Church's reaction to gradual secularization and religious pluralization (the rise of Pentecostalism and other forms of evangelical Protestantism) and to the gradual disentangling of the tight connection between the Catholic Church and the popular masses.

During the second half of the twentieth century, the Catholic Church in Latin America has gradually taken steps away from a Constantinian understanding of the Church. It has loosened its bonds with the powerful elites, becoming a voice of social critique and proactively missionary. It has acquired an understanding of itself as a denominational church with clear demarcation lines, vis-a-vis the state, popular cultures, and other faith communities.[50] This gradual process of demarcation has had different expressions (e.g., Catholic Action, liberation-oriented theology, and social critique) as well as what I would call—using George Weigel's term—evangelical Catholicism, of which Charismatic Catholicism is a prime example.[51] After the decline of liberation theology's influence and the implementation of New Evangelization initiatives, the agendas of the bishops and the CCR have gradually become more alike. In the latest CELAM document (Aparecida, 2007), the bishops partly apply the same missionary language used by the Charismatic Renewal. They call for all baptized to have a "personal encounter with Jesus Christ" and to become "missionaries and disciples."[52] The frequent use of words such as "mission," "Spirit," "encounter with Jesus,"

50. Chesnut, *Competitive Spirits*, 84; Thorsen, *Charismatic Practice*, 143.
51. Weigel, *Evangelical Catholicism*.
52. Fifth General Conference of the Bishops of Latin America and the Caribbean, "Concluding Document," §226.

"conversion," "experience," "joy," and "fire" are striking and have been interpreted by many observers as a sign of Pentecostal and Charismatic Christianity's influence.[53] This development has led scholars such as Gastón Espinosa and Andrew Chesnut to speak of a general Pentecostalization of Christianity in the region, whereas I more modestly speak of an "incipient Pentecostalization" of the Catholic Church in Latin America.[54]

Charismatic Influence and the Future

The final question to address in this chapter is how the Charismatic understanding and nuances of pneumatology and ecclesiology might influence Latin American Catholicism in the future—and which challenges this raises. With the rise of Charismatism, the experience of the Holy Spirit's workings has been broadened, and the strong, almost exclusive connection between the Spirit and the sacraments administered by ordained clergy has been loosened in the faithful's understanding. On the one hand, this "democratization" of the Holy Spirit is a prerequisite for the flowering of the universal priesthood described in this chapter. On the other hand, there is a risk of over-evaluating the subjective and experiential side of the Spirit's workings, thereby undermining the objective character of the faith—i.e., that God is present and acts through the sacraments (*ex opera operato*), despite the sometimes weak faith and lack of experience on the part of the faithful and/or their priests.

As noted above, the institutional Church has made considerable strides towards the ideals and priorities of the Charismatic Renewal. Like the Renewal, the Catholic Church is today proactively missionary, has a strong confessional identity, and is demanding in its expectations of the faithful, while at the same time involving the laity in the Church's work and life. Despite the fact that Charismatic Renewal and the Church in Latin America move in tandem to a higher degree than before regarding the task of the New Evangelization, it is my impression that Charismatic practice and spirituality are still, to some degree, at odds with mainstream Catholicism. With such a huge popularity, there is no doubt that the Charismatic Renewal will influence the face of the Catholic Church in the region and contribute to the ongoing Catholic pluralization. As a whole, Catholicism is living through a period

---

53. See, for example, Suess, "Die missionarische Synthese," 72; Arntz, "Einführung in Aufbau," 56; Libanio, "Conferencia de Aparecida," 44; and Thorsen, *Charismatic Practice*, 159.

54. Chesnut, "Latin American Charisma"; Espinosa, "Pentecostalization"; Thorsen, *Charismatic Practice*.

of awakening, and observers such as the late Edward L. Cleary, OP, argued that, in some ways, Latin America—contrary to the US and Europe—is the only place where a traditionally Catholic region is seriously implementing the reforms of Vatican II.[55] Regarding the missionary understanding of being Church and the question of raising the faithful to a vibrant and personal faith, the CCR and institution are in tandem.

The only serious "loser" is the traditional, unpretentious, low-practicing folk Catholicism, which is the target of the New Evangelization and the continental mission campaign. These days, this form of Catholicism has few defenders. The Latin American bishops describe this group as people whose faith has been "reduced to mere baggage" of "fragmented devotional practices" which do not "convert the life of the baptized" and hence, would not "withstand the trials of time."[56] Personally, I would like to warn against a too particularistic ecclesiology, which easily blocks out all those with a small, rudimentary faith and irregular practice.[57] The Church in Latin America should not—in this enthusiastic spirit of renewal—abandon its roomy and inclusive character. Not all the baptized will be fire-born "missionary disciples," and bishops ought to be reluctant to look down on the unpretentious, everyday Catholicism whose practitioners, at first glance, may pale somewhat in comparison to the extroverted Charismatic or the dedicated lay missionary depicted in the Aparecida Document. There should also be room for the less enthusiastic; during my 2009 fieldwork, an elderly neighbor said it well, sighing when confronted with yet another mission initiative in the parish led by Charismatics: "There is too much hallelujah in the Church nowadays."[58]

Bibliography

Alberoni, Francesco. *Movement and Institution*. New York: Columbia University Press, 1984.

Arntz, Norbert. "Einführung in Aufbau und Inhalt des Schlussdokuments der 5. Generalversammlung des Episkopats von Lateinamerika und der Karibik." *Zeitschrift für Missionswissenschaft und Religionswissenschaft* 92 (2008) 48–67.

Barrett, David B., et al. *World Christian Trends, AD 30–AD 2200: Interpreting the Annual Christian Megacensus*. Pasadena, CA: William Carey Library, 2001.

Boff, Leonardo. *Church, Charism, and Power: Liberation Theology and the Institutional Church*. New York: Crossroad, 1985.

55. Cleary, *How Latin America*.
56. Fifth General Conference of the Bishops, "Concluding Document," §12.
57. Thorsen, *Charismatic Practice*, 215.
58. Thorsen, *Charismatic Practice*, 106.

Chesnut, R. Andrew. *Competitive Spirits: Latin America's New Religious Economy.* Oxford: Oxford University Press, 2003.

———. "Latin American Charisma: The Pentecostalization of Christianity in the Region." In *New Ways of Being Pentecostal in Latin America*, edited by Martin Lindhardt, 1–14. Lanham, MD: Lexington, 2016.

Cleary, Edward L. *How Latin America Saved the Soul of the Catholic Church.* Mahwah, NJ: Paulist, 2009.

———. *The Rise of Charismatic Catholicism in Latin America.* Tallahassee, FL: University Press of Florida, 2011.

Conferencia Episcopal de Guatemala (CEG). *Renovados en el Espíritu: Instrucción Pastoral Colectiva de los Obispos de Guatemala sobre la Renovación Carismática.* Guatemala City: CEG, 1986.

Espinosa, Gastón. "The Pentecostalization of Latin American and U.S. Latino Christianity." *Pneuma* 26 (2004) 262–92.

Fifth General Conference of the Bishops of Latin America and the Caribbean. "Concluding Document: Aparecida." Bogotá, Colombia, May 13–31, 2007. http://www.celam.org/aparecida/Ingles.pdf.

Freston, Paul. *Evangelicals and Politics in Asia, Africa, and Latin America.* Cambridge: Cambridge University Press, 2001.

Gooren, Henri. "The Catholic Charismatic Renewal in Latin America." *Pneuma* 34 (2012) 185–207.

———. "Conversion Careers: Entering and Leaving Church among Pentecostals, Catholics, and Mormons." In *Conversion of a Continent: Contemporary Religious Change in Latin America*, edited by Edward L. Cleary and Timothy Steigenga, 59–70. New Brunswick, NJ: Rutgers University Press, 2007.

International Catholic Charismatic Renewal Services (ICCRS)'s Doctrinal Commission. *Baptism in the Holy Spirit.* Vatican City: ICCRS, 2012.

Libanio, João B. "Conferencia de Aparecida: Documento Final." *Revista Iberoamericana de Teología* 6 (2008) 23–46.

Kärkkäinen, Veli-Matti. *Pneumatology: The Holy Spirit in Ecumenical, International, and Contextual Perspective.* Grand Rapids: Baker Academic, 2012.

Mariz, Celia L., and Marjo de Theije. "Localizing and Globalizing Processes in Brazilian Catholicism: Comparing Inculturation in Liberationist and Charismatic Catholic Cultures." *Latin American Research Review* 43 (2008) 33–54.

McDonnell, Kilian, and Arnold Bittlinger. *The Baptism in the Holy Spirit as an Ecumenical Problem.* Notre Dame, IN: Catholic Charismatic Renewal Services, 1972.

Ospina Martínez, María A. "'Satanás se "desregula"': Sobre la paradoja del fundamentalismo moderno en la Renovación Carismática Católica." *Universitas Humanística* 61 (2006) 135–63.

Pew Forum on Religion and Public Life. *Religion in Latin America: Widespread Change in a Historically Catholic Region.* Washington, DC: Pew Research Center, 2014.

———. *Spirit and Power: A Ten-Country Survey of Pentecostals.* Washington, DC: Pew Research Center, 2006.

Suess, Paulo. "Die missionarische Synthese nach Aparecida." *Zeitschrift für Missionswissenschaft und Religionswissenschaft* 92 (2008) 68–83.

Thorsen, Jakob Egeris. *Charismatic Practice and Catholic Parish Life: The Incipient Pentecostalization of the Church in Guatemala and Latin America.* Leiden: Brill, 2015.

Várguez, Luis. "Constructing and Reconstructing the Boundaries of Tradition and Modernity: The Catholic Church and the Catholic Charismatic Renewal in the Holy Spirit." *Convergencia: Revista ee Ciencias Sociales* 46 (2008) 175–204.

Weigel, George. *Evangelical Catholicism: Deep Reform in the Twenty-First-Century Church.* New York: Basic, 2013.

Zimmerling, Peter. *Die charismatischen Bewegungen: Theologie-Spiritualität: Anstösse zum Gespräch.* Göttingen: Vandenhoeck and Ruprecht, 2002.

3

The Contribution of Pentecostalism to the International Community: Opportunities for Socioreligious Transformation in Africa and Beyond

Clement Majawa

Introduction

Today, the encounter of Pentecostalism and African cultural heritage is misunderstood. It is at a crossroads and often leads to challenges and chain reactions in both the Church and society. Each challenge has a character of its own and needs a unique path to transformation. The objective of this chapter is to critically examine the evolution and contribution of the emerging Pentecostal churches and Charismatic spiritualities to the socioreligious agenda, and social transformation in Africa and the international community. There is no doubt that there are many African religious values which have been sidelined—or forgotten, lost, or renounced—due to various reasons. Thus, there is an urgent need to rediscover, reclaim, and restore such transforming beliefs and virtues like humanness (*Ubuntu*) in the light of the Pentecostal revival in Africa and world Christianity. These should be interpreted with Christian wisdom in order to contribute and offer a spiritual "renaissance" to personal, cultural, and global opportunities of liberation, development, and transformation. As Africa summons up its genus, ethos, and cultural strength, it should be able to draw on its religious patrimony and common good. How Pentecostalism is helping the realization of this quest is a central concern of this paper.

The Methodology

The methodology adopted is the historic-empirical survey research design, descriptive analytical approach, and the "two-way-theological-conversion" in a given context, employing pertinent literature, oral interviews, questionnaires, and participant observation as tools for eliciting information. This approach critiques and listens to the other with dialectical discipline so as to avoid bias, armchair conclusions, and generalizations. Pentecostalism dialogues with and encounters the African spirituality of humanness (*Ubuntu*) "through the spirit we are called to and integrated life leading to transformation."[1] Pope Pius XII, in his 1939 encyclical *Summi Pontificatus*, called for necessity to respect "unity and values of the human race" and "unity of religious coexistence,"[2] part of which are their diverse cultures: "what wonderful vision which makes us contemplate the human race in the unity of its origin in God; unity of the redemption wrought by Christ for all through the Holy Spirit."[3] Charles Pfeiffer states that the two-way theological conversion removes all ambiguities from interreligious and intercultural engagements and leads the diverging peoples to the universal Christian concord.[4] Pentecostal Christianity must help other cultures to rediscover their righteous values and give opportunities to improve and share them with the global community.[5] African spirituality has many supernatural endowments, sacred symbols, and values of solidarity that can be cherished and cultivated in the Christian Pentecostal traditions; to that end, on different occasions, John Paul II, for example, called for dialogue with African traditional religion and values.[6] This expression of African genus, ethos, and spirituality has similar orientations to Christian Pentecostalism. Geoffrey Ronald Mphikitso acknowledges that African humanness (*Ubuntu*) and religious phenomena have many socio-spiritual values to offer to the global context of Pentecostalism.[7]

The main argument of this chapter is that Pentecostalism is a universal Christian redemptive phenomenon which, through the power of the Holy Spirit, is experienced and brings transformative change and renewal in all cultures and religions worldwide. This charismatic reality inspires and

---

1. Palmer, *Hidden Wholeness*, 12.
2. Pius XII, *Summi Pontificatus*, 3.
3. Pius XII, *Summi Pontificatus*, 3.
4. Pfeiffer, *New Combined Bible Dictionary and Concordance*, 43–44.
5. Pius XII, *Summi Pontificatus*, 44.
6. Isizoh, "Dialogue with African Traditional Religion," §5.
7. Mphikitso, *Dynamism of Pentecostal Christianity*, 98.

empowers all traditions to make socioreligious reconstructive contributions to world Christianity. The investigation argues that there is an ongoing resistance and denunciation from some leaders and agents of evangelization. Others tend to see Pentecostalism as a divisive movement in the body of Christ, or see Pentecostal groups as confusing or anarchic. There is still a lot of ignorance and intolerance surrounding the Pentecostal phenomenon. The Church has not articulated, substantively, the Pentecostal catechesis or offered the contributions of Pentecostal religious values to world Christianity. Godfrey Whitaker, in *Pentecostalism and African Orthodoxy*, reveals that "today Pentecostalism is resented by some mainstream churches and preventing it to resonate with universal orthodoxy of unity in the Holy Spirit. The Holy Spirit has a universal history of letting African and other traditional spiritualities be acknowledged, enlightened, and reborn in the Worldwide Pentecostalism."[8] Finally, this chapter aims to present a new face of universal Pentecostal spirituality with the manifestation of *Ubuntu* consciousness which is a somewhat different way of understanding and interpreting Pentecostalism in the worldwide Christianity.

Pentecostal Transformational Change

One of the major aspects of Jesus' ministry was humanitarian service and bringing transformational change through the proclamation of the good news, healing, miracles, exorcism, caring for the sheep, and renewing people's lives through the power of the Holy Spirit. In fact, Jesus quotes Isa 61:1–3 in Luke 4:18–19: "The Spirit of the Lord is upon me, because he has anointed me, to bring glad tidings to the poor. He has sent me to proclaim liberty to the captives and recovery of sight to the blind, to let the oppressed go free, and to proclaim a year acceptable to the Lord."[9] This redemptive ministry of holistic change was clearly demonstrated in the numerous miracles of healing, feeding the multitude, and liberating the social outcasts. This ministry of deliverance, liberation, and transformation was left to the apostles for posterity. In *The Holy Spirit and Charismatic Renewal in Africa and Beyond*, I argue that Christianity is a catalyst of social change in any context. Pentecostalism is a redemptive opportunity for transformation and renewal of the whole person, whole church, and whole global community.[10] According to Robert Peel, "Powerful spiritual experience, new socio-psycho-somatic needs, values, techniques, and roles, new political, economic

8. Whitaker, *Pentecostalism and African Orthodoxy*, 64.
9. *African Bible*.
10. Majawa, *Holy Spirit and Charismatic Renewal*, 56.

and religious systems are interconnected in the Spirit of the Lord."[11] The mainstream missionary churches and African independent churches had earlier evangelized many African countries with the introduction of some civilizing phenomena. According to Boniface Chafwathandumea, Christianity which is rooted in Pentecost experience (Acts 1:1–13) should be involved in upholding the gifts and fruits of the Holy Spirit, renewal, social change, reformation, and development in such areas as socioeconomic, educational, religious, moral, political, and medical perspectives. He further highlighted and categorized the expected Pentecostal transformative role of the church in the twenty-first century thus:

a. preaching God's Word;

b. healing and deliverance;

c. humanitarian services;

d. educational development;

e. employment generation;

f. social and ethical development;

g. governance by example;

h. improved economy; and

i. spiritual and moral development.[12]

The Holy Spirit and Pentecostal experiences are forces behind such pneumatic transformation for all. The Pentecostal Spirit is the heart and soul of Christian life. This pneumatic grace was not grasped at the level of the institutional church, but it was later revealed through its spirituality and witness.[13] The soul of renewal is the grace of Pentecostal refreshment offered to all Christians. The Pentecostal Renewal Movement is becoming a spiritual stimulus for the transformation of the church and society worldwide. The Pentecostal renewal is "like yeast that a woman took and mixed in with three measures of flour until all of it was leavened" (Luke 13:21). Thus, the significant growth of Pentecostalism in Africa has much to contribute to world Christianity. On January 2, 1979, John Paul II told the International Catholic Charismatic Renewal Services (ICCRS) Council that the Catholic Charismatic Renewal "is a very important component in the total renewal

---

11. Peel, *Christian Science*, 23–25.
12. Chafwanthandumea, *Towards Reformation of Christian Pentecostalism*, 95.
13. John, *Spurred by the Spirit*, 34.

of the Church . . . ."[14] The pope confirmed Cardinal Suenens to guide the evolution of ICCRS in the Church.[15]

African Vision and Pentecostal Regeneration

Africa is rich in traditional values and communitarian supernatural charismas which are manifested in its worldview. John Mbiti refers to Africa as religiously notorious.[16] Both Robert Chawanangwa and John Mary Waliggo describe African culture as having roots in Egyptian civilization and North African Christianity as having a life force and a spiritual capacity to preserve and regenerate its traditions into a distinctive unifying consciousness for the global contexts.[17] Laurenti Magesa suggests that the African socio-spiritual contribution to efforts for global change is its deep religious consciousness.[18] African culture was, is, and will remain unique because of its immense human, natural, and religious customs and riches. Magesa points out that "[r]eligion and belief in the essence of what the primal African worldview stood for still lives on. In this sense, African spirituality is not something of the past; it is current and real."[19] Allan Anderson then argues that this African spiritual phenomenon and hierarchy of community values is what motivates Africa to share with the world what she is and what she has. Africa is not an island; it has to, and does, interact and share with the international community her religious opportunities, perceptions of life, and common good.[20] Thus, Walter Hollenweger observes that there is intrinsic unity between African culture, the gospel culture, and the Pentecostal culture. The three cultures are questing for recognition and dialogue in international Pentecostalism.[21]

In *African Values as a Contemporary Catalyst for Global Change*, Dickson Phulamtenga revealed that, for Africans in the twenty-first century,

14. Pesare, *"Then Peter Stood Up,"* 76.

15. ICCRS, "Pope John Paul II Confirms."

16. Mbiti, *African Religions and Philosophy*, 24.

17. See Chawanangwa, *Church in Africa in Need*, 38–39; and Waliggo, *African Religious Values*, 22–24.

18. Magesa, *What is Not Sacred?*, 22.

19. Magesa, *What is Not Sacred?*, 15.

20. Anderson and Hollenweger, *Pentecostals after a Century*, 190. Also, Anderson and Otwang, *Tumelo*, 32–33. The argument is further developed in chapter 8 of Anderson, *African Reformation*.

21. Armitage, *Christian Charisma*, 107. Dayton, *Theological Roots of Pentecostalism*. See also Dempster et al., *Called and Empowered*; Dempster et al., *Globalization of Pentecostalism*. Cf. Faupel, *Everlasting Gospel*.

communion and service include rediscovery of a traditional ethos and promoting evangelization of African cultures so as to add interfaith value to the world at large.[22] Christian values and African spirituality should not contradict but should complement each other. In 1975, Paul VI made a prophetic statement which would later encourage the process of integrating Pentecostal dignity with authentic African spirituality: "The split between the Gospel and culture is without a doubt the drama of our time, just as it was of other times. Therefore, every effort must be made to ensure a full evangelization of culture and to let Christianity enrich the cultural religions. They have to be regenerated by an encounter with the Gospel."[23]

Marcellino Douglas states that African cultural transformation has to dialogue and engage Pentecostal experiences for future renewed Christian communion.[24] Thus, Pentecostalism is urged to dialogue with African values for holistic transformation.[25] The study of African culture and Christianity is crucial today because of the paradigm shift of the center of Christian gravity worldwide: from the global North to the global South.

Prof. Peter Mhlambani Zwide observes that Pentecostalism is witnessed in many forms with diversified pneumatic spiritualities.[26] Allan Anderson cites that the older "prophet-healing" African Independent Churches (AICs), the "classical" Pentecostals, and the emerging new Pentecostal churches have all responded to the existential needs of the African worldview. As David Maxwell points out, even the older Pentecostal churches—whether AICs or those founded by Western missions—can lose their Pentecostal vigor and dynamism through a process of religious bureaucratization, spiritual ethnicization, and structural stratification.[27] Anderson goes on to state that many of these vigorous new churches were influenced by the Pentecostal and charismatic movements in Europe and North America and by established Pentecostal mission churches in Africa. Thus, Anderson and Otwang write emphatically that we cannot understand

---

22. Phulamtenga, *African Values*, 101.

23. Paul VI, *Evangelii Nuntiandi*, 20.

24. Douglas, *Africa and Pentecostalism*, 97.

25. Hamilton, *Pentecostalism*, 50–51.

26. Zwide, *Reviving Pentecostalism*, 132. See also Asamoah-Gyadu, "Church in the African State," 56.

27. Maxwell, "Witches, Prophets, and Avenging Spirits," 313; Gifford, *African Christianity*, 31; Anderson, *Zion and Pentecost*, chapter 9. See also Kalu, "Third Response," 3. For further insights on Pentecostalism and New religious movements, see Asamoah-Gyadu, "Traditional Missionary Christianity"; Kalu, "Third Response," 7.

African Christianity today without also understanding these movements of revival, renewal, and Pentecostalism.[28]

The Second Vatican Council's *Nostra Aetate* confirms that there is something divine and gracious in all cultures because all stem from one God. All share a common destiny, namely God (Wis 8:1; Acts 14:17; Rom 2:6–7; 1 Tim 2:4), and all religions have something good to offer and share with others. Thus, men and women look to their different religions for an answer to the unsolved riddles of human existence.[29] As Daniel Amadankhawa writes in *African Traditional Religion and Its Impact on World Christianity,* African peoples and religions have deep religious therapeutic experiences that can enrich Christian faith and morals. Such traditional healing beliefs, counseling practices, and therapeutic witnesses are a traditional grace that can deepen the understanding of the Church's healing ministry and Pentecostal regeneration.[30] Cornelius Onuh and Joachim Chingwenembe make a powerful contention that the church and civil society are in need of holistic regeneration. The two socioreligious values are reciprocal symbiotic Pentecostal facets. Thus, the church and international community should engage in a serious conversation of transformative universalization of human values and socioreligious structures for the common good. Thus, all people are invited to participate in this noble project of global humanization.[31]

For the last few centuries, Africa has been at the crossroads, surviving from the institutional evil of slavery and colonialism on one hand, and on the other, struggling to embrace the foreign religion of Christianity, Islam, and Hinduism at the expense of its own African Traditional Religion (ATR). In many traditional contexts, there is unbecoming parallelism between Christianity and traditional beliefs. Prof. Emmanuel Olembuntine invites us to look critically to Africa, where many ancient traditional assets were despised, forgotten, lost, or destroyed, and then to begin inquiring and discovering more opportunities in the lost facets of the past and, in the light of Pentecostal wisdom, begin to see how orthodox Christian charisma is being reborn and

---

28. Anderson and Otwang, *Tumelo*, 32–33.

29. Paul VI, *Nostra Aetate*, 1. Vatican II Council was the twenty-first ecumenical council of the Catholic Church, convoked by Pope John XXIII and opened on October 11, 1962, at St. Peter's Basilica in Rome. About 2,500 bishops participated from 1962 to 1965. The Council had a threefold mandate of discussing the role and relevance of the Church on (a) the renewal of the Church; (b) the challenges of modernism; (c) and ecumenism. The ecumenical program and conclusions were contained in sixteen documents. Cf. *Catechism of the Catholic Church*, 111, 597, 748, 816, 1232, 1388, 1557, 1571, 1656, and 2068.

30. Amadankhawa, *African Traditional Religion*, 77.

31. Onuh and Chigwenembe, *Culture of Alternative Theology*, 33–34.

witnessed in the Church and society in Africa and international community.[32] Charismas which are founded in the Holy Spirit are evident in all cultures. With one exception (1 Pet 4:10), it is only in the New Testament's Pauline writings that we find the word *charisma* used. The main references are found in 1 Cor 12–14; Rom 12:3–8; Eph 4:1–16; and Gal 5:13–26. The word *charisma* is used to convey gratuity and benevolence, usually referring to God's gift granted to the individual. Paul introduces the word *charisma* in the context of the organization of the church and Christian community.

In *African Cultures in Conversation with Christian Faith*, Raphael Dingaka Zulu reveals that the cumulative influences of African culture may be viewed as a powerful river that impacts everyone living on its shoreline. In addition, numerous tributaries from other continents feed this massive cultural river with values of civilization, politics, government, art, education, religion, and other permeating influences.[33] People from various parts of the world come to Africa to interact with this river of life for a diversity of reasons. Some came with a missionary agenda, others with hopes of discovery. There were those who came with scientific objectives; others were slave traders or colonizers, and some came to Africa to exploit its natural resources.[34] However, all these excruciating experiences have helped in the rediscovery, rebirth, and reconstruction of some lost, condemned, or forgotten values toward the new transformation of orthodox global Pentecostalism for Africa and beyond. African culture is becoming more prophetic to the international community in the preservation of religious and moral worldviews.

Pentecostal Expansionism in Africa

As David Barrett and T. M. Johnson reveal, the Pentecostal movement today, in its various expressions, represents roughly over 25 percent of the world's Christians.[35] Estimates for all those associated with global Pentecostalism range from 500 to 600 million, and the numbers are increasing at a fast rate on all the continents. These figures show that many people in the Christian world see Pentecostalism as an attractive value to many of their challenges

---

32. Olembuntine, *Recovering and Rediscovering African Values*, 65–66.

33. Zulu, *African Cultures in Conversation*, 72–73. See also McClung, *Azusa Street and Beyond*, 51. Cf. Dempster et al., *Called and Empowered*, 207. For more Pentecostal and charismatic insights, see Saayman, "Reflections on the Development," 42, 51.

34. Guyson, "Of False Prophets and Profits."

35. Barrett and Johnson, "Global Statistics," 286–87.

of life.[36] As Malcolm McVeigh explains, there is much statistical research about expansionism and the effects of Pentecostalism in the northern and southern hemispheres.[37] At the current rate of growth, informed researchers like Grant McClung, George Kimberly, and Patrick Bartley predict some one billion adherents by 2025, as an outgrowth of the dynamic diffusion throughout the Southern hemisphere of Asia, Africa, and Latin America.[38] The future of Christendom worldwide will be Pentecostal in nature and mission with renewing fire from Africa.

The expansionism of Pentecostal experiences in Africa has diversified factors. Among the most prominent features of the Pentecostal gospel in Africa and probably the most important part of Pentecostal evangelism and church recruitment are the following: spiritually and emotionally enriching prayers; the laying on of hands; security; resting in the Lord; speaking in tongues; prosperity; protection from evil; and counseling, healing, visiting, and caring for the sick, the poor, prisoners, orphans, widows, the elderly. The problems of disease, superstition, and evil affect the entire African community and are not simply relegated to individual pastoral care. People are looking beyond African physiognomy and social structure for something spiritually permanent and transformative. As Cox observes, African Pentecostals are increasing with great pneumatic impact every day and everywhere. They are providing a setting in which the African conviction—that spirituality, prayers, social security, healing, and deliverance from all evils belong together—is dramatically enacted.[39] Furthermore, Asamoah-Gyadu states that one of the reasons Pentecostalism has flourished so well in Africa is that "its emphasis on the experience of the Holy Spirit with specific manifestations that make worship both heart-felt and body-felt experience."[40]

---

36. Huns, *Future of the Practice of Pentecostal Awareness*, 27–28.

37. McVeigh, *God in Africa*, 27.

38. Barrett and Johnson, "Global Statistics," 284–85.

39. Cox, *Fire from Heaven*, 247. See also Dempster et al., *Called and Empowered*. Cf. Dempster et al., *Globalization of Pentecostalism*. See also Ma, "Global Shift," 62–70. Cf. Macchia, *Baptized in the Spirit*. See Johnson, "Key Findings of Christianity," 156–64; Kärkkäinen, *Pneumatology*; White, *Spreading of Pentecostalism*, 67–68; Yong, "Not Knowing Where the Wind Blows," 81–112.

40. Asamoah-Gyadu, "Church in the African State," 56. For more clarification of the argument, see Asamoah-Gyadu, *Contemporary Pentecostal Christianity*; Asamoah-Gyadu, "Pentecostalism and the Influence," 138–61.

Christianity in Africa[41]

	Christians		Catholics		Protestants, Anglicans, and Independents	
	In millions	% of total population	In millions	% of total population	In millions	% of total population
1900	10	9%	2	2%	2	2%
1970	144	40%	45	13%	53	15%
1990	276	45%	91	15%	162	26%
2005	411	46%	147	17%	253	29%

By many standards, Africa's population is growing at the fastest rate ever. Pentecostal Christianity continues to spread to many African countries. Thus, the Pentecostal and charismatic phenomena should be at the center of African and world Christianity.[42] As Robert Theweralatha states, African philosophy, sociology, spirituality, and integrity has more to offer to the global institutions and religions.[43] In his book, *Pentecostal Awareness in Global Christianity*, Raphael Lewis adds that religious Pentecostalism in Africa is original in its traditional luminous experience, and this is bringing personal and communal fascination to the international community.[44] Thus, Pentecostalism is growing rapidly, bringing new ways of living the Word of God, witnessing to the Spirit of the Lord, and being a renewed church in the world. Luke Thendolafewa and George Mumderanji agree that, due to the popularity of Pentecostal spirituality today, many people are fond of using the following statement at home, at work, when traveling, at the hospital, in school, etc.: "I am saved. I was saved on this day. I am a born-again Christian so I have stopped this or that sinful

---

41. Barrett et al., *World Christian Encyclopedia*, 283–90; 580–85. See also Pew Forum, *Global Christianity*.

42. Hearns, *Power of Pentecostalism*, 32. See also Majawa, *Holy Spirit and Charismatic Renewal*, x–xii; Gros, "Significance of Global Pentecostalism," 430; Robeck Jr., "Holy Spirit and the Unity of the Church," 354.

43. Theweralatha, *Richness of African Spirituality and Religious Experience*, 47. Tsokalida, *Spread of Pentecostal Beliefs*, 58–59. Kalu, "Third Response," 3–7. Cf. Haar, "Standing Up for Jesus," 224; Gifford, *African Christianity*, 62–63, 95, 233–34. For more Pentecostal conversation on the Christian movements in the light of the Holy Spirit, see McGee, "Pentecostal Missiology," 275–82.

Hearns, *Power of Pentecostalism*, 32. See also Majawa, *Holy Spirit and Charismatic Renewal*, x–xii.

44. Lewis, *Religious Pentecostalism and Societal Harmony*, 98.

or unrighteous behavior!" There is a special witnessing to Pentecostal relationship in Africa and elsewhere.[45]

Many people are witnessing the transformative spiritual values of African Pentecostalism. As Alfred Nyontho Mvume observes, Pentecostalism in Africa is playing a major role in people's lives. Those within or outside the Church acknowledge Pentecostal witnessing with appreciation. Pentecostal and charismatic Christianity's involvement in Africa has been felt at all levels of African life—in economics, education, the judiciary, health, and politics. Marriages and jobs have been saved, and social services are done with a human face.[46] Jenkins remarks that the greatest challenge regarding Pentecostalism, the charismatic movements, charismatic gifts, etc., is the misunderstanding and misinterpretation of the nature and mission of the Holy Spirit in our lives and communities.[47] In continuity with the African religious paradigm, Pentecostal and charismatic Christianity have proven successful in Africa because of their supernatural values and openness to the religious communality as well as their cultural interventionist, oral philosophy, and theological forms that resonate with traditional African spirituality. In *The Power of Pentecostal Christianity in Africa in the New Millennium,* Peter Shadreck Simatei's research revealed that at least two-thirds of Pentecostal Christians are in the developing world, and some believe Pentecostalism is emerging as the de facto way of being Christian in the southern hemisphere.[48] Experts on world religions say that, today, Pentecostalism should be understood as the most visible expression of a whole series of deep religious reconfigurations associated with globalization and universal common good.

---

45. Thendolafewah and Mumderanji, *Pentecostalism Is Influencing,* 11–12.

46. Mvume, *Pentecostal and Charismatic Christianity,* 98–99. See also Land, *Pentecostal Spirituality;* Martin, *Tongues of Fire;* Martin, *Pentecostalism.*

47. Jenkins, *Christianization of Charismatic Gifts,* 13. See also Au, "Asian Pentecostalism," 31–38; Ma, "Global Shift," 62–70; Macchia, *Baptized in the Spirit.*

48. Simatei, *Power of Pentecostal Christianity,* 77. Cf. Dempster, "Eschatology, Spirit Baptism, and Inclusiveness," 155–88: "The overall purpose of my chapter is to develop a Christian social ethic that provides a theological and ethical rationale for the Pentecostal church to carry on its mission of blending together the tasks of evangelism, strengthening the church's own congregational life in worship and *koinōnia,* and creating social ministries for people both inside and outside the church, which promote human welfare, social justice, and personal dignity. This holistic vision of church mission and ministry is designed to affirm the growing sense of Christian social concern among Pentecostals in the various sectors of the movement, which has generated an increasing movement of people to new habitats of pneumatic inclusiveness because of the power of the Holy Spirit."

Pentecostalism through African Humanness (*Ubuntu*)

The meaning of the concept *ubuntu,* or *umunthu,*[49] is ontologically captured by Laurenti Magesa who says that *ubuntu* refers to perfect humanity in African indigenous spirituality.[50] *Ubuntu* entails the goodness and perfection of human values within the African worldview. Thus, Magesa argues that the human quest of goodness implies the effort to avoid everything that indicates aversion to growth into human wholeness or *ubuntu.*[51] Augustine Musopole, a Malawian scholar, speaks of *umunthu* in this way: "to be human in Africa is to be a reconciled person-in-community-and-communion responsibly living out the integrity of one's humanness in all spheres of life and thus contributing to the development and realization of what we have called the good village or community and harmony in the *cosmos. Umunthu* (humanness) is the expression of the image of God in us and this sacred value leads into transformative relationship characterized by integrity, wisdom, and common good shared with universal family."[52]

Theologically, *ubuntu* (African humanness or *africana humana*) is rooted in Genesis 1:27: "God created man [and woman] in his own image." In each man or woman, God puts the dignity and sacredness of "divineness" and "humanness." *Umunthu* has these two relational essentials that define a human being's origin, mission, and destiny in the history of salvation. Gerald Chigona and Lawrence Magudumu justify this position with

---

49. *Ubuntu* as a form of African philosophy thus blends potential, imagined, or actual gifts and the rich values of Africa to the wider world: a specific appreciation of time, being, and personhood; African drum, music, and dance; orality and orature; kingship; and healing rituals in which trance and divination play major roles. All of the cultural achievements and opportunities provide a socioreligious framework for learning and experiencing a transformation of the interior life. The African humanness (*ubuntu*) which is at the core of human existence has to be put in its rightful place for easy interaction and communication with the spiritual world in Africa. It is a fact also that cultural institutionalized rituals and practices, which are denounced and sidelined by secularized ideologies, lose much of their significance in interreligious dialogue and interfaith engagement. In the hands of academicians, *ubuntu/hunhu* has become a key concept to evoke the unadulterated forms of African social life before the European conquest.

This concept and understanding of *ubuntu* (perfect humanity) is found in almost all African ethnic groups. Magesa observes that these African traditional communities describe the same value of ultimate or accomplished humanness: *Ubuntu* (the Zulu, Xhosa, and Ndebele in South Africa); *Botho* (the Sotho and Tswana in Botswana); *Umunthu* (the Chewa or Nyanja in Malawi); *Obuntu* (the Ganda in Uganda); *Utu* (the Swahili in East and Central Africa); *Unhu* (the Shona in Zimbabwe); *Obunu* (the Kwaya/Jita in Tanzania)—Magesa, *What is Not Sacred?*, 13.

50. Magesa, *What is Not Sacred?*, 134.

51. Magesa, *What is Not Sacred?*, 133.

52. Musopole, *Being Human in Africa*, 34–35.

the understanding that the *umunthu* model or *ubuntu* paradigm begins with the human person who is immersed in the world within the exigencies and dynamics of history. It is not a model that contains glory a priori as is the case in the models of the African king, chief, village headman, diviner, healers, medicine man/woman, dream interpreter, counselor, and ancestor. Rather, it is a model that takes into account the people's cultural values and ideals, their failures, and their successes as they evolve towards the perfect state of *ubuntu* which has as its full realization within an inculturated African theology the belief in Jesus our Savior who sent the Holy Spirit to be with us.[53]

With his divine and human natures, it is Jesus Christ who elevates and transforms African humanness and values—*ubuntu*—to become paradigms of re-evangelizing, renewing, and recreating the face of Africa and the international community through the gifts of the Holy Spirit. The phenomenon of Pentecostalism is a socio-moral pastoral praxis for promoting personal renewal, deeper evangelization, and holistic transformation. *Ubuntu* Pentecostalism is suggesting that the spirituality and praxis of Pentecostalism worldwide, which is in the power and working of the Holy Spirit, should engage the whole person who is created in the image of God (Gen 1:27). Thus, in the light of African cultural values, Pentecostalism should embrace the values of initiation rites from birth to death. It should embrace the rich values of the preservation of life and supernatural traditions as manifested in the categories of drums, song, and dance. It should dialogue with the experiences of family life and respect for the elders and ancestors as witnesses in religion, prayer, and sacrifices, etc. These values of the African life cycle provide an opportunity to contribute a new communal standard of existence in global Pentecostalism. Lovemore Mbigi, explicating this rich concept, summarized the role of Ubuntu spirituality in Pentecostal Christianity in Africa and beyond in this way: "It is important that African culture, including the collective concept of *Ubuntu*, should develop fast enough to cope with contemporary secularism, materialism, relativism, modern technological, economical, social, and political challenges" and help Christianity in Africa become relevant on the international platform.[54]

---

53. Chigona, *Umunthu Theology,* 74. See also Magudumu, *Umunthu Anthropology,* 41–44.

54. Mbigi, *Ubuntu,* 147.

Contribution of "*Ubuntu* Pentecostalism" to World Transformation

The value of African humanness (*africana humana*), or *ubuntu*, is a gift from God. It defines human nature, mission, and destiny in relation to God the creator. Many *ubuntu* values are unique—sense of family and community, sacredness of life, respect and commitment to elders, sense of shame, holistic healing of a person, hospitality—and should be preserved, conversed with, and integrated into the physionomy and spirituality of Pentecostalism in Africa. The dialogue and engagement with these values create an opportunity of spiritual transformation and are important phenomena to the spiritual worldview and social commitment even though they are not widely known among many Pentecostals or Catholics. These African values of *ubuntuism* are resources for religious and educational growth, economic and political integrity, and social and pastoral ministry.

As Pentecostalism on the African continent searches for its identity, it is appreciative of the traditional value of ubuntu and, at the same time, is also critical of some modern revolutionary ideas. It is working hard to portray the image of the family experience and the religious communitarian worldview to the international community. I recommend more research and Catholic-Pentecostal ecumenical initiatives based on the *ubuntu* philosophy and spirituality in both local and global contexts. The Pentecostal charismatic renewal movements will need to develop a robust, inculturated catechesis and spirituality for the Christian identity in a plural world for a Church with a Pentecostal and ecumenical commitment.

This is done in the light of the Holy Spirit who enables and engenders Pentecostal unity. The unitive work of the Holy Spirit is taking form worldwide on a record-breaking scale. Many countries are experiencing and being enriched by the gifts and fruits of the Holy Spirit in personal, religious, socioeconomic, political, and globalized contexts. Such pneumatic unification is manifested with special power and values in Africa. The Spirit is at work in Africa. Clement Donaldson affirms that the Holy Spirit is renewing the face of Africa through Pentecostal faith and practice. Despite the various challenges the continent is facing, the Spirit is instrumental in rediscovering, reviving, and enhancing the powerful African values related to life, family, sharing, ancestors, initiation rites, perseverance, caring for the sick and elders, sense of shame, psychosomatic counseling, preservation of nature, experiences of joy through dance and song, etc.[55] Through Pentecostalism, the Spirit is creating forms of grassroots unity, dialogue, and

---

55. Donaldson, *Holy Spirit Renewing*, 76–77.

renewal in the Church and society for the transformation of all people. Like other parts of the world, Africa wants truth, justice, peace, development, and transformation. As John 16:13 says, "When the Spirit of truth comes, he will guide you into all truth." The Spirit enables accurate memory and holistic renewal. The Spirit in Africa is reminding the people of the values of the good news, the Kingdom of God, and the global transformative communion. As part of the "Body of Christ," Africa has many converging values, virtues, and assets to share with the international community.

Conclusion

Pentecostalism is a socioreligious phenomenon for all. African Pentecostalism has a universal mission, to bring transformative humanization into Africa and the world. The *Ubuntu* Pentecostalism is a religious spirituality of life and wholeness; its import, value, creativity, and relevance go far beyond the limits and confines of Africa. The Holy Spirit blows where he wills; therefore, through the Holy Spirit, *Ubuntu* Pentecostalism is a universal concept and experience that brings to all cultures, religions, and countries a renewed, reformed, and inspired life of experiencing Christ as Lord and Savior. Kgalushi Koka observes: "*Ubuntu* (humanness) is not an African peculiarity, nor a property of Black people. *Ubuntu* Pentecostalism is a universal concept and spirituality that is characterized by attributes of omnipresence (everywhere), omniscience (all-knowing), omnisophia (all wisdom), omniphilia (all loving), and benevolence. It embraces all people, all cultures, and all religions alike. It is an endowment from the one (Supreme Principle of Principles) to the human race. It transcends all human-made barriers. The *Ubuntu* Pentecostalism permeates geographical boundaries, ethnicity, race groupings, religious affiliations, cultural settings, gender disparity, political ideologies, etc. It reaches out to all and makes interpersonal communications and relations possible."[56] *Ubuntu* Pentecostalism brings all people together and makes them *One* Village in the belief and practice of the Holy Spirit. *Ubuntu* Pentecostalism becomes a universal socioreligious catalyst for promoting transformational universal brotherhood, Christian re-humanization, and Pentecostal communion. In *Ubunthu Theology: Path of Integral Liberation Rooted in Jesus of Nazareth,* Gerald Chigona reveals that even religious skeptics or lands where Christianity has previously had a long history but are now in need of re-evangelization would appreciate

---

56. Koka, "African Renaissance," 11.

this universal pneumatic outlook; *Ubuntu* is a theology and a Pentecostal experience of renewal and re-humanization.[57]

Finally, through Pentecostalism with an inculturated face (*Ubuntu* values), the Holy Spirit is a catalyst for interreligious dialogue and embracing African spirituality for the transformation of universal Christian spirituality. The African spirituality and life force continue to commend traditional philosophy and oral narrative that have developed from the experience of *Africana humana*[58] and *Pax Africana*,[59] while reclaiming its socioreligious values, significant literary tradition, and role in informing and shaping global Christianity which is focusing on inculturated Pentecostal evangelization for the twenty-first century and beyond. Thus, in the light of Pentecostalism, the Holy Spirit is uniting the international community. Through the Holy Spirit, African *Ubuntu* Pentecostalism is playing a major role in transcending some limiting, negative factors and helping Africa to rediscover its treasured values and develop its rightful place in the international agenda. It is also helping to reconstitute and transform some unjust worldly bureaucratic policies and systems. The Holy Spirit is working to bring about substantive unity, peace, justice, and development in the world. Pentecostalism in Africa is creating Spirit-led grassroots structures to help those in need, liberate those oppressed by many sociopolitical vices, and deliver those in immoral and unrighteous institutionalized evil. The promise of the Holy Spirit is to guide the Church and society into all truth: "When the Spirit of Truth comes, He will guide you into all truth" (John 16:13). Africa is in the moment of Pentecostal truth.

Bibliography

The African Bible: Biblical Text of the New American Bible. Nairobi: Paulines, 1999.

Agwegwebe, George. *The Implementation of the "Africa Synod" Teaching and Spirituality*. Nairobi: Focus, 2009.

Amadankhawa, Daniel. *African Traditional Religion and Its Impact on World Christianity*. Rome: Editrice Pontificia, 2006.

Anderson, Allan. *African Reformation: African Initiated Christianity in the Twentieth Century*. Trenton, NJ: Africa World, 2000.

———. *An Introduction to Pentecostalism: Global Charismatic Christianity*. Cambridge: Cambridge University Press, 2004.

———. *Moya: The Holy Spirit in an African Context*. Pretoria: University of South Africa, 1991.

---

57. Chigona, *Umunthu Theology*, 78.
58. Lekuleku, *Revisiting African Traditions*, 52.
59. Mazrui, *Africans*.

———. *Zion and Pentecost: The Spirituality and Experience of Pentecostal and Zionist/Apostolic Churches in South Africa.* Pretoria: University of South Africa, 2000.

Anderson, Allan, and Edmond Tang. *Asian and Pentecostal: The Charismatic Face of Christianity in Asia.* Oxford: Regnum, 2005.

Anderson, Allan, and Samuel Otwang. *Tumelo: The Faith of African Pentecostals in South Africa.* Pretoria: University of South Africa Press, 1993.

Anderson, Allan, and Walter Hollenweger, eds. *Pentecostals after a Century: Global Perspectives on a Movement in Transition.* Sheffield: Sheffield Academic, 1999.

Armitage, Thomas. *Christian Charisma and Transformation of World Communities.* Sydney: Encounter, 1995.

Asamoah-Gyadu, Kwabena. "The Church in the African State: The Pentecostal/Charismatic Experience in Ghana." *Journal of African Christian Thought* 1 (1998) 51–57.

———. *Contemporary Pentecostal Christianity: Interpretations from an African Context.* Eugene, OR: Wipf & Stock, 2013.

———. "Pentecostalism and the Influence of Primal Realities in Africa." In *The Many Faces of Global Pentecostalism*, edited by Harold Hunter and Neil Ormerod, 138–61. Cleveland, TN: Centre for Pentecostal Theology, 2013.

———. "Traditional Missionary Christianity and New Religious Movements in Ghana." Masters thesis, University of Ghana, 1996.

Atiemo, Abamfo O. *The Rise of the Charismatic Movement in the Mainline Churches in Ghana.* Accra: Asempa, 1993.

Au, Connie. "Asian Pentecostalism." In *Handbook of Pentecostal Christianity*, edited by Adam Stewart, 31–38. DeKalb, IL: Northern Illinois University Press, 2012.

Auch, Ron. *Pentecostals in Crisis.* Green Forest, AR: New Leaf, 1988.

Barrett, David B. "AD 2000: 350 Million Christians in Africa." *International Review of Mission* 59 (1970) 39–54.

———. *African Initiatives in Religion.* Nairobi: East African Publishing, 1971.

———. *Schism and Renewal in Africa: An Analysis of Six Thousand Contemporary Religious Movements.* Nairobi: Oxford University Press, 1968.

Barrett, David B., et al. *World Christian Encyclopedia: A Comparative Study of Churches and Religions in the Modern World.* London: Oxford University Press, 2001. http://www.bible.ca/global-religion-statistics-world-christian-encyclopedia.htm.

Barrett, David B., and T. M. Johnson. "Global Statistics." In *New International Dictionary of Pentecostal and Charismatic Movements*, edited by Stanley M. Burgess and Ed M. Van der Maas, 283–302. Grand Rapids: Zondervan, 2002.

Bongmba, Elias Kifon, ed. *The Routledge Companion to Christianity in Africa.* New York: Routledge Taylor & Francis, 2016.

Bosch, David J. *Transforming Mission: Paradigm Shifts in Theology of Mission.* Maryknoll, NY: Orbis, 1991.

Catechism of the Catholic Church. 2nd ed. Vatican City: Libreria Editrice Vaticana, 2000.

Cairns, Earle. *Christianity Through the Centuries: A History of the Christian Church.* 2nd ed. Grand Rapids: Zondervan, 1981.

Carroll, Jackson W., et al., eds. *Handbook for Congregational Studies.* Nashville: Abingdon, 1986.

Chafwanthandumea, Boniface. *Towards Reformation of Christian Pentecostalism in Africa.* Nairobi: MIAS, 2011.

Chawanangwa, Robert. *The Church in Africa in Need of Pentecostal Values*. George Town: Rosen, 2011.

Chethimattam, John. "Mission and Fellowship of Religion." in *Third Millennium: Indian Journal of Evangelization* 7 (2004) 9–10.

Chigona, Gerald. *Umunthu Theology: Path of Integral Liberation Rooted in Jesus of Nazareth*. Balaka: Montfort Media, 2002.

Coleman, Simon. *The Globalization of Charismatic Christianity: Spreading the Gospel of Prosperity*. Cambridge: Cambridge University Press, 2000.

Corten, André, and Ruth Marshall, eds. *Between Babel and Pentecost: Transnational Pentecostalism in Africa and Latin America*. Bloomington, IN: Indiana University Press, 2001.

Cox, Harvey. *Fire from Heaven: The Rise of Pentecostal Spirituality and the Reshaping of Religion in the Twenty-First Century*. Reading, MA: Addison-Wesley, 1995.

Dayton, Donald. "Pentecostal/Charismatic Renewal and Social Change: A Western Perspective." *Transformation* 5 (1988) 7–13.

———. *Theological Roots of Pentecostalism*. Peabody, MA: Hendrickson, 1987.

Dempster, Murray W. "Eschatology, Spirit Baptism, and Inclusiveness: An Exploration into the Hallmarks of a Pentecostal Social Ethic." In *Perspectives in Pentecostal Eschatologies: World without End*, edited by Peter Althouse and Robby Waddell, 155–88. Cambridge: James Clarke, 2012.

Dempster, Murray W., et al., eds. *Called and Empowered: Global Mission in Pentecostal Perspective*. Peabody, MA: Hendrickson, 1991.

———. *The Globalization of Pentecostalism: A Religion Made to Travel*. Oxford: Regnum, 1999.

Donaldson, Clement. *The Holy Spirit Renewing the Face of the Earth*. New York: AMACOM, 2009.

Douglas, Marcellino. *Africa and Pentecostalism in the Twenty-First Century*. Windhoek: St. Gabriel, 2003.

Duffield, Guy P., and Van Cleave, Nathaniel M. *Foundations of Pentecostal Theology*. Los Angeles: L.I.F.E. Bible College, 1987.

Durasoff, Steve. *Bright Wind of the Spirit: Pentecostalism Today*. Englewood Cliffs, NJ: Prentice-Hall, 1972.

Dzobo, Noah K. "African Ancestor Cult: A Theological Appraisal." *Reformed World* 38 (1985) 333–40.

Erickson, Millard J. *Postmodernizing the Faith: Evangelical Responses to the Challenge of Postmodernism*. Grand Rapids: Baker, 1998.

Faupel, David. *The Everlasting Gospel: The Significance of Eschatology in the Development of Pentecostal Thought*. Sheffield: Sheffield Academic, 1996.

Freston, Paul. *Evangelicals and Politics in Asia, Africa, and Latin America*. Cambridge: Cambridge University Press, 2001.

Gifford, Paul. *African Christianity: Its Public Role*. London: Hurst, 1998.

———. *The Christian Churches and the Democratization of Africa*. Leiden: Brill, 1995.

———. *Christianity, Development, and Modernity in Africa*. London: Hurst, 2015.

———. *Ghana's New Christianity: Pentecostalism in a Globalizing African Economy*. London: Hurst, 2003.

———. *New Dimensions in African Christianity*. Nairobi: All African, 1992.

Gros, Jeffrey. "The Significance of Global Pentecostalism for Catholic Ecumenism." *Emmanuel Journal* (September 2011) 427–31; 434–46.

Gutierrez, Benjamin F., and Dennis Smith, eds. *In the Power of the Spirit: The Pentecostal Challenge to Historic Churches in Latin America.* Louisville, KY: Presbyterian Church (USA) Worldwide Division, 1996.

Guyson, Nangayi. "Of False Prophets and Profits: Meet the Pentecostal Preacher Taking on the Prosperity Gospel." *African Arguments.* September 12, 2016. http://africanarguments.org/2016/09/12/of-false-prophets-and-profits-meet-the-pentecostal-preacher-taking-on-the-prosperity-gospel/.

Haar, Gerrie ter. "Standing Up for Jesus: A Survey of New Developments in Christianity in Ghana." *Exchange* 23 (1994) 225–36.

Hamilton, Andrew. *Pentecostalism on the Work of the Holy Spirit and World Christianity.* Sydney: Coldhill, 2002.

Hanciles, Jehu. *Beyond Christendom: Globalization, African Migration, and the Transformation of the West.* New York: Orbis, 2009.

Hardacre, Helen. "Ancestors: Ancestor Worship." In *The Encyclopedia of Religion,* Vol.1, edited by Mircea Eliade and Charles J. Adams, 263–68. New York: Macmillan, 1987.

Hearns, Patrick. *The Power of Pentecostalism in Influencing the African Culture and Religion.* Oxford: Clarendon, 2008.

Henderson, David W. *Culture Shift: Communicating God's Truth to Our Changing World.* Grand Rapids: Baker, 1998.

Hollenweger, Walter. *Pentecostalism: Origins and Development Worldwide.* Peabody, MA: Hendrickson, 1977.

———. *The Pentecostals: The Charismatic Movement in the Churches.* London: SCM, 1972.

Huns, William. *Future of the Practice of Pentecostal Awareness.* Johannesburg: Zondervan, 2007.

Ilo, Stan Chu. *The Church and Development in Africa: Aid and Development from the Perspective of Catholic Social Ethics.* Eugene, OR: Pickwick, 2014.

International Catholic Charismatic Renewal Services (ICCRS) Newsletter. "Pope John Paul II Confirms the Mandate of Card. Suenens." January–February 1979. http://www.iccrs.org/en/pope-jpii-confirms-mandate-of-card-suenens/.

Isizoh, Chidi Denis. "Dialogue with African Traditional Religion in Sub-Saharan Africa: The Changing Attitude of the Catholic Church." In *Christianity in Dialogue with African Traditional Religion and Culture,* edited by Chidi Denis Isizoh, 1–42. Vatican City: Pontifical Council for Interreligious Dialogue, 2001.

Jenkins, Gerald. *Christianization of Charismatic Gifts.* London: Anthem, 2009.

Jenkins, Philip. *The New Christendom: The Coming of Global Christianity.* London: Oxford University Press, 2001.

———. *The New Faces of Christianity: Believing the Bible in the Global South.* New York: Oxford University Press, 2006.

John, Cyril. *Spurred by the Spirit: The Catholic Charismatic Renewal in the New Millennium.* New Delhi: NCO, 2007.

John Paul II. *Ecclesia in Africa: The Church in Africa.* Washington, DC: U.S. Catholic Conference, 1996. http://w2.vatican.va/content/john-paul-ii/en/apost_exhortat ions/documents/hf_jp-ii_exh_14091995_ecclesia-in-africa.html.

Johnson, Todd. "Key Findings of Christianity in its Global Context, 1970–2020." *International Bulletin of Missionary Research* 37 (2013) 156–64.

Kalu, Obgo U. *African Pentecostalism: An Introduction.* London: Oxford University Press, 2008.

———. "The Third Response: Pentecostalism and the Reconstruction of Christian Experience in Africa, 1970–1995." *Journal of African Christian Thought* 1 (1998) 1–21.

Kaphagawani, Didier. *African Conceptions of Personhood and Intellectual Identities.* London: Routledge, 1998.

Kärkkäinen, Veli-Matti. *Pneumatology: The Holy Spirit in Ecumenical, International, and Contextual Perspective.* Grand Rapids: Baker Academic, 2002.

Katongole, Emmanuel. *The Sacrifice of Africa: A Political Theology for Africa.* Grand Rapids: Eerdmans, 2011.

Kirwen, Michael. *African Cultural Knowledge: Themes and Embedded Beliefs.* Nairobi: Maryknoll Institute of Africa Studies, 2005.

Koka, Kgalushi. "The African Renaissance in the Context of African Humanism." Paper presented at the conference "Ubuntu: From Philosophy to Practice," Durban, South Africa, August 5–6, 1999.

Land, Steven J. *Pentecostal Spirituality: A Passion for the Kingdom.* Sheffield: Sheffield Academic, 1993.

Lekuleku, John. *Revisiting African Traditions for Relevant Christianity in Contemporary Times.* London: Bloomsbury, 1923.

Lewis, Raphael. *Religious Pentecostalism and Societal Harmony.* London: Collins, 2009.

Linden, Ian. *Global Catholicism: Diversity and Change Since Vatican II.* London: Hurst, 2009.

Luvis-Nuñez, Agustina. "Approaching Caribbean Theology from a Pentecostal Perspective." In *The Many Faces of Global Pentecostalism,* edited by Harold Hunter and Neil Ormerod, 126–38. Cleveland, TN: CPT, 2013.

Ma, Wonsuk. "A Global Shift of World Christianity and Pentecostalism." In *The Many Faces of Global Pentecostalism,* edited by Harold Hunter and Neil Ormerod, 62–70. Cleveland, TN: CPT, 2013.

Macchia, Frank D. *Baptized in the Spirit: A Global Pentecostal Theology.* Grand Rapids: Zondervan, 2006.

Magesa, Laurenti. *Anatomy of Inculturation: Transforming the Church in Africa.* Maryknoll, NY: Orbis, 2004.

———. *What is Not Sacred? African Spirituality.* Maryknoll, NY: Orbis, 2013.

Magudumu, Lawrence. *Umunthu Anthropology and New Vision of Africa.* Oxford: Intellect, 2009.

Majawa, Clement. *African Christian Reconciliation.* Nairobi: Kijabe, 2009.

———. *The Holy Spirit and Charismatic Renewal in Africa and Beyond.* Nairobi: Kijabe, 2007.

Marans, Noam E. "Commentary: John XXIII and John Paul II: Two Catholic Saints for the Jews." *Religion News Service,* April 24, 2014. https://www.washingtonpost.com/national/religion/commentary-john-xxiii-and-john-paul-ii-two-catholic-saints-for-the-jews/2014/04/24/93330820-cbd3-11e3-b81a-6fff56bc591e_story.html?utm_term=.f85fd0b95a94.

Mariz, Christopher. *Coping with Poverty: Pentecostals and Christian Base Communities.* Philadelphia: Temple University Press, 1994.

Martin, David. *Pentecostalism: Their World, Their Parish.* Oxford: Blackwell, 2002.

———. *Tongues of Fire: The Explosion of Protestantism in Latin America.* Oxford: Basil Blackwell, 1990.
Mascarenhas, Fio. *Catholic Charismatic Renewal: A Handbook for Leaders.* New Delhi: NCO, 1997.
Maxwell, David. "Witches, Prophets, and Avenging Spirits: The Second Christian Movement in North-East Zimbabwe." *Journal of Religion in Africa* 25 (1995) 309–35.
Mazrui, Ali. *The Africans: A Triple Heritage.* New York: Little Brown, 1987.
Mbigi, Lovemore. *Ubuntu: The Spirit of African Transformation Management.* Pretoria: Knowledge Resources, 1997.
Mbiti, John. *African Religions and Philosophy.* Oxford: Heinemann Educational, 1969.
McClung, Grant. *Azusa Street and Beyond: Pentecostal Missions and Church Growth in the Twentieth Century.* South Plainfield, NJ: Bridge, 1986.
McGee, Gary. "Pentecostal Missiology: Moving Beyond Triumphalism to Face the Issues." *Pneuma: The Journal of the Society of Pentecostal Studies* 16 (1994) 275–82.
McVeigh, Malcolm. *God in Africa: Conception of God in African Traditional Religion.* Cape Cod, MA: Claude Stark, 1974.
Menkiti, Ifeanyi. "Person and Community in African Traditional Thought." In *African Philosophy: An Introduction,* edited by Richard A. Wright. Lanham, MD: University Press of America, 1984.
Montgomery, Patrick. *Pentecostal Dynamics in African Contexts.* Capetown: Random House, 2011.
Mphikitso, Geoffrey Ronald. *Dynamism of Pentecostal Christianity for World Transformation.* Cape Town: Lugard, 2010.
Murove, Munyaradzi Felix. *African Ethics: An Anthology of Comparative and Applied Ethics.* Scottsville, South Africa: University of Kwazulu-Natal Press, 2009.
Musopole, Augustine. *Being Human in Africa: Toward African Christian Anthropology.* New York: Peter Lang, 1994.
Muwewe, Douglas. *The Bridge between African Spirituality and Christian Pentecostalism.* London: Olympia, 2009.
Mvume, Alfred Nyontho. *Pentecostal and Charismatic Christianity in Africa: A Continuing or Discontinuing Religious Factor.* Cleveland: Pilgrim, 2008.
Nyamiti, Charles. "African Ancestral Veneration and its Relevance to the African Church." *African Christian Studies* 9:3 (1993) 14–37.
———. *Christ Our Ancestor: Christology from an African Perspective.* Gweru: Mambo, 1984.
———. "The Mass as Divine and Ancestral Encounter between the Living and the Dead." *African Christian Studies* 1 (1985) 28–48.
O'Connor, Edward. *The Pentecostal Movement in the Catholic Church.* Notre Dame, IN: Ave Maria, 1971.
Oden, Thomas. *The Rebirth of African Orthodoxy: Return to Foundations.* Nashville: Abingdon, 2016.
Olembuntine, Emmanuel. *Recovering and Rediscovering African Values for Christian Transformation.* Cambridge: Anthem, 2011.
Onuh, Cornelius, and Joachim Chigwenembe. *The Culture of Alternative Theology and Responsible Pentecostalism.* Johannesburg: Leiden, 2006.
Orobator, Agbonkhianmegbe, ed. *Reconciliation, Justice, and Peace: The Second African Synod.* Maryknoll, NY: Orbis, 2011.

Palmer, Parker James. *A Hidden Wholeness: The Journey Toward an Undivided Life.* San Francisco: Jossey-Bass, 2004.

Paul VI. *Evangelii Nuntiandi: On Evangelization in the Modern World.* Washington, DC: U.S. Catholic Conference, 1976. http://w2.vatican.va/content/paul-vi/en/apost_exhortations/documents/hf_p-vi_exh_19751208_evangelii-nuntiandi.html.

———. "Homily at the Conclusion of the Symposium Organized by the Bishops of Africa." July 31, 1969, Kampala (Uganda). https://w2.vatican.va/content/paul-vi/en/homilies/1969/documents/hf_p-vi_hom_19690731.html.

———. *Nostra Aetate: The Declaration on the Relation of the Church to Non-Christian Religions.* Washington, DC: National Catholic Welfare Conference, 1965. http://www.vatican.va/archive/hist_councils/ii_vatican_council/documents/vat-ii_decl_19651028_nostra-aetate_en.html.

Peel, Robert. *Christian Science: Its Encounter with American Culture.* Boston: Henry Holt, 1958.

Pesare, Oreste. *"Then Peter Stood Up—" (Acts 2:14): Collection of the Popes' Addresses to the Catholic Charismatic Renewal from Its Origin to the Year 2000.* Vatican City: International Catholic Charismatic Renewal Services, 2000.

Petersen, Douglas. *Not by Might nor by Power: A Pentecostal Theology of Social Concern.* Oxford: Regnum, 1996.

The Pew Forum on Religion and Public Life. *Global Christianity: A Report on the Size and Distribution of the World's Christian Population.* Washington, DC: Pew Research Center, 2011. http://www.pewforum.org/2011/12/19/global-christianity-regions.

———. *Spirit and Power: A Ten-Country Survey of Pentecostals.* Washington, DC: Pew Research Center, 2007. http://www.pewforum.org/2006/10/05/spirit-and-power/.

Pfeiffer, Charles. *The New Combined Bible Dictionary and Concordance.* New York: Baker, 1973.

Phulamtenga, Dickson. *African Values as a Contemporary Catalyst for Global Change.* London: National Society/Church House, 1998.

Pius XII. *Summi Pontificatus: The Unity of Human Society.* New York: American, 1939. http://w2.vatican.va/content/pius-xii/en/encyclicals/documents/hf_p-xii_enc_20101939_summi-pontificatus.html.

Poewe, Karla O. *Charismatic Christianity as a Global Culture.* Columbia, SC: University of South Carolina Press, 1994.

Robeck, Cecil M., Jr. "The Holy Spirit and the Unity of the Church: The Challenge of Pentecostal, Charismatic, and Independent Movements." In *The Holy Spirit, the Church, and Christian Unity: Proceedings of the Consultation Held at the Monastery of Bose, Italy, 14–20 October, 2002,* edited by Doris Donnelly, et al., 353–82. Leuven: Leuven University Press, 2005.

Saayman, Willem A. "Some Reflections on the Development of the Pentecostal Mission Model in South Africa." *Missionalia* 21 (1993) 40–56.

Sawyer, Harry. *God: Ancestor or Creator? Aspects of Traditional Beliefs in Ghana, Nigeria, and Sierra Leone.* London: Influx, 1970.

Scharer, Matthias, and Hilberath Bernd. *The Practice of Communicative Theology: An Introduction to a New Theological Culture.* New York: Crossroad, 2008.

Schreiter, Robert. *Faces of Jesus in Africa.* Maryknoll, NY: Orbis, 1991.

Simatei, Peter Shadreck. *The Power of Pentecostal Christianity in Africa in the New Millennium.* New York: Costello, 2003.

Stanley, Grenz. *A Primer on Postmodernism.* Grand Rapids: Eerdmans, 1996.

Suenens, Leon-Joseph. *Charismatic Renewal: A Grace, a Challenge, and a Mission.* Vatican: ICCRS, 2000.
———. *A Controversial Phenomenon: Resting in the Spirit.* Dublin: Veritas, 1997.
———. *Memoirs and Hopes.* Dublin: Veritas, 1992.
Synan, Vinson. *Aspects of Pentecostal-Charismatic Origins.* Plainfield, NJ: Bridge-Logos, 1975.
———. *The Holiness-Pentecostal Tradition: Charismatic Movements in the Twentieth Century.* Grand Rapids: Eerdmans, 1997.
Thendolafewah, Luke, and George Mumderanji. *Pentecostalism Is Influencing Socioeconomic Life.* New York: Palgrave, 2009.
Theweralatha, Robert. *The Richness of African Spirituality and Religious Experience.* London: St. George, 2010.
Tsokalida, John. *The Spread of Pentecostal Beliefs in the Northern Hemisphere.* St. Louis: Dover, 2011.
Uzukwu, Elochukwu. *A Listening Church: Autonomy and Communion in African Churches.* Maryknoll, NY: Orbis, 1996.
Waliggo, John Mary. *African Religious Values and Christian Transformation in the History of the Church.* Nairobi: East African Educational, 1988.
Walls, Andrew. *The Cross-Cultural Process in Christian History: Studies in the Transmission and Appropriation of Faith.* Maryknoll, NY: Orbis, 2002.
———. *The Missionary Movement in Christian History: Studies in the Transmission of Faith.* Maryknoll, NY: Orbis, 1996.
Wanjala, Frederick. *Basics of African Theology: A Cogent Mentor in Charles Nyamiti.* Rome: Litografia Leberit, 2008.
Whitaker, Godfrey. *Pentecostalism and African Orthodoxy.* Sydney: Mondial, 2009.
White, Matthew. *The Spreading of Pentecostalism and its Impact in the World Today.* Scottsville, ZA: Kwazulu-Natal, 2011.
Yong, Amos. "Not Knowing Where the Wind Blows: On Envisioning a Pentecostal Charismatic Theology of Religion." *Journal of Pentecostal Theology* 14 (1999) 81–112.
Zahan, Dominique. *The Religion, Spirituality, and Thought of Traditional Africa.* Chicago: University of Chicago Press, 1979.
Zuesse, Evan. *Ritual Cosmos: The Sanctification of Life in African Religions.* Athens, OH: Ohio University Press, 1979.
Zulu, Raphael Dingaka. *African Cultures in Conversation with Christian Faith.* Blantyre, MW: Jhango Heinemann, 1998.
Zwide, Peter Mhlambani. *Reviving Pentecostalism and African Independent Churches.* London: Ellis, 2009.

PART TWO

Spiritual Warfare and Healing

4

Spiritual Warfare and Healing in Kenyan Neo-Pentecostalism

PHILOMENA NJERI MWAURA

Introduction

Since the 1970s, there has been an explosion of Pentecostalism globally and especially in the global South, notably Africa, Asia, and Latin America. This new wave of Pentecostalism has been labeled as charismatic or neo-Pentecostal Christianity and, on the African continent, has become a significant phenomenon. In Kenya, Pentecostal and charismatic Christianity have become an important feature of the country's religious landscape, commanding a massive following. Some of the prominent characteristics of this type of Christianity are its focus on pneumatic elements like spirit baptism, speaking in tongues, salvation by conversion, instantaneous sanctification, revival, deliverance, healing, spiritual warfare, exorcism, and miracles.

In this article, I discuss the subjects of spiritual warfare, healing, and deliverance in Kenyan neo-Pentecostalism, drawing examples from some of the neo-Pentecostal churches (NPCs), especially in the city of Nairobi's Jesus is Alive Ministries (JIAM) and Faith Evangelistic Ministries. Beginning by examining the roots and characteristics of Kenyan neo-Pentecostalism, I attempt to argue that healing, deliverance, and spiritual warfare are not just theological categories but also concepts and practices/rituals that offer spaces for empowerment in an environment that engenders dehumanization and disempowerment in every sense of the word. It seeks answers to the following questions: How do Pentecostals[1] understand healing, deliverance,

---

1. While Pentecostal Christianity was introduced to Kenya by American missionaries in the early twentieth century, a new wave of revival within Christianity in

and spiritual warfare? What mechanisms do they employ to mediate healing? What is the meaning of healing, deliverance, and spiritual warfare in the self-understanding of the individual and the churches? The article uses a cultural model to analyze healing, deliverance, and spiritual warfare in Kenyan neo-Pentecostalism.

The Origins of Kenyan Neo-Pentecostalism

In the last four decades, a new strand of Pentecostalism has emerged not only in Kenya but also throughout Africa and the rest of the world. To distinguish it from the classical Pentecostal churches of the early twentieth century, this new strand has been designated as modern Pentecostalism, neo-Pentecostalism, and charismatic Christianity. Ogbu U. Kalu regards this phenomenon as the third response of Africans to the missionary message.[2] It is also regarded as the fastest growing strand of Christianity; for example, in 2007, Amos Wako, the then Kenyan attorney general, revealed while speaking to church leaders that there were approximately 8,520 registered churches and that sixty applications were submitted every month. He also asserted that the attorney general's department was overwhelmed by increasing demand for the registration of churches and was facing difficulty processing 6,740 pending applications by various religious organizations. Thousands of these churches have sprung up in all of the nation's major towns, and some are huge megachurches while others are too small to be called churches, though they nevertheless add to the numbers. According to newspaper reports, the Registrar General's office is overwhelmed by increasing demands for registration of these new churches.[3]

According to a survey by the Pew Forum on Religion and Public Life, the Pentecostal/Charismatic movement accounts for more than half of Kenya's population. The survey also found that approximately seven in ten Protestants in Kenya are either Pentecostal or charismatic, and about a third of Kenyan Catholics surveyed can be classified as charismatics.[4]

Due to the proliferation of neo-Pentecostal churches, Kenya has evolved into a strong Pentecostal and charismatic culture as is evidenced by the

---

Africa since the 1970s to the present has resulted in a new type of Pentecostalism that has been variedly labelled as charismatic or neo-Pentecostal. This is what is addressed in this article. The preferred term for the phenomena is "charismatic Christianity" or "neo-Pentecostal churches/Christianity."

2. Kalu, *Power, Poverty, and Prayer*, 135.
3. Ndegwa, "Over 6,000 Churches," 6.
4. Pew Forum, "Spirit and Power," 83.

numerous instances of open-air rallies, crusades, revival meetings, miracle centers, healing and deliverance ministries, street preaching, bus evangelism, and televangelism. Writing about Nigeria, Ruth Marshall observes that "literally thousands of new churches and evangelical groups have cropped up in cities and towns forming broad-based religious movements which are rapidly becoming a powerful new social and religious force."[5] Though Marshall is writing about Nigeria, this observation also resonates well with the Kenyan context. A few examples of such churches in Kenya are the following: the Deliverance Churches of Kenya headed by Bishop Mark Kariuki; Neno Evangelism Ministries of Apostle James Ng'ang'a; Jesus is Alive Ministries of Bishop Margaret Wanjiru; Faith Evangelistic Ministries (FEM) of Teresia Wairimu; and Maximum Miracles Centers of Bishop Pius Muiru.

The explosion of neo-Pentecostalism is attributed to a combination of factors, including according to Ogbu Kalu: Pentecostal ferment before 1970; the increase of the Word of Faith movement; the proliferation of prosperity preachers; the African roots of Pentecostalism in the African worldview; a global outpouring of the Holy Spirit;[6] the emergence of young university evangelical Christian leadership; rapid urbanization; and the collapse of African economies. This growth has equally been necessitated by aggressive evangelism, church planting, lay mobilization, lively music, the celebratory nature of worship, and claims of healing and deliverance.

The Kenyan religious landscape had already been prepared for neo-Pentecostal Christianity by classical Pentecostal missionaries—the Assemblies of God—from America and Canada in the 1920s and the East African Revival Movement in the 1930s. As early as 1927, revival had occurred in the Friends African Mission (Quakers) in Kaimosi, western Kenya. The revival stressed personal salvation and the importance of receiving the Holy Spirit as a sign of sanctification. Confession of sins and speaking in tongues were later stressed by the African converts as evidence of receiving the Holy Spirit. The emergence of the revival was an African reaction to a Christianity that did not adequately address Africans' spiritual needs. This Pentecostal experience resulted in the emergence of African Instituted Churches (AICs) of the spiritual/Zionist variety.

The East African Revival started in Rwanda and spread to Uganda, Kenya, and Tanzania. Commonly referred to as the *Balokole* ("saved ones" in the Luganda language) or *Ahonoki* ("saved ones" in Gikuyu), the revival evolved within missionary churches. Mark Winters defines the movement as "a revival in which nominal or 'backslidden' Christians are 'revived' in

5. Marshall, "Pentecostalism in Southern Nigeria," 7–32.
6. Kalu, *Power, Poverty, and Prayer*, 141–46.

their commitment to the faith; it is not primarily a movement of charismatization affecting non-Christians."[7] The movement was interdenominational, interracial, and interethnic. It was also a response to the perceived lethargy of missionary Christianity and its having been compromised to worldliness. It emphasized the experience of personal salvation through the blood of Jesus, personal holiness, asceticism, confession of sins, hard work, and reliability. One of its characteristics was to hold fellowship meetings in churches once a week, in divisions once a month, and in districts every year. There were national conventions and regional ones held regularly in each East African country. The fellowship meetings included Bible readings, expositions of Bible passages, personal testimonies, confession of sins, and offers of repentance and response by those to be saved. The Balokole Movement empowered the laity—literate and illiterate—to testify for Jesus. This impacted the evolution of patterns of ministry that were different from those in mainline churches.

In the 1960s and 1970s, American evangelists such as Billy Graham and T. L. Osborne visited Kenya, and this helped the revivalists to discover that revival was a worldwide phenomenon, entailing more than revival preaching—for example, other charismatic gifts such as healing. In schools and colleges, revival work was carried out by the Kenya Students Christian Fellowship. University ministry had regular missions to the whole university every three years. A network of hall prayers and Bible study sessions were planned to enhance Christian nurturing to university student communities. In high schools and junior colleges, Christian unions were organized to facilitate spiritual nurturing through prayers and Bible studies. Camps were organized in key regional schools to train students in holistic spiritual growth. Leaders of the revival were generally lay men and women who had little theological formation, but they worked tirelessly to involve the schools and colleges. Many lay people who were involved in the revival later became prominent personalities and even founded churches and parachurch organizations—for example, Joe Kayo, founder of the Deliverance Church; David Kimani, founder of Bethel Mission; and Reverend Margaret Wangari, presiding bishop of the Church of the Lord.

The churches they founded are dotted all over the country. The crystallization of the revival movement into churches is attributed not only to the charismatic nature of the preachers and their powerful and relevant messages that transcended barriers of gender, class, and age but also to the problem in which mainline churches found themselves after Kenya's independence in 1963. They were mostly concerned with managing churches

---

7. Winter, "Balokole and the Protestant Ethic," 69.

and developing their social ministries in education and health, and they lacked the adequate personnel for pastoral work in schools and other educational institutions. These were years of transition, and Nigeria, as Ojo reports, had a similar experience of revival.[8]

Since the 1980s, Pentecostal fellowships, ministries, and churches have proliferated, some founded by indigenous Kenyans and others founded by international evangelists from Europe, Asia, America, and other parts of Africa. Itinerant televangelists such as Reinhardt Bonke, Benny Hinn, Morris Cerulo, Joyce Meyer, Cecil Stewart, Emmanuel Eni, and David Yongi Cho have graced the Kenyan capital of Nairobi and other major towns. As Mugambi observes, these personalities preside "over personal enterprises not directly related to any specific denominations . . . they claim to have spiritual gifts and charismatic powers of preaching and faith-healing."[9] The emphasis in these campaigns has been a "spiritual renewal" and numerical expansion of Christianity. It is evident from this discussion that there is a continuum between African Instituted Churches of the spirit type, revival within mission Christianity, and the current wave of neo-Pentecostalism.

Spiritual Warfare, Deliverance, and Healing

What is spiritual warfare? The following passage from St. Paul's letter to the Ephesians is often quoted by Pentecostals to depict the paradoxical life of Christians: ". . . our struggle is not against flesh and blood, but against the rulers, against the authorities, against the powers of this dark world and against the spiritual forces of evil in the heavenly realms" (Eph 6:12 NIV).

This passage seems to imply that Christians must live their lives in opposition to "the powers of this dark world." For Pentecostals, going through life is spiritual warfare. Spiritual warfare has several sources, including concepts of evil in the traditional African worldview and the biblical worldview. As Kalu observes, "the challenge for Christianity is how one should witness the gospel in a highly spiritualized environment where recognizing the powers has not been banished in a Cartesian flight to objectivity and enlightenment. The power question is ultimate and suffuses an African Primal worldview with charitable institutions, demanding an answer from the new African change agents and pointing to the need for community in change."[10]

---

8. Ojo, "Deeper Life Bible Church," 135–37. See also Ojo, "Charismatic Movement," 114–18.

9. Mugambi, "Evangelistic and Charismatic Initiatives," 121.

10. Kalu, *Power, Poverty, and Prayer*, 178.

As we shall see, these challenges in the African worldview resonate with the biblical world of Jesus' time.

During his ministry, Jesus treated Satan and demonic forces as real enemies, frequently casting them out and thus setting people free whom he called "prisoners" and "oppressed" (Luke 4:18). From these and other passages in Scripture, Pentecostals have conceptualized Christianity as a continuous warfare between the forces of light and darkness, the Kingdom of God and the kingdom of Satan. Because of their faith in Christ Jesus and having been redeemed, they believe that they have been given the power to cast out demons and heal the sick. This is done through positive and bold prayer and fasting. Asamoah-Gyadu[11] observes that "prayer is understood to have the power to stir the supernatural by decimating the powers of evil and releasing the anointing of the Spirit."[12] Thus, in Pentecostal thought, prayer is an activity inspired primarily by a certain understanding of the workings of the Holy Spirit and the believers' source of empowerment.

Certain principles govern the way spiritual warfare operates in the universe. Among them is the scriptural fact that there is a very close relationship between what goes on in human life and what goes on in the spiritual realm. Scripture also shows that humans can do things that thwart the enemy's plans such as prayer and other acts of obedience to God. Since the relationship between the spirit and the human worlds is very close, whatever is done in the human world has great implications in the spirit world. One of the rules seems to be that when human beings honor and obey a spirit being, that being is enabled to do more of what it wants in the human realm. Thus, when people obey God, God is able to do more of his will among human beings that otherwise would be impossible.[13]

Conversely, when people obey Satan, Satan is enabled to do more of his will. Prayer, then—along with fasting, repentance, forgiveness, righteousness, and every other human attitude and behavior that stands in obedience to God—can be seen as acts of war and means of enabling God to accomplish his plans in the human sphere. Related to prayer and intercession in spiritual warfare are intimacy and authority prayer.[14] The former refers to the type of prayer that requires one to have "intimacy with God, be in conversation, fellowship and having the ability to listen to God's promptings. The latter implies taking Jesus' authority over conditions that are against God's will and asserting His power against that

---

11. Asamoah-Gyadu, *Contemporary Pentecostal Christianity*, 35.
12. Asamoah-Gyadu, *Contemporary Pentecostal Christianity*, 35.
13. Kraft, "Spiritual Warfare," 1092.
14. Kraft, "Spiritual Warfare," 1092.

on the enemy."[15] This is following Jesus' example of commanding demons to release their grip on victims. It is asking his authority to heal people, to break the enemy's power over objects or places. Through this kind of prayer, war is waged against the enemy.

Another important part of spiritual warfare is the concept of "power encounters."[16] This is reminiscent of the encounters between Moses and the pharaoh (Exod 7–12) and between Elijah and the prophets of Baal (1 Kings 18). The concept of "power encounters" is virtually synonymous with the concepts of spiritual warfare, agreeing that healing and deliverance from demons are power encounters. This ministry is seen as one large power encounter that includes numerous smaller ones in which Jesus freed people from the power of Satan through healing and deliverance. It is argued that these encounters qualify as genuine power encounters since they involve pitting the power of God to bring freedom against the power of Satan to keep people in bondage.[17]

Kraft[18] observes that, according to Scripture, there are two levels of spiritual warfare: the ground level and cosmic level. When Jesus cast out demons from people, he was operating on the ground level, and when Elijah confronted the prophets of Baal, he was engaged in cosmic level combat. Ground level warfare, according to neo-Pentecostals, involves dealing with spirits that inhabit people. These could be of three kinds: (1) family spirits that give power through the dedication of successive generations; (2) occult spirits; and (3) ordinary demons that attack through anger, lust, greed, an unwillingness to forgive, illnesses that don't heal, repetitive misfortunes, death, etc. Cosmic level warfare involves dealing with territorial spirits over regions and nations, evil ancestral spirits, and institutional spirits such as those attached to churches, governments, and educational institutions.

Ogbu Kalu argues that, in African Pentecostalism and its conceptualization of power, evil and good resonate with the indigenous African theology of the world which is built on an alive universe in which power is central. The "world is suffused with powerful forces in competition; human beings manipulate the services of the good gods against the machinations of the evil ones in the quest of abundant life."[19] He further argues that, though the Pentecostals accept the meaning of cosmos as the material universe, they are not ignorant of the other aspect of cosmos—worldly affairs, that is—worldly

15. Kraft, "Spiritual Warfare," 1092.
16. Kraft, "Spiritual Warfare," 1093.
17. Kraft, "Spiritual Warfare," 1093.
18. Kraft, "Spiritual Warfare," 1094.
19. Kalu, *Power, Poverty, and Prayer*, 153.

goods, endowments, pleasures, and allurements that seduce one away from God. An evil power is perceived to be behind the cosmos, and friendship with it equals enmity with God. These views are also shared by the members of Jesus is Alive Ministries, whose bishop has established a very vibrant and strong deliverance ministry to deal with demonic forces.

Some scholars have argued that African Christians have enlarged their understanding of demons to include African concepts of evil, witchcraft, sorcery, magic, evil ancestral spirits, and bad omens. Brigit Meyer, in *Translating the Devil*,[20] argues that local converts absorbed the missionary images and representations of evil. Other scholars argue that local Christianity emerged by reconceptualizing indigenous powers and biblical powers. Regardless of the various arguments to understand spiritual warfare and spiritual powers, African Pentecostals have developed their own theology, finding ways of understanding the realm of evil and innovative ways to deal with existential realities in their contexts. Hence, as Kalu further observes, African Pentecostals "have equated principalities and powers, and demons with the various categories of spirits in the primal world view and as enemies of 'man' and God. They reinforce the explanations of cause and effect in the primal world view before providing a solution beyond the purviews of indigenous cosmology. They rework the Pauline structure with native ingredients."[21] It is important to note that the aim of spiritual warfare and encounters is not an end in itself. Relationship with God, incessant reading of Scripture to empower one with the Word of God, and building a strong relationship with God are very essential components. Any approach that ignores the love and other fruits of the Spirit and the truth of the gospel is incomplete and unbalanced. At this juncture, I will explore what healing and deliverance entail and their relationship with spiritual warfare.

What is Healing and Deliverance?

Jesus is Alive Ministries (JIAM) is one of the NPCs in Kenya that devotes itself to the ministry of deliverance as its core business and identity. According to Bibiana Chege,[22] a member of JIAM, healing deals with illness although it also refers to total well-being. Deliverance, on the other hand, deals with power of evil and seeks to free those bound by evil in some way.[23] It is a ministry of authority, taking up the command of Jesus to set the captives free and

---

20. Meyer, *Translating the Devil*, cited in Kalu, *Power, Poverty, and Prayer*, 152.
21. Kalu, *Power, Poverty, and Prayer*, 153.
22. Interview with the author on January 7, 2016.
23. See also Gifford, *African Christianity*, 98–111.

cast out demons. She further says that, in rare cases, people are possessed by demons or tormented or harassed by evil spirits. Jesus Christ gave his authority to the church to cast out evil spirits and set people free. He thus sent his disciples to proclaim the kingdom and to heal and deliver those in bondage. They receive their mandate from this command (Luke 10:17). Healing and deliverance, therefore, support each other for there can be no deliverance without healing, and healing often involves deliverance. If the two are not linked, one runs the risk of seeing deliverance as isolated spiritual warfare with ongoing battles and struggles carried out in a virtual vacuum. People who are bonded to evil spirits are also wounded, hurting, and in need of healing. Another JIAM member observed that, "spiritual bondage is almost rooted in a deep wounded-ness that needs to be touched with healing love."[24] He further said that the ministry of deliverance and healing must center on people, not demons. The goal is human wholeness, involving all the dimensions of being: will, mind, body, spirit, soul, and his/her context.

The worldview that underlines the NPCs' conceptualization of deliverance and healing is derived (even though they deny it) from both the African tradition and biblical conceptions. It is a holistic worldview that perceives God, humanity, nature, and the spirit world as concerned with the wholeness of life and relationships. In African religion, these relationships are ones of power. In the African religious worldview, the moral universe is perceived, as earlier stated, to consist of powers or forces which constantly and necessarily interact with one another. As Magesa argues, "Power in the African moral universe is not an abstraction: it does not exist apart from relationships. Relationships establish power and give it meaning, purpose, and specific identity."[25]

Power is correctly understood not as a "noun"—a state, a quality—but precisely as a "verb"—an act, a dynamic reality. These realities' existence is only possible because of the power relations they share. God is God, because he sustains and cares for the elements; God has put together and ordered the universe. Conversely, apart from sharing in this sustenance and care, according to their own being, all other elements likewise cease to exist. Being cut off from this relationship—due to personal or communal wrongdoing, manipulation of mystical powers (on the part of human beings) to harm others through witchcraft, or sorcery and magic—contributes to illness and lack of well-being. It destroys the equilibrium necessary for individual, family, and communal well-being.

---

24. Author's interview with Eileen Mathea on January 8, 2016.
25. Magesa, "Power in African Religion," 2.

This worldview is very real in JIAM and Faith Evangelistic Ministry's (FEM's) understanding of deliverance and healing. It is also complemented by the biblical understanding of illness and misfortune as arising from personal and communal sin, curses, Satan, and demonic forces. By virtue of their emphasis on the prominence of the Holy Spirit and the immediacy of God's presence, these NPCs possess a strong interventionist theology evidenced especially in their attitude toward healing for the sick and deliverance for the demonically possessed or oppressed.

In NPCs, just as in other Christian churches and African religion, healing has to do with praying for the restoration of health to the physically sick as well as deliverance from the bondage of evil spirits perceived to be involved in a variety of crises including chronic joblessness, family discord, lingering illnesses, premature deaths, accidents, problematic children, and other misfortunes. Illness is, therefore, broadly understood to be whatever hinders individuals, families, and communities from attaining well-being. As Asamoah-Gyadu argues, in Pentecostal discourse, "It is believed that sometimes spirits do not take possession of victims, but they may remotely control one's life in negative ways by afflicting with diseases... in such cases, a person is described simply as being oppressed by evil powers."[26]

In Kenya, as is generally true throughout Africa, traditional spirits and ancestors have survived in the African imagination. So, too, the belief in sorcery and witchcraft; consultation of witches, wizards, and sorcerers; generational curses; and evil omens. It is believed among neo-Pentecostal and charismatic churches that associating with these traditional institutions renders one vulnerable to demonic influences of possession and oppression. Healing and deliverance operate to liberate victims from the encumbrances of such demonic powers. Healing which is done in the name of the Trinity, therefore, implies being freed from demonic influences and curses, such that people may enjoy health and wholeness or God's fullness of life understood to be available in Christ. Healing also results in liberation, the acquisition of a new identity, and reintegration into society and, thereby, peace and reconciliation in all realms of being.

The Healing and Deliverance Process in NPCs

Generally, although most NPCs do not have elaborate healing and deliverance rituals, they do still employ some methods in their mediation of healing. All these methods are based on biblical teaching, but in some NPCs, they are culturally specific and have been reinforced by traditions that exist within

26. Asamoah-Gyadu, *Contemporary Pentecostal Christianity*, 35.

mainline churches. The healing process is steeped in ritual and symbolism. According to Victor Turner, ritual is "prescribed formal behaviour for occasions not given over to technological routine, having reference to beliefs in mystical beings or powers."[27] Ritual actions gather life together, as it were, for those participating in it. Its symbols are intended to lead participants to dimensions of reality deeper than that which is merely visible. As Zuesse argues, "ritual immerses us in process and becoming, forces us back into the concrete, and makes us recognize our body,"[28] since the body is the microcosm of the universe. The types of healing and deliverance rituals that are prominent may rightfully be identified as therapy, identity, salvation, social intensification, and revitalistic. Healing rituals serve several social and spiritual functions. They portray, in symbolic form, certain values as well as cultural orientations. They create or recreate the categories through which human beings perceive reality. As Turner poignantly observes, "Ritual conjures models of public behavior that might once have been consistent with such conditions as provided by ecological, economic, or political factors but which have now lost their efficacy. New models may incompletely reflect new conditions, but they coexist with other models and may contradict them."[29]

Hence, even if certain ritual activities may not appear purposive, they have effects upon participants which influence their subsequent behavior. Whether communion, healing, or general purification, rituals renew the community, express shared beliefs, integrate the community, and reorient it and individuals towards further submission to God's protection and care. For example, in his analysis of Ndembu cults of affliction, Turner observes that the rituals "turn painfully destructive impulses and social tensions and even mental and physical illnesses into affirmative communal experiences."[30] Symbols, particularly in a religious context, have a metaempirical purpose. Every religious act or object in healing is charged with significance which is, in the final act, symbolic since it refers to supernatural values or forms. Symbols are not a replica of objective reality but reveal something deeper and more fundamental. As Beane observes, "Symbols are capable of revealing a modality of the real or a condition of the world which is not evident on the plane of immediate experience."[31]

In the context of NPCs, reserves of spiritual power are ritually built up and utilized in such a manner as to redress or eradicate the effects of

---

27. Turner, *Forest of Symbols*, 11.
28. Zeusse, *Ritual Cosmos*, 328.
29. Turner, *Forest of Symbols*, 7.
30. Turner, *Drums of Affliction*, 197.
31. Eliade et al., *Myths, Rites, Symbols*, 347.

human and nonhuman mystical agents that affect the individual. In an analysis of Zionist[32] healing rituals in South Africa, Kiernan distinguishes between "powers" and "specifics" utilized by Zionist prophets.[33] He argues that specifics are contingent infusions of spiritual power designed to cope with problems: drinking a portion of water and ashes transmits power sufficient to alleviate stomach pains, having been blessed for this purpose. While "specifics" are exhausted in their application and are thus renewable, "powers" are permanent and lasting endowments. Some belong personally to gifted individuals such as prophets; others are attached to the functions of membership or of office within the community.[34] These "specifics" and powers are imbued with *Umoya*—literally spirit, breath, air—which is expanded to counteract evil. Kiernan further adds that powers of status and office are given through a ritual act of conferral, and all conferred power is used in the manner of weapons. Therefore, unlike specifics which are used to arrest or reverse an undesirable condition already contracted, conferred powers are designed to ward off impeding mystical attacks: to repel rather than to expel. This weaponry resides in clothing, flags, and staves.[35]

Although Jesus is Alive Ministries does not employ elaborate healing rituals, and they reject traditional African practices, nevertheless, they practice numerous forms of rituals. Examples include their use of anointing oil, mantles and white clothing, photographs of those in need of healing and deliverance; the laying on of hands, causing people to fall down or be slain by the spirit; their use of revelations through prophecies, rebuking the devil and his demons and exorcising them. The "anointed men and women of God" are invested with powers to deliver, exorcise, and heal. On every Tuesday evening, there is a deliverance service. Teachings on deliverance are also held regularly for the benefit of church members, so that they can learn how to protect themselves from the wiles of the enemy.

The interpretations of the causes of lack of prosperity, poor health, unhappy marriages, phobias, emotional complexes, soul ties, spiritual/demonic marriages, and other problems also have a strong cultural determinant. Most illnesses or misfortune are perceived to arise from family conflicts, witchcraft, and demonic attacks. As Arthur Kleinman observes, "diseases and illness are explanatory concepts rather than entities in themselves. They can be understood only within defined contexts of meaning

---

32. Zionist churches are African Instituted Churches of the spiritual type. Like NPCs, they are Pentecostal but much more Africanized and inculturated.

33. Kiernan, "Weapons of Zion," 13.

34. Kiernan, "Weapons of Zion," 13.

35. Kiernan, "Weapons of Zion," 13.

and social relationship. Culture influences the patterning of sick roles in a society, and sickness has different social significance within different cultures. Thus, illness may be perceived as punishment for wrongdoing or possession by an alien spirit. In the latter case, possession may be accepted, and the role of such a possessed person is functional and accepted within the culture."[36] While spirit possession may be accepted as a sign for one to be a healer in traditional culture, in Pentecostal theology, the spirit is dealt with through exorcism and deliverance.

Discussion of NPCs' Healing and Deliverance

Using James Dow's framework of symbolic healing,[37] I shall try to analyze the NPCs' spiritual warfare, healing, and deliverance. According to Dow, this framework can be used to describe and explain all forms of "symbolic," "cultural," "spiritual," or "folk" healing. Following the theories of Talcott Parsons,[38] Dow outlines the steps in this process as

- constructing the cultural myth of health with its healing symbols;
- persuading the sick person that the sickness can be explained and cured by the myth;
- attaching the emotions of the sick person to particular symbols within the myth; and
- manipulating the symbols to effect healing.[39]

Dow understands community as a multi-layered, biocultural system in which the layers are connected by key signals. The symbolic community is connected to the individual through "myth" or "symbols," which are the central content of the commonly held view of the cosmos. He notes that the healing symbol works on two levels: general and specific. The general symbol, or myth, exists within the symbolic framework of the culture as an accepted sign of health, healing, or power. It is a culture-specific symbol, a cultural myth. Jesus, for example, is such a symbol among NPC Christians, and so are ancestors or God among African communities. Particularized symbols for the sick person are constructed from these general myths or symbols in the healing process by "letting Jesus come into your life," or "speaking in tongues," or discovering the identity of the ancestor. Dow

36. Kleinman, *Patients and Healers*, 73.
37. Dow, "Universal Aspects of Symbolic Healing," 56–69.
38. Parsons, "On Concepts of Influence," 37–62.
39. Dow, "Universal Aspects of Symbolic Healing," 56–57.

refers to these symbols as "transactional symbols," and they are available for symbolic healing. The mechanisms by which the transactional symbols are manipulated by the healer are highly culture-specific. They include the laying on of hands; casting out demons; identifying sorcery; applying, drinking, or bathing in anointing oil; calling upon the blood of Jesus; fighting the devil with the fire of the Holy Ghost, etc.

According to Dow, the central aim of the symbolic healing process is the transaction of emotions, which he says "are generalized media that link the self and somatic system . . . (they) have an integrative function. They summarize complex processes at a lower level in a single message to a higher level."[40] Dow assumes that particular symbols can be translated into emotions and, thus, be effective in the biosphere. A healer or therapist has the ability to find the various symbols and thus effect in the patient not only a new sense of meaning but a reshaping of emotions which can involve healing. However, the mediating process between symbol and emotion is not clear, and this is the weakest point of his argument, for he reduces healing to psychological processes, a mere transfer of emotion. Nevertheless, his model has the advantage that it can treat religious healing as a psychological, social, cultural, and spiritual event.

In the NPCs, the key spiritual agents are God, Jesus, the Holy Spirit, ancestors, evil spirits (*mapepo, jinns*), Satan, demons, witches, sorcerers, priests, pastors, anointed men or women of God, prophets, and healers. Illnesses are, as a rule, understood as emanating from human and spiritual sources. These sources of sickness and misfortune simultaneously affect the body, spirit, social relations, and the sense of the cosmos. In the healing ritual, particularly that performed by anointed men and women of God in NPCs, African ideas crop up in the following four ways:

1. The anointed man or woman of God and patient relate to a shared truth, a myth that generalizes their special life, experience, and values, and that is structured by the symbols present in their cultural context. The practice of the healer consists in being able to express the myth in relation to the concrete situation. Prayers, testimonies, and preaching indicate the "myth" of the NPC to be that life is a continual battleground for the struggle between the forces of good and evil, mirroring the socio-economic and political context of frustration, hopelessness, and despair. The traditional channels can no longer guarantee the longed-for harmony and well-being. However, God (*Nyasaye, Were, Ngai, Murungu*), the spirit of God (*Roho*), and Jesus Christ are symbols of the expectation that good will be victorious at last. The dangers of life can be escaped

40. Dow, "Universal Aspects of Symbolic Healing," 56–57.

only through confession of sin, repentance, and forgiveness, which implies radical conversion to the Trinitarian God. The healing ritual is the sign of that conversion and of acceptance by God.

2. Through the process of diagnosis, usually done through prophetic revelation, the healer explains to the patient that a personal problem is to be understood as a disturbed relation. Since they share in the same myth, it is therefore understood that there is a disturbance in the general myth. The sharing of a common worldview (myth) between the patient and the anointed man or woman of God is essential to the therapeutic process, for it enhances the patient's growth in faith and trust in the healer and healing ritual. It is this relationship and the faith of the patient in the healer's ability that elicits the healing. Therefore, the healer applies a particular diagnosis. Complex images of illness appear, all linked to mental suffering, bodily infirmities, and social isolation. The healer reveals the causes in destructive spirits associated with Satan.

3. The healer connects the problems with particular elements of the common myth and so names the factors that are afflicting the patient: spirits of the dead, *mapepo* and *jinns,* sent through witchcraft, curses, demonic attacks, etc.

4. By bringing these mythological elements into due order, the healer removes what is disturbing the myth. The patient experiences the recreation of the good cosmos as a new ordering of his/her consciousness and his/her feelings. He/she is set free to reestablish a new relation to his/her body and, particularly important in Africa, to his/her social environment. Exorcism regularly takes place on an individual and communal basis in the NPCs like Neno Evangelism Centre and Jesus is Alive Ministries. It takes the form of rebuking evil spirits/ demons, and expelling and binding them using the Bible. It is Jesus on whom the pastor calls to drive out the evil spirits. The patient may fall down and go into a trance. The expulsion is usually achieved as the patient collapses and gains consciousness with a calm, happy expression, and it is assumed that the spirit of God has entered the patient. The service is brought to an end with prayers of thanksgiving, testimonies of victory, song, and a sermon of explanation.

As Ustorf argues, "religious healers of every provenance have the special quality of revealing the meaning of healing for concrete existence in the microcosm of the human body. Symbolic behaviour is able to create identity amid individual and historic change."[41] In light of the process Émile Durkheim

---

41. Ustorf, "Das Heilen in den unabhängigen Kirchen Schwarzafrikas," 198–210.

explains in *The Elementary Forms of Religious Life*, sociologist Gary Easthope describes the healing process as transformation of identity in the person as a result of transformation or change in the socialization process.[42] The healing process involves the reconstruction of a person's identity in terms of the more positive symbols of the new social or religious grouping in which the person is healed. The patient is socialized into the new world, and this is experienced as healing. Identity change is always a transcendental process, since it involves giving up one's identity so that a new identity and a new self-understanding can emerge. In the NPCs, this identity is articulated in the saying that one becomes a "child of the church family," or enters the register of members if they had not already. The church becomes a protective healing community, and they experience themselves as immune to attacks of Satan and *mapepo* (evil spirits) and fortify themselves with the "weapons of the spirit."

The receptive attitude of the patient is especially meaningful in the fourth stage, when healing is experienced. It is not an act of self-determination. The patient experiences liberation and is elevated to a transcendental level. Indigenous ideas of healing are developed and reinterpreted in biblical words. The old powers are not simply replaced, but the reality they describe serves to articulate the liberating, biblical God. Possession by evil ancestral or other spirits is no longer interpreted as a positive sign but symbolizes destructive forces. These forces are no longer to be appeased but must be driven out. This is done in the name of God (*Mungu*, in Kiswahili; *Were; Ngai; Nyasaye; Murungu*) who is unambiguously identified with the triune God. He is the healing power, "everlasting life and health."

Conclusion

Healing, spiritual warfare, and deliverance are crucial to NPC theology. They are a factor in the appeal of these churches for causal explanations of illness, and the solutions provided are derived from Scripture and reflect the cultural understanding of the same. Healing and deliverance and spiritual warfare are also metaphors for understanding lived realities and their impact on the well-being of individuals and communities. When properly effected, spiritual warfare, deliverance, and healing result in self-understanding, liberation, and well-being; they lead to individual and community reintegration and resolution of what ails relationships.

It is, however, important to exercise caution with regard to certain practices in NPC healing rituals that may render patients vulnerable to

---

42. Easthope, *History of Social Research Methods*. For Durkheim's thought, see Durkheim, *Elementary Forms*, 116–24.

exploitation and abuse by unscrupulous "healers." One such practice is the demand for money. When money becomes an important constituent of the healing process, it may divert attention from the source of healing who is God and lead patients and adherents to regard it as an important instrument. Some healer-pastors encourage patients with chronic illnesses like cancer, diabetes, hypertension, etc., to get off medication. This can result in loss of faith and even death when healing does not occur. Victims can also become immobilized, abdicating their moral agency, if they rely too much on the pastor-healer and an over-spiritualization of evil and problems. Nevertheless, the healing rituals in the NPCs represented by Jesus is Alive Ministries, Neno Evangelistic Centre, and Faith Evangelistic Ministries have been efficacious, to some extent, in the sense that healing results in self-understanding and acceptance of one's situation.

Bibliography

Asamoah-Gyadu, Kwabena. *Contemporary Pentecostal Christianity: Interpretations from an African Context*. Oxford: Regnum, 2013.
Dow, James. "Universal Aspects of Symbolic Healing: A Theoretical Synthesis." *American Anthropologist* 88 (1986) 56–69.
Durkheim, Emile. *The Elementary Forms of Religious Life*. Translated by Karen E. Fields. New York: Free Press, 1986.
Easthope, Gary. *A History of Social Research Methods*. London: Longman, 1974.
Eliade, Mircea, et al., eds. *Myths, Rites, Symbols: A Mircea Eliade Reader*. Vol 2. New York: Harper and Row, 1976.
Gifford, Paul. *African Christianity: Its Public Role*. London: Hurst, 1998.
Kalu, Ogbu U. *Power, Poverty, and Prayer: The Challenges of Poverty and Pluralism in African Christianity, 1960–1996*. Trenton, NJ: Africa World, 2006.
Kiernan, J. P. "The Weapons of Zion." *Journal of Religion in Africa* 10 (1979) 13–31.
Kleinman, Arthur. *Patients and Healers in the Contexts of Culture*. Berkeley: University of California Press, 1980.
Kraft, Charles H. "Spiritual Warfare: A Neocharismatic Perspective." In *The New International Dictionary of Pentecostal and Charismatic Movements*, edited by Stanley M. Burgess and Ed M. Van der Mass, 1091. Grand Rapids: Zondervan, 2002.
Magesa, Laurenti. "Power in African Religion." *Wajibu* 14 (1999) 2–3.
Marshall, Ruth. "Pentecostalism in Southern Nigeria: An Overview." In *New Dimensions in African Christianity*, edited by Paul Gifford, 7–32. Nairobi: All Africa Conference of Churches, 1992.
Meyer, Brigit. *Translating the Devil: Religion and Modernity among the Ewe in Ghana*. Trenton, NJ: Africa World Press, 1999.
Mugambi, Jesse N. K. "Evangelistic and Charismatic Initiatives in Post-Colonial Africa." In *Charismatic Renewal in Africa: A Challenge for African Christianity*, edited by Mika Vähäkangas and Andrew Kyomo, 111–44. Nairobi: Acton, 2003.

Ndegwa, Alex. "Over 6,000 Churches Awaiting Registration." *The Standard*. September 4, 2007.

Ojo, Matthews. "The Charismatic Movement in Nigeria Today." *International Bulletin of Missionary Research* 19 (1995) 114–18.

———. "Deeper Life Bible Church of Nigeria." In *New Dimensions in African Christianity*, edited by Paul Gifford, 135–56. Nairobi: All Africa Conference of Churches, 1992.

Parsons, Talcott. "On Concepts of Influence." *Public Opinion Quarterly* 27 (1963) 32–62.

Pew Forum on Religion and Public Life. "Spirit and Power—A Ten-Country Survey of Pentecostals." Washington, DC: Pew Research Center, 2006. http://assets.pewresearch.org/wp-content/uploads/sites/11/2006/10/pentecostals-08.pdf.

Turner, Victor. *The Drums of Affliction: A Study of Religious Processes among the Ndembu of Zambia*. London: Hutchinson, 1968.

———. *Forest of Symbols: Aspects of Ndembu Ritual*. New York: Cornell University Press, 1967.

Ustorf, Werner. "Das Heilen in den unabhängigen Kirchen Schwarzafrikas: Ein Versuch interkulturellen Verstehens." *Zeitschrift für Mission* 13 (1987) 198–210.

Winter, Mark. "The Balokole and the Protestant Ethic: A Critic." *Journal of Religion in Africa* 14 (1983) 58–73.

Zuesse, Evan, M. *Ritual Cosmos: The Sanctification of Life in African Religions*. Athens, OH: Ohio University Press, 1979.

5

Locating Exorcisms and Faith Healing in African Pentecostalism within Constructive Postmodernity

ZORODZAI DUBE

Introduction

"In the name of Jesus, re-le-ase and go!" Every Sunday and during midweek prayer meetings, African Pentecostal pastors rebuke demons in stern voices. Exorcism and faith healing are so central to African Pentecostalism that there is no church service that ends without confronting the evil spirits. Some of the "evil spirits" commonly identified and subsequently cast out are the demons of unemployment, hunger, poverty, and sleeplessness. It is notable, in view of socioeconomic realities in Zimbabwe, that these demons correspond to the social needs of the people: hunger, poverty, and unemployment.[1] Some demons are physiological, such as the demons that attack the back, legs, and eyes.

This study, using examples from Zimbabwe, approaches the subject from a sociohistorical perspective by exploring the social, economic, and political contexts within which the exorcisms and healing take place. It shall be argued that the exorcisms and healings, far from being a spiritual warfare, seem to respond to social consequences due to the corruption of African leaders and the negative effects of global capitalism. In this claim, I agree with scholars such as Terrence Ranger and Paul Gifford[2] who explore the connections between particular religious phenomenon to African realities

---

1. Dube, "Casting Out Demons," 352.
2. Gifford, *Ghana's New Christianity*, ix.

such as economics and politics. Adding to these voices, this study primarily investigates the manner in which exorcisms and faith healing open new spaces of identity and survival vis-à-vis the local and global realities. As such, exorcism and faith healing are not only coded protest voices but also spaces of re-articulation and re-energizing through the creation of alternative fictive kinship which cushions against the hegemony of corruption and capitalism. This is achieved by resocializing subjects into moral and ethical citizens who, instead of imitating the evils of local African leaders, conceive themselves as self-sustaining because of the God-power within. The perspective that helps to unpack these dynamics is constructive postmodernism, which is associated with theorists such Dirk Hebdige,[3] Jean Baudrillard,[4] and Paul Heelas[5] who explore the alternative or subcultural identities articulated by these movements.

Are the Current Voices on the Subject Sufficient?

Before I focus on my own perspective, a brief overview of major approaches is necessary. Like any other field of study, approaches to African Pentecostalism are varied and raise plural issues. Generally, three dominant perspectives concerning the study of African Pentecostalism can be discerned. The first category, which has a majority of voices and is followed by many in the academy, takes a comparative and inculturation approach by comparing African diviners to African Pentecostal prophets or healers.[6] Scholars in this category agree that African Pentecostalism repackages the enchanted African worldview of healing and spiritual warfare with Christian regalia. Informed by postmodern paradigms, they regard African Pentecostalism as a global ambassador in reviving and recovering some of the African thought forms, especially concerning healing and exorcism.

The second category, similar to the first, comprises scholars that celebrate the emergence of African Pentecostalism as something unique from Africa—a spirituality buoyed on the wings of globalization with an implicit intention to revive global Christianity. Unlike the first category that is interested in comparison between African tradition and African Pentecostalism, this methodology explores ways that African Pentecostalism takes advantage of trends in globalization, technology, and migration. As if to excavate something positive from the challenges associated with

---

3. Hebdige, *Subculture*, 3.
4. Baudrillard, *Seduction*, 37.
5. Heelas, *Spiritualties of Life*, 23.
6. Shoko, *Karanga Indigenous Religions*, 12. Kalu, *African Pentecostalism*, 64.

global capitalization's evils, such as immigration, African Pentecostalism is hailed as a unique form of Christianity from Africa destined for the entire globe. Prominent African scholars in this category are Afe Adogame[7] and Matthews Ojo.[8] Though started in Africa, African Pentecostalism has global networks which function as identity havens and economic exchange routes, and thus implicitly describe African Pentecostalism as a positive new phenomenon coming from Africa to the rest of the world. However, perhaps due to sensitivity toward a rationalized Western worldview, scholars in this category put less emphasis on issues such as exorcisms and faith healing. They speak less enthusiastically about exorcism and spiritual healing, fearing the accusations of being primitive and less scientific.

The third category incorporates gender and masculinity perspectives in the study of African Pentecostalism. Examples of African scholars in this category are Adriaan van Klinken[9] and Sarojini Nadar,[10] for whom healing and exorcism reveal the cunning shrewdness of Pentecostal leaders who use their religious tricks to abuse women. Voices within this category are interested in the question of power dynamics within the movement, and they argue that African Pentecostalism exudes all forms of African patriarchy and masculinity. Paradoxically, although there are many women at such gatherings—as prophetesses, teachers, and deacons—scholars who address African Pentecostalism from this perspective see it as a phenomenon that must be critically examined because of the African patriarchal culture's inherent traits that persist in some versions of Pentecostalism and perpetuate the subordination of women in marriages. Klinken and Nadar also highlight the idea that African Pentecostalism thrives within poor communities where people are made to prove their faith by drinking or eating inappropriate substances, such as grass and rats. The type of African Christianity that Ojo and Adogame discuss—one that takes advantage of the opportunities of globalization and technology—is vastly different from the brand of African Pentecostalism found in African villages. The new versions that have mushroomed in the African villages and townships are geared towards demonstrations of power, and, in these assemblies, abuse happens in the name of Jesus.[11]

---

7. Adogame and Gerloff, "Introduction," 1–9.
8. Ojo, "Religion, Public Space, and the Press," 233.
9. van Klinken, "Male Headship as Male Agency," 204.
10. Nadar, "Palatable Patriachy and Violence," 551.
11. Recently, in South Africa, there have been cases of Africa Pentecostal pastors who force their followers to eat grass and rats and drink gas.

Critique of Current Approaches and a Way Forward

The first and second categories of African scholars that I mentioned take a descriptive and phenomenological approach, which leaves unanswered the question as to which variable makes African Pentecostalism attain a global outreach or which aspects strengthen African identities—poverty or economics. African Pentecostalism involves global outreach, not because it is interested in missionary work, but as a survival strategy. African churches with Western links are materially richer than their cousins next door. Typically, African Pentecostal churches use their members who study in Europe as links to establish churches abroad. My argument is augmented by the fact that, besides immigrant church members and intermarriages, African churches in the Diaspora have not succeeded in evangelizing or converting local people. One may equally argue, in agreement with Ogbu Kalu, that African Pentecostalism is reinforcing African patriarchal ideas. This is not because Christian ideas and African tradition are being blended, but because religion is used as a shield to respond to the vicissitudes associated with the negative effects of global capitalism and the local corruption of African leaders. Thus, notably missing in Afe Adogame's argument concerning African Pentecostalism's global outreach is the economic variable that African Pentecostalism responds to economic challenges, locally and abroad.

Instead of making the case for the entire continent, this study focuses on Zimbabwe through three broad sections. The first section attempts to establish the sociopolitical context, with reference to Zimbabwe, where exorcisms and healing are taking place. This section also contains the argument that the healing and exorcisms are theological statements that refract the sociopolitical challenges faced by the people. The second section looks into the rise and *mundus operandi* of various African Pentecostal movements in Zimbabwe. The last section, the main contribution of this study, explores how African Pentecostalism, besides providing coded protest language, provides alternative survival strategies, ethical instructions as a strategy for good citizenship, and a personal sense of agency.

Political and Economic Uncertainties in Zimbabwe

Until 2000, when the country's economic and political fortunes began to change for the worse, African Pentecostal movements were not visible on issues of healing and exorcism. Instead, African Initiated Churches (AICs) and traditional diviners (*sangoma*) were the go-to methods for faith healing. On the other hand, classical Pentecostalism, from which came many of the

African Pentecostals (such as the Apostolic Faith Church which is linked to the Asuza Revival) was famous for preaching holiness, rapture, and morality. However, by the year 2000, with the rapid collapse of the Zimbabwean economy and the chaotic political climate, African Pentecostalism began to be associated with healing and exorcism.

In order to understand how politics intertwined with religious developments in Zimbabwe, one needs to start as far back as 1980. In 1980, Zimbabwe attained its political liberation after a protracted liberation war against the British settler government which was led by Ian Smith.[12] Between 1980 and 1990, the euphoria of political independence was significantly high, and the country was internationally regarded as the "darling of Africa."[13] Several factors contributed to this golden period. First, Mugabe's reconciliatory tone after 1980 was a great relief to many who feared that a possible episode of vengeance might occur. Second, the economic structure did not change, which pleased the minority white citizens and foreign investors; land and the entire agricultural sector, the main backbone of the economy, remained in the hands of the few white farmers known as the Zimbabwe Farmers Union. It is not clear why Mugabe did not suddenly restructure Zimbabwe's economy. However, it is possible to postulate that, beginning in 1980, Mugabe became preoccupied with

1. the fragile internal politics as a result of the ethnic tension among the minority Ndebele tribe and the majority Shona tribe, which shifted the focus away from the former colonizer and the need to restructure the economy;

2. the lessons from the neighboring country, Mozambique, which had paid a hefty price for chasing away and destroying all colonial institutions and acted as a deterring metaphor against radical economic change; and

3. the achievement of Zimbabwe's independence during the "global triumph of capitalism." The fall of the Soviet Union in 1989 saw many African countries adopting the Economic Structural Adjustment Program (ESAP), a capitalist economic framework which had negative effects on people's livelihoods. Thus, despite political independence, the colonial economic institutions remained intact and reinvigorated.[14]

---

12. I stress political independence because economists and political scientists, in view of globalization and imperialism, realize that political independence did not translate to economic independence in most African countries.

13. Chitando, "Come Down, O Lord," 334.

14. Fukuyama, "End of History," 3.

By 1990, most African countries, including Zimbabwe, swallowed the bitter pill of liberal economic policies in the form of a Structural Adjustment Program (SAP).

As an economic policy, SAPs were projected to ensure fiscal prudence, which would stimulate economic growth through privatization and decentralization. However, privatization left the African economies vulnerable to corrupt leaders and corrupt international companies that did not provide revenue to the local governments. Many scholars have argued that the negative effects of capitalism were not envisaged.[15] As Adorno and Horkheimer,[16] Alain Touraine,[17] and Alan Bond[18] said, regrettably, economic liberalism benefited few—mostly those with the means to compete on a liberalized, economic playing field. Consequently, as the years progressed, the gap between the rich and the poor widened in most African countries. While seeking to maximize profits, industries infringed on people's livelihood by retrenching many from their employment. In Zimbabwe, growing dissatisfaction led to constant protests, almost daily. Local musicians such as Leonard Zhakata and Simon Chimbetu captured the growing sadness through music that chronicled people's pain due to rising inflation, retrenchments, and deplorable living conditions.[19] In addition, gospel musicians also mushroomed, consoling people facing the painful realities of life. Mostly through their lyrics, gospel musicians exhorted people to trust God, while some cried for immediate divine intervention.[20] The hope for *nirvana* turned out to be hell on earth for many.

Come 2000: Changing Political Tides

Due to economic hardships and the lack of dividends from political liberation, by the year 2000, people had already lost hope for the promised nirvana. They wanted an alternative political solution. In addition to pressures associated with the global international capitalism, the corruption at home by Mugabe's government was evident: politicians were rich while the ordinary people were poor. Consequently, demand began to grow for "Mugabe to go." Led by workers' movements which later metamorphosed into the

15. Horkheimer and Adorno, *Dialectics*, 5. Wallerstein, "Introduction," 6.
16. Horkheimer and Adorno, *Dialectics*, 5.
17. Touraine, *Post-Industrial Societies*, 9.
18. Bond, *Elite Transition*, 42.
19. Vambe, "Version of Subversion," 164.
20. Chitando, "Come Down, O Lord."

opposition party called the Movement for Democratic Change (MDC), the protesting voices gained followers from across the country. If the national mood was a litmus test, then it was clear that Mugabe would have vacated the presidency by 2002. However, like a caged lion, Mugabe instead initiated the chaotic land reform program. In what could be regarded as a divide-and-conquer strategy, Mugabe introduced a controversial land reform program, basically annexing all land that was in the hands of the white people. Instead of venting their anger on Mugabe, the rowdy peasant farmers—who had previously lost their land to the white farmers through the Native Land Act and Land Husbandry Act of the 1930s—regarded Mugabe as a hero. Mugabe managed to shift the people's anger from accusing him of corruption to the minority white farmers who were now accused of sabotaging the country's economic progress. The loot was extended to his supporters who also saw the rampage as a reversal of colonial land policy. However, land reform program received mixed reactions from the urban dwellers who accused Mugabe of political gamble. These people needed food which was no longer coming due to land inversion. Consequently, the country was politically divided between the loyal, rural peasant farmers and the sieged urban dwellers. To cement his grip on power, Mugabe revived the liberation war sentiments through music and propaganda.[21]

The land reform received international condemnation, especially from America, Britain, Australia, and New Zealand. These countries hastily slapped Zimbabwe with economic sanctions, crippling its hope of self-sustenance. The economic sanctions put a strain on the vulnerable poor who had, for years, endured the corruption of their political leaders and the negative effects of global capitalism. Sanctions shattered the country's production base, which was mainly agriculture. What followed was the predictable demise of the country's economic sector and the closing of major factories and industries, all of which had repercussion on the people's livelihoods.

In response, people demonstrated on the streets but faced the heavy arm of the police and the army. Brutalized and hopeless, the people found that the only remaining survival route was to jump the border into neighboring countries such as South Africa, Zambia, Mozambique, and Botswana. In addition, due to lack of medicine, hospitals became places to welcome the "angel of death." Today, the situation in Zimbabwe has worsened: people are starving, and most urban dwellers cultivate small pieces of available land. People import almost everything. Zimbabwe is in economic woe, and the only hope any Zimbabwean has is to find a passport and escape the "burning house."

---

21. Chitando, "Come Down, O Lord," 334.

Since 2000, elections in Zimbabwe have been marred by violence and intimidation, even though Mugabe won in 2002. Like an Islamic *muezzin*,[22] Mugabe used the only national television channel as a political mouthpiece to accuse the West of imperialism and attempts to change the regime through economic sanctions. As the economy worsened, so too did the political climate. Mugabe had trained militias to terrorize the public and imprison supporters of opposition. Economists have determined that Zimbabwe has succeeded in overtaking Somalia as the poorest country on the continent. Millions of Zimbabweans are in the Diaspora; even though Mugabe was ousted in 2017 and elections were held in July 2018, life remains very hard and unbearable for many Zimbabweans. What is happening in Zimbabwe is a reflection in some ways of what is happening in many African countries that experience random political violence, disillusionment with the political establishment, ill health, and unemployment.

The Rise of Prophets and the Spiritual Fathers

Given the context, I now move to locate the *modus operandi* of African Pentecostal preachers. As mentioned, African Pentecostalism exists in different forms, and new ones emerge each day. However, the type of Pentecostal movements that are of interest to this study are ones that are found in many African towns and villages, where they are distinctly different from those that migrate abroad. They put emphasis on faith healing and exorcism and see demons as the cause of all people's experiences. In these movements, there are spirits of poverty and unemployment, as well as spirits that cause people to remain unmarried or to encounter misfortunes in work or everyday life.

Given the chaotic political context and versatile economic climate due to local and global forces, the rise of African Pentecostal preachers may not be a coincidence. As economic challenges and political disillusionment thicken, prophets heighten their stern rebuke: "In the name of Jesus, I rebuke you, spirit of illness, poverty, unemployment, lack of shelter, hunger . . . re . . . lease and go!" The Prophets, who masquerade under the guise of divine wisdom, tell people that they have answers to almost everything—finance, marriage, health, and prosperity. "There is nothing impossible with God," they thunder to large crowds in hoarse, yet persuasive, voices. Sometimes, specific diseases and conditions are addressed, and the crowd shouts "Amen" in response: "You, HIV, tuberculosis, cancer, diabetes, back pain . . . you have no place in the presence of God; go away!"

---

22. The chosen person at the mosque who leads the call for daily prayer.

One day, I was in attendance at one of these crusades. When I heard the pastor mention my own medical condition, I felt some psychological relief and shouted, "Amen!"

With modern technology, it is now easy to get a feel for the way these pastors carry out their business. For example, in a YouTube video, well-known prophet Emmanuel Makandiwa prophecies that massive oil reserves would be discovered in Zimbabwe. In the same video, he also predicts the explosion that took place in China and prophecies to his audience about businesses, property, health, and economic prosperity. Some prophecies are very specific in detail. For example, the prophet would mention a person's exact name, surname, address, type of clothing, and personal problems. To an onlooker who suspends rationality, the performance is persuasive, because one wonders how the pastor came to know such intimate and personal information. Public opinion is divided, with some labelling the prophets as charlatans or magicians. I prefer to see them as individuals who are able to tap into the people's religious worldview and offer a religious explanation for reality, and, given the lack of an alternative meaningful social canopy, people believe them.

Importantly, while the country is battling with unemployment, poverty, an inefficient health sector, and political chaos, the pastors are stretching a spiritual canopy. *Casting out Demons in Zimbabwe* and *Jesus and Afro-Pentecostal Prophets* show connections between the rise of Afro-Pentecostal prophets and the country's economic fortunes. These works argue that, though confined to church buildings, prophets speak indirectly to the public challenges facing the people—poverty, hunger, and unemployment—not as structural issues but as consequences of the devil. The healing and exorcisms within African Pentecostal churches seem like a coded disavowal or a desire for alternative economic and political framework. They negate the immediate context and simultaneously promise sudden divine intervention.

That religious exorcisms are symptomatic of deep social problems is not a new argument or perspective. In *Wretched of the Earth*, Franz Fanon[23] suggests, in reference to Algeria's situation of colonialism, that the dramatic healings and exorcisms express a disavowal against French colonialism. Fanon's view differs from Sigmund Freud,[24] who sees religion as an illusionary drug that shrouds concrete reality. In light of the economic and social challenges within most African states, there is a kernel of truth in viewing exorcisms as coded protest. I differ from Fanon in that, while he seems to see

---

23. Fanon, *Wretched of the Earth*, 55.
24. Freud, *Civilization and its Discontent*, 46.

exorcisms as hopeless protests from caged people, I read the exorcisms and healings as disavowals that signify agency rather than passivity.

African Pentecostal Prophets as Constructive Postmodern Practitioners

Similar to Zimbabwe, the subjects within oppressive structures do not yield to power but contest and express alternatives. This argument is the major contribution of this study. The task is to unpack how exorcism and faith healing in Zimbabwe contest and express an alternative view of reality. It is then possible to locate African Pentecostalism within constructive postmodernism.[25] Constructive postmodernism acknowledges power structures, but unlike Foucault's view,[26] power is not institutionalized, pervasive, and asymmetric. Power can be contested, and new identities, in contrast to "docile" bodies, can emerge. Thus, constructive postmodernity articulates "new identities, communities and even utopias in the face of increasing ephemerality and social life that lacks foundation."[27] The approach "seeks new connections and syntheses that might offer alternatives to the negative aspects of modernism."[28] It "combine[s] the benefits of modernity with values and qualities that it believes were devalued by modernism as an ideology" and "represent[s] new and often surprising combinations and crossovers of codes and discourses, but also challenges to grand narratives."[29]

How does African Pentecostalism fit this description? The answer is that a majority of African Pentecostal churches are found in urban centers, places characterized as ephemeral in terms of economics and politics. Once independent, most young Zimbabweans move into urban centers which, even today, are their only hope of finding employment. In fact, in comparison to the rural areas, urban cities can be places of employment as maids, gardeners, clerks, or factory workers. As the economic fortunes of the country shift with factories and hospitals closing, there is no production in urban centers. In towns, the corruption of African politicians and the negative effects of global capitalism converge. Survival in the form of subsistence is paramount, yet risky. In the Zimbabwean context, it is

---

25. Constructive postmodernism reacts to previous explanations (mostly Karl Marx—see Callinicos, *Against Postmodernism*) that only see society as dominated by class interests. Instead, constructive postmodernity is interested in non-class identities such as fashion, clubs, charity organizations, or sports.

26. Foucault, *Archaeology of Knowledge*, 10.

27. Thompson, "Social Pluralism," 588.

28. Thompson, "Social Pluralism," 588.

29. Thompson, "Social Pluralism," 588.

plausible to view African Pentecostalism as (1) movements that seek to rearticulate identities in view of local and global disruptions; (2) movements that seek to offer a utopian or alternative view of reality vis-à-vis globalization and capitalism; and (3) movements that encourage personal agency. Therefore, the question is: how do exorcism and faith healing act as the ultimate expression of contesting evils in public space, yet also offer an alternative constructive vision of reality?

Healing and Exorcism as Alternative Citizenship

One of the negative effects of global poverty and neoliberalization in Africa is the creation of unexpected social realities for most Africans. While fighting colonialism, Africans hoped for united and prosperous communities where the state would be the ultimate arbitrator in matters of politics and economy. In most African states, the current reality is dispossession: most people are poor compared to the few African elites and global traders whose presence does not profit the local people. Economic dispossession is not merely a lack of material; it also creates violence, the symptoms of which find expression within the African household and community.

The pain and anger resulting from political failure and poverty are notable in the language used in exorcisms. In high and harsh voices, African leaders cast out demons of poverty, unemployment, lack of personal economic progress, and many other evils; these demons are real social issues that face the people. Given the political chaos and malleability of context, the exorcism's mythical and chaotic, violent language plausibly articulates a disavowal against the current political establishment. Mythical language captures or describes chaotic situations that demand an urgent need for change. In the exorcism, the desired change is indeed urgent; it is a demand for health, employment, and food.

On the other hand, African Pentecostal movements as constructive postmodernism offer an alternative view of reality, which comes in two forms. One form is that of a desire for alternative leadership. As religious leaders, the Pentecostal pastors offer solutions to problems affecting marriage, finance, and retirement. Their teaching is regarded as crucial for survival within such volatile spaces. This echoes Max Weber[30] and Durkheim's assertion that charismatic leaders arise within contexts that are characterized by *anomia* or lawlessness. Largely, postcolonial African realities characterized by political instability and economic failure are *anomic* spaces. A second alternative view of reality comes in the form of exorcisms, which

30. Weber, *Protestant Ethic*.

create alternative spaces similar to what Dirk Hebdige calls "communities of common aspiration."[31] African Pentecostal gatherings are characterized by people with the concrete desire for survival, which they feel is becoming difficult due to economic hardships. As a solution, alternative forms of kinship exist within the communities through the sharing of small gifts, such as salt, cooking oil, clothes, shelter, and other necessities. In some churches, announcements are made each Sunday for people who are looking for jobs as gardeners, receptionists, and maids. Thus, the church has become a place to create survival networks. Other churches encourage members to employ their own youth instead of outsiders.

As postmodern constructivists, African Pentecostals may be described as an alternate vision of family and country. Within these gatherings, family ties based on blood are no longer useful; they are demonized. Instead, members are encouraged to develop new (fictive) fathers, mothers, brothers, and sisters based on Jesus. According to them, religious ties are stronger than blood ties. In these gatherings, the pastor is the spiritual father while his wife is the spiritual mother, and church members are supposed to be obedient to the father and mother. Concerning this, Sarojini Nadar[32] and Adriaan van Klinken[33] make the valid observation that African Pentecostals seem to duplicate patriarchal asymmetric social order within the church. Importantly, because they take an inward look through the creation of alternative social ties, most African Pentecostals disregard national politics; instead, they focus on prayer. National politics are seen negatively as violent and possibly leading to death. Thus, Christians are taught not to vandalize property or riot but to work hard, love, and be obedient citizens. It is plausible that African Pentecostalism regard themselves as alternative communities of citizens and leaders. In this regard, exorcisms are based on a belief in dual and competing powers: the corrupt national government and the spiritual citizens within African Pentecostal movements. Given the tensions associated with multiculturalism, Pentecostalism projects a global environment characterized by inclusivity, and, in terms of ethos, it transcends the narrow identities associated with the household and nationality.

Healing and Exorcism as an Alternative Health System

As a postmodern constructive space, African Pentecostalism deals with the suffering and poverty that causes so much disease and death in Africa.

31. Hebdige, *Subculture*, 10.
32. Nadar, "Palatable Patriachy and Violence," 551.
33. van Klinken, "Male Headship as Male Agency," 204.

Rising income inequality in Africa is a direct effect of capitalism. African Pentecostalism makes us redefine and broaden our definition of sickness. African Pentecostals pray and cast out the demons that cause headaches, back pain, leg pain, and sleeplessness. Such conditions are somatic conditions, resulting from the body's inability to cope with particular social and economic pressures. By casting out demons that cause the body to be sick, African Pentecostals disavow structural conditions that cause sickness. Thus, sickness does not only emanate from viruses and bacteria but has multiple causes. The idea that sickness has a psychosomatic dimension is present within African traditional culture. Recently, we have heard similar ideas espoused by talk show hosts such as Dr. Phil, Oprah, and Dr. Oz. Thus, to heal is to restore individuals, or the community, to well-being. In the case of a community, healing means ridding a community of those negative aspects that corrode its well-being. The spiritual dimensions of sickness are crucial as a postmodern constructivism within African Pentecostalism.

African Pentecostals employ various strategies to restore health to the physical body and the community. One such approach is to deal with the individual by inculcating moral uprightness, emphasizing the avoidance of behaviors such as drinking beer, smoking, and having multiple sexual partners. These seemingly unrealistic moral injunctions have direct, positive consequences on the body. Another strategy is to encourage and teach strong family values, which mostly happens at fellowship events. Such fellowship takes place once a week, usually on Saturdays. Through religious teachings, the household, which feels the negative pinch of capitalism and corruption, is taught to rid itself of grudges, bitterness, jealousy, etc., all vices that cause headaches, back pain, and ultimately, block God's blessings.

African Pentecostals have a broad utopian vision in which good morality may produce accountable citizens. Healing within the African Pentecostal church could be said to summarize all that is bad about current African communities: lack of service delivery and medicine, sickness, and the general atmosphere of chaos. Thus, African communities are sick and need exorcism. In contrast to holiness movements where the end goal is to go to heaven, within African Pentecostalism, good health habits are markers of utopian identity, reinvigorating the African dream of better and healthier communities.

Prayer as Protest

Lastly, as postmodern constructivists, African Pentecostalism inculcates a sense of agency. One way to express agency is through prayer, which is an acquisition of divine power and resilience. Prayer is protest. In the realm of prayer, the individual is a god, and he/she recovers agency. All households in Zimbabwe are prayer centers where people meet for all-night prayers. During the beginning of the year, most churches in Zimbabwe adopt ten days of prayer and fasting; some have extended this period to thirty days. It is a time to "live and stay in the supernatural," and the omnipresent, omniscient, and powerful God is internalized. God is within the believer, and the believer is a god. Thus, believers can command, cast out demons, or do anything, because they are part of the supernatural. Paul Heelas, who studied postmodern spiritualties, argues that, in view of the harsh capitalistic environment, believers internalize and consume God.[34] However, prayer may not be the best strategy to deal with corrupt African leaders and the negative effects of global capitalism. Regardless, people are actively coming up with alternative survival strategies.

Conclusion

This study locates African Pentecostalism's exorcisms and faith healing within constructive postmodernism, which traces the creativity of postmodernity subjects dealing with oppressive local and global structures. First, we noted that African Pentecostalism does not operate in a vacuum. Instead, these are movements that seem to respond to issues, particularly within postcolonial African states. Zimbabwe is a good example of a postcolonial state that gradually slipped from economic glory into political and economic chaos. Like many African states, Zimbabwe is led by a corrupt government that values nepotism over accountability and transparency. In addition, multinational companies that invest in Africa and in Zimbabwe pay no revenue towards the livelihood of the local people and, thus, exacerbate neocolonialism and imperialism. Therefore, in view of World War II's aftermath of imperialism, colonialism, and global capitalism, African communities are questioning the dividends of political independence and democracy.[35] Instead of developing strong national governments that care for the needs of the people, African states have lost bargaining power due to the overwhelming power of global capitalism. In addition, at-home corruption, nepotism, and violence reign supreme. These realities are not answered by another wave of liberation war. Instead, African Pentecostalism provides spaces for disavowal and alternative engagement through healing and

---

34. Heelas, *Spiritualties of Life*, 5.

35. Fukuyama, "End of History," 3. Harvey, *Condition of Postmodernity*, 14. Wallerstein, "Introduction," 6.

exorcism. In this way, these spaces fit the description of constructive, postmodern spaces. In these spaces, exorcisms may be seen as a form of protest. African Pentecostalism also provides an alternative vision of the country by building new family ties. Unlike the African governments known for violence against their citizens, African Pentecostal communities are taught to work hard and be peaceful. They also preach individual and community morality, which indirectly creates accountable citizens. Instead of passively suffering, believers are called to pray and actively live their lives. Though African Pentecostalism is not igniting a revolution, it is alternatively helping people to be strong in view of local and global challenges.

Bibliography

Adogame, Afe, and Roswith Gerloff. "Introduction." In *Christianity in Africa and the Diaspora: The Appropriation of a Scattered Heritage,* edited by Afe Adogameet, et al., 1–9. London: Continuum, 2008.

Baudrillard, Jean. *Seduction.* Paris: Galilee, 1983.

Bond, Patrick. *Elite Transition: From Apartheid to Neoliberalism in South Africa.* Pietermaritzburg: University of Natal Press, 2000.

Callinicos, Alex. *Against Postmodernism: A Marxist Critique.* Cambridge: Polity, 1989.

Chitando, Ezra. "Come Down, O Lord! Music Protest and Religion in Zimbabwe." *Scriptura* 96 (2007) 334–47.

Dube, Zorodzai. "Casting Out Demons in Zimbabwe: A Coded Political Posturing." *Exchange* 41 (2012) 352–63.

———. "Jesus and Afro-Pentecostal Prophets: Dynamics within the Liminal Space in Galilean and in Zimbabwe." *HTS Teologiese Studies/Theological Studies* 71 (July 2015) 1–6.

Fanon, Francis. *Wretched of the Earth.* New York: Grove, 1963.

Foucault, Michel. *Archaeology of Knowledge.* London: Routledge, 2002.

Freud, Sigmund. *Civilization and its Discontent.* New York: Norton, 1962.

Fukuyama, Francis. "The End of History." *The National Interest* 16 (Summer 1989) 3–18.

Giddens, Anthony. *The Consequences of Modernity.* Cambridge: Polity, 1990.

Gifford, Paul. *Ghana's New Christianity: Pentecostalism in a Globalizing Africa.* Indianapolis: Indiana University Press, 2004.

Harvey, David. *The Condition of Postmodernity: An Enquiry into the Origins of Cultural Change.* Oxford: Blackwell, 1989.

Hebdige, Dirk. *Subculture: The Meaning of Style.* London: Routledge, 1979.

Heelas, Paul. *Spiritualties of Life: New Age Romanticism and Consumptive Capitalism.* Oxford: Blackwell, 2008.

Horkheimer, Max, and Theodor Adorno. *The Dialectics of Enlightenment.* New York: Herder and Herder, 1972.

Kalu, Ogbu. *African Pentecostalism: An Introduction.* Oxford: Blackwell, 2008.

Nadar, Sarojini. "Palatable Patriarchy and Violence against Wo/men in South Africa: Angus Buchan's Mighty Men's Conference as a Case Study of Masculinism." *Scriptura* 102 (2009) 551–61.

Ojo, Matthews. "Religion, Public Space, and the Press in Contemporary Nigeria." In *Christianity and Social Change in Africa*, edited by Toyin Falola, 233–50. Durham, NC: Carolina Academic Press, 2005.

Shoko, Tabona. *Karanga Indigenous Religions in Zimbabwe: Health and Well-Being*. Aldershot, UK: Ashgate, 2007.

Thompson, Kenneth. "Social Pluralism and Postmodernity." In *Modernity: An Introduction to Modern Societies*, edited by Stuart Hall, et al., 564–95. Oxford: Blackwell, 1996.

Touraine, Alain. *Post-Industrial Society: Tomorrow's Social History, Class, Conflict, and Culture in the Programmed Society*. New York: Random House, 1971.

Vambe, Maurice. "Version of Sub-Version: Trends in Chimurenga Music in Post Independent Zimbabwe." *African Study Monographs* 25 (2004) 167–93.

van Klinken, Adriaan. "Male Headship as Male Agency: An Alternative Understanding of a 'Patriarchal' African Pentecostal Discourse on Masculinity." *Religion and Gender* (2011) 104–24.

Wallerstein, Immanuel. "Introduction: The Lessons of the 1980s." In *Geopolitics and Geoculture: Essays on the Changing World-System*, edited by Immanuel Wallerstein, 1–18. Cambridge: Cambridge University Press, 1991.

Weber, Max. *The Protestant Ethic and the Spirit of Capitalism*. London: Routledge, 1930.

6

Francis MacNutt and the Globalization of Charismatic Healing and Deliverance

CANDY GUNTHER BROWN

The career and teachings of Francis MacNutt (1925–) offer a revealing window onto the globalization of Charismatic healing, deliverance, and spiritual warfare practices. MacNutt has been credited with catalyzing the spread of the global Catholic Charismatic Renewal throughout Latin America in particular. MacNutt's experiences in Latin America, Africa, and Asia in turn shaped his teachings on healing by deepening his confidence in the availability of supernatural healing and accentuating his emphasis on deliverance from evil spirits. MacNutt also played a distinctive role in healing the centuries-old rift between Catholics and Protestants; building trust with medical professionals and psychotherapists; and making divine healing and deliverance into a "normal" part of the Christian life. MacNutt contributed to the supernaturalism and the democratization of global Christianity by offering accessible teachings on healing and deliverance to lay Christians as well as Catholic and Protestant ministers.

Factors Contributing to MacNutt's Leadership in Charismatic Healing

A number of factors contributed to MacNutt's extraordinary degree of influence on the global Charismatic movement and its renewed interest in divine healing and deliverance. One element is the length and timing of his ministry career. Born in 1925, MacNutt was ordained a Dominican priest in 1956. He gained his introduction to Charismatic renewal in 1967 while in his early forties. In the 1970s, he traveled full-time, conducting Charismatic conferences globally. However, in 1980, he married Judith Sewell and did not receive dispensation for laicization until 1993. Although MacNutt lost much of his influence among Catholics during the 1980s, his impact among Protestants continued and augmented. Francis and Judith MacNutt formed Christian Healing Ministries in 1981, which they relocated to Jacksonville, Florida, in 1987 at the invitation of the Episcopal Diocese of Florida. The MacNutts continued to travel widely to minister among predominantly Protestant groups. MacNutt regained influence among Catholics in the 1990s and 2000s. In 2001, the Pontifical Council for the Laity invited Francis and Judith MacNutt to a special meeting with one hundred and fifty international participants to discuss healing and deliverance ministry.[1] In 2007, the Vatican's International Catholic Charismatic Renewal Service cosponsored with Christian Healing Ministries a six-day conference, a School for Healing Prayers for Leaders, that brought together four hundred and fifty Catholic leaders from forty-two countries. A similar conference followed in 2008. Also in 2008, the Second International Institute for Catholic Charismatic Leadership Formation invited MacNutt to the Vatican.[2] Although he retired in 2008, MacNutt continued to accept speaking invitations from around the world well into his eighties. As late as 2015, he agreed to speak at Oral Roberts University, though health issues forced him to cancel.[3]

MacNutt's academic, as well as his ministerial, experiences and credentials prepared him to take a leadership role in promoting interest in healing within and beyond the Catholic Church. MacNutt recounts that his "involvement in the healing ministry came about in a very natural way. I was first prepared by my desire to become a doctor, a desire which was nearly fulfilled in 1944, when I was accepted by Washington University Medical School in St. Louis, Missouri."[4] He was, however, drafted during World War II, just ten days before he would have started medical school. In the army, he served in an operating room as a surgical technician. After the war, he earned a BA from Harvard University, an MFA from the Catholic University of America, and a PhD in theology from the Aquinas Institute. He taught homiletics and wrote three books on preaching while on the faculty at the Dominican seminary in Dubuque, Iowa.[5] This training in oral and written communication as well as academic research skills prepared MacNutt

1. MacNutt, *Practice of Healing Prayer*, 11.
2. Cleary, *Rise of Charismatic Catholicism*, 38.
3. Oral Roberts University, "Oral Roberts University Hosts Celebration."
4. MacNutt, *Healing*, 8.
5. Christian Healing Ministries, "Francis S. MacNutt, PhD."

to disseminate his teachings by preaching at numerous conferences and by writing ten books on healing.

MacNutt's background as a Catholic, and as a Dominican in particular, also laid the groundwork for his interest in divine healing. As MacNutt recounts, Roman Catholics had a "tradition of saints blessed with extraordinary gifts, including healing, the one that is still used as a test for canonization. Consequently, most traditional Catholics have little difficulty in believing in divine healing. What was difficult was to believe that healing could be an ordinary, common activity of Christian life."[6] Likewise with deliverance from evil spirits, "the pastoral practice of the Catholic Church has always accepted the power of spirits as a real force in human affairs, although recent times have seen the ministry of deliverance played down."[7] Upon entering the Dominican Order, MacNutt's training included reading about the lives of saints in which "healing seemed an everyday occurrence."[8] MacNutt attributes his influence among diverse audiences to his Thomistic Dominican training, which emphasized finding the good across traditions. As a Dominican priest, MacNutt formed relationships with other priests and sisters, especially fellow Dominicans, some of whom he would later encounter again while itinerating abroad among missionaries. MacNutt also learned from his failures. As a priest, he was often approached by people seeking counsel, sometimes through referrals from their psychiatrists, but MacNutt found himself at a loss as to how to help.

MacNutt was among the first Catholic priests to embrace Charismatic renewal and perhaps the first modern Catholic priest to develop an international healing ministry, but he was not so far ahead of his times that he lacked followers. Unaware of the now-legendary February 1967 "Duquesne weekend" in Pittsburgh, where the Catholic Charismatic Renewal (CCR) broke out among Catholic professors and college students, MacNutt experienced his own "Baptism with the Holy Spirit" at a Protestant retreat in Tennessee in August 1967.[9] A foundation had already been laid by the growth of the Charismatic renewal in the 1960s among mainstream Protestants, Vatican II's acceptance of Protestants as "separated brethren," and an endorsement of the exercise of Charismatic gifts.[10] In 1972, the Church restored the sacrament of Extreme Unction to its original name, Anointing

6. MacNutt, *Healing*, 10.
7. MacNutt, *Power to Heal*, 75.
8. MacNutt, *Healing*, 8.
9. Foster, "Interview."
10. Paul VI, *Unitatis Redintegratio* and *Lumen Gentium*.

of the Sick, and expanded its applicability from those who are at the point of death to anyone who has begun to be in danger of death.[11]

The CCR placed little emphasis on healing during its early years. Instead, leaders focused on the experience of baptism with the Holy Spirit and the charisms of speaking in tongues and prophecy. There were no national US healing conferences between 1967 and 1974. Leaders wanted to prevent a focus on a "selfish need to get healed" over the "more important need for spiritual growth."[12] MacNutt played a pivotal role in validating the healing ministry as facilitating, rather than detracting from, the spiritual growth of those healed and others to whom healthy Christians could more effectively minister. In 1974, the National Service Committee selected "healing" as the theme of the International Conference on Charismatic Renewal at Notre Dame and invited MacNutt to conduct a public healing service.[13] In anticipation of the conference, Ave Maria Press asked him to write a book, *Healing*, which he did in just three months, in time for the event.[14] The conference drew 35,000 attendees.[15] The book and conference propelled healing "to the center of Charismatic religious praxis."[16] *Healing* won a wide readership through its "balanced," nonsensationalist approach, honesty about failure, and nonjudgmental, encouraging tone. One million copies had been sold by 2008, including translations into Spanish, Portuguese, Chinese, Japanese, and German.[17] MacNutt also helped found the Charismatic Concerns Committee (later, the Charismatic Leaders Fellowship) and played a major role in the Kansas City Charismatic Conference of 1977 that drew 40,000 participants.[18]

MacNutt contributed to the ecumenical nature of the Charismatic movement by bringing Catholics and Protestants together. As a priest in the 1970s, he regularly ministered alongside Protestant clergy and laity.[19] In a personal conversation with MacNutt in the 1970s, Father Ralph Rogawski, a fellow Dominican priest who was a missionary in Bolivia, put it this way:

> "Your greatest gift is not praying for healing, although many people think that it is. No, your gift is really in bringing people

11. Paul VI, *Sacram Unctione Infirmorum*.
12. Ryan, "Restoring the Gifts of Healing," 3.
13. Chesnut, *Competitive Spirits*, 67.
14. Foster, "Interview."
15. MacNutt, *Practice of Healing Prayer*, 136.
16. Chesnut, *Competitive Spirits*, 67.
17. Foster, "Interview."
18. Cleary, *Rise of Charismatic Catholicism*, 38, 37.
19. Foster, "Interview."

together who usually are apart. This comes so naturally to you that you may not even notice it. But you can talk to groups that most people can't. For example, you are an American, and you don't know Spanish. Most Americans with your background can't get a hearing in Latin America—even if they do know Spanish. But yet people in South America want to hear whatever you have to say."[20]

MacNutt similarly brought unlikely groups together in the United States. Unusual for a minister of divine healing, MacNutt succeeded in winning a hearing among medical professionals. In 1976, he founded the Association of Christian Therapists with the goal of encouraging the integration of prayer for healing into medical and psychological treatments.[21] In 1978, he produced a half-hour documentary film, *The Power of Healing Prayer: A Hospital Visit*, that concludes with the Chief of Medical Staff at St. Vincent's Hospital and Medical Center in Toledo, Ohio endorsing prayer for healing as a valuable addition to the medical armamentarium.[22] In 2000, MacNutt coauthored with a doctor and nurse a peer-reviewed article published in the *Southern Medical Journal*; the study reported beneficial effects of intercessory prayer on patients with rheumatoid arthritis.[23]

Catalyst for Global Charismatic Renewal

Historians generally agree about the pioneering influence of the United States on the global CCR and of MacNutt in particular. The historian Edward Cleary describes the CCR as "largely a U.S. innovation" and MacNutt as "one of the founders" of the global Catholic Charismatic movement.[24] During the 1970s, MacNutt itinerated full-time, ministering in thirty-one countries on five continents.[25] It was in this formative period that he developed his theology of healing and deliverance and wrote several books. He characteristically worked with a team of Catholics and Protestants, including women as well as men, to preach entry-level "Life in the Spirit" retreats that focused more on healing than on speaking in tongues. As MacNutt

20. MacNutt, "What I Needed to Hear."
21. Christian Healing Ministries, "Francis S. MacNutt, PhD."
22. MacNutt, *Power of Healing Prayer*.
23. Matthews et al., "Effects of Intercessory Prayer."
24. Cleary, *Rise of Charismatic Catholicism*, 12, xi.
25. Christian Healing Ministries, "Francis S. MacNutt, PhD"; Foster, "Interview"; MacNutt, "What I Needed to Hear"; Cleary, *Rise of Charismatic Catholicism*, 38.

described his approach, "My main theme for retreats was usually the Holy Spirit—especially as shown in healing."[26]

Latin America

Historians trace the beginnings of the CCR in Latin America to retreats and conferences led by MacNutt and a handful of other Catholic and Protestant Charismatic pioneers. The historian Andrew Chesnut describes the CCR in Latin America as an "imported religious product from the United States" and notes that MacNutt "played a pivotal role in establishing the CCR in several Latin American nations."[27] Chesnut reports that "many, if not most, of the original CCR groups in Latin America were founded by ecumenical pastoral teams," including MacNutt and other Dominican and Jesuit priests, often working side by side with Protestants.[28] Cleary affirms that MacNutt "proposed the new paradigm of the Charismatic Renewal" and "provided the first spark for the Catholic Charismatic movement in several Latin American countries."[29] MacNutt made a dozen month-long visits to Latin America during the 1970s. Specifically, his "impetus for starting the movement was felt in the following countries: Bolivia and Peru, 1970; the Dominican Republic, 1971; Guatemala, Mexico, and Costa Rica, 1972; and Colombia and Chile, 1972."[30]

MacNutt exerted an influence in Latin America by working on several levels, conducting retreats for priests and conferences for broader audiences, as well as personally mentoring long-term missionary priests who subsequently "incorporated his ideas into their own retreats for the grassroots communities."[31] Teaming up with Methodists Joe Petree, Tommy Tyson, and others, MacNutt visited Bolivia, Costa Rica, Peru, and Ecuador in 1970 and 1971. He and his team began in Bolivia with a series of three retreats conducted in English and attended primarily by a few Bolivian Catholics and some Bolivian Protestants, as well as foreign missionaries. Those who experienced baptism with the Holy Spirit went back to their Spanish-language ministries to lead others into experiences of Spirit baptism and healing. Attending these retreats were hundreds of Catholic missionaries from the United States and Canada, many of them

26. MacNutt in Cleary, *Rise of Charismatic Catholicism*, 30.
27. Chesnut, *Competitive Spirits*, 66, 67.
28. Chesnut, *Competitive Spirits*, 67.
29. Cleary, *Rise of Charismatic Catholicism*, 30.
30. Cleary, *Rise of Charismatic Catholicism*, 30.
31. Cleary, *Rise of Charismatic Catholicism*, 32.

experiencing baptism with the Holy Spirit, after which they returned to their parish and school ministries to pass on the experience and recruit lay leaders for the movement. Conducting "Life in the Spirit" retreats in Spanish hastened the spread of the movement among the populace.[32] Among the sites MacNutt visited was the Templo Bíblico of the Evangelical Association of Bible Churches in San José, Costa Rica, one of the first centers of Protestant Charismatic renewal in Central America.[33]

In 1973, MacNutt convened the First Latin American Leadership Conference in Bogotá, Colombia. He made a particular effort to bring in priests he knew who were working in *barrios populares*, or poorer neighborhoods, in order to build Christian community in these areas. Twenty-three leaders from the Dominican Republic, Mexico, Puerto Rico, Costa Rica, Venezuela, Peru, and Bolivia sent representatives.[34] MacNutt persuaded attendees that "the renewal of the church in Latin America would be brought about through a revival of the healing ministry."[35] Priests and sisters with "long, active records in working for social justice . . . discovered in healing prayer a power for liberating people from inner problems and physical sickness."[36] The conference concluded with the creation of the influential Encuentro Carismático Católico Latinoamericano (ECCLA), or Latin American Catholic Charismatic Encounter.[37] The second meeting of the ECCLA, held in 1974, attracted 220 participants, many of them laity, from seventeen Latin American countries.[38]

The 1970s was a period during which liberation theology and Christian base communities (CEBs, from the Spanish *comunidades eclesiales de base*) had wide appeal. Cleary describes CCR as a "revitalization movement that offers a clear and popular alternative to liberationist Christian base communities."[39] MacNutt encountered resistance at first from Catholic missionaries who were, in his words, "strongly identified with the poor and were working for greater social justice." He recalled years later that "initially they were prejudiced against what I was saying because they associated my themes with those emphasized by some North American televangelists who stressed the 'health and wealth' gospel. It always took several days to

32. Cleary, *Rise of Charismatic Catholicism*, 31, 189, 190.
33. Hocken, "Charismatic Movement," 498.
34. Cleary, *Rise of Charismatic Catholicism*, 69, 70.
35. MacNutt, *Healing*, 31.
36. MacNutt, *Healing*, 31.
37. Cleary, *How Latin America Saved*, 61–62.
38. Cleary, *Rise of Charismatic Catholicism*, 71.
39. Cleary, *How Latin America Saved*, 62.

convince the missionaries that I was not preaching a gospel that is too comfortable to be real."[40] MacNutt won over many of the missionaries, having the easiest time with Dominicans who already knew him from their time in the United States, and "many of them eventually put the double emphasis of the baptism of the Spirit and social justice together in one vision." Several missionaries in Bolivia "understood the vision of combining the message of the Church's preferential option for the poor, together with the need of the power of the Spirit."[41] Likewise, leaders in Colombia found that the Charismatic movement offered a "strong spiritual basis that they felt had been missing in their busy lives."[42] As a result of this integration, the CEBs actually became "vehicles for the spread of Charismatic renewal."[43] This happened as priests and laity came to rely on the "Holy Spirit as a source of unity among fragmented lives and families and as a source of healing."[44] For example, one of the priests whom MacNutt mentored felt inspired by the new teachings to start a rehabilitation house for drug addicts.[45] MacNutt concluded from his experiences in Latin America that "praying for the healing of our inner being will help as much as anything toward the creation of a just society,"[46] because "justice cannot be brought to a society until there are just people; and people cannot be just until they are healed of the hurts and wounds of the past."[47]

Native Americans

Likewise, Native American Christians in Montana interviewed in 2009 credit conferences led by MacNutt in 1976 with initiating a ten-year period of renewal.[48] Historian Mark Clatterbuck cites three factors that help to explain the scope and intensity of renewal: supernaturalism, community, and ecumenism. First, it proved advantageous that CCR shared with traditional Native religions an emphasis on "physical manifestations of the Divine," or "direct, immediate, and sensibly perceived contact with God."[49] Second, renewal

40. MacNutt in Cleary, *Rise of Charismatic Catholicism*, 30.
41. MacNutt in Cleary, *Rise of Charismatic Catholicism*, 30.
42. Cleary, *Rise of Charismatic Catholicism*, 49.
43. Cleary, *Rise of Charismatic Catholicism*, 32.
44. Cleary, *Rise of Charismatic Catholicism*, 32.
45. Cleary, *Rise of Charismatic Catholicism*, 33.
46. MacNutt, *Healing*, 21.
47. MacNutt, *Healing*, 23.
48. Clatterbuck, "In Native Tongues," 153, 155.
49. Clatterbuck, "In Native Tongues," 177.

engendered a sense of community that crossed tribal affiliation. Third, the emphasis on direct, experiential encounter with God encouraged active participation by Native, lay Catholics as well as crossover between Catholic and Pentecostal churches that had previously had little interaction.

Asia

MacNutt also ministered in several countries in Asia. For example, in 1978, he led a series of conferences in India; four hundred priests and thirteen bishops attended two retreats for clergy, and twenty thousand people attended a healing conference. MacNutt equipped two hundred priests to go into the crowd to pray for healing.[50] By the 2000s, the Catholic Charismatic movement in India had grown to a million members, organized into ten thousand prayer groups.[51]

Africa

MacNutt's influence extended to Africa as well. In 1974, a group of Dominican missionaries in Nigeria invited MacNutt to spend six weeks preaching in six different cities. The context was that Nigerian "seminarians were afraid of witch doctors putting curses on them." According to MacNutt, the "dedicated missionaries had decided that the native seminarians were superstitious and needed to be enlightened." The missionaries first called in a psychologist from a local university to assuage the seminarians' worries by offering "psychological explanations" for strange sicknesses. When the psychologist failed to persuade the seminarians, the missionaries invited MacNutt to come "see if the seminarians might be right."[52]

What MacNutt observed in Nigeria strengthened his belief in the reality of demons—and his concern about the inadequacy of Western mission strategies. "We would be praying with a group when suddenly a man would fall down in the aisle and start displaying the signs that often indicate the presence of a demon. The Nigerians understood immediately what was going on." By contrast, "some of the European missionaries, meanwhile, were heading toward the door," interpreting the incident as a "throwback to the primitive religion from which they were trying to rescue the people."[53]

50. MacNutt, *Healing Reawakening*, 202.
51. MacNutt, *Deliverance*, 298.
52. MacNutt, *Deliverance*, 58–59.
53. MacNutt, *Deliverance*, 59.

Because the Catholic missionaries would not minister deliverance, the Nigerians went to Pentecostal churches comfortable with deliverance, with the result that "the missionaries themselves told us that these Pentecostal churches were growing at an explosive rate."[54] MacNutt concludes that

> "the Africans understood the biblical worldview far better than we did, and seemed more in touch with some basic spiritual realities. Western churches have come to recognize their pride in imposing European church architecture on African peoples and have mostly repented of it. But in a far more important realm, they are still imposing their Western spiritual bias. These Africans know by experience the reality of an evil power that destroys, and of witch doctors with the power to heal. Unless Catholic and mainline Protestant missionaries exhibit a greater power, the Nigerians will flock to the Aladura churches or will continue to revert to their native witch doctors in time of need."[55]

MacNutt's conclusions about deliverance and missions in Nigeria would later be confirmed by his experiences in other countries. The historian Ogbu Kalu said of MacNutt's tour of Nigeria that "the priests treated the team with much suspicion because of imbibed pattern of ministerial formation, but the lay people lapped up the opportunity and the import of the challenge was not lost on the rulers of the synagogue who had to ensure that their flock would not drift away. These are aspects of the origin of the Catholic charismatic movement."[56]

The Connection between Healing and Deliverance

As MacNutt began to pray for divine healing, he quickly discovered that "healing prayer is not always enough."[57] MacNutt argued from his experiences in healing ministry and from his study of the Bible and Catholic literature that "evil spirits exist, that they can cause sickness, and that they can also heal by removing the sickness they cause."[58] In listing reasons why people might not be healed from a physical affliction despite prayer, MacNutt included the possibility of an unmet need for deliverance from evil spirits. Healing and deliverance from evil spirits are thus two sides of a

---

54. MacNutt, *Deliverance*, 59.
55. MacNutt, *Deliverance*, 59–60.
56. Kalu, "Passive Revolution," 275.
57. MacNutt, *Deliverance*, 23, 26.
58. MacNutt, *Power to Heal*, 74.

single coin. Deliverance is "a part of healing in the broader sense of freeing us from all the evil that burdens us and prevents us from being fully alive and free."[59] MacNutt considered "evil" to be real, not merely metaphorical. "Evil is, at its root, demonic and too great for us to overcome . . . Through prayer—prayer for healing and prayer for deliverance—we become channels for Jesus to heal and to free people (as well as institutions and societies) from the evil that weighs them down."[60]

MacNutt did not seek a deliverance ministry, but he "got involved through experience, not theory." He recalled that "in 1972 a case was thrust upon me that forced me to learn more." Although this incident occurred in the United States, notably it involved a Brazilian immigrant whose "father had consecrated her to an evil spirit in a satanic ritual in Brazil."[61] This incident proved not to be an isolated example. One thing that convinced MacNutt of the reality of evil spirits was that "demonized people all over the world behave in the same ways when we pray for them."[62] MacNutt referred repeatedly to common phenomena or "symptoms" that "we find in all parts of the world."[63] As MacNutt described, "I might be conducting a healing service in a chapel, for example, praying quietly for the people who come forward asking for physical healing, when suddenly, with no outward provocation, a man's face contorts and he shouts something like, 'We hate you!'" Far from being uncommon, "usually when we pray for a sufficiently large number of people, several erupt with disturbing behavior," or someone "falls to the ground, then starts rolling around and shouting."[64]

MacNutt distinguishes between the formal rite of "exorcism," which only a priest can perform and only with permission from a bishop, and "deliverance," as a much broader field of ministry, in which laity can participate or take a leading role. Whereas the need for exorcism is, in MacNutt's view, rare, the need for deliverance is quite common.[65] Exorcism is required in cases of full demonic possession, whereas more often individuals—Christians included—are only partially "demonized" or "infested" by demons.[66] MacNutt expresses concern that "Roman Catholic thought on deliverance tends to concentrate on exorcism and permission to perform it, granted by a

---

59. MacNutt, *Healing*, 167.
60. MacNutt, *Deliverance*, 52.
61. MacNutt, *Deliverance*, 26.
62. MacNutt, *Deliverance*, 25.
63. MacNutt, *Deliverance*, 76.
64. MacNutt, *Deliverance*, 24.
65. MacNutt, *Deliverance*, 72.
66. MacNutt, *Deliverance*, 73–74.

bishop to a priest." If, as in the vast majority of cases, "someone complaining about a demonic presence" fails to pass tests for possession (for instance, by levitating or speaking an unknown foreign language), the Church will not call an exorcist. As a result, "thousands of people are denied the help they desperately need."[67] MacNutt included a chapter on deliverance in his 1974 book, *Healing*, expanding his teachings into a full-length book, *Deliverance from Evil Spirits*, in 1995. Although recognizing that deliverance is even more controversial than healing, MacNutt did not feel free to omit teaching on the subject given the widespread need for it.

Addressing European and North American audiences, MacNutt explicitly speaks to demands for evidence. When it comes to physical healing, MacNutt cites scientific studies—one of which he coauthored—to adduce evidence that prayer improves health.[68] On the subject of deliverance, by contrast, MacNutt acknowledges that there is no scientific evidence that demons exist. He concedes that "the demonic world cannot be seen, measured, or placed under a microscope. We are dealing with an unseen, mysterious world of fallen spirits. A spirit, by definition, is a 'non-material' being." Consequently, "every evidence we have indicating the presence of a demon is bound to be ambiguous since we do not see the evil spirit itself, but only what it causes people to do. These effects of its presence, moreover, can be explained in some other way." For example, when someone's voice changes eerily, "the voice might be a sign of multiple personality disorder" rather than a demon.[69]

Reciprocal Influences of Global Experiences on MacNutt's Theology and Practice

MacNutt bases his teachings on healing and deliverance on the Bible and his own experiences—many of which took place while ministering outside the United States or to individuals who had spent time abroad. MacNutt recalled in 2014 that "the most remarkable example of healing through soaking prayer I have ever seen took place after a retreat my team gave in Colombia, South America. Towards the end of the retreat, members of our team ended up praying for a young woman with a withered leg."[70] After countless hours of prayer, the leg grew several inches and straightened, enabling the woman to walk. MacNutt also recounts meeting an Anglican

---

67. MacNutt, *Deliverance*, 73.
68. Matthews et al., "Effects of Intercessory Prayer."
69. MacNutt, *Deliverance*, 53.
70. MacNutt, "Soaking Prayer."

priest in England who had been cursed by a "witch doctor" while a missionary in Africa; "when we prayed, the curse lifted off, the spirits manifested, and the physical difficulties disappeared. It sounds weird but we find these things quite a bit."[71] MacNutt also claims to have ministered to priests in Latin America "who had been hexed after work in the barrios."[72] Similarly, MacNutt recalls that "in 1977 I met a fine priest in India, Fr. Rufus Pereira, who in two brief years had prayed to free more than four hundred individuals from demonic influence . . . During one conference, five cases of possessed surfaced while I was speaking."[73]

As an itinerant minister, MacNutt listened respectfully to the stories of priests and people in other countries, rather than joining the ranks of foreign missionaries who devalued indigenous beliefs as superstitious. To the contrary, MacNutt accepted the supernatural worldviews he encountered in Latin America, Africa, and Asia as better attuned to reality than the demythologizing efforts of European and North American missionaries. MacNutt explains:

> "The people of every culture I have visited, except the European, are eager to share their experiences of a spiritual world that oppresses them. Nor do they understand why many missionaries seem to have less belief in these demonic forces than they do. The missionaries, meanwhile, are trying to educate the people not to fear this dark world of 'spirits.' If only they will accept our more advanced, scientific worldview (so we think), they will become like us and no longer be tormented by an irrational fear of demons."[74]

MacNutt concludes from such experiences that "one of the reasons we have not succeeded in bringing the Gospel to many cultures is simply that we do not fully understand what Jesus Christ came to bring."[75] MacNutt cites the relative failure of Christian missionary activity in Japan as an example. When MacNutt visited Japan in 1978, he found that even this "advanced, sophisticated" culture experienced the "activity of evil spirits. He noted that Japanese New Religions which focus on healing and deliverance were growing much more rapidly than Christianity, indicating that "the people themselves feel a great need for healing and deliverance, and

---

71. MacNutt, in Brown, "From Sickness to Priestly Abuse."
72. Brown, "From Sickness to Priestly Abuse."
73. MacNutt, *Deliverance*, 114.
74. MacNutt, *Deliverance*, 58.
75. MacNutt, *Deliverance*, 58.

that perhaps the basic preevangelism of Christianity (as it was in Jesus' own ministry) should be healing and deliverance."[76]

MacNutt blames the legacy of the Enlightenment for the emasculation of Western Christianity. "A rationalistic, scientific worldview that assumed there is no reality beyond the natural, material universe . . . has so affected Western Christianity that we automatically regard the work of the supernatural with skepticism and rule out the world of angels and demons."[77] Even in European countries, "only in the past few centuries, under the influence of the Enlightenment, have Christians come to question the reality of such experiences. Yet demonic encounters remain frequent; it is just that people [in the Western world] are ashamed to own up to them."[78] MacNutt argues that "prayer for deliverance is just as important for us in North America or Europe as it is in Africa or Asia, but we do not seem to realize it."[79] In MacNutt's view, "other cultures that we may regard as primitive are ahead of us in many ways; they are more in touch with spiritual reality and the world of the supernatural."[80] Indeed, "most of the world finds it hard to fathom why we are so ignorant about the spirit world."[81]

Pastoral and Missiological Implications

MacNutt's concerns are pastoral and missiological. He worries that inattention to healing and deliverance needlessly abandons hurting people and drives them to seek help from the occult and non-Christian religions. MacNutt recalls that "when I was in Venezuela, the missionaries there estimated that 80 percent of Venezuelans go to a witch doctor or curandero when they feel oppressed."[82] It seems anomalous to MacNutt that "so few churches consider the possibility of the curse as a real pastoral concern, when so much traditional pagan religion not only believes in it but concentrates on seeking blessings and avoiding curses through the rituals of their native priests (shamans)."[83] MacNutt warns:

---

76. MacNutt, *Deliverance*, 60.
77. MacNutt, *Deliverance*, 48.
78. MacNutt, *Deliverance*, 56.
79. MacNutt, *Deliverance*, 288.
80. MacNutt, *Deliverance*, 298.
81. MacNutt, *Deliverance*, 57–58.
82. MacNutt, *Deliverance*, 62.
83. MacNutt, *Deliverance*, 101.

> "Even Christians will seek the help of their curandero, or whatever the healer is called in their culture, if the Christian bishops, priests, and ministers do not believe in praying for healing. My own experience leads me to a firm conviction in the reality of the demonic realm and of its power to curse and to heal. These powers are ultimately destructive and enslaving; it is important to recognize them, rather than to deny them, and to learn to apply the power of the Holy Spirit in healing, so that sick people will not be driven to seek help from an alien and dangerous source."[84]

In MacNutt's view, missionaries work at a serious disadvantage when they understand less about spiritual warfare than do local representatives of other religions. "The power of evil spirits invoked by cursing is a primary component of most native religions. The ability of witch doctors to impose curses, hexes, and spells, and to lift them off, gives them power and respect based on fear. When Christians do not understand their own religion, they are at a disadvantage in trying to convert pagans, who may better understand the reality of spiritual warfare."[85] MacNutt argues pointedly that "ministers of the Gospel need to stop passing the buck by denying that demonic oppression exists or by simply referring people to psychiatrists or counselors when what is needed is deliverance."[86] MacNutt worries that many people continue to suffer as a result of such negligence.

MacNutt warns, moreover, that missionary efforts to counteract local superstitions do a disservice. Based on decades of traveling ministry, MacNutt reflects:

> "In every culture except the European (and those influenced by the European, such as our own), I have found that ordinary people have a lively appreciation of spiritual bondage and the reality of demonic forces. They are waiting to hear the good news that they can be freed by the power of God. While we think we are bringing these other 'less enlightened' cultures into Christian truth, what we are really doing is converting them to a Western (that is, Western-since-Descartes) view of humanity and the world, which is prejudiced against a number of spiritual practices we label as superstitious. One of the 'superstitions' our missionaries want to eradicate is the belief of these people in the presence and activity of evil spirits."[87]

84. MacNutt, *Power to Heal*, 75.
85. MacNutt, *Deliverance*, 105.
86. MacNutt, *Deliverance*, 31.
87. MacNutt, *Deliverance*, 57–58.

MacNutt recognizes that his claims about the demonic realm "may sound very primitive and scientifically unsupportable to many readers," but he urges his Western audiences that the extensive experiences of people across many cultures supply compelling empirical evidence.[88]

Deliverance, Spiritual Warfare, and Social Justice

MacNutt's personal ministry focuses on deliverance of individuals rather than spiritual warfare over entire regions. Nevertheless, he describes Peter Wagner and others who do address territorial spirits as "Christian pioneers" who are "discovering an important dimension of intercession that needs to be taken seriously."[89] MacNutt has also interacted extensively with liberationists in Latin America and those who work for social justice in other parts of the world. His evaluation is that "what is missing among those who take a stand for social justice and against institutional injustice is that they do not, for the most part, recognize that demons and evil spirits really exist, and that, until we deal with them, we cannot successfully destroy the kingdom of Satan." Such individuals are "keenly aware of aspects of societal evil" but may have had negative experiences with certain Christians who have "used their belief in demons as a ploy to avoid taking personal responsibility for evil."[90] MacNutt seeks to bring together the ministries of deliverance, spiritual warfare, and social justice, for "there are demonic, personal powers that control regions, societies, political systems, and institutions . . . there are also evils to which we are blind that influence the same regions, nations and societies, in which our human greed and selfishness become institutionalized."[91] Moreover, "the larger issues of injustice will be helped when individuals in society are themselves made whole . . . we also need to work together to create a more peaceful, just society. It's no either/or; it's both/and."[92]

Healing, deliverance, and spiritual warfare are, in MacNutt's view, central rather than peripheral aspects of the gospel. After he began preaching outside the United States, MacNutt came to realize, "I was not preaching the Gospel fully because I did not fully understand the need for the power to heal and free people from evil spirits. . . . Only when we are able to free the oppressed and heal those suffering from the curse of sickness

---

88. MacNutt, *Power to Heal*, 75.
89. MacNutt, *Deliverance*, 264.
90. MacNutt, *Deliverance*, 267.
91. MacNutt, *Deliverance*, 268.
92. MacNutt, *Healing*, 21.

can we really preach Christ's basic message: The Kingdom of God is at hand and the kingdom of Satan is being destroyed."[93] Indeed, "[a] major theme in the New Testament is the clash between the Kingdom of God and the kingdom of Satan." MacNutt clarifies: "Nor do I propose that the ministry of exorcism is simply one minor ministry among many that need to be resurrected in today's Church but that Jesus' ministry of deliverance is central to an understanding of the Gospel."[94] Emphatically, "*The Gospel is not meant merely to teach doctrine, but necessarily includes the power to free, to save, and to heal.*"[95] Moreover, "the entire New Testament shows that Jesus was not primarily a Teacher (although He was an extraordinary Teacher) but that His chief title is Savior or Redeemer. The traditional title Savior means, of course, that He actually saves us; He rescues us from a real danger, from something evil." Consequently, "to the extent that we no longer realize the reality of the supernatural power of the demonic realm—against which we are powerless in our own unaided humanity—we no longer sense the need for a Savior, for Jesus Christ."[96] Thus, in MacNutt's assessment, the battle between kingdoms simply cannot be ignored if Christians are to preach the real gospel.

Retrospect and Prospect

Reflecting on the history and prospects of Charismatic renewal near the end of his lengthy ministry career, MacNutt expresses more optimism about the trajectory of Christianity in the global South than in Europe and North America. In writing the introduction to the 2009 edition of *Deliverance from Evil Spirits*, MacNutt recalls that "forty years ago I experienced real difficulties when asked to pray to free people from demonic influence. Some religious authorities forbade me, mainly because they were convinced that a belief in demons was primitive superstition." MacNutt found that "educated Christians want to rid the world of primitive talk about Satan and 'demons behind every bush.' Scholars regarded exorcism as worse than superstition because it might discourage people from getting the psychological help they desperately needed."[97] By 2009, deliverance ministry had become "more acceptable," yet "profound skepticism remains" especially among Western

---

93. MacNutt, *Deliverance*, 71.
94. MacNutt, *Deliverance*, 38.
95. MacNutt, *Deliverance*, 71; emphasis original.
96. MacNutt, *Deliverance*, 38–39.
97. MacNutt, *Deliverance*, 17.

academics.[98] As a result, "in Asia, Africa, and Latin America the charismatic renewal is exploding, while in Europe and the United States, it's stalled.... it's stabilized and been domesticated."[99]

The supernatural worldviews prevalent in the global South facilitate the rapid spread of Christianity. It is because people outside the Western world recognize "the reality of evil spirits and the power of witch doctors and shamans" that they also "respond readily to preaching and ministry that promise to set them free."[100] In the global South, "as in the early Church, ordinary people interpret the Bible literally and have no intellectual problem casting out evil spirits and asking Jesus to heal the sick."[101] MacNutt concludes that "this renewed emphasis on preaching that the Kingdom of God is at hand, and that Satan's kingdom is being destroyed, helps us understand why Pentecostal and charismatic churches are growing at such an extraordinary rate in the developing world."[102] Looking ahead, "the main centers of Christianity twenty-five years from now are no longer going to be Rome and Geneva and New York, but they are going to be New Delhi, Lagos, and other such exotic centers."[103] By implication, if Christians in North America and Europe are to regain their lost influence, they too need to recognize and respond to Satan's kingdom by preaching the Kingdom of God, healing the sick, and casting out demons.

Bibliography

Brown, Michael H. "From Sickness to Priestly Abuse, Expert Cites Mostly Hidden Role of Evil Spirits." *Spirit Daily*, December 1, 2015. http://www.spiritdaily.net/macnutt.htm.

Chesnut, R. Andrew. *Competitive Spirits: Latin America's New Religious Economy*. New York: Oxford University Press, 2003.

Christian Healing Ministries. "Francis S. MacNutt, PhD." *Christian Healing Ministries*. https://www.christianhealingmin.org/index.php?option=com_content&view=article&id=488:francis-macnutt&catid=140:about-us1&Itemid=209.

Clatterbuck, Mark. "In Native Tongues: Catholic Charismatic Renewal and Montana's Eastern Tribes (1975–Today)." *U.S. Catholic Historian* 28 (Spring 2010) 153–80.

Cleary, Edward L. *How Latin America Saved the Soul of the Catholic Church*. New York: Paulist, 2009.

———. *Rise of Charismatic Catholicism*. Gainesville: University Press of Florida, 2011.

98. MacNutt, *Deliverance*, 40.
99. MacNutt, in Foster, "Interview."
100. MacNutt, *Deliverance*, 40.
101. MacNutt, *Deliverance*, 15.
102. MacNutt, *Deliverance*, 40.
103. MacNutt, in Foster, "Interview."

Foster, David Kyle. "Interview: Francis and Judith MacNutt." *Mastering Life: Pure Passion TV*. September 1, 2008. http://purepassion.us/web/index.php?option=com_k2&view=item&id=35:interview-francis-judith-macnutt&Itemid=147.

Hocken, Peter D. "Charismatic Movement." In *The New International Dictionary of Pentecostal and Charismatic Movements*, edited by Stanley M. Burgess and Eduard M. van der Maas, 477–519. Grand Rapids: Zondervan, 2002.

Kalu, Ogbu. "Passive Revolution and Its Saboteurs: African Christian Initiative in the Era of Decolonization, 1955–1975." In *Missions, Nationalism, and the End of Empire*, edited by Brian Stanley, 250–77. Grand Rapids: Eerdmans, 2003.

MacNutt, Francis. *Deliverance from Evil Spirits: A Practical Manual*. Grand Rapids: Chosen, 2009.

———. *Healing*. Revised and expanded edition. Notre Dame, IN: Ave Maria, 1999.

———. *The Healing Reawakening: Reclaiming Our Lost Inheritance*. Grand Rapids: Chosen, 2006.

———. *The Power of Healing Prayer*. Oaklawn, IL: CharCom, 1978.

———. *The Power to Heal*. Notre Dame, IN: Ave Maria, 1977.

———. *The Practice of Healing Prayer: A How-To Guide for Catholics*. Ijamsville, MD: Word Among Us, 2010.

———. "Soaking Prayer." *Healing Line* (Winter 2013/14) 3–5. http://christianhealingmin.org/media/downloads/HL/pdf/201304_Winter_HL.pdf.

———. "What I Needed to Hear." *Healing Line* (January/February/March 2013) 3. http://christianhealingmin.org/media/downloads/HL/pdf/201301_Jan-Mar_HL.pdf.

Matthews, Dale A., et al. "Effects of Intercessory Prayer on Patients with Rheumatoid Arthritis." *Southern Medical Journal* 93 (2000) 1177–86.

Oral Roberts University. "Oral Roberts University Hosts Celebration of Healing Academic Conference and Tent Crusade." *ORU News*, March 23, 2015. http://www.oru.edu/news/oru_news/20150323_celebration_of_healing.php.

Paul VI. *Dogmatic Constitution of the Church: Lumen Gentium*. Boston: Pauline, 1965. http://www.vatican.va/archive/hist_councils/ii_vatican_council/documents/vat-ii_const_19641121_lumen-gentium_en.html.

———. *Sacram Unctione Infirmorum: On the Sacrament of Anointing of the Sick*. Washington, DC: U.S. Catholic Conference, 1973. https://w2.vatican.va/content/paul-vi/en/apost_constitutions/documents/hf_p-vi_apc_19721130_sacram-unctionem.html.

———. *Unitatis Redintegratio: Decree on Ecumenism*. Boston: St. Paul, 1964. http://www.vatican.va/archive/hist_councils/ii_vatican_council/documents/vat-ii_decree_19641121_unitatis-redintegratio_en.html.

Ryan, Barbar Shlemon. "Restoring the Gifts of Healing: Reflections on Thirty-Five Years of Healing Ministry. *PentecostToday* 28 (October/November/December 2003) 3–4. https://www.nsc-chariscenter.org/wp-content/uploads/PT/OND2003_pt1.pdf.

PART THREE

Relationships between Catholics and Protestant Pentecostals

7

Catholic–Pentecostal Relations in Asia: Conflict and Cooperation

Simon Chan

Introduction

In this paper, the term *Pentecostal* or *Pentecostalism* refers mainly to classical Pentecostal denominations but includes indigenous movements, independent churches, and denominations which share certain family resemblances with classical Pentecostalism, including practices and doctrines, even though many of these churches and movements do not call themselves Pentecostal. The term *charismatic* is reserved for the Catholic charismatics or those cases where a historical distinction needs to be made between the older, classical Pentecostals and the newer charismatics. This is admittedly an oversimplification, but there is currently such a profusion of terms, which are not always understood in the same way, that introducing them without careful qualification is likely to lead to confusion.[1]

As in many other parts of the world, Pentecostals in Asia are sometimes accused of proselytism, but more frequently their relationship in Asia can be better described as cautious and benign. This paper will consider the factors giving rise to these situations. Their relationship will be considered from the institutional as well as grassroots perspectives. If there is any contact between them at the institutional level, it is almost always indirect, within a broader framework involving other Christian churches or non-Christian religions. The institutional perspective will be discussed from

---

1. Barrett et al., *World Christian Encyclopedia* lists fifty-nine categories under the first three waves of renewal (Pentecostal, Charismatic, and Neocharismatic) and creates sixteen neologisms; see 19–21.

three such contexts: (1) The Catholic-Pentecostal Dialogues in the West; (2) the Catholic-Protestant relationship arising from the different socio-political realities in Asia; and (3) the relationship between the Catholic Church in Asia and Rome and its impact on local Catholic-Pentecostal relations. At the grassroots level, I will look at various exchanges that are taking place between Pentecostals and Catholics.

The Catholic-Pentecostal Dialogues

Since its early days, Pentecostalism has displayed a strong ecumenical impulse. As David Bundy, a Pentecostal historian, notes:

> Ecumenism has been an essential and foundational quest of Pentecostalism. Despite the pressures, from within and without, to succumb to the temptation of sectarian values, the tradition has maintained an ecumenical dimension as a core value.[2]

Bundy cites many examples of early Pentecostal leaders who were deeply involved in ecumenical endeavors: William Seymour, Thomas Ball Barratt, Lewi Pethrus, Donald Gee, and David du Plessis. Their involvement was all the more remarkable coming at a time when relations between the Catholic Church and the more conservative wing of Protestantism was almost unheard of. This tradition continues today with people like Carmelo Álvarez, Gameliel Lugo, Cecil M. Robeck Jr., Steven J. Land, Cheryl Bridges Johns, and Bishop James Tyson.

But historically, the relationship between Catholics and Pentecostals had been, to put it mildly, bumpy. Cecil Robeck Jr., who has been involved in the Catholic-Pentecostal Dialogues for many years, notes that the most difficult situation is in Latin America where Pentecostalism is regarded as a "sect" because of its aggressive proselytism.[3] Part of the problem may have to do with the Catholic Church itself. Its highly institutionalized structure makes it difficult to accommodate even its own spiritual movements. As one Catholic writer notes, with reference to the Catholic Charismatic Renewal and Basic Ecclesial Communities, "the more dynamic they are the more 'extra-parochial' they tend to be."[4] Thus, it is not surprising that a Catholic lay movement like El Shaddai in the Philippines exists in an uneasy relationship with the Church.[5]

2. Bundy, "Ecumenical Quest of Pentecostalism."
3. Robeck, "Achievements," 164.
4. Prior, "Jesus Christ," 3.
5. Wiegele, *Investing in Miracles*.

For the Catholic Church, the challenges posed by the Pentecostals in Catholic-majority countries make the Catholic-Pentecostal Dialogues a matter of some urgency.[6] These dialogues have been going on since 1972—a remarkable achievement in itself. Yet, a lot of Asian Catholic and Pentecostal leaders are not aware of it, not well-informed about it, or simply ignore it. In a paper presented at the Asian Convention of the Pontifical Council for Culture in 2006, this was how John Manfred Prior put it:

> For thirty-four years, the official conversation between the Catholic Church and Classical Pentecostals has to be the greatest secret of the ecumenical movement! It is an extraordinary, even prophetic dialogue between the largest Christian church and the fastest growing Christian movement. Catholic/Pentecostal understanding has deepened and mutual respect fostered. I am not aware of any echoes in Asia nor am I aware that any of the documentation has been published in Asia. The reports of the Five Phases should inspire conversations at the local level between Catholic charismatics, classical and indigenous Pentecostals together with activists in basic Christian communities. Without in any way neglecting ongoing contact with mainline churches, thirty-four years after Pentecostals and Catholics engaged in dialogue it is not too soon for the Catholic Churches of Asia to open up to indigenous Pentecostal communities.[7]

There are a number of reasons for the gross negligence on both sides. On the Pentecostal side, Pentecostal representatives to the Dialogues are usually not official representatives of (although they are mostly endorsed by) their respective denominations, and consequently, their ecumenical work is not likely to be noticed by their denominations. Some of the Pentecostal denominations may even be quite hostile to *any* kind of ecumenical dialogues, not to mention dialogue with Catholics.[8] Within many Pentecostal constituencies, the words "ecumenical" and "ecumenism" carry very negative connotations, as noted by the Pentecostal delegation at the first Global Christian Forum (GCF).[9] There was no lack of overtures from ecumenical bodies to the Pentecostal "establishment" such as the World Pentecostal Fellowship (PWF), but they were received with indifference.[10] Further, most, if

---

6. Robeck, "Achievements," 167.
7. Prior, "Jesus Christ," 50.
8. Robeck, "Achievements," 170–71.
9. van Beek, *Revisioning Christian Unity*, 71.

10. For example, when the Secretaries of Christian World Communions sought the participation of the PWF, the gesture was rebuffed. Robeck renewed this appeal to the PWF in January 2014 and proposed that either the chairperson or secretary of the

not all, of the Pentecostal representatives have come from the West. Robeck notes the practical difficulty of getting Pentecostal participants from the global South, because, among other things, Pentecostal participants have to find their own funding.[11] Finally, until recently, the prevailing view of many Pentecostals, including most Asian Pentecostals, was that Catholics were not Christians; therefore, they should be regarded as suitable candidates for evangelization rather than as partners in dialogue.

As an outsider, it is difficult to know for certain the reason the Catholic Church in Asia has ignored the Catholic-Pentecostal Dialogues. One possibility is that the primary focus of the Federation of Asian Bishops Conference (FABC) has been on the "triple dialogue" with Asian cultures, Asian religions, and the poor.[12] Relations with other Christian churches was not, until recently, within their purview. Asian Catholic theologians do not appear to show much interest either, if one were to look at some of the titles and themes of doctoral dissertations written on the FABC's focus. Of the dissertations written between 1985 and 2008, there is not a single one dealing with relations with Protestants, let alone Pentecostals.[13] This is rather surprising in view of the fact that exchanges between the FABC and the Christian Conference of Asia (the regional organization of the WCC) have been going on since 1996 under the banner "Asian Movement for Christian Unity."[14] One could only surmise that Pentecostals were seen as problematic rather than as suitable dialogue partners. Thus, while Pentecostal-Catholic relations may have thawed in the West, there is still much mutual suspicion and ignorance in Asia.[15]

Catholics may accuse Pentecostals of "aggressive proselytizing,"[16] but they have also sought to learn from Pentecostals. This can be seen at the Conference of Catholic Bishops in India which devoted its Ninth Plenary (January 9–12, 1997) to discussing "the rise and growth of Neo-Pentecostalism, which poses a challenge to the Catholic Church."[17] The Indian bishops did not speak of proselytism but focused mostly on the Church's need to develop a holistic response to the Pentecostal challenge by promoting what

---

PWF be represented, but again, the proposal was rejected. See Robeck, "Ecumenism and Ecumenical Opportunities," 1.

11. Robeck, "Ecumenism and Ecumenical Opportunities," 6.
12. "First Bishops' Institute," 4–5.
13. Kroeger, *Theology from the Heart of Asia*.
14. Jones, "Global Christian Forum," 16.
15. Locke, "Call."
16. Locke, "Call," 9.
17. Conference of Catholic Bishops of India, "Neo-Pentecostals."

they termed "God-experience." "God-experience" could be enhanced by emphasizing "the primacy of the Word of God in Christian living," "fostering fellowship in the church," and developing "pastoral care with a personal touch." Each of these areas of concern is followed up with practical recommendations; for example, to promote the Word of God in Christian living, they recommended that it "be proclaimed with faith and *unction* so that it touches the hearts of people." Further, daily reading of the Bible should be encouraged in the family; Bible study groups and prayer groups ought to be promoted; Bible conventions should be held with special emphasis on God-experience, with testimonies of people who have experienced the power of the Word of God in their lives . . . .[18]

It is clear from this small sampling of statements from the Ninth Plenary that the Indian bishops were aware of their own deficiencies in "God-experience." Thus, one of the positive outcomes of the Pentecostal challenge is that Asian Catholics are becoming more aware of the need to develop a Pentecostal-like spirituality with an explicit emphasis on pneumatology within the framework of Catholic teaching.[19]

But since the beginning of the twenty-first century, formal exchanges have been taking place within the larger ecumenical framework. The formation of the WCC-initiated Global Christian Forum (GCF) in 2002 sought to bring Catholic, Orthodox, mainline Protestant, evangelical, and Pentecostal churches and organizations together by creating a "neutral space" that makes it easier for evangelicals and Pentecostals, unused to the formal patterns of discussion in the WCC, to participate.[20] At its first global gathering in Limuru, Kenya, in 2007, the first two papers were presented by Pentecostals: Wonsuk Ma, an Assemblies of God scholar from Korea, and Cheryl Bridges Johns from the Church of God (Cleveland, Ohio). Ma acknowledges that Pentecostals have sometimes been offensive and intolerant, because many first-generation Pentecostals had experienced new life in Christ, so real to them that they simply could not keep it to themselves.[21] Johns, in her paper, argues that Pentecostalism in the global South needs to be understood on its own terms rather than within the framework of the Christianity of the global North. If this approach is taken, ecumenism cannot be undertaken in its old forms but must be reconceptualized to take account of a different kind of—but equally important—contribution

---

18. Conference of Catholic Bishops of India, "Neo-Pentecostals," §-17 *passim*. Emphasis added.
19. Conference of Catholic Bishops of India, "Neo-Pentecostals," §8.
20. Jones, "Global Christian Forum," 4.
21. Ma, "Discerning What God is Doing," 83.

of the global South, especially Pentecostalism.²² In different ways, both Ma and Johns are seeking to carve out for Pentecostals their own unique space within the larger Christian community.

The second global gathering of GCF took place in Indonesia in October 2011, and its theme had an unmistakable Pentecostal undertone: "Life Together in Jesus Christ, Empowered by the Holy Spirit."²³ The third GCF global gathering—held in Tirana, Albania, in 2015 on the theme "Discrimination, Persecution, Martyrdom: Following Christ Together"—reveals some tension between the Pentecostals and the Orthodox. The Pentecostals expressed certain general reservations: "We see the need to equip our churches to stand with the suffering church. But we are not comfortable with the emphasis on some social issues." For his part, his Eminence Anton Audo, Archbishop of Aleppo of the Chaldeans, Chaldean Catholic Bishopric of Aleppo, was much more explicit: "I understand the suffering of Pentecostals in our countries. It also seems that sometimes they . . . want to teach us how to be Christian."²⁴ Clearly, Pentecostals have much work to do to clear themselves of this widespread perception.²⁵ Despite the minor spat, GCF is a remarkable achievement as far as Pentecostals are concerned. It provides a safe space for all participants, not so much to engage in theological discussions as to share testimonies and reflect on common concerns. It is a space that is clearly welcoming to Pentecostals whose basic modus operandi is not theological dialogues. Most simply lack the confidence and expertise to engage in such conversations; they are more adept at joint evangelistic campaigns, "festivals of praise," and mission partnership with parachurch organizations, about which they are quite ready to share their practical expertise. Besides the global gatherings, the third Asian regional GCF meeting was held at the Assemblies of God Yoido Full Gospel Church in Seoul, South Korea, from November 12–16, 2010. Such a broad-based ecumenical gathering in a Pentecostal church was unprecedented. In this meeting, the existing relationship between the FABC and CCA in the Asian Movement for Christian Unity was reaffirmed. In addition, it recommended that the AMCU "seek ways of including also the Pentecostals of

---

22. Johns, "When East Meets West."
23. Cain, "Manado 2011," line 12.
24. "Discrimination, Persecution, Martyrdom," 12.
25. But to set things in perspective, in Asia it appears that the Orthodox seem to have an issue not only with Pentecostals but also with Catholics over proselytism. As Met. Dr. Youhanon Mar Demetrios from India states in no uncertain terms: "Lest one interprets this response as a broadside only against the Evangelicals and Pentecostals, I have to add that proselytism is one of the serious issues that the Orthodox Churches see in their relationship with the Catholic Church." Demetrios, Challenges of Proselytism," 146.

Asia in the movement."[26] This recommendation was realized when the fifth AMCU gathering in December 2010 welcomed a representative from the Asia Pentecostal Society.[27] Through these forums, Pentecostals and Catholics are beginning to engage each other but only in gatherings involving other Christian bodies.

Pentecostal-Catholic Cooperation on Public Issues

In matters of mutual concern that affect their common life as citizens, Pentecostals and Catholics in Asia do come together but again, within the broader framework of Protestant-Catholic cooperation. The level of practical cooperation, however, differs from country to country. To a large extent, engagement between Catholics and Protestants is affected by their sociopolitical situations. In contexts where the Christian minority faces a common threat, there is a high level of cooperation. Political exigencies often force Christians of all persuasions to work closely together. For instance, in the face of persistent attacks on Christian churches by Hindu militants, the United Christian Forum of Human Rights in India was formed. It brings together the Roman Catholic Church and the Evangelical Fellowship of India which includes a number of Pentecostal churches and organizations. Similarly, in Myanmar, the law proscribing religious conversion drew a concerted response from the Catholic, Protestant, and Evangelical (including Pentecostal) churches.[28] In Malaysia, the Catholic Bishops' Conference, the Council of Churches of Malaysia, and the National Evangelical Christian Fellowship (which includes Pentecostal churches) have come together to form the Christian Federation of Malaysia (CFM). On matters that affect all Christians, it would be the CFM that issues a unified Christian response. Such was the case not long ago when Christians were forbidden to use the word *Allah* for God in the Malay Bible. In such a context, the question of proselytism among Christians is not even raised.

In Singapore, there are fewer formal exchanges between Catholics and Protestants compared to Malaysia. This has to do with a very different sociopolitical climate; there are no perceived threats that force Catholics and

---

26. Pasaribu, "An Ecumenical Encounter," 55–56.

27. AMCU, "Fifth Asian Movement for Christian Unity," line 5. However, the latest AMCU gathering in 2013 does not mention Pentecostal participation. See AMCU, "Common Statement of the Sixth Meeting." In an e-mail to the author, the past president of the Asia Pentecostal Society, Joseph Suico, says that the APS has been inactive for the past five years. This may explain its absence at the last AMCU gathering.

28. Hmung, "Religious Conversion and the Law," 71.

Protestants to stand together. This lack of cooperation is quite palpable. For example, even when addressing significant issues of common concern, such as human sexuality and biomedical ethics, the National Council of Churches of Singapore (NCCS) and the Catholic Church will usually issue separate public statements. To my knowledge, there has not been any joint statement between the NCCS and the Catholic Church on issues of mutual concern. Any *official* engagement between the churches occurs *indirectly* at interreligious forums such as the Interreligious Organization and the government-initiated Presidential Council for Religious Harmony. It seems that the only regular official engagement comes once a year in the Week of Prayer for Christian Unity. During this time, Catholics and NCCS churches hold combined services in both Catholic and Protestant churches, but not in the Pentecostal churches, even though the largest Pentecostal denomination, the Assemblies of God, is a member of the NCCS.[29]

Ecumenical Relations in Asia vis-à-vis Rome

So far, most of the formal engagements between Catholics and Pentecostals in Asia have been indirect. If there is to be any direct engagement, it would most probably come as a result of some *directive* from Rome. The reason for this is that Asian bishops are generally quite amenable to the Vatican's policies and directions. Evidence of this can be seen in the responses of the FABC to the pre-synodal *Lineamenta* and post-synodal apostolic exhortation, *Ecclesia in Asia,* promulgated in connection with the Year of Jubilee in 2000 following the Asian Synod. With the possible exception of the bishops from Japan and India,[30] the Asian bishops' responses tend to follow the direction charted by Rome.[31] One possible reason is that Asian bishops are generally more theologically conservative and readier to toe the line than break ranks, unlike some of their Western

---

29. But exchanges occur at an unofficial level—for example, at Trinity Theological College (TTC). As an ecumenical theological college of the mainline Protestant churches, it provides a congenial environment for various exchanges between Catholics and Protestants. Catholic priests and religious have been invited to speak at the college chapel (but so far this initiative has not been reciprocated). In the past, Catholic seminarians, mostly from the Redemptorist order, were sent to TTC for some of their courses, mostly in the field of biblical studies and languages. And over the years, TTC has graduated a few Canossian sisters.

30. Even for Japan and India, one wonders if the outspoken reactions to the *Lineamenta* represent the views of the more radical theologians rather than the bishops'. There is good reason to suspect that the views and concerns of bishops and theologians do not always coincide. See the analysis of Nick Chui, "On Being Catholic," 12–19.

31. For the various responses, see Kroeger and Phan, *Future of the Asian Churches.*

counterparts. They faithfully reflect the conservative ethos of the Church's grassroots members. This means that changes emanating from the Vatican are also likely to be reflected in changes in the Church in Asia. In light of this tendency, I think there is reason for hope. The last quinquennium (the sixth) of the Catholic-Pentecostal Dialogues ended in 2015. The Dialogues have certainly brought about mutual understanding and removed some of the prejudices on both sides, although as indicated earlier, the fruits of these Dialogues have not been widely disseminated in Asia, nor have they provided the catalyst for an Asian version of it, even though some of the issues like proselytism are just as real in some parts of Asia, especially the Catholic-majority Philippines, as elsewhere.

But things may be changing for the better under the current pope. Compared to the previous two popes, Francis is perhaps far more open to Pentecostals. According to Catholic Charismatic, Peter Hocken, Francis developed a very positive relationship with Pentecostal pastors when he was archbishop of Buenos Aires. His understanding of the renewal of the Church through baptism in the Spirit was in no small part the result of these personal relationships. Hocken thinks that the prayer of some Pentecostal pastors for the archbishop through the laying on of hands has had a decisive impact on the new direction of the Catholic Church under Francis.[32] Although this aspect of Francis's work does not get any press attention, it could have very important ramifications for Catholic-Pentecostal relations in Asia. Given the general tendency of the Asian bishops to toe the Vatican line, we Pentecostals hope that this irenic spirit will positively impact future relations between Catholics and Pentecostals in Asia. All that is needed is some form of directive from Rome.

Grassroots Exchanges between Catholics and Pentecostals

The potential for better cooperation and deeper engagement is likely to lie in the informal exchanges taking place between Catholics and Pentecostals at the grassroots level. I will focus on three kinds of exchanges: shared experiences, shared ideas, and shared resources.

Shared Experiences

The Catholic charismatic renewal came to Asia in the 1970s, just a few years after it began in the US. But for some years, the reality did not quite hit

32. Hocken, *Azusa*, 165–69, 205.

home for non-Catholics, because the Catholic renewal was mostly confined to Catholic communities and local parishes. But the increasing use of social media has created greater awareness of and direct contact with each other. When Pentecostals begin to come into contact with Catholics who are "filled with the Spirit," they are forced to ask themselves some hard questions: Are they *really* filled with the Spirit? If they are, what about their Mariology and many other beliefs and practices which are deemed "unbiblical"? However, over time, even the most intransigent Pentecostals cannot help noticing similarities and a kindred spirit: Catholic charismatics speak in tongues, pray to Jesus, raise their hands, dance and sing in the Spirit—just like we do! They appear to be truly in touch with God, and what's more, they sing our songs. It's like a repeat of the Cornelius story in Acts 10: "They have received the Holy Spirit just as we have" (Acts 10:47). So, who are we to say that Catholics are not Christians?

But it would take several more decades before these shared experiences found concrete expressions in cooperative ventures. Since 2013, the Singapore Archdiocesan Catholic Council for Ecumenical Dialogue, an "Ad Hoc Protestant Team," and Alpha Singapore, have jointly organized an annual Ecumenical Charismatic Healing Service. According to the *Catholic News*, the aim is "to give Protestants and Catholics the opportunity to worship God, commit to love one another, and minister the Lord's healing as one."[33] What brings them together was their common Pentecostal experience. The current Catholic Archbishop of Singapore is charismatic, and so are some of the leaders of the Protestant team, including the Methodist and Lutheran bishops. Interestingly, the Protestant participants are represented by an ad hoc team rather than the NCCS. Within the NCCS, the charismatic renewal continues to divide member churches. Ironically, the Assemblies of God, a member of the NCCS, has not been involved in this Healing Service, although individual members are represented.[34] The reason is not hard to find: within the AG, there are still some diehards who refuse to believe that Catholics are Christians.

Shared Ideas

Between Pentecostal and Catholic charismatics, there has been considerable cross-fertilization of ideas and practices. One example is El Shaddai, a Catholic lay-led movement in the Philippines with more than eight million followers internationally and which shares with some Pentecostal groups an

33. "Archbishop Goh, Bishops from Other Churches to Hold Healing Service."
34. "Archbishop Goh, Bishops from Other Churches to Hold Healing Service."

emphasis on the prosperity gospel. Its founder, Brother Mike Velarde, speaks of "seed faith" borrowed from Oral Roberts, and "word of faith" or "faith confession" derived from Kenneth Hagin.[35] Its *modus operandi* comes from Pat Robertson's *The 700 Club*.[36] The difference between El Shaddai's founder and Pentecostal prosperity preachers is that Brother Mike's movement is officially recognized as a lay Catholic movement, whereas most Protestant prosperity preachers tend to disassociate themselves (or were disassociated from) classical Pentecostal denominations. El Shaddai's prosperity teaching has also created tension with the Catholic Church in the Philippines,[37] but El Shaddai is too valuable for the Catholic Church to be sidelined. It is probably the most effective Catholic answer to Pentecostal proselytism. With El Shaddai, Catholics have no compelling reason to join a Pentecostal church. The difference between El Shaddai and the earlier Catholic Charismatic Renewal movement is that Brother Mike preaches a prosperity gospel that resonates deeply with the poor. These are the people who would have gravitated toward a Pentecostal megachurch.

On the Pentecostal side, a growing number of Pentecostals are rediscovering Catholic spiritual resources, such as the sacraments, the liturgy, and even episcopacy. This has resulted in the formation of a number of "convergence" churches, which seek to integrate charismatic, evangelical, and sacramental dimensions of church life, such as the International Communion of the Charismatic Episcopal Church (ICCEC), founded in 1992; the Communion of Evangelical Episcopal Churches (1993); and its sister communion, the Communion of Convergence Churches (2005). The ICCEC is especially strong in the Philippines, perhaps because its rich sacramental life, elaborate rituals, and colorful pageantry—along with a strong charismatic emphasis—resonate deeply with grassroots Catholics.[38]

In addition to shared ideas, both the Pentecostals and Catholic charismatics share a common language of worship. One cannot underestimate the power of a shared language in transcending barriers, especially at the grassroots level. When both sides discover a spontaneous and unaffected capacity to shout "Hallelujah!" and "Praise the Lord!" or to sing "Shine, Jesus Shine," they immediately sense a shared spiritual affinity which no amount of formal dialogue could produce.

35. Wiegele, *Investing in Miracles*, 6–8.
36. Wiegele, *Investing in Miracles*, 18–21.
37. Wiegele, *Investing in Miracles*, 25, 40.
38. The Cathedral of the King, founded by a former Assemblies of God missionary, is perhaps the best known. http://www.cathedraloftheking.org.

Shared Resources

In a globalized world, spiritual resources are widely marketed and shared. Many local Catholic parishes use the Alpha Course for their "New Evangelization." The Alpha Course was produced by the Anglican charismatic Holy Trinity Church Brompton in London, with international "franchises" in several Asian countries. The course includes a session in which people pray for believers to be "filled with the Holy Spirit."[39] For deepening the spiritual life, the Catholic Charismatic Renewal (CCR) runs a program called Life in the Spirit Seminar (LISS) which, among other things, aims to "help those who come to the seminars to yield to the action of the Holy Spirit in their lives."[40] This program is used in many parishes in Asia.[41] The teaching of the CCR concerning baptism in the Spirit is surprisingly closer to the classical Pentecostal's than that of Third Wave evangelical charismatics, as seen in the following statement:

> The baptism of the Holy Spirit is a gift of God which we can choose to receive *after* we become Christians (Acts 1:4-5, Luke 11:11-13), and the purpose of this gift is to *empower* every believer for being a witness of Christ to a hurting and unbelieving world (Acts 1:4-8, Luke 24:49). The usual outward evidence that we have received the baptism of the Holy Spirit is not that we "feel" anything but that we are able to begin praying in tongues by the Holy Spirit.[42]

Another shared resource is charismatic songs. Most Pentecostals may not be aware of the many modern Catholic songs from GIA Publications and Oregon Catholic Press, but many Catholics are familiar with Vineyard music and Hillsong. Even if there is a bit of trade imbalance in the Pentecostals' favor, the use of common resources helps to assuage suspicion on the part of the Pentecostals: if Catholics sing our songs and use our evangelistic materials, they can't be very different from us.

---

39. Session 10, "How Can I Be Filled with the Holy Spirit?" *Alpha Guide*, 55–60.

40. Catholic Charismatic Renewal-Archdiocese of Miami, "Life in the Spirit Seminar."

41. For example, the Archdiocese of Singapore lists LISS as one of its regular events: https://www.catholic.sg/participate/returning-catholics.

42. "Baptism of the Holy Spirit," lines 1–7.

Conclusion

Unlike in Latin America, the Pentecostal-Catholic relationship in Asia has been less acrimonious, with the possible exception of the Philippines which, in many ways, shares similar cultural characteristics with Latin America. In fact, compared to relations with the Orthodox, the Pentecostal-Catholic relationship has been much more cordial in recent years. Two factors stand out that account for the peculiar way Pentecostals and Catholics relate to each other in Asia. One is their minority status in most Asian countries, which forces them to work together for their own common good. The other is their shared experience of the Holy Spirit. Catholicism in Asia and in much of the global South has been influenced more by Pentecostalism than by the Orthodox Church.[43]

In addition, the Global Christian Forum, by creating a congenial environment for Pentecostals, could well be the most important catalyst for Pentecostals to engage with other Christian bodies on an unprecedented scale. GCF "is focused more on birthing, extending, and deepening relationships between churches than on theological dialogue producing consensus texts. Its theological mode is more testimonial and doxological than theoretical and analytical."[44] This is clearly in deference to the Pentecostals who are more comfortable sharing their testimonies than engaging in formal theological dialogue. So, in the spirit of the GCF, let me end with a testimony. It's the story of my wife. Born in the Philippines, she was baptized as an infant in the Catholic Church but grew up in the United Church of Christ in the Philippines (UCCP). While a student in Manila, she experienced Spirit baptism in an Assemblies of God church and brought the Pentecostal experience back to her local church. After our marriage, we settled in Singapore. As a choir director and voice trainer, she travels extensively in Southeast Asia to give vocal and choral workshops. In one of these workshops in East Malaysia, a Catholic choir director approached her for help. Soon, she was getting requests from other parish choirs. When the new translation of the Roman Missal was introduced in 2011, she was traveling regularly to East and West Malaysia to help choirs, priests, and seminarians learn the new chants. On one occasion, a parish choir on a recruitment drive approached their priest, asking him to let her

---

43. The highly developed pneumatology of Orthodoxy may, ironically, be the main reason for its lack of interest in the Pentecostal experience. One commonly heard response from Orthodox Christians when dealing with certain Pentecostal experiences is: "We already have them!" What they mean is that many Pentecostal experiences are embodied, but differently expressed, in their liturgy.

44. "How the GCF Engages with Participants," lines 21–23.

share her testimony during Sunday Mass. Because that was not allowed under canon law, the priest resorted to some creative casuistry. He delivered a five-minute homily and gave the rest of the time to her.

On another occasion, upon learning that she was baptized as an infant in a Catholic church, another priest welcomed her to the Eucharist. "But I was re-baptized as an adult in a Protestant church," she replied. "That's not a problem," he said, "Your first baptism is the valid one." It is often at the level of interpersonal relations that mutual trust develops, and where there is trust there is goodwill. Hopefully, in the future, we will see more constructive engagements at the institutional level from such grassroots exchanges between Catholics and Pentecostals.

The need for such engagements is perhaps greater for the Pentecostals than the Catholics. One area where Pentecostals could learn from Catholics is in the discernment of spirits. Since the 1980s, many Pentecostals in Asia have become deeply enamored of the "supernaturalism" of the Third Wavers. Some of the extraordinary spiritual phenomena border on the bizarre such as glory cloud, gold dust, and grave soaking emanating from Bill Johnson's Bethel Church in Redding, California. Many Pentecostals sense that something is seriously wrong but are at a loss over how to deal with it. They would benefit greatly from the Catholic Church with its long history of discerning between the Spirit of God and other spirits.[45] It would make an appropriate subject for a Pentecostal-Catholic dialogue in Asia today.

Bibliography

The Alpha Guide. London: Alpha International, 2016.
"Archbishop Goh, Bishops from Other Churches to Hold Healing Service." *The Catholic News* 64, September 21, 2014. http://catholicnews.sg/index.php?option=com_content&view=article&id=10351:archbishop-goh-bishops-from-other-churches-to-hold-healing-service&catid=485:september-21-2014-vol-64-no-19&Itemid=473.
Asian Movement for Christian Unity (AMCU). "Common Statement of the Sixth Meeting of the Asian Movement for Christian Unity (AMCU VI)." December 5, 2013, Bangkok, Thailand. http://cca.org.hk/home/asian-movement-for-christian-unity-amcu.
———. "The Fifth Asian Movement for Christian Unity (AMCU V): A Joint Statement." December 4, 2010, Bangkok, Thailand. http://www.catholic.org.tw/en/News/News315a.html.
"Baptism of the Holy Spirit." *The Burning Bush Charismatic Prayer Group*. http://www.burningbush.sg/ccr/bhs.htm.

---

45. See, for example, Poulain, *Graces of Interior Prayer*, and Groeschel, *A Still Small Voice*.

Barrett, David, et al. *World Christian Encyclopedia: A Comparative Survey of Churches and Religions in the Modern World*. 2nd ed. Oxford: Oxford University Press, 2001.
Bundy, David. "The Ecumenical Quest of Pentecostalism." *Cyberjournal of Pentecostal-Charismatic Research* 5 (February 1999). http://pctii.org/cyberj/cyberj5/bundy.html.
Cain, Kim. "Manado 2011—An Overview." *Global Christian Forum*. http://www.globalchristianforum.org/manado-overview.html.
Catholic Charismatic Renewal-Archdiocese of Miami. "Life in the Spirit Seminar." http://www.miamiccr.com/life-in-the-spirit-seminar.html.
Chui, Nick. "On Being Catholic and Singaporean in the Third Millennium: Identity and Mission with Reference to *Ecclesia in Asia*." MTS thesis. John Paul II Institute for Marriage and Family, 2011.
Conference of Catholic Bishops of India (CCBI). "Neo-Pentecostalism: A Pastoral Response." In *Charisms, Movements and Communities in the Church: A Pastoral Overview. FABC Papers* 79 (September 1997) 6–12. http://www.fabc.org/fabc%20papers/fabc_paper_79.pdf.
Demetrios, Youhanon Mar. "The Challenges of Proselytism in the Context of Christianity in Asia." In *The Mission of God: Studies in Orthodox and Evangelical Mission*, edited by Mark Oxbrow and Tim Grans, 143–47. Oxford: Regnum, 2015.
"Discrimination, Persecution, Martyrdom: Following Christ Together." *Global Christian Forum News* 1 (2016) 1–2. http://www.globalchristianforum.org/docs/2016.01%20GCF%20News%20EN.pdf.
"The First Bishops' Institute for Missionary Apostolate of the Federation of Asian Bishops' Conferences." *FABC Papers* 19 (1979) 1–19. http://www.fabc.org/offices/csec/ocsec_fabc_papers.html.
Groeschel, Benedict. *A Still Small Voice*. San Francisco: Ignatius, 1993.
Hocken, Peter. *Azusa, Rome, and Zion*. Eugene, OR: Pickwick, 2016.
"How the GCF Engages with Participants." *Global Christian Forum*. http://www.globalchristianforum.org/how-GCF-engages-participants.html.
Hmung, Van. "Religious Conversion and the Law: A Case Study from Myanmar with Ecumenical Perspective and Response." *Asia Journal of Theology* 29 (April 2015) 64–73.
Johns, Cheryl Bridges. "When East Meets West and North Meets South: The Reconciling Mission of Global Christianity." In *Revisioning Christian Unity: The Global Christian Forum*, edited by Huibert van Beek, 93–101. Oxford: Regnum, 2009.
Jones, Sarah Rowland. "The Global Christian Forum: A Narrative History." In *Revisioning Christian Unity: The Global Christian Forum*, edited by Huibert van Beek, 3–36. Oxford: Regnum, 2009.
Kroeger, James H. *Theology from the Heart of Asia: FABC Doctoral Dissertations*. Quezon City, PH: Claretian, 2008.
Kroeger, James H., and Peter C. Phan, eds. *The Future of the Asian Churches: The Asian Synod and Ecclesia in Asia*. Quezon City, PH: Claretian, 2002.
Locke, John. "The Call to a Renewed Church in Asia and the Challenge of Religious Fundamentalism." *FABC Papers* 92m (January 2000) 1–16. http://www.fabc.org/fabc%20papers/fabc_paper_92m.pdf.
Ma, Wonsuk. "Discerning What God is Doing Among His People Today: A Personal Journal." In *Revisioning Christian Unity: The Global Christian Forum*, edited by Huibert van Beek, 80–92. Oxford: Regnum, 2009.

Pasaribu, Yustin. "An Ecumenical Encounter with the Global Christian Forum (GCF): Asia Regional Meeting." *Praxis: Newsletter of the World Student Christian Federation Asia Pacific* 3 (2010)/1 (2011) 18–19. https://issuu.com/praxisenews/docs/2010_2011-praxis-n3_1.

Poulain, Augustin. *The Graces of Interior Prayer*. Reprint. Whitefish, MT: Kessinger, 2010.

Prior, John Manfred. "Jesus Christ, the Way to the Father: The Challenge of the Pentecostals." *FABC Papers* 119 (October 2006) 1–65. http://www.fabc.org/fabc%20papers/fabc_paper_119B.pdf.

Robeck, Cecil M. Jr. "The Achievements of the International Pentecostal-Catholic Dialogue." In *Celebrating a Century of Ecumenism: Exploring the Achievements of International Dialogue*, edited by John A. Radano, 163–94. Grand Rapids: Eerdmans, 2012.

———. "Ecumenism and Ecumenical Opportunities for Pentecostals." Unpublished document prepared for the members of the executive committee, Advisory Council and Advisory Committee of the Pentecostal World Fellowship. Used by permission.

van Beek, Huibert, ed. *Revisioning Christian Unity: The Global Christian Forum*. Oxford: Regnum, 2009.

Wiegele, Katherine L. *Investing in Miracles: El Shaddai and the Transformation of Popular Catholicism in the Philippines*. Honolulu: University of Hawaii Press, 2005.

8

"Do Not Quench the Spirit": Some Thoughts on the International Roman Catholic–Pentecostal Dialogue

Cecil M. Robeck Jr.

Introduction

Although the International Roman Catholic-Pentecostal Dialogue has been in existence for nearly forty-five years and has completed six rounds of discussion ranging from five to eight years each, many people still do not know of its existence. This stems, in part, from the fact that many people do not realize how much Pentecostals and Roman Catholics hold in common. Due to popular stereotypes and caricatures they believe Catholics and Pentecostals ought to—or that they do—exist in two separate worlds, or at two ends of a very broad spectrum.[1] It is also the case that, until relatively recently, those leading many of the Pentecostal denominations have not been particularly interested in pursuing any type of formal ecumenical engagement. Some of them have actively worked against it.[2]

---

1. In his first *Prolusio* to the plenary meeting of the Pontifical Council for Promoting Christian Unity, given in November 2001, Cardinal Walter Kasper countered the argument that Pentecostals and Catholics are so different. See Kasper, "Present Situation and Future," 11–20. This was also the position noted by the Catholic co-chair, McDonnell, in "Improbable Conversations," 163.

2. In North America, this has only recently changed. The Pentecostal and Charismatic Churches of North America (PCCNA), which includes Canada and Mexico, named Dr. David Cole its liaison to the Greater Christian Community, effective November 1, 2012. On February 25, 2016, the PCCNA introduced its Christian Unity Commission to its members for the first time. So far, there is no other body on a regional, national, or international level that has taken such an action, and even some member churches of the PCCNA still have questions regarding its value.

There are several reasons for this lack of Pentecostal interest. First, the Pentecostal Movement is still quite young; it is little over a century old. During its first century of existence, it has been preoccupied with reaching the world through evangelism and mission, while attempting to determine its role as a "renewal movement" within the one Church of Jesus Christ. Thus, some of its energy has been spent on questions of organization and institutionalization. Second, because Pentecostals often found themselves marginalized, criticized, and in some cases persecuted by the ancient churches (Catholic and Orthodox), many of the Reformation-era churches (Lutheran, Reformed, Anabaptist, and Anglican), and many post-Reformation bodies such as Baptists, Methodists, and various Holiness churches,[3] most Pentecostals were not interested in participating with them in any of their ecumenical activities. Third, many Pentecostals viewed the formation of such organizations as the World Council of Churches—the most visible global attempt to organize ecumenical efforts—as an exercise in compromise, making possible relationships at the expense of "truth," and thus, participating in something that held the potential of undermining the church and its task of proclaiming the gospel to the world.[4]

What kind of dialogue is this paper exploring? There are different types of bilateral dialogues. Some, such as Catholic-Orthodox, Catholic-Anglican, or Catholic-Lutheran are working towards unity, possibly even institutional unity. Others, such as the Catholic-Pentecostal Dialogue, are aimed at greater understanding. There are also some more complex contexts of dialogue in this regard especially when one asks whether this dialogue is between one church (Catholic) and one church (Pentecostal). Is it a dialogue between one church (Catholic) and many churches (Pentecostal)? Is it a dialogue between one church (Catholic) and a Movement (Pentecostal)? The answers continue to be elusive, since Pentecostals are still working on issues of origin and identity.[5]

A second major factor is the disparity between Catholic and Pentecostal educational requirements for their leaders. While Catholic priests and theologians receive a minimum of seven years of theological training, that is not the case for Pentecostals where a Divine call and a good testimony may be all that is considered necessary. In 2000, the Assemblies of God in the United States surveyed its ministers and found that:

- 4.3 percent have no ministerial training;

---

3. See Robeck, "Holy Spirit and the Unity of the Church," 353–55.

4. See "Bylaws of the General Council of the Assemblies of God, Article IX.B, Section 11," in *Minutes of the Fiftieth Session*, 131–32. See also Taylor, *Second Coming*, 177.

5. McClymond, "'I Will Pour Out of My Spirit upon All Flesh,'" 356–74.

- 12 percent have no education beyond high school;
- 27.4 percent have completed a ministry certificate or correspondence course;
- 55.6 percent have attended Bible College, but only 41.3 percent of those completed a bachelor's degree (BA or BS);
- 12.4 percent have a master's degree (MA or MDiv);
- 9.9 percent hold a seminary degree;
- 2.8 percent hold an advanced degree in ministry.[6]

The Assemblies of God, which numbers sixty-eight million members and adherents around the world, is not alone. My son is writing a dissertation on a Pentecostal denomination in El Salvador, where the average pastor appears to have only a third-grade education. Such educational disparity sometimes makes communication difficult, even when goodwill is in place.

Finally, while it is the case that those involved in this important dialogue are people of goodwill, the opinions expressed even by clergy around the world are not always positive. While the Pontifical Council for Promoting Christian Unity has made it clear for years that the classical Pentecostal denominations are not to be numbered among the "sects,"[7] in many places that message has not been fully received.[8] Similarly, in many places, Pentecostals are still highly critical of the Catholic Church.[9] So there is, clearly, much work to be done.

While the Second Vatican Council was still underway, however, letters were exchanged between David du Plessis[10] and Augustin Cardinal Bea

---

6. "Fact* Survey Results," 9.

7. Cassidy, "Prolusio," 122.

8. See the term "sectas" in the popular dictionary Bravo, *Vocabulario de la religiosidad popular*, 173. See also Alta/Baja California Bishops, "Dimensions of a Response to Proselytism," 667, which seems to assume that Pentecostals seek members at any cost.

9. Many Pentecostals, especially in Latin America, think of the Catholic Church in that region as "pagans disguised as Christians" as evidenced in the language used by d'Epiney, *Haven of the Masses*, 170. See also Jeter de Walker, *Siembra y Cosecha*, 2:163–64 where she speaks of syncretism and idolatry in Bolivia.

10. David du Plessis was born in South Africa. He was a minister with the Apostolic Faith Mission of South Africa and served as its general secretary from 1936 to 1947, when he moved to Switzerland and helped to organize the Pentecostal World Conference [now Fellowship]. He served as the organizing secretary from 1947 to 1952 and again from 1955 to 1958. In 1948, he moved once again, this time to the United States, where for two years, he was affiliated with the Church of God (Cleveland, Tennessee). In 1952, he transferred to the Assemblies of God where he pastored and then went on to help spread the Charismatic Renewal across all denominational lines. His work ecumenically led to his nickname, "Mr. Pentecost." His openness to ecumenism led to

that would ultimately lead to the establishment of an international theological dialogue between the Roman Catholic Church and Pentecostals. This exchange began in September 1964. In a letter co-signed by Cardinal Bea (then president of the Secretariat for Promoting Christian Unity) and by Archbishop [of Utrecht, Netherlands] Johannes Willebrands (then secretary of the Secretariat for Promoting Christian Unity), the Pentecostal, David du Plessis, was invited "under private title" and with "all the rights and facilities" given to "Delegated Observers" to participate in the third round of the Second Vatican Council as a "Guest of the Secretariat" [for Promoting Christian Unity].[11]

Another eight years would pass before the first session of the International Roman Catholic-Pentecostal Dialogue was held. It began on June 20, 1972.[12] Following the death of Cardinal Bea, Archbishop Willebrands was elevated to the presidency of the Secretariat on April 12, 1969, and two weeks later he was named cardinal. Bishop Basil Meeking served as his under-secretary. During this same period (1968–1970), David du Plessis and Fr. Kilian McDonnell, a Benedictine monk from St. John's Abbey in Collegeville, Minnesota, became friends. Fr. McDonnell had begun his important research on the Charismatic Renewal and on Pentecostalism,[13] and the two spoke many times about their common interests. In September 1970, David du Plessis joined Bishop Basil Meeking and Bishop Pierre Duprey of the Secretariat, along with Fr. Kilian McDonnell and ten other Catholic and Pentecostal representatives. Theirs was the first of three preliminary meetings that paved the way for the Dialogue. The second meeting would take place in June 1971, and a third, smaller meeting between the two "steering committees" took place the following October. By June 1972, it seemed that everything was in place to begin a formal Dialogue.[14]

---

discipline by the Assemblies of God, which defrocked him in 1962; he was not restored to ministerial status until 1980. He died in 1987.

11. Augustin Cardinal Bea, personal correspondence to David J. du Plessis, September 7, 1964.

12. For a full report and analysis of this first round of discussions, see Bittlinger, *Papst und Pfingstler*.

13. Among McDonnell's works are (with Arnold Bittlinger) *The Baptism in the Holy Spirit as an Ecumenical Problem; Charismatic Renewal and the Churches; The Charismatic Renewal and Ecumenism; Presence, Power, Praise: Documents on the Charismatic Renewal*; (with George Montague) *Christian Initiation and Baptism in the Holy Spirit: Evidence from the First Eight Centuries*. It was Fr. McDonnell who gave us the category, "Classical Pentecostal Churches," in his 1976 volume.

14. For an overview of these sessions see Sandidge, *Roman Catholic/Pentecostal Dialogue*, 62–75.

In a sense, everything was in place, but there were two important facts that posed difficulty. First, there was no institutional support from any Pentecostal body. While the Catholic Church would be officially represented in this dialogue, there was no comparable body representing Pentecostals. The Pentecostals would be represented only by the integrity and goodwill of David du Plessis and those whom he managed to gather with him to speak to the Catholic team. Second, David du Plessis had difficulty recruiting Pentecostal leaders who were both competent and sufficiently confident to participate in such an international theological discussion. No one in the Pentecostal Movement had done such a thing before.

Second, the educational level required for ordination in most Pentecostal groups is still quite low. It is still possible to be ordained with little more than a Divine call and a compelling testimony. Because of this fact alone, few were prepared to engage in active ecumenical dialogue at any level of sophistication. They simply lacked the academic resources that would be necessary in a genuine theological exchange at a meaningful level.[15] While du Plessis was able to include a few close friends who occupied leadership positions in their respective denominations as well as two Pentecostal scholars,[16] the participants on the Pentecostal team who were most adequately trained were drawn from various Protestant, Anglican, and Orthodox charismatics. Indeed, virtually all papers presented on behalf of the Pentecostal team during the first Quinquennium were presented by Charismatics rather than Pentecostals.

The First Quinquennium

As one might surmise, the reports from the first five years of the Dialogue had limited value as a representation of classical Pentecostals. It was valuable in that, for the first time, it brought a small number of Pentecostals into direct contact with Catholic leaders and theologians, though it did not make good use of the two Pentecostal scholars on the Pentecostal team. The fact that the Pentecostal team included a sizable number of Charismatics who had experienced a life-transforming experience of baptism in the Holy Spirit but who were not classical Pentecostals is sufficient to demonstrate the naïveté of David du Plessis and the initial Pentecostal steering

---

15. For an overview of the problems that continue to plague the Assemblies of God, see for instance, Robeck, "Pentecostal Ecumenism," 34:2, 113–32 and 35:1, 5–17.

16. The two scholars were Dr. Russell P. Spittler, who held a PhD in early Christianity from Harvard University, and Dr. Vinson Synan, who held a PhD in American religious history from the University of Georgia.

committee. They assumed that, because these Charismatics had shared a common experience of baptism in the Spirit, they would also be able to represent Pentecostal interests. But on many subjects, they did not.

Both the Secretariat for Promoting Christian Unity and the Pentecostal steering committee soon recognized that this was not a tenable model if the Catholics were going to learn what they wanted to know about classical Pentecostals.[17] The subject of baptism, for instance, quickly became a team-dividing issue when the classical Pentecostals contended for the baptism of believers by immersion, and the Charismatics on the Pentecostal team argued for the validity of infant baptism.[18] Thus, before the second round of the Dialogue began, the decision was reached to limit participation on the Pentecostal team to those who were members of various classical Pentecostal congregations or denominations and to end further participation by Charismatics who were members of Protestant, Anglican, and Orthodox denominations.[19]

---

17. Through his research, Fr. Kilian McDonnell, OSB, offered the definition of classical Pentecostals as "those groups of Pentecostals which grew out of the Holiness Movement at the beginning of the [twentieth] century." See McDonnell, *Charismatic Renewal and the Churches*, 2.

18. The issue of baptism was picked up once again during the Dialogue's third round (1985–1989), when Dr. Jerry L. Sandidge and Dr. Cecil M. Robeck Jr., both Assemblies of God ministers, were invited to present the paper on baptism in August 1988. The paper revealed that Pentecostals around the world believe in and practice water baptism in very different ways. Initially, the Pentecostal co-chair, Justus du Plessis, argued strongly not to allow this paper to be presented. He was quickly joined by most of the other members of the Pentecostal team, who criticized Robeck, in particular, for pointing out these differences. Robeck argued that, while the majority of Pentecostals practiced believers' baptism using the Trinitarian formula, it was important for Catholics to know of the diversity of theology and practice on the subject within the Pentecostal Movement and to see that the Pentecostal team was honest about Pentecostal diversity. Catholics around the world were likely to run into these differences, and if only one line were taken in the Dialogue, its value would be undermined. In the end, the Catholic co-chair, McDonnell, intervened. The paper was presented and was very well received, with McDonnell calling it the "most honest paper yet delivered" by the Pentecostals. It was subsequently published in a slightly abridged form. Cf. Sandidge and Robeck, "Ecclesiology of *Koinōnia* and Baptism," 504–34.

19. The only exception to this rule was Dr. Howard M. Ervin, a member of the American Baptist Convention and professor at Oral Roberts University, who argued that he was, for all intents and purposes, a classical Pentecostal because he shared their theology. His publications include *And Forbid Not to Speak with Tongues*; *These Are Not Drunken as Ye Suppose*; *This Which Ye See and Hear*; *Conversion-Initiation and Baptism in the Holy Spirit*; and *Spirit Baptism*.

The Second Quinquennium

In a sense, the decision to continue the Dialogue only with representatives from classical Pentecostal churches beginning with the second round of discussions (1977–1982) amounted to a re-introduction of the Dialogue partners and a new beginning for the Dialogue. The beginning of this round was complicated, however, by the fact that the Catholic co-chair, Fr. Kilian McDonnell (who prepared the Catholic paper in 1977), suffered a heart attack and was not able to attend the opening week of meetings. Furthermore, Dr. Vinson Synan, who wrote and presented the Pentecostal paper that year, left before discussion of either paper began.

The Dialogue's second round was further stymied by the death of Pope Paul VI on August 6, 1978, and the sudden and unexpected death of Pope John Paul I on September 28, 1978. His death required the Dialogue to postpone its second year of discussion until 1979, after Pope John Paul II was in place.[20]

The remaining years of the second round of discussions included some staff changes on both sides, with a small but growing number of Pentecostals with varying levels of academic training, making presentations. The Pentecostal team was maturing in its ability to respond to Catholic questions with questions of their own, and this was demonstrated through conversations that were held beginning in 1980 on such topics as healing, worship, Church as communion, sacraments versus ordinances, Tradition and tradition, and finally on Mary, and ministry. Still, a variety of issues arose that made life difficult for the Pentecostal team. David du Plessis's health had begun to fail, and it was clear that he could no longer lead effectively. Thus, in 1983, questions were raised about the future of the Dialogue. As a result, the co-chairs, David du Plessis and Fr. Kilian McDonnell, both resigned their positions after serving for ten years together. Both would continue on their respective steering committees in an emeritus status. Justus du Plessis, a younger brother of David's, was invited to serve as the Pentecostal co-chair. After further review, the Secretariat asked Fr. Kilian McDonnell to resume as the Catholic co-chair. A new round of discussions would begin in 1985.

Jerry Sandidge, an Assemblies of God missionary working in campus ministries at the University of Leuven in Belgium, would soon face professional difficulties for his activity in the Dialogue, beginning in 1983. In his role at the university, Sandidge was subject to oversight from the Division of Foreign Missions of the Assemblies of God in the United States. He had entered a doctoral program at the Catholic University of Leuven in which

---

20. Sandidge, *Roman Catholic/Pentecostal Dialogue*, 191–200.

he had chosen as his dissertation topic the international Roman Catholic-Pentecostal Dialogue. Unfortunately, a press release that noted that he had presented the Pentecostal paper on Mary in 1983 led to several controversial news reports which resulted in significant backlash from some Pentecostal leaders. As a result, Sandidge was instructed by the executive director of the Division of Foreign Missions to disengage from the Dialogue and to drop the study of the Dialogue as the topic of his PhD dissertation or lose his missionary appointment. Sandidge continued to work on his proposed dissertation, however, while attempting to negotiate with his director for an alternative solution, but his requests were consistently denied. Still, he managed to receive his PhD in 1985, and in 1987 his dissertation was published.[21] Following much prayer and considerable anguish, Sandidge gave up his missionary appointment in 1987.[22] Meanwhile, he had been invited by du Plessis to join the steering committee as the new secretary for the Pentecostal team. He returned to the United States, where he took academic appointments first at Oral Roberts University and then at Regent University, and finally, he was invited to serve as the senior pastor of Evangel Temple, a leading Assembly of God congregation in Springfield, Missouri, that was ecumenically open. He served there until his death in 1992.

Perspectives on *Koinōnia*

With Dr. Jerry Sandidge now serving as the secretary of the Pentecostal steering committee, some changes were made regarding how participants were selected. Sandidge believed that the Pentecostal team needed to include more Pentecostal scholars. To that end, he made use of his connections with the Society for Pentecostal Studies, an academic organization made up primarily of faculty members in Pentecostal and Charismatic schools, as well as graduate students and professors who were studying or teaching at various other seminaries and universities. As a result, the academic level of the papers presented by Pentecostals began to improve.

Dr. Miroslav Volf and his brother-in-law, Dr. Peter Kuzmič (at that time, the founding director of the Biblijsko Teološki Institut in Osijek, Yugoslavia, now Croatia), were invited to give the Pentecostal presentation on "*Koinōnia* and the Communion of Saints" in 1985. They were both members of the Krístova Pentecostal Crkva in Yugoslavia.[23] Dr. Cecil M. Robeck, then

21. Sandidge, *Roman Catholic/Pentecostal Dialogue*.
22. Sandidge, *Roman Catholic/Pentecostal Dialogue*, 339–40.
23. After completing his PhD, Volf took a position for several years in systematic theology at Fuller Theological Seminary in Pasadena, CA. In 1994, he resigned from

serving as assistant dean for academic programs and assistant professor of Church history at Fuller Theological Seminary, was invited to join the Pentecostal steering committee in 1985. Robeck presented the Pentecostal paper, "The Holy Spirit and the New Testament Vision of *Koinōnia*" in 1986.[24] In 1987, the Pentecostal paper on "*Koinōnia*, Church, and Sacraments" was presented by Dr. Howard Ervin, professor of Old Testament at Oral Roberts University. And in 1988, Sandidge and Robeck teamed up to present the Pentecostal paper, "The Ecclesiology of *Koinōnia* and Baptism."

With this round, the Dialogue became much more focused. The steering committees had met and decided to study *koinōnia*. It was a topic then under discussion by the Commission on Faith and Order of the World Council of Churches. It was a topic that found resonance in the *communio* language of the Decree on Ecumenism 4 (*Unitatis Redintegratio*), and the concept of *koinōnia* as communion was not foreign to Pentecostals. Each year, the topics received considerable discussion and reflection, and in the end, they yielded a report titled "Perspectives on *Koinōnia*." Thus, for the first time, the report provided a more or less comprehensive understanding of a single theme. Its most significant contribution was probably the recognition that Catholics and Pentecostals represent two genuine Christian families who share in a real, "though imperfect, communion" with one another, in keeping with the claims of the Second Vatican Council.[25]

The third round of the Dialogue (1985–1989) became the subject of a doctoral dissertation completed by Fr. Paul D. Lee in 1994 at the Pontifical University of St. Thomas Aquinas in Urbe.[26] Its focus was on what Fr. Lee termed the "pneumatological ecclesiology," which he believed could be found in the report. He concluded that the report "contribut[ed] to an ecumenical understanding of the Church in a way which is more theologically satisfying because of the inherent attention to the economy of the Spirit."[27] Dr. Veli-Matti Kärkkäinen, a minister within the Finnish Pen-

---

the Dialogue for professional reasons. Subsequently, he received an appointment in theology from Yale Divinity School. Dr. Kuzmič continued to work in Osijek, Croatia, but also received an appointment as Distinguished Professor of World Missions and European Studies at Gordon-Conwell Theological Seminary in South Hamilton, Massachusetts.

24. In 1992, Robeck was invited to leave the administration of Fuller Theological Seminary and join the full-time faculty, where he now serves as professor of Church history and ecumenics.

25. See "Perspectives on *Koinōnia*." §55. Cf. *Unitatis Redintegratio*, 4.

26. Lee, *Pneumatological Ecclesiology in the Roman Catholic-Pentecostal Dialogue*. Dr. David Cole included a lengthy section on the third round in his dissertation, "Pentecostal *Koinōnia*," 103–89.

27. Lee, *Pneumatological Ecclesiology*, 271.

tecostal Movement, completed his dissertation shortly thereafter. Rather than focusing only on the third round of the Dialogue, Kärkkäinen chose to review the Dialogue's treatment of pneumatology from the beginning (1972–1989), completing his dissertation in 1998 at the University of Helsinki.[28] Like Fr. Lee, Dr. Kärkkäinen found the pneumatological approach in this Dialogue to be consistent with what he saw elsewhere in ecumenism, namely that the use of pneumatology was "one of the most promising recent developments in ecumenical theology"[29] to date.

The acknowledgment by both the Pentecostal and Catholic teams that Catholics and Pentecostals are undeniably linked to one another by the mysterious reality of the Holy Spirit, through whom they share in some way in genuine communion, however imperfect it might be, ultimately led to the challenging question raised by members of the Catholic team: "If we are both part of the Christian community, that is, if we are both part of the People of God, why do you Pentecostals insist on proselytizing our people?" It was a question that raised considerable discussion as the steering committees met with one another. Dr. Jerry Sandidge argued strongly that the Dialogue should take this question head-on. He contended, "If we can't take on the issues that most deeply separate us, we have no business continuing with this Dialogue." Justus du Plessis joined him in advocating for this position as did the Catholic members of the steering committee, Msgr. John A. Radano and Msgr. Juan Usma Gomez, who both served on the staff of the Pontifical Council for Promoting Christian Unity.

On the other hand, the Catholic co-chair, Fr. Kilian McDonnell, and Dr. Cecil Robeck of the Pentecostal steering committee believed that the Dialogue had not reached sufficient maturity to be able to address such a controversial topic directly. McDonnell stated simply, "If you take this topic on, we will bury you!" McDonnell did not offer his comment in a derogatory fashion, but stated it from his perspective as a matter of fact, since the topic of proselytism carried with it deep emotional baggage in both camps. His fear was that the Dialogue could be destroyed if it became confrontational.

Evangelization, Proselytism, and Common Witness

As a result, at the conclusion of the third round, the steering committee put the question to all the participants serving on both teams. McDonnell and Robeck were quickly outvoted. After further negotiation within the steering committee that contextualized the issue of proselytism, the topic for round

---

28. Kärkkäinen, *Spiritus ubi vult spirat*.
29. Kärkkäinen, *Spiritus ubi vult spirat*, 425.

four was announced as "Evangelization, Proselytism, and Common Witness." The Dialogue's fourth round began in Emmetten, Switzerland, on July 14, 1990. Msgr. Juan Usma Gomez, the person on the staff of the Pontifical Council for Promoting Christian Unity who was primarily responsible for the Catholic-Pentecostal Dialogue, would go on to complete his PhD dissertation on this fourth round at St. Thomas Aquinas in Urbe in 2001.[30]

The fourth round began with a discussion on evangelization. Dr. Gary B. McGee, professor of Church history and Pentecostal studies at the Assemblies of God Theological Seminary, was teamed up with Fr. Karl Müller, SVD, director of the Missiological Institute in St. Augustin, Germany. Müller was the initial drafter of the Decree on the Church's Missionary Activity (*Ad Gentes*) that was adopted on December 7, 1965, at the Second Vatican Council. McGee had authored a two-volume history of Assemblies of God Missions titled *This Gospel Shall Be Preached*.[31] While the discussion of McGee's and Müller's presentations demonstrated a common concern for evangelization by both communities, it also led to further discussion the following year which revealed various lacunae in the positions held by each. The link between evangelization and social justice demonstrated clearly that the social teaching of the Catholic Church is much more developed than that within Pentecostalism. That is not to suggest that Pentecostals have no social teaching or social programs but rather that the theological foundation for such things has not yet been adequately developed. At the same time, the Pentecostals suggested that Catholics might do well to re-think the role of individuals in the evangelization process, both in spreading the message and in demonstrating that individuals had received the message. Their sense was that the Catholic faithful would benefit from clear instruction on how to share their faith with others.

As the discussion progressed, it also became clear that one of the significant reasons that Pentecostals could be accused of "proselytism" was that many Pentecostals do not recognize most confessing Catholics as actually being Christians. Part of that stems from the fact that Catholics do not always share their faith clearly, but this is somewhat due to the fact that Pentecostals do not observe signs that they might recognize as marks of spiritual transformation in Catholic lives. The question begins with who each community understands to be fully "Christian" and how these individuals become fully incorporated into the ongoing life of their respective

---

30. Usma Gómez, *Evangelización, Proselitismo y Testimonio Común*.

31. His work, *Miracles, Missions, and American Pentecostalism*, would be published posthumously.

communities. This question would become the foundation for the fifth round of discussions which began in 1998.

Two significant events took place in the beginning of the fourth round. First, Justus du Plessis made clear in the Dialogue's second meeting in July 1991 that he intended to resign. In a difficult meeting in Venice, Italy, members of the Pentecostal team elected Cecil M. Robeck Jr. to succeed him. Second, two weeks after the third meeting of this round, Dr. Jerry Sandidge died at the age of fifty-two. Thus, the two people who had raised the issue of proselytism most forcefully, Sandidge and du Plessis, were gone from the scene, and the two who had opposed the topic most strongly, McDonnell and Robeck, were now charged with overseeing that the discussion was adequately addressed.

In spite of these events, the Dialogue continued without interruption. The steering committee soon recognized that further discussion was required on evangelization; indeed, it would take four full years of discussion before the groundwork had been laid to address the difficult issue of proselytism. Papers by Fr. Karl Müller, SVD, and Cecil Robeck helped to frame the discussion on proselytism.[32] At the end of the 1994 meeting, it was agreed that, while two further papers would be added to the conversation on proselytism—one by Fr. Kilian McDonnell, OSB, and the other by Dr. Walter Hollenweger, professor of mission at the University of Birmingham, England—reflections on the subject of common witness would also need to be included. Then, the Dialogue would be ready to move forward to frame its fourth report.

The significance of this fourth round on "Evangelization, Proselytism, and Common Witness," came first in the fact that both communities were able to sit down in a civil and respectful manner and discuss some very contentious issues that could possibly cause further discord and division between them. That such discord did not arise is a testimony to the growing trust that had emerged over their time spent together, including daily times of prayer. The discussions were sometimes intense. For instance, an entire day was spent debating whether the word "persuasive" could be used in the report when describing the type of preaching that should be done when proclaiming the gospel. To some, it sounded like coercion. To others, it was simply an attempt to bring people to a point of decision. But in the end, the dialogue partners believed that they had accomplished something important.

---

32. Much of this paper was ultimately published as Robeck, "Mission and the Issue of Proselytism," 2–8.

For the first time, Catholics and Pentecostals had addressed the problem of proselytism *together*. They agreed on definitions and on the need to condemn the practice of proselytism, while also describing some of the factors that lead to its practice. As a result, they were able to find a "more excellent way" forward, pointing to the possibility that Catholics and Pentecostals could actually evangelize together. That such an agreement could be reached did not mean that all Catholics or all Pentecostals might agree with every statement in the report, but it set a standard by which to measure and call to account their actions. In his *Habilitationsschrift* undertaken at the University of Helsinki, Dr. Veli-Matti Kärkkäinen analyzed and assessed this fourth round of the Dialogue.[33]

As the Dialogue participants shared their understandings of the reasons people proselytize, several factors emerged. Zealous Christians of all stripes are not necessarily satisfied only with experiencing the goodness of God. They want to share it, sometimes indiscriminately and without wisdom. For others, it is a matter of believing, for whatever reason, that others are not truly Christian and are in need of salvation. They may believe that someone belongs to the "wrong" church, or doesn't attend church often enough, or engages in some practice or in some habit that is viewed as not sufficiently representative of what a Christian should do or how a Christian should live.

On Becoming a Christian

It was these things that led the fifth round of the International Roman Catholic-Pentecostal Dialogue to address the questions of how one becomes a Christian and how the respective community nurtures young believers in such a way as to integrate them into the fullness of life in the church. Dr. Karen Jorgenson Murphy pursued the study of this fifth round in her PhD dissertation, providing a year-by-year account and assessment.[34] The Belgian theologian, Dr. Jelle Creemers of the Evangelische Theologische Faculteit in Leuven, focused primarily upon the theological methodology employed throughout the Dialogue's first five rounds, though he also included a section describing the fifth round of discussions.[35]

---

33. Kärkkäinen, *Ad ultimum terrae*.

34. Murphy, "On Becoming a Christian."

35. In its dissertation format, it was titled "Ecumenical Dialogue with a Non-Institutional Movement: A Systematic-Historical Analysis of Pentecostal Involvement in the International Roman Catholic-Classical Pentecostal Dialogue (1972–2007)." It has since been published by T. & T. Clark as Creemers, *Theological Dialogue with Classical Pentecostals*.

The fifth round focused on how Catholics and Pentecostals view the way(s) one becomes a Christian. It is far too easy to say that Catholics believe that people become Christians simply by undergoing baptism and that Pentecostals believe that people become Christians simply by making a public confession of faith. However, as participants discussed such stereotypes, it became clear that, in both cases, these moments mark the beginning of a lifelong process of spiritual transformation that can be described as conversion.[36] There is much more to becoming a Christian and becoming fully integrated into the ongoing life of the church than such initial steps might suggest. Indeed, the Pentecostal team was greatly encouraged when the Catholic Rite of Christian Initiation of Adults (RCIA) was explained to them. It helped them to understand more easily what was expected in the initial formation of young believers within the Catholic Church.[37]

The Dialogue's fifth round was also somewhat experimental. Repeatedly from the third round of discussion onward, Pentecostals argued that the early fathers of the church were their fathers as much as they were the fathers of the Catholic Church, even though these two Christian families granted different levels of authority to the fathers.[38] Thus, in 1997, the steering committees of both teams agreed that they would include material from the fathers of the church throughout each section of the fifth report. This proved to be a very difficult task, in large part because most of the Pentecostal participants lacked expertise in the patristic era. In spite of this weakness, the effort proved to be one that enriched the entire report. The teams worked together to identify important theological insights from the fathers, but equally important was the inclusion of testimonies by various fathers of the church in which Pentecostals could easily recognize the language of experience and affectivity that is familiar to them and in which they see much value. At the same time, it lengthened the report significantly.

Throughout the eight years of this round of discussions, participants set forth their understandings on the nature of conversion; the role of faith in "conversion-initiation"; the importance and significance of discipleship and formation; the legitimate place for experience in the Christian walk; and their understandings of "baptism in the Holy Spirit" and its role in the spiritual development of Christians. While much of the document contains common affirmations, there are areas where the teams could not reach a

---

36. See International Roman Catholic-Pentecostal Dialogue, "On Becoming a Christian," para. 45, 51, 75, 88, and 91.

37. International Roman Catholic-Pentecostal Dialogue, "On Becoming a Christian," para. 48–52.

38. See International Roman Catholic-Pentecostal Dialogue, "On Becoming a Christian," para. 10–13, 185, 266–70.

common understanding and where further discussion might have contributed to further agreement. Unfortunately, the question of how long to spend on this round came into play. As a result, there are a couple of sections—for instance, on "The Role of Experience in Becoming a Christian"—where differences were left in such an unresolved state that the Pentecostals and Catholics made separate statements on the subject.[39] In spite of such difficulties, the team was able to reach a series of convergences on the subject that was received with great appreciation as the following comment demonstrates: "Through our dialogue on the role of experience in Christian faith and community, we Pentecostals and Catholics are grateful to God for the mutually illuminating insights that our conversations have provided."[40] Participants concluded the report on a high note, noting that:

> Each of us has learned a great deal about the ways in which the other fosters faith, conversion, discipleship and formation, understands experience, and the Baptism in the Holy Spirit. As we reflected on the scriptures and the witness of the early church writers, and as we heard the way our partners in this dialogue engage in fostering the Christian life in those who come to the faith, we recognize in each other a deep commitment to Christ. Although Pentecostals and Catholics may give different emphases on aspects of becoming a Christian, each fosters the Christian life for the glory of God. Knowing this helps overcome misunderstandings or stereotypes we may have had about each other.... We have found much that we share together. Although we have significant differences still on some questions, we are able because of our study in this dialogue, to call one another brothers and sisters in Christ.[41]

"Do Not Quench the Spirit"

The sixth round of discussion ran from 2011 to 2015, and the report is still under embargo while it works its way through the process that the Vatican

---

39. International Roman Catholic-Pentecostal Dialogue, "On Becoming a Christian," 153–74 outlined the Pentecostal understanding while para. 175–83 outlined the Catholic understanding of experience.

40. International Roman Catholic-Pentecostal Dialogue, "On Becoming a Christian," para.184.

41. International Roman Catholic-Pentecostal Dialogue, "On Becoming a Christian," para. 284.

requires of all such documents. Upon completion, the Pontifical Council for Promoting Christian Unity forwards each report to the Congregation for the Doctrine of the Faith. It is reviewed by the Congregation, and a Catholic theologian is invited to offer a review as well. Once the review is received and the document is published in the *Information Service* of the Pontifical Council for Promoting Christian Unity, it is free to be released and published elsewhere. All reports to date have been published in a variety of Pentecostal venues, though most frequently they have appeared in *Pneuma: The Journal of the Society for Pentecostal Studies*.[42]

The topic of the sixth round provided a bit of a break from the previous three, picking up on themes mentioned in earlier rounds while also striking out into new territory.[43] Historically, relations between Pentecostals and Catholics throughout Latin America could often be described as difficult. At best, Pentecostal denominations have been described as "sects"[44]—as tools of the Central Intelligence Agency[45] and as instruments of the religious right[46]—by Catholics in Latin America, and in his famous 1992 speech in Santo Domingo, Dominican Republic, to the bishops of Latin America, Pope John Paul II even referred to them as "rapacious wolves."[47] On the other hand, Pentecostals have treated Catholics in the region, often enough, as though they were not Christians at all. They have labeled them as syncretistic, idolatrous, and much in need of conversion.[48]

In 2008 and 2009, the Pentecostal co-chair, Dr. Cecil M. Robeck Jr., met with Bishop Brian Farrell, secretary of the Pontifical Council for Promoting

---

42. The International Roman Catholic-Pentecostal Dialogue's first three reports on this Dialogue were published together in *Pneuma: The Journal of the Society for Pentecostal Studies* 12 (Fall 1990) 85–142. The fourth phase's report, "Evangelization, Proselytism, and Common Witness," appeared in *Pneuma* 21 (Spring 1999) 11–51 and in the *Asian Journal of Pentecostal Studies* 2 (January 1999) 105–51. The first four documents were published sequentially in Vondey, *Pentecostalism and Christian Unity*, 101–98. The fifth, "On Becoming a Christian," was too long for publication in *Pneuma* but was published in Vondey, *Pentecostalism and Christian Unity*, 95–216.

43. "Final Report (1972–1976)," para. 37 and 38–41, 45 f; "Final Report (1977–1982)," para. 31–40; "Perspectives on *Koinōnia*," para. 67; International Roman Catholic-Pentecostal Dialogue, "Evangelization, Proselytism, and Common Witness," para. 40–41.

44. Serbin, "Latin America's Catholics," 405–6; "Vatican Reports," 2–10; Haynes, "Brazil's Catholics Launch 'Holy War,'" 74–75; Bravo, *Vocabulario*, 173.

45. This claim was noted in Stoll, *Is Latin American Turning Protestant?*," 32, 99.

46. Stewart-Gambino and Wilson, "Latin American Pentecostals," 234–38.

47. "Opening Address to Fourth General Conference" 326, para. 12. Fr. Edward L. Cleary, OP, and I worked together to note the significance of this comment in Cleary, "John Paul Cries 'Wolf,'" 7–8, and Robeck, "What the Pope Said," 30–31.

48. Jeter de Walker, *Siembra y Cosecha*, 19–20.

Christian Unity, and Msgr. Juan Usma of the Council's staff, to plan the sixth round of the Dialogue. Msgr. Usma and Cardinal Walter Kasper had recently completed trips to several Latin American cities where some bishops had voiced concerns regarding certain Pentecostal claims, notably on the role of prophetic gifts and the nature of healing. They wondered what classical Pentecostals believed about these things and whether Pentecostals ever exercised discernment regarding these charisms. As a result, Msgr. Usma, Bishop Farrell, and Dr. Robeck agreed that such questions provided the Dialogue sufficient opportunity to clarify the positions on these subjects. Further conversation between Robeck and Dr. David Cole, secretary to the Pentecostal team, affirmed that decision.

With this scenario as its backdrop, new teams were chosen. In what was potentially the strongest Pentecostal team to date, participants came from the United States, Finland, Ghana, the Netherlands, Great Britain, and the Philippines. It included the president of the Church of Pentecost, an executive presbyter and district superintendent from the Assemblies of God in the US, and the general secretary of the Assemblies of God in the Philippines. It also included scholars who were officially designated by their denominations, such as the Pentecostal Movement in Finland, the Verenigde Pinkster Evangeliegemeenten in the Netherlands, the Elim Pentecostal Church of Great Britain and Ireland, the International Church of the Foursquare Gospel, and the Open Bible Church. The sixth round held its opening meeting in Rome, and the official title given at the beginning of this round was "Charisms in the Church: Their Spiritual Significance, Discernment and Pastoral Implications." At the end of the Quinquennium, however, the title was changed to "'Do Not Quench the Spirit': Charisms in the Life and Mission of the Church."

While there were genuine concerns raised by some Latin American bishops regarding the charisms that would be addressed, the report of the sixth round began with an uplifting introduction. This may be due, in large part, to the place that the Charismatic Renewal has found within the Catholic Church.[49] Estimates of the number of Charismatics in the Catholic Church range from 120 to 200 million, realistically about 11 percent of all Catholics worldwide.[50] In his last book, *The Rise of Charismatic Catholicism in Latin America*, the late Fr. Edward L. Cleary, who spent much of his life studying Pentecostals and Charismatics in Latin America, claimed that

---

49. Since June 1993, the International Catholic Charismatic Renewal Services (ICCRS) office has received formal Vatican recognition.

50. Johnson et al., "Christianity 2016," 26; note that by mid-2016, there were 656,606,000 Pentecostals/Charismatics in global Christendom, but they do not state how many Catholic Charismatics are part of that number.

Catholic Charismatics in Latin America "number 73 million of the some two hundred million Catholic Charismatics in the world."[51] The World Assemblies of God Fellowship, which constitutes the largest Classical Pentecostal denominational body in the world is roughly 67 million.[52]

The report of the sixth round of discussion begins with the following affirmation:

> Catholics and Pentecostals rejoice in the renewed emphasis given in recent decades to charisms in the life and mission of the Church. Together they affirm that the Holy Spirit has never ceased to bestow his charisms on Christians in every age to be used for the spread of the gospel and the upbuilding of the Church. Over the past century, the experience of charisms has taken a more central role, thanks largely to the witness of the Pentecostal and Charismatic movements. Catholic and Pentecostals are very grateful to the Lord for bestowing these divine gifts. At the same time, they recognize that the exercise of charisms is sometimes a source of tension and concern in various parts of the world.[53]

The continued openness that the Catholic Church has historically held in relation to such charisms as healings and miracles may well be the reason that it has found a way to welcome its large and healthy Charismatic Renewal as a valid manifestation in Catholic life. On the other hand, many of the churches that emerged during and after the Protestant Reformation seem to have redefined certain charisms for a more modern or "enlightened" understanding, or they rejected any possible use for certain of the biblical charisms in the modern period, thereby confining them to the apostolic or the immediate post-apostolic period.[54]

---

51. This number was first reported in Barrett et al., *World Christian Encyclopedia*, 1:20, Table 1–6a. Firm numbers, however, are extremely difficult to discern because they are self-reported. In a special report—Nucci, "Charismatic Renewal and the Catholic Church," 1—the author claimed that there were one hundred and sixty million Catholic Charismatics at the time of writing (Cleary, *Rise of Charismatic Catholicism in Latin America*, ix). I cannot account for the estimate of two hundred million Catholic Charismatics worldwide that Cleary claims to exist. In Allen, *Future Church*, 375–413, the author views the Pentecostalization of the Catholic Church as one of the top ten trends facing Catholics globally.

52. The figure of 67,290,023 is provided in Assemblies of God, 2014 Summary Statistical Report.

53. International Roman Catholic-Pentecostal Dialogue, "'Do Not Quench the Spirit,'" para. 1–2.

54. John Calvin, for example, equated prophecy with preaching; see Calvin, *Commentaries on the Epistles of Paul*, 269; Warfield, *Counterfeit Miracles*; Ruthven, *On the Cessation of the Charismata*; Ash, "Decline of Ecstatic Prophecy," 236, 250.

The title for this round, "Do Not Quench the Spirit," is an imperative taken from 1 Thess 5:19, which calls into question such redefinitions and limitations. Thus, the teams began with what Catholics and Pentecostals hold in common regarding the charisms, affirming first that their understanding of charisms is rooted in Scripture and that they affirm "the charismatic nature of the entire Church."[55] Charisms are "gifts of the risen and ascended Lord Jesus through the Holy Spirit (cf. Eph 4:8–12)," "given to all believers (1 Cor 12:7, 11)," "operative when Christians rely upon the power of the Holy Spirit to proclaim the gospel and to serve one another."[56] With such foundational affirmations in place, the Dialogue studied, with considerable agreement, the gifts of prophecy and healing. They called for those who exercise these charisms to do so in ways that are consistent with Scripture and the teaching of the Church, and to do so while living lives of good character.[57]

The most difficult issue that the Dialogue studied was that of discernment. When the Church is confronted by so many different voices, even "Pentecostal" or "Charismatic" voices, it is forced to discern the voice of the Lord. Sometimes, the task of discernment may seem daunting, even impossible. But the Lord of the Church has given to both through Scripture and through the charisms bestowed by the Holy Spirit, people and ways of making proper judgments on this wide array of voices. It was at this point where Pentecostals and Catholics engaged in a type of tug of war.

Catholics have a long tradition of discernment; one need be reminded only of the Exercises of St. Ignatius. Discernment appears to be the result of a rational process that seeks "the truth and will of God," while taking into consideration evidence such as we might find being given in the Jerusalem Council in Acts 15, where information is presented and a decision is rendered. While Pentecostals were willing to accept this definition as one valuable way that discernment is accomplished, they pressed the Catholic team to go beyond mere rationalism in the discernment process. The apostle Paul spoke of a charism called the "discernment *of spirits*" (1 Corinthians 12:10), and the apostle John exhorted his readers throughout Asia Minor to test *the spirits* to see whether they are from God" (1 John 4:1). Pointing to the apostle Paul's response to the girl with the spirit of divination (Acts 16:16–18), the Pentecostal team asked whether there was not more to the issue than lay below the surface; that is, whether it might also include at

---

55. International Roman Catholic-Pentecostal Dialogue, "'Do Not Quench the Spirit,"' para. 9, 15.

56. International Roman Catholic-Pentecostal Dialogue, "'Do Not Quench the Spirit,"' para. 10, 11, and 13.

57. International Roman Catholic-Pentecostal Dialogue, "'Do Not Quench the Spirit,"' para. 46–47.

some level a "trans-rational," or intuitive, form. In the end, they agreed that this was true.[58] A very similar discussion took place on this subject in the World Alliance of Reformed Churches-Pentecostal Dialogue.[59]

Once the definition was settled, participants moved to the more difficult question of authority and its pastoral implications.[60] Within the Catholic Church, there is a clear hierarchy of authority and responsibility. For Pentecostals, while there are levels of authority, it is vested much more broadly among the people of God. While some preliminary answers were reached in this discussion, it is clear that more study is needed on how authority is understood and how it functions within these two important traditions of the One Church of our Lord Jesus Christ.

Bibliography

Allen, John L., Jr. *The Future Church: How Ten Trends are Revolutionizing the Church.* New York: Doubleday, 2009.

Alta/Baja California Bishops. "Dimensions of a Response to Proselytism." *Origins: CNS Documentary Service* 19 (March 15, 1990) 667.

Ash, James L. "The Decline of Ecstatic Prophecy in the Early Church." *Theological Studies* 37 (1976) 227–52.

Assemblies of God. 2014 Summary Statistical Report. http://agchurches.org/Sitefiles/Default/RSS/AG.org%20TOP/AG%20Statistical%20Reports/2015%20%28year%202014%20reports%29/Online%20Stats%202014.pdf.

Barrett, David B., et al. *World Christian Encyclopedia: A Comparative Survey of Churches and Religions in the Modern World.* 2nd ed. Oxford: Oxford University Press, 2001.

Bea, Augustin Cardinal. Personal correspondence to David J. du Plessis. September 7, 1964. Secretariat for Promoting Christian Unity (SPCU), Prot. No. A 2613/64.

Bittlinger, Arnold. *Papst und Pfingstler: der römisch katholischen-pfingstliche Dialog und seine ökumenische Relevanz.* Frankfurt am Main: Peter Lang, 1978.

Bravo, Benjamín. *Vocabulario de la religiosidad popular.* Mexico City: Dabar, 1992.

Calvin, John. *Commentaries on the Epistles of Paul the Apostle to the Romans and the Thessalonians.* Grand Rapids: Eerdmans, 1961.

Cassidy, Edward Idris Cardinal. "Prolusio." *Information Service* 84:3–4 (1993) 122.

Cleary, Edward L. "John Paul Cries 'Wolf': Misreading the Pentecostals." *Commonweal* 119:20 (November 20, 1992) 7–8.

———. *The Rise of Charismatic Catholicism in Latin America.* Gainesville, FL: University Press of Florida, 2011.

---

58. International Roman Catholic-Pentecostal Dialogue, "'Do Not Quench the Spirit,'" para. 84, 89, 96.

59. For a Pentecostal understanding of discernment, see "Experience in Christian Faith and Life," 18–27, para. 72–113, especially para. 74–82.

60. International Roman Catholic-Pentecostal Dialogue, "'Do Not Quench the Spirit,'" para. 91–102.

Cole, David. "Pentecostal *Koinōnia*: An Emerging Ecumenical Ecclesiology among Pentecostals." PhD diss., Fuller Theological Seminary, 1998.

Creemers, Jelle. "Ecumenical Dialogue with a Non-Institutional Movement: A Systematic-Historical Analysis of Pentecostal Involvement in the International Roman Catholic-Classical Pentecostal Dialogue (1972–2007)." PhD diss., Catholic University of Leuven, 2014.

———. *Theological Dialogue with Classical Pentecostals: Challenges and Opportunities.* Ecclesiological Investigations, Vol. 23. London: Bloomsbury T. & T. Clark, 2015.

d'Epiney, Christian Lalive. *Haven of the Masses: A Study of the Pentecostal Movement in Chile.* London: Lutterworth, 1969.

Ervin, Howard M. *And Forbid Not to Speak with Tongues.* Hazlett, NJ: Paraclete, 1962.

———. *Conversion-Initiation and Baptism in the Holy Spirit.* Peabody, MA: Hendrickson, 1984.

———. *Spirit Baptism: A New Testament Investigation.* Peabody, MA: Hendrickson, 1987.

———. *These Are Not Drunken as Ye Suppose.* Plainfield, NJ: Logos International, 1968.

———. *This Which Ye See and Hear.* Plainfield, NJ: Logos International, 1972.

"Experience in Christian Faith and Life: Worship, Discipleship, Discernment, Community, and Justice." *Reformed World* 63 (March 2013) 2–44.

"Fact* Survey Results: A 2000 Survey of Assemblies of God Churches." Springfield, MO: Office of the General Secretary, 2000.

"Final Report (1972–1976)." *Pneuma* 12 (Fall 1990) 85–95.

"Final Report (1977–1982)." *Pneuma* 12 (Fall 1990) 97–115.

Haynes, Gary. "Brazil's Catholics Launch 'Holy War'." *Charisma* 19 (May 1994) 74–75.

International Roman Catholic-Pentecostal Dialogue. "'Do Not Quench the Spirit': Charisms in the Life and Mission of the Church: Report of the Sixth Phase of the International Catholic-Pentecostal Dialogue (2011–2015)." http://www.vatican.va/roman_curia/pontifical_councils/chrstuni/pentecostals/rc_pc_chrstuni_doc_2011-2015_do-not-quench-the-spirit_en.html.

———. "Evangelization, Proselytism, and Common Witness: The Report from the Fourth Phase of the International Dialogue 1990–1997 between the Roman Catholic Church and Some Classical Pentecostal Churches and Leaders." *AJPS* 2 (January 1999) 105–51.

———. "Evangelization, Proselytism, and Common Witness: The Report from the Fourth Phase of the International Dialogue 1990–1997 between the Roman Catholic Church and Some Classical Pentecostal Churches and Leaders." *Pneuma* 21 (Spring 1999) 11–51.

———. "On Becoming a Christian: Insights from Scripture and the Patristic Writings with Some Contemporary Reflections: The Report from the Fifth Phase of the International Dialogue between Some Classical Pentecostal Churches and Leaders and the Catholic Church (1998–2006)." *Information Service* 129 (2008) 162–215.

Jeter de Walker, Luisa. *Siembra y Cosecha.* Springfield, MO: Assemblies of God, Division of Foreign Mission, 1985.

Johnson, Todd M., et al. "Christianity 2016: Latin America and Projecting Religions to 2050." *International Bulletin of Mission Research* 40 (2016) 26.

Kärkkäinen, Veli-Matti. *Ad ultimum terrae: Evangelization, Proselytism, and Common Witness in the Roman Catholic Pentecostal Dialogue (1990–1997).* Studien zur interkulturellen Geschichte des Christentums, Vol. 117. Frankfurt am Main: Peter Lang, 1999.

———. *Spiritus ubi vult spirat: Pneumatology in Roman Catholic-Pentecostal Dialogue (1972–1989)*. Helsinki: Luther-Agricola-Society, 1998.

Kasper, Cardinal Walter. "Present Situation and Future of the Ecumenical Movement." *Information Service* 109:1–2 (2002) 11–20.

Lee, Paul D. *Pneumatological Ecclesiology in the Roman Catholic-Pentecostal Dialogue: A Catholic Reading of the Third Quinquennium (1985–1989)*. Rome: Pontifical University of St. Thomas in Urbe, 1994.

McClymond, Michael. "'I Will Pour Out of My Spirit upon All Flesh': A Historical and Theological Meditation on Pentecostal Origins." *Pneuma* 37 (2015) 356–74.

McDonnell, Kilian. *Charismatic Renewal and the Churches*. New York: Seabury, 1976.

———. *The Charismatic Renewal and Ecumenism*. New York: Paulist, 1978.

———. "Improbable Conversations: The International Classical Pentecostal/Roman Catholic Dialogue." *Pneuma* 17 (1995) 163–74.

McDonnell, Kilian, ed. *Presence, Power, Praise: Documents on the Charismatic Renewal*. 3 vols. Collegeville, MN: Liturgical, 1980.

McDonnell, Kilian, and Arnold Bittlinger. *The Baptism in the Holy Spirit as an Ecumenical Problem*. Notre Dame, IN: Charismatic Renewal Services, 1972.

McDonnell, Kilian, and George Montague. *Christian Initiation and Baptism in the Holy Spirit: Evidence from the First Eight Centuries*. Collegeville, MN: Liturgical, 1991.

McGee, Gary B. *Miracles, Missions, and American Pentecostalism*. American Society of Missiology Series, Vol. 45. Maryknoll, NY: Orbis, 2010.

———. *This Gospel Shall Be Preached: A History and Theology of Assemblies of God Foreign Missions*. 2 vols. Springfield, MO: Gospel, 1986.

Minutes of the Fiftieth Session of the General Council of the Assemblies of God, with Revised Constitution and Bylaws, Fiftieth General Council, Washington, DC, July 31–August 3, 2003. Springfield, MO: General Secretary's Office, 2003.

Murphy, Karen Jorgenson. "'On Becoming a Christian': The Fifth Quinquennium of the International Roman Catholic-Pentecostal Dialogue in Historical-Theological Perspective." PhD diss., Fuller Theological Seminary, 2013.

Nucci, Alessandria. "The Charismatic Renewal and the Catholic Church." *The Catholic World Report*. May 18, 2013. http://www.catholicworldreport.com/Item/2269/the_charismatic_renewal_and_the_catholic_church.aspx.

"Opening Address to Fourth General Conference of Latin American Episcopate." *Origins: CNS Documentary Service* 22:19 (October 22, 1992) 326.

"Perspectives on *Koinōnia*." *Pneuma* 12 (Fall 1990) 117–42.

Robeck, Cecil M., Jr. "The Holy Spirit and the Unity of the Church: The Challenge of Pentecostal, Charismatic, and Independent Movements." In *The Holy Spirit, the Church, and Christian Unity: Proceedings of the Consultation held at the Monastery of Bose, Italy (14–20 October 2002)*, edited by Doris Donnelly, et al., 353–81. Leuven: Leuven University Press, 2005.

———. "Mission and the Issue of Proselytism." *International Bulletin of Missionary Research*, 20 (1996) 2–8. http://www.internationalbulletin.org/issues/1996-01/1996-01-ibmr.pdf.

———. "Pentecostal Ecumenism: Overcoming the Challenges—Reaping the Benefits." *Journal of the European Pentecostal Theological Association (JEPTA)* 34:2 (2014) 1:113–32.

———. "Pentecostal Ecumenism: Overcoming the Challenges—Reaping the Benefits." *JEPTA* 35 (2015) 2:5–17.

———. "What the Pope Said." *Commonweal*, 119:22 (December 18, 1992) 30–1.

Ruthven, Jon Mark. *On the Cessation of the Charismata: The Protestant Polemic on Postbiblical Miracles*. Journal of Pentecostal Theology Supplement Series, Vol. 3. Sheffield: University of Sheffield Academic Press, 1993.

———. *On the Cessation of the Charismata: The Protestant Polemic on Post-Biblical Miracles*. Revised ed. Tulsa: Word and Spirit, 2011.

Sandidge, Jerry L. *Roman Catholic/Pentecostal Dialogue [1977–1982]: A Study in Developing Ecumenism*. Studien zur interkulturellen Geschichte des Christentums, Vol. 44. Frankfurt am Main: Peter Lang, 1987.

Sandidge, Jerry L., and Cecil M. Robeck Jr. "The Ecclesiology of *Koinōnia* and Baptism: A Pentecostal Perspective." *Journal of Ecumenical Studies* 27 (1990) 504–34.

Serbin, Ken. "Latin America's Catholics: Postliberationism?" *Christianity and Crisis* 52 (December 14, 1992) 405–6.

Stewart-Gambino, Hannah W. Wilson, and Everett Wilson. "Latin American Pentecostals: Old Stereotypes and New Challenges." In *Power, Politics, and Pentecostals in Latin America*, edited by Edward L. Cleary and Hannah W. Stewart-Gambino, 227–46. Boulder: Westview, 1997.

Stoll, David. *Is Latin American Turning Protestant? The Politics of Evangelical Growth*. Berkeley: University of California Press, 1990.

Taylor, G. F. *The Second Coming of Jesus*. Franklin Springs, GA: Pentecostal Holiness Church, 1916.

Usma Gómez, Juan F. "Evangelización, proselitismo y testimonio común: un estudio crítico de la cuarta fase del diálogo internacional católico-pentecostal (1990–1997)." PhD diss., Pontifical University of St. Thomas Aquinas in Urbe, 2001.

"Vatican Reports on Sects, Cults, and New Religious Movements." *Origins: CNS Documentary Service* 16 (May 22, 1986) 2–10.

Vondey, Wolfgang, ed. *Pentecostalism and Christian Unity: Continuing and Building Relationships*. Eugene, OR: Pickwick, 2013.

———. *Pentecostalism and Christian Unity: Ecumenical Documents and Critical Assessments*. Eugene, OR: Wipf & Stock, 2010.

Warfield, Benjamin. *Counterfeit Miracles*. London: Banner of Truth Trust, 1918.

9

Perceptions of the Holy Spirit in the African Initiated Churches: Lessons for Christianity in Africa

Laurenti Magesa

Introduction

African Initiated Churches (AICs) are also variously referred to as African "instituted," "independent," or "indigenous" churches,[1] or again as "African Initiatives in Christianity."[2] To characterize these churches as "spirit-centered," "spirit-led," or "spirit-filled" institutions or movements is certainly a generalization, but it is far from being a falsification. This assertion about them may be considered sweeping or oversimplified only in the sense that different AICs place dissimilar emphases on the involvement of spirits and the Holy Spirit in their creeds and faith experience. But that each and every one of them places a premium on the activity of spirits—and specifically the Holy Spirit—in the life of their adherents and, comprehensively, in the activities of the church in general, and in worship in particular, is something that cannot be gainsaid. It is perfectly accurate to affirm that AICs are founded on and operate under the strong belief in the power of spirit existence in the world. Consequently, for the AICs, all church endeavors—from the calling of the founder to the structures of the church, the church's preaching, and all ministries there—are based on and clearly marked by the conviction that the spirits and the Holy Spirit act

---

1. Pobee and Ositelu, *African Initiatives*, 29–34.
2. Pobee and Ositelu, *African Initiatives*, 29–34. This is also the title of the study by Pobee and Ositelu.

continuously within the church, manifested in a special way through the activities of the church's leaders.

This principle operative in the AICs has distinctively African indigenous religious roots, where everything in existence, whether visible or invisible, inherently and inevitably sustains spiritual aspects and manifests spiritual effects in all existence as appropriate. Early European anthropologists studying the features of African religion desperately sought to classify them according to their own philosophical approach to religion. Since the European methodology consisted not only in the distinction, but actually in the supposed separation between the "sacred" and "profane" perceptions of creation and nature, they could only pigeon-hole the integrated vision of African spirituality and religion as "animism." They accordingly branded African ritual expressions as "animist"; that is, having to do with spirit beings. Of course, they meant this in a pejorative sense, as in the main, they considered the African perception of spirits as superstitious at best. In their view, spirits were either nonexistent or evil. To approach them in the way the Africans did was, therefore, deemed unacceptable. Heavily informed by these anthropological studies, Christian missionaries from the West, in turn, made the eradication of African beliefs in spirits one of their major and primary evangelizing objectives.

The effort of Christian missionaries in Africa to eliminate indigenous belief in spirit-beings was ironical, given the testimony of the Scriptures about the reality of their existence in the world and their activity manifested in various ways among human beings. Reading both the Old and New Testaments, one does not fail to notice this conviction held by the biblical authors, and the history of Christianity affirms it in its metaphorical or practical dimensions. Immersed in their own indigenous view of the world where the reality and activity of spirits are fully acknowledged, many of the AICs' founders consequently noticed this discrepancy in missionary teaching. In contrast, they underlined the centrality of belief in spirits in their teaching and religious practices.

Among most Africans today, the belief that all nature has a "soul," or some form of spirit force, has remained substantive. It exists either openly or clandestinely in all forms of religious expressions. In general, Islam in Africa does not make much ado about it. Considering Islamic popular practice in this respect, it could be said, in fact, that it tolerates or even accepts it. However, mainline, classical, or mission churches originating from Europe and America—including Catholic churches and the Protestant churches of the Reformation, in particular—remain very much ill at ease with it. A famous example from the Catholic Church is that of Archbishop Emmanuel Milingo of Lusaka, Zambia, who was forced to resign from his episcopal see by Vatican authorities because he was involved in faith healing activities.[3] These were interpreted in the West as "witchcraft" practices. The exception in Christianity today, but in a rather different way, includes the wide range of emerging Pentecostal churches and other charismatic movements currently gaining ground in all parts of the African continent.

While clearly and strongly affirming the power and presence of the Holy Spirit in their activities, most Pentecostal churches operating in Africa, however, neither share nor accept the African spiritual conviction about the ubiquitous consciousness of the spirits or the spiritual nature of all existence. On the contrary and, indeed, paradoxically, many Pentecostal movements are much more vocal in vilifying the African viewpoint, oftentimes even more stridently than the mainline variety of Christianity. In so many ways, when approaching Pentecostalism, Africans entrenched in this belief are considered lacking in full Christian faith. Thus, in these churches' eyes, African "converts" who continue to hold on to the belief in spirits forfeit the possibility of the Holy Spirit working fully within and among them. African Pentecostals are, therefore, often obliged to abandon wholesale acceptance of the existence of spirits other than the "Holy Spirit." It is as if, for Pentecostalism in Africa, faith in Christ is completely antithetical to belief in spirits. The latter is often subsumed under the pejorative category of "evil spirits."

At the end of the day, the attitude of most Pentecostal churches would appear to be antithetical to African beliefs in the existence and powers of spirits. But as is the case with so many other so-called "Christian" things in Africa, where core values of African spirituality and religiosity are at stake, where they are disparaged and not taken into serious account, African Pentecostals' understanding of spirits as either nonexistent or evil is usually more apparent than it is real. In practice, belief in the spirits (and also in the Holy Spirit) continues to have a strong grip on them. This becomes evident in situations of grave need when African Pentecostal adherents easily and openly take recourse to the powers of spirits. For them, the Christian reality of the existence of the Holy Spirit and the ubiquitous presence of cosmic spirits need not be perceived as diametrically opposed. Often, they are perceived to tend to the same goal of affirming the fullness of life in the world.

Similarity of Perceptions of Spirits and the Holy Spirit

Concerning the Holy Spirit and spirits, there is an essential notional resemblance between African religion, mission Christianity, and the AICs. This

---

3. Milingo, *World in Between; Demarcations*; Haar and Ellis, "Spirit Possession and Healing," 185–206.

has to be explored in order to understand their approaches to this dimension of religious belief. The association has not always been cordial in practice, however. Whereas, as we have just mentioned, African religion holds as incontestable the universal spiritual consciousness of all creation and affirms that there is a cosmic spirit at the core of its spiritual and religious awareness and practice, mission Christianity's stances on the issue have been different, at least as far as practice is concerned. At any rate, official Christian teaching so circumscribes its approach to the Holy Spirit and the existence of spirits as to cause it the proverbial death of a "thousand qualifications." Mission Christianity is, in general, rather shy about the efficacy of spirits, particularly where the activity of spiritual beings among humans is concerned. In contrast with African religion and spirituality, which never expend energy trying to deny the activities of the spirits in the world but take them for granted, much effort is spent in most forms of mission Christianity in Africa trying to regulate their empirical manifestations even when their existence may, in principle, be embraced and proclaimed.

The AICs' position on the Holy Spirit is very close to the experience of African religion and spirituality, however. It should be said right away that this affinity is one of the reasons many of the AICs emerged as separate and distinct churches from the Christian mission churches. While some AICs are original creations by African pioneers (hence the designations African "initiated" or "indigenous" churches), many broke away from European mission churches in protest. These are those labelled "independent" churches in the strict sense. Apart from obvious dissatisfaction with missionary doctrinal strictures against some of the African customs regarded by Africans as good and essential to their social and spiritual survival (such as the practice of polygamy), as well as the general paternalistic attitudes of white colonialists and missionaries toward black people (for a long time, Africans could not hold high offices or unsupervised leadership positions in these churches), there were other causes of the discontent. Specifically, many AICs started as a rebellion against forms of liturgical practices in mission churches which seemed to deny or contradict their own belief in the ubiquitous presence of the Holy Spirit. In this respect, three issues were prominent in the revolts:

1. the doctrinal and practical denial of the power of spirits, in particular ancestral spirits;
2. the absence in mission churches of practical evidence of healing through the power of these spirits and the divine Spirit; and

3. some forms of worship in mission churches which African Christian converts considered too sedate and uninspiring—unworthy, in their view—of the dynamic presence of the Holy Spirit and spirits in people's lives.

The Significance of Ancestral Spirituality

African religion and spirituality as well as the AICs firmly believe in ancestral spirits. "The dead are not dead," as the Senegalese poet, Birago Diop, so picturesquely put it. The dead are not "under the earth" as lifeless objects.[4] In both the African and AICs' beliefs, the ancestors live on as spirits, and exercise strong influence on the living. Actually, they are the foundation of religion in as much as they represent most immediately to the people the power of the Divine. There can be no complete and authentic human community without access to the ancestors, who bring together in their person divine power and human longing for life. They make present to humanity the fullness of life, which is the ultimate goal of human existence. The tradition the ancestors have established and keep on confirming in the different clans of the human community makes human life in the universe possible, as well as the existence of the entire universe itself. The ancestors' spirits permeate the universe: they live on in the rustling trees, in the growing plants, in the running waters, and in everything and everyone that exists.[5] Failure in any way to pay attention to the ancestors amounts to repudiation of community and, consequently, diminishment of life itself. This is how the spirituality of African religion and that of the AICs see the role of ancestral spirits.

For both African religion and the AICs, God often intervenes in human and universal life through the agency of the ancestors and other spirits. Ancestral (and other) spirits are God's spokespersons and agents for social order and harmony. While the Divinity is, as a rule, not easy to reach and interact with, the ancestors are, comparatively, readily accessible whenever necessary though the intervention of the elders or various experts in the community, namely, diviners and oracles. The ancestors are unambiguous in their instructions about where human responsibility lies concerning its own welfare. The ancestors are benevolent to humanity, because they have a vested interest in the flourishing of human life: their existence as ancestors is dependent exclusively on the continuation of human life in this world, particularly through childbearing and naming

---

4. For the full English text of Diop's poem, "The Dead Are Not Dead," see Wiredu, *Companion to African Philosophy*, 379.

5. Abaka, "Ancestor Veneration," 72.

(nominal reincarnation). In African belief systems, ancestors survive only when they are remembered through their descendants' being named after them. It is for this reason that, in African religion and spirituality, the cult of the ancestors is omnipresent and deep. It manifests itself in many forms. In various fundamental ways, most AICs incorporate this African religious conviction, as well as some of its expressions, in their religious approaches.[6] In worship and prayer, the names of the ancestors are never far away from the hearts and mouths of the people. They call upon them to bring blessings to or to ward off disaster from the community.

When mission Christianity objected to ancestor veneration and, worse, characterized it as evil or devil worship, it made a grave attack against the kingpin of African spirituality and religion. Few Africans could radically accept Christianity because of this. If denial of ancestral spirits and their influence in life defined a true Christian, then most African converts to Christianity became Christians in name only. Ancestral veneration runs very deep in African people's blood and bones. And when, down the line, many of the AICs' founders noticed how Israel's ancestors were revered, not only in the Hebrew Scriptures (the Old Testament) but throughout the history of Christianity, they were not slow to see the incongruence. If the names of Abraham, Moses, David, Solomon, and so on continue to be held in high religious esteem by Christians as, in their reading, they were by Jesus Christ himself, they wondered what could be evil or unchristian about remembering and venerating the ancestors of their own African clans and communities. Furthermore, if the church could choose and hold up dead (mostly European) Christian individuals as ancestors to be emulated in the church, they could not understand why good men and women who were models of righteous living for their clans and communities in Africa could not be held up as such in Christian religious worship. Many AICs, therefore, logically incorporated ancestor veneration rituals in their worship routines.

Healing and Exorcism (or, Ministry of Deliverance)

An indispensable dimension in ancestral veneration is the desire for comprehensive healing of mind, soul, and body. Experiencing daily illnesses and other indispositions that afflict the individual and society at large in their physical, mental, and spiritual lives, African religionists and AIC members continuously call upon the ancestors to help reestablish health in their individual persons and communities. Physical illness and any kind of social dissention is, to them, a sign of disharmony, manifesting divine and ancestral

---

6. Schmidt, "Role of Ancestors and Living-Dead."

displeasure. Healing, therefore, constitutes the responsibility of restoring good relationships with the invisible powers or, in other words, of consolidating harmony, wholeness, and wholesomeness to the body, mind, and the social fabric of the community. This happens through the power of the ancestors and other good spirits and, supremely for the AICs, through the intervention the Holy Spirit. The activities of good, benevolent spirits must be courted in prayers and worship, and that of malevolent spirits, (of which there are also many judging by the problems women and men experience in the world) must be expelled. This obligation cannot be ignored if life in its integrity is to be preserved and enhanced. The worst agent for evil or destruction of life that must be continually dealt with is subsumed by African religionists and AIC members under the general concept of "witchcraft." This feature of African and AICs' spirituality, fundamentally fought against by mission Christianity, is perhaps the most paramount and evident in the worship services of both African Religion and AICs, as Bernhard Udelhoven, for example, demonstrates in an extensive case study of Zambia.[7]

In African and AICs' spirituality, witchcraft is not an abstract "notion" of a theoretical evil existing in a vacuum. We may say that, in these perceptions, witchcraft implies the spirit or spirits of relentless evil inhabiting an individual or individuals with or without their cooperation. In every case, however, witchcraft is the greatest evil that can affect a person and profoundly contradicts the role of ancestral spirits and the Holy Spirit. Anyone afflicted with witchcraft power must be exorcized for their own good and that of society above all. Anyone suffering from the effects of witchcraft must be healed or delivered from its influence. This is necessary if community and universal life is to continue and flourish. And so, healers and exorcists are indispensable in this spiritual approach. How else can the therapeutic and blessed restorative power of God, the ancestors, and the benevolent spirits be identified and harnessed for the sake of human and universal well-being except through these experts' charisms?

Again, since witchcraft as evil is more or less always present in society, manifesting itself through various physical and psychological diseases and social conflicts of various kinds and at various dimensions, the need for these religious figures will always be urgent. Healers and deliverers are there not only to diagnose the spiritual causes of disharmony in society and the universe, but also to prescribe the means, either spiritual or physical or both, to deal with "witchcraft" problems in very practical ways. It follows that healing and cleansing rituals, which are generally referred to as "deliverance," are part and parcel of prayer and worship services in the AICs, as

---

7. Udelhoven, *Unseen Worlds*.

Opoky Onyinah illustrates in the case of Ghana.[8] Lack of this ministry is a serious lacuna in some forms of Christianity in Africa.[9]

Obviously, these healing and deliverance services take different forms in different Christian institutions and movements, from the extreme step of separating and banishing the possessed, or witches, from the rest of the community (excommunication), or giving witches anti-witchcraft concoctions to drink so as to confirm their witchcraft if there is any doubt about it (witch hunting), to praying intensely over the afflicted in order to drive out the evil spirit(s) possessing them. The latter is the more common practice in AICs. In most AICs, healing and deliverance are done only in the name of Jesus, but in others, deliverance is achieved through the power of God and the ancestors that is bestowed to an exorcist. Therefore, it is common for the pastor, or some of the church leaders endowed with such spiritual power, to stand at the entrance of the worship space in order to "sniff out" (as they often describe the practice) anyone needing deliverance from witchcraft, for, as already mentioned, the afflicted individuals themselves may not be aware of their condition. The people identified as stricken by spiritual evil are usually grateful for this awareness. Whatever the case, there is invariably a cleansing and exorcism session during every AIC worship service, either through mechanical methods like drinking or sprinkling of holy water, or automatically and remotely through the spiritual-sensory agency of the leader-healers in the congregation. By the mere extension of hands over the worshipers and praying for them, the afflicted individuals may be healed by the power of the Holy Spirit or spirits.

It is important to emphasize the fact that all AICs engage in this ministry in various ways, but some prominent examples may be mentioned. In Kenya, these include the Jerusalem Church of Christ of Prophetess Mary Sinaida Akatsa in the Kawangware settlement on the outskirts of Nairobi, as well as the Legio Maria Church (also known as Maria Legio or Legio Maria of African Church Mission) spread throughout the country and beyond.[10]

Worship in the AICs is principally a struggle against practical evil, anything that threatens life. This perception is again drawn from the spirituality of African religion. There are no prayers for very remote contingencies or possibilities that can only be imagined, like "going to heaven" (becoming an ancestor). In this case, one prays for children, health, wealth, and good company, because these are what assure eventual ancestorship. The actual road that must be traveled is what should occupy reflection, because when

---

8. Onyinah, "Deliverance as a Way of Confronting Witchcraft."
9. Manala, "Witchcraft and Its Impact."
10. Kustenbauder, "Believing in the Black Messiah"; Neupert, "Journey to Nairobi."

this is done correctly, the goal is an assured consequence not to be fretted about. The prayers of African religion and the AICs, therefore, differ markedly from those of the mainline Christian churches which are often acontextual, cerebral, and abstract.

Manner of Worship

The practical nature of worship in the AICs again derives from African religiosity as is apparent in their worship services or liturgies. AIC liturgies demand the involvement of the whole of the worshiper's body and soul as well as that of the entire congregation. Characteristic features of AICs' liturgies are singing, clapping, and dancing individually and together. And if a person is being exorcised, there is crying and wailing. There is nothing to be ashamed of or embarrassed about in this. There is always an emotive and passionate, not merely an intellectual or rational, dimension to these liturgies. On Sundays in many an African city like Nairobi, for example, there will be many groups of variously sized AICs marching on the streets and chanting and dancing in unison to the rhythm of drums, trumpets, and cymbals. Some students of AICs' worship culture have argued that AICs tend to worship in the open air, because they cannot afford to construct buildings. A more accurate observation, however, has been suggested that open-air worship may be a deliberate preference of AICs, because it is not constrictive; it offers worshipers more freedom of movement and bodily expression and provides closer involvement with raw, physical nature where many of the spirit-forces reside. Even where there are buildings for worshiping purposes, therefore, there will usually be a minimum of furniture (chairs or benches), usually for a few presiders.

Another element cherished in AICs' worship services is speaking in tongues ("glossolalia"). Rather than indicating the direct influence of African religion (although it is not entirely foreign to it), this aspect of AICs is more immediately drawn from the Hebrew and Christian Scriptures, where it is invariably interpreted as an act of the Spirit (or spirits). The Old Testament prophets were often characterized by this spirit and, on account of its irresistible influence on the individual concerned, sometimes displayed what were, even in their day, certainly odd or eccentric (not to mention "bizarre") forms of behavior (e.g., Isa 20, Jer 13, Hos 1, Ezek 1, 3, 27). Not infrequently, under the power and stimulus of the Spirit of God, prophets lived and worked in groups or in bands (1 Sam 10:5). Under instruction from the same Spirit, they were often impelled in spite of themselves to deliver to the contemporary powers-that-be news that was hard for the latter to swallow. Two interesting examples are Jonah's mission to Nineveh, as well as the encounter between the prophet, Nathan, and King David over Uriah's wife, Bathsheba (Jonah, 2 Sam 12:1-25). But this was characteristic of all prophets whose messages are described at length in the Old Testament. The typical phrase with which they introduced their message was, "Thus says the Lord," indicating that it was the Spirit of God that was driving them to say what they said and to act in the way they did. In the New Testament, the spiritual gifts of prophecy and speaking in tongues are taken for granted by Paul (1 Cor 12), even if he is careful to establish some guidelines to keep the latter in proper use (1 Cor 14).

However, the exuberant mood always demonstrated in AICs' conduct of worship draws directly from the African spiritual belief in the unity of all creation: God is in everything and everything is in God. This unity of all creation, of the invisible and visible reality, comes together in the human person intensely at worship. In worship, song and dance—including all the material, linguistic, and bodily signs and symbols used there—are intended to bring this unity into consciousness, to pragmatically demonstrate it, and to promote and strengthen it. Only when these are present can liturgy truly fulfill its purpose as the most concentrated moment that combines and brings together all the vital powers of the universe for the goal of achieving fullness of life. Liturgy should be and should be seen to be physically, mentally, and spiritually therapeutic, according to the AICs.

The Story of the Spirit in African Christianity: Lost in Translation?

Belief in the Holy Spirit (and also spirits, good and evil) is part of the Christian church's tradition, as we have noted. And again, as we have shown above, in the Hebrew Scriptures, the Spirit of God is a constant agent in the process of salvation history, from creation to Israel's deliverance from slavery in Egypt and beyond; the Spirit of God is present when and even if God himself is not visible. The Spirit, whom the Wisdom literature of the Old Testament understands in the feminine gender as indeed "Wisdom," was the authority upon which not only the patriarchs, but more evidently and concretely the prophets, understood their divine vocation and mission and acted among the people. Once again, the Spirit personified the call of God from the time of Abraham and Moses onwards. The divine Spirit is the overpowering Force that impels them to speak in favor of justice for the people of Israel.

But the same vision has also been one of the central and indispensable aspects of the Christian faith, forming her self-understanding and her living tradition from earliest times. Since the fourth century CE—specifically according to the doctrine defined and promulgated by the Council of Nicaea in 325 and subsequently substantially reaffirmed by the Council of Constantinople in 381—the Holy Spirit was defined officially as the Third Person of the Divine Trinity. The Council of Constantinople asserted this as part of the definitive Christian creed on the Trinitarian question: that the Holy Spirit is "the Lord, the Giver of Life, who proceeds from the Father, who with the Father and the Son is worshiped and glorified together, who spoke by the prophets." These are the words of the profession of faith in the Nicene-Constantinopolitan Creed recited every Sunday in the Catholic liturgy of the Eucharist, a succinct formula of the Christian perception of the Holy Spirit's nature and activity in the world. Together with the Father and the Son, the Holy Spirit is God, but the Father and the Son act through the Spirit. The activity of the Holy Spirit is the manifestation of the wholeness of the Divinity through which divine favor is experienced and known in the world.

In the Christian Scriptures, Jesus is appropriately described as "Word" or *Logos*, preexistent with God before the foundations of the universe, and who, with God, created the universe, and in and through whom the universe achieves its redemption (John 1:1–4). As David L. Edwards notes,

> Jews would connect the word *Logos* with the mighty Word of the Lord which came to the prophets; with the Spirit and Glory which had descended from time to time; with the personified (and female) Wisdom pictured as God's agent in the creation of a wonderful world and in the inspiration of humanity; and with the religious law believed to express God's wisdom.[11]

In African spirituality, the power of the word of the elder, as that of the community in the AICs, is comparable to this Christian perception. For African spirituality, in the word of the elder consists wisdom, which is the life of the community. Similarly, in the spirituality of the AICs, someone who rebels against the consensus of the community (usually arrived at in the process of palaver or common deliberation) is someone who has, or actually *is*, an evil spirit.

But if the theoretical notion of the Holy Spirit has been more or less constant in Christianity, the practice inspired by this understanding was stifled as Christianity was translated to Africa. This seems to have been deliberate. Several reasons for the discrepancy can be adduced. A major one

11. Edwards, *Christianity*, 19.

was cultural: on account of its long gestation in Europe, Christianity gradually lost its dynamic flexibility and adaptability. It became culturally rigid, with people increasingly considering its European expression as definitive and unchangeable. In addition to this was the cultural bigotry of Europeans in general and European anthropologists in Africa, as we have noted, serving as the intellectual references of missionaries to the African continent. Despite the fact that Christian belief was permeated with acceptance of spiritual existences from the very beginning (and, in fact, stood or fell on this belief), European missionaries to Africa, influenced by the nineteenth-century Enlightenment movement, could not bring themselves to accept the African appropriation and expression of it in their own cultural contexts. Given the doctrines on the Holy Spirit, it is baffling that missionaries balked even at the African characterization of God as "the Great Spirit!" Again, given their own cult of the saints (especially in Catholic Christianity), it is difficult to understand, except in terms of cultural prejudice, that European Christian missionaries to Africa would categorically forbid every form of ancestral veneration by African Christian converts, considering all African ancestral spirits as evil spirits and their veneration as either superstition or idolatrous heathenism or both.

Listening to the narrative of the Scriptures and the history of western Christianity (or, reading it, for those who eventually could do so themselves), most Africans saw that what was condemned as unchristian in their belief and practices about the spiritual reality was believed and practiced in the West itself, even if in different forms. At any rate, numerous African Christian converts instinctively knew that they could not abandon their spirituality and religiosity as western Christianity demanded of them, without alienating themselves from their own identity as Africans. So, what has been the result? The Christianity of the mission churches has not been able to penetrate deeply into the African mind, heart, and soul. This is now universally acknowledged. However, since Christianity bore a very attractive spiritual message for Africans, and because African converts needed to find "a place to feel at home"[12] there, African initiatives to create that space arose, developed, and continue to proliferate in the form of AICs. The contention here is that there is something the mainline Christian churches in Africa today can learn from the AICs in the areas of theology, pastoral ministry, and worship.

---

12. Welbourn and Ogot, *Place to Feel at Home*.

Inspiration for the Mainline Christian Churches: Worship and Pastoral Practice

Theologically, what John S. Pobee and Gabriel Ositelu II have observed should be kept in mind by the mainline mission churches in Africa. In contrast to the latter where the theological emphasis is Christology, "[t]he former have a central focus on the work and experience of the Holy Spirit, manifested in prophecies, baptism, and faith-healing."[13] Of course, it does not mean that AICs ignore the place and role of Jesus Christ, but they feel his presence much more in the activity of the Holy Spirit among the people (John 16:5–7) through the above-mentioned manifestations, including the propensity to speak in tongues on certain occasions (Acts 2:14). In this, they are much more in line with the spirituality of African religion than the mission churches. According to Pobee and Ositelu, the AICs' "nativistic" nature "signals the heightened sense of pride in race, nation, or tribe on the basis of which these churches sought to purge themselves of foreign influences."[14] But in terms of Christian theology, an important motivation for the founding of AICs was to give Christianity an African "heart," as Robert Schreiter puts it, so that the Christian faith would be understood and lived in terms of African culture.[15]

The importance of taking context seriously is now an acknowledged principle in doing theology. That all theology is contextual is an indisputable fact. For the past several decades, this has been reiterated many times by all mission churches. For example, Pope Francis underlines it in *Evangelii Gaudium*. There, he insists that Christian theology must take the existence of different cultures as a blessing and a source of spiritual wealth and not a threat to Christian revelation or unity. Warning against the tendency in the mission churches to homogenize theological expression, he says:

> We cannot demand that peoples of every continent, in expressing their Christian faith, imitate modes of expression which European nations developed at a particular moment of their history, because the faith cannot be constricted to the limits of understanding and expression of any one culture. It is an indisputable fact that no single culture can exhaust the mystery of our redemption in Christ.[16]

---

13. Pobee and Ositelu, *African Initiatives*, 34.
14. Pobee and Ositelu, *African Initiatives*, 32.
15. Schreiter, *Constructing Local Theologies*, 150.
16. Francis, *Evangelii Gaudium*, 118.

The same applies to other dimensions of the church's life—to liturgical worship, for instance. Mission churches, the Catholic Church in particular, present to the African Christian forms of worship that are overly regimented, individualistic, rationalistic, and almost empty of emotional content. The prayers are cerebral and, in the African context, hardly applicable to the needs of the moment. To many Africans, this is not holistically human and is certainly uninspiring. It is devoid of the participation and sharing that they expect should lead to authentic community. As Pobee and Ositelu again observe, the flexibility that we find in the worship arrangements of the AICs may be interpreted as a protest or "an African dissatisfaction with a Christianity that is too cerebral [and too institutionalized] and does not manifest itself in acts of power in the Spirit and Spirit possession."[17]

Pastorally, the apparent contradiction in the historic mission churches between belief in the Holy Spirit and spirits (doctrinally) and hesitancy about spirit-driven human expression and activity, especially in situations of worship, baffles many an African Christian. One such perplexed individual was a participant in a discussion in 2009, in Kabwe, Zambia, about the Catholic Church's approach to witchcraft. Frustrated to the point of exasperation by the contradictions he perceived in Catholic approaches to this phenomenon, he exclaimed to Fr. Bernhard Udelhoven:

> You priests are divided. Some priests cast out demons with holy water. Others say there are no demons. Others refer the possessed to the charismatics. Some pray for those attacked by witchcraft in novenas and healing Masses. Others come to bless their houses. Others say that witchcraft does not exist. If there is no common line among you priests, no wonder we are all confused![18]

This individual captures the actual situation that besets the pastoral approaches of mainline Christian churches toward witchcraft, the spirits, spirit possession, and the Holy Spirit in African Christianity. In short, if there is a common belief in the Holy Spirit among the churches, there are very few shared interpretations of how this doctrine should be applied in concrete situations in Africa. Pastorally, this is far from helpful. Despite possible problems of fickleness that may affect the AICs (some believers claiming to act at the prompting of the Spirit), there is need for a cohesive approach to the reality. Faced with situations of doctrinal and pastoral confusion, some guidelines for proper behavior must be put in place. St. Paul sets a good example of how to confront these problems (1 Cor 14). But even such Pauline

17. Pobee and Ositelu, *African Initiatives*, 34.
18. Udelhoven, *Unseen Worlds*, 1.

correctives must be situated in each concrete situation; in other words, they must be contextualized to bear Christian fruit.

Conclusion

That "[a]ll Christians are committed to be filled with the Spirit" is a central position of Christian belief," as Billy Graham asserts. "Anything short of a Spirit-filled life is less than God's plan for each believer."[19] The Holy Spirit is the active agent of God in the church and in the world. This is what AICs believe: that the Holy Spirit "speaks," "intercedes," and "testifies." The Holy Spirit "leads," "commands," "guides," and "appoints."[20] Throughout time, the Holy Spirit heals, performs miracles, and causes people to speak in tongues. All of this should not be strange or surprising to a Christian. Mission churches in Africa can learn and gain much from this stance of the AICs. What the mission churches must hold AICs accountable for is perhaps the Pauline dimension of "distinguishing the spirits" (1 Cor 12:30), to always try to see to it that the authentic fruits of the Holy Spirit and the good spirits, namely, the fruits of "love, joy, peace, patience, kindness, goodness, faith, gentleness, and self-control" (Gal 5:22–23)—prevail in all things. Following the advice of the apostles in the early church concerning diversity, we might similarly assert that, if the AICs sincerely keep these instructions, they will do well (Acts 15:29).

Bibliography

Abaka, Edmund. "Ancestor Veneration." In *The Oxford Encyclopedia of African Thought*, edited by Francis Abiola Irele and Biodun Jeyifo. Oxford: Oxford University Press, 2010.

Bongmba, Elias Kifon, ed. *The Routledge Companion to Christianity in Africa*. New York: Routledge, 2016.

Edwards, David L. *Christianity: The First Two Thousand Years*. New York: Orbis, 1997.

Francis. *Evangelii Gaudium: The Joy of the Gospel*. Rome: Libreria Editrice Vaticana, 2013.

Graham, Billy. *The Holy Spirit*. Nashville: Word, 1988.

Haar, Gerrie Ter, and Stephen Ellis. "Spirit Possession and Healing in Modern Zambia: An Analysis of Letters to Archbishop Milingo." In *African Affairs: The Journal of the Royal African Society* 87:347 (1988), 185–206.

Kustenbauder, Matthew. "Believing in the Black Messiah: The Legio Maria Church in an African Christian Landscape." *Nova Religio* 13 (2009) 11–40.

---

19. Graham, *Holy Spirit*, 114.
20. Graham, *Holy Spirit*, 2–4.

Manala, Matsobane J. "Witchcraft and Its Impact on Black African Christians: A Lacuna in the Ministry of the Hervormde Kerk in Suidelike Afrika." HTS Teologiese Studies / Theological Studies 60 (2004) 1491–511. https://hts.org.za/index.php/hts/article/view/635/536.

Milingo, Emmanuel. *The Demarcations*. Lusaka: Teresanium, 1982.

———. *The World in Between: Christian Healing and the Struggle for Spiritual Survival*. New York: Orbis, 1985.

Neupert, Memo. "Journey to Nairobi: Five Days with Mary Akatsa." Share International Archives. October 15, 2005. http://share-international.org/archives/M_appearances/Map_mnjourney.htm.

Onyinah, Opoky. "Deliverance as a Way of Confronting Witchcraft in Modern Africa: Ghana as a Case History." *Cyberjournal for Pentecostal-Charismatic Research* 10 (July 2001). www.pctii.org/cyberj/cyberj10/onyinah.html.

Ositelu, Rufus Okikiolaolu Olubiyi. *African Instituted Churches: Diversities, Growth, Gifts, Spirituality, and Ecumenical Understanding of African Initiated Churches*. Hamburg: LIT, 2002.

Pobee, John S., and Gabriel Ositelu. *African Initiatives in Christianity: The Growth, Gifts, and Diversities of Indigenous African Churches: A Challenge to the Ecumenical Movement*. Geneva: WCC, 1998.

Schmidt, Gregor. "The Role of Ancestors and Living-Dead in the Life of Kenyan Christians." Master's thesis, Maryknoll Institute of African Studies, 2005.

Schreiter, Robert J. *Constructing Local Theologies*. New York: Orbis, 1985.

Udelhoven, Bernhard. *Unseen Worlds: Dealing with Spirits, Witchcraft, and Satanism*. Lusaka: FENZA, 2015.

Welbourn, Frederick B., and Bethwell A. Ogot. *A Place to Feel at Home: A Study of Two Independent Churches in Western Kenya*. London: Oxford University Press, 1966.

Wiredu, Kwasi, ed. *A Companion to African Philosophy*. Malden, MA: Blackwell, 2004.

10

The Catholic Charismatic Renewal as Ecumenical and Intercultural Experiment in Africa

LUDOVIC LADO, SJ

In the second edition of his well-known book, *The Holiness-Pentecostal Tradition*, Vison Synan has a good chapter on the "Catholic Charismatic Renewal," which opens with the statement: "Perhaps the greatest surprise in the whole Pentecostal tradition was the sudden appearance of Catholic Pentecostalism in 1967."[1] "Sudden," because it took most Catholics by surprise. But the "greatest surprise," indeed, is the rapidity with which the Catholic Church accepted this Protestant import which came to be known first as "Catholic Pentecostalism" and then later, as "Catholic Charismatic Renewal." From a mere semantic perspective, juxtaposing "Catholicism" and "Pentecostalism" in those days was ecumenical progress, or even revolutionary. How could one be "Catholic" and "Pentecostal" at the same time? The combination was potentially confusing, and it came as no surprise that the Catholic Church finally settled for "Catholic Charismatic Renewal" as the name for its own brand of Pentecostalism. This terminological cosmetic is the first illustration of the two major points that I want to make in this paper, but I will do so from an African perspective. The first argument is that the acceptance of features of Pentecostalism in the Catholic Church was indeed a major ecumenical breakthrough at the end of the 1960s. The second is that, nevertheless, time has shown that this concept has been accepted in a distinctively Catholic way, and this is manifest in the ways that the Catholic Charismatic Renewal (CCR) embodies Catholic forms of Pentecostalism. I am writing from an African context, within which I have done

---

1. Synan, *Holiness-Pentecostal Tradition*, 234.

ethnographic work on Catholic Charismatic groups in the past fifteen years, in an attempt to highlight the domestication and localization processes at work, both within the Catholic Church and at the grassroots levels.[2] As a number of authors have indicated, Pentecostalism, including its Catholic forms, has been relatively successful in sub-Saharan Africa, and I will also be discussing some of the religious, cultural, and social factors which might explain this success. But first, one must consider what scholars are saying about the relative success of the Pentecostal and Charismatic movements in African Christianity in general and in the Catholic Church in particular. They suggest, on the whole, that this success appears to be a response to needs improperly addressed in mission churches—primarily, the need for a holistic approach to salvation.

Appraising the Pentecostal Needs of Catholics in Africa

Why are people attracted to what the Pentecostal and Charismatic offers in the context of Africa, both outside and within the Catholic Church? And what are scholars saying about it? The existing literature on Pentecostalism has extensively documented the flow of Christians from missionary churches to Pentecostal and Charismatic groups. Scholars have formulated various reasons to account for this religious mobility.

The first set of reasons emphasizes the holistic approach to salvation, consistent with the African worldview which, according to its adherents, is more appealing than otherworldly approaches attributed to missionary churches. According to Allan Anderson, "They responded to the existential needs of the African Worldview. They have all offered a personal encounter with God through the power of the Spirit, healing from sickness, and deliverance from sickness and deliverance from evil in all its manifestations: spiritual, social, and structural."[3] Matthews Ojo further suggests that "[i]ndependent Pentecostal and Charismatic movements continue to spread, because they are pragmatic in their approach to social and religious issues and are also responding to the existential needs of Africans within the contemporary situations of sociopolitical disequilibrium."[4]

The second set of reasons given for the success of these new movements relates to the management of power in hierarchical mission churches. For Mwaura, the Pentecostal and Charismatic movement "empowers the young to challenge the authority of the elders who have dominated

2. Lado, *Catholic Pentecostalism*, 170–90.
3. Anderson, *African Reformation*, 168.
4. Ojo, "Transnational," 169.

religious leadership in the mainline churches . . . ."[5] As Allan Anderson puts it, "The new churches give opportunity not afforded by patriarchal and gerontocratic religious that have lost their Charismatic power," or they emerge "in reaction to the bureaucratization process in established churches."[6] In the same line of arguments, Omenyo suggests that "[g]enerally, the activities can be seen as a reaction to a conservative 'alien' Western Christianity with concomitant imported patterns of ministry, liturgical forms, hymnody, and theological emphasis."[7]

The third set of reasons revolves around the multidimensional crisis tearing apart our societies and the search to find new bearings after the colonial modernity's destabilization of traditional religious and social structures. For example, Laurenti Magesa describes Pentecostal and Charismatic groups as "communities of affliction" in the sense that "[t]hey arise and flourish as responses to real or perceived crisis in the social, political, economic, and religious environments of contemporary society . . . an order that has happened to make very many people uncertain, unsettled, and threatened in their lives."[8] According to Ojo, "Pentecostal religion as a purveyor of Modernity and its emphasis on personal empowerment seem to offer greater openings to the global world; hence, its attraction to the young, mobile, educated people seeking self-realization amidst the deteriorating socioeconomic and political situations in the continent."[9] Gifford sums up this argument about economic and political deprivation in the Ghanaian context in the following words:

> We have touched on other important reasons for Charismatic growth and recapitulate some here. The worship is participative and exhilarating. Testimonies enable nonprofessionals and the voiceless generally to express themselves and be heard. Where cell groups exist, they can provide a sense of solidarity. Charismatic churches provide employment in a country where employment is scarce . . . . Yet, these churches have proliferated primarily because they profess to have answers to Ghana's real problems, expressed in an idiom to which many Ghanaians naturally respond. The ills that beset Ghanaians are often explained

---

5. Mwaura, "Role," 183.
6. Anderson, *African Reformation*, 168–70.
7. Omenyo, "Charismatization," 12.
8. Magesa, "Charismatic," 30.
9. Ojo, "Transnational," 169.

in terms of spiritual forces, and many of these religious leaders claim the powers to control these forces.[10]

Questions arising from this debate include the following: Is the Catholic approach to salvation not holistic enough? Is faith in the Catholic Church more intellectual than experiential and pragmatic? It should be humbly acknowledged that, if people are leaving the Catholic Church to join other religious groups, it means they are missing something that they seem to find elsewhere. This is true of any religious mobility. Cardinal Walter Kasper, the former president of the Pontifical Council for the Promotion of Christian Unity, suggests that before dwelling on the shortcomings of these new movements, "[i]t is above all necessary to do a pastoral examination of conscience and to critically ask ourselves: why are so many Christians leaving our Church? We should not begin with the question of what is wrong with the Pentecostals but with the issue of our pastoral shortcomings. How can we respond to this new challenge with a liturgical, catechetical, pastoral, and spiritual renewal?"[11]

If we do consider that the CCR emerged as a result of Protestant Pentecostalism's influence on the Catholic Church, then the acceptance of the Charismatic predicament within the Catholic Church can also be interpreted as a strategic move in a context of religious competition, an attempt to manage the risk of the outflow of Catholics to Pentecostal churches. But has the CCR responded to the Pentecostal needs of Catholics? What are scholars saying about what attracts people to the CCR specifically?

Indeed, some scholars have interpreted the openness of mainline churches to the influence of Pentecostalism in strategic terms: "By strategically opening themselves to Charismatic influence, the mainline churches have not only stemmed numerical loss but have experienced real growth."[12] In the same line of thought, another scholar writes: "Historic missions accommodate Charismatic renewal groups and phenomena within their ranks, because their survival has come to depend on how open they are to a Pentecostalist culture."[13] I will argue that this view is overstated, for it seems to overestimate the proportion of Catholics actually influenced by the Charismatic renewal groups. It fails to take into account the fact that the majority of Catholics are not members of Charismatic renewal groups and have a very limited knowledge of its nature. Meinrad Hebga, one of the pioneers of the CCR on the continent, speaks of "a tacit connivance between

10. Gifford, *Ghana's New Christianity*, 196.
11. Kasper, "Le Dialogue," 22.
12. Mwaura, "Role," 190.
13. Asamoah-Gyadu, "I Will Put My Breath," 196.

the civilization of the rhythm, of the collective therapy, and of divination with some aspects of Charismatic renewal: songs and dances, ministering to the sick, proclamation of inspired messages."[14] Furthermore, he invokes three main reasons for the Charismatic Renewal's attractiveness: the laity's quest for autonomy from the clergy; the diaconia of the sick (quest for divine favors: healing, fertility, work, success, etc.); and the rhythm and dance that is consonant with the inner being of Africans. He challenges Jean Marc Ela, who had argued that the social and economic crisis of African countries was the main reason for the rapid growth of the CCR in Africa.[15] Magesa, for his part, describes Charismatic groups as "communities of affliction,"[16] where spiritual solutions are offered for social problems. Although Hebga acknowledges the relevance of the social crisis factor, he thinks it is simplistic to reduce the Charismatic Renewal to a mere opium or space of "evasion" from hardships of daily life.[17] Eric de Rosny mentions the dynamics of affectivity which put feelings and emotions at the heart of religious experience, lived as a process of the inner transformation of the self.[18] Writing on the "charismatization" of mainline churches in general, Cephas Omenyo mentions the opportunity it gives to lay Christians to exercise leadership in a church that is traditionally dominated by the clergy: "A major characteristic of Charismatic Renewal is the recognition it gives to lay ministries. They encourage the general participation of all members to play a vital role in their churches' diaconia and mission in general."[19]

What are Catholic Charismatics Saying?

Why do Catholics join CCR groups? From my exploratory research on about fifteen Charismatic groups operating in different parishes in the city of Yaoundé (Cameroon), it appears that the reasons fall into two main categories: spiritual and social, or material. I understand that the spiritual reasons explicitly refer to the search for spiritual growth, while social reasons pertain to the quest for spiritual solutions to problems of a social nature such as marriage, infertility, and sickness. The results indicated that spiritual reasons are, by far, predominant. These reasons can further be classified according to the nature of people's expectations or needs. Some are related to a

---

14. Hebga, "Le Mouvement," 67–75.
15. Ela and Luneau, *Voici le Temps des Héritiers*, 150.
16. Magesa, "Charismatic," 27–44.
17. Hebga, "Le Mouvement," 67–75.
18. de Rosny, "Renouveau," 667–78.
19. Omenyo, "Charismatization," 18.

quest for spiritual growth, expressed as the need for "conversion and change in my life," or "I felt I needed to grow in my faith." This first sub-category of reasons emphasizes the person's desire to progress in his or her spiritual life, and the CCR is perceived as offering that possibility. The second sub-category of spiritual reasons voiced by CCR members pertains to prayer. Sample responses include the following: "need to pray differently"; "for love of prayer of praise and adoration"; "to learn to pray"; "to pray with others"; and "to learn to pray in tongues." These responses dwell on the desire not only to learn how to pray better but also to pray with others, especially prayers of praise, adoration, and intercession. The need for spiritual fellowship is also emphasized: it is not just a matter of learning to pray but also of learning to pray with others and for others. Some respondents insisted they were attracted to CCR because of the "singing," which is an aspect of praise and adoration. Singing here implies, of course, dancing and other bodily and emotional expressions. One respondent mentions his desire to learn to pray in tongues, which is a major issue in some Charismatic groups. This leads us to the third sub-category of spiritual reasons, the search for the gifts of the Holy Spirit. A few say they joined the movement to seek the power to fight evil spirits in their lives. One person writes: "I had a revelation." This probably indicates his or her conviction to have access to special spiritual experiences, and the CCR is perceived here as a space for these extraordinary experiences. The last sub-category of responses mentions the need to deepen one's knowledge of the Bible: "I joined the group so that I could know more about the Bible."

The social reasons for joining the CCR include various problems such as childlessness, school failure, sickness, lack of success in life, etc. First among the reasons in this category is the quest for healing, especially physical healing. Here, spiritual solutions are sought for social or physical problems; in short, people often expect miracles in situations of despair after the failure of ordinary solutions. In these cases, suspicions of evil interference (witchcraft or the devil) are never far from people's minds. And explaining their motivations, some people simply wrote: "I had many problems." Among the other reasons for joining a CCR, and which hardly qualify as spiritual or social, are the following: "out of curiosity"; "my parish priest didn't want the sacred heart group I wanted to start"; "a friend told me about it"; and "following my parents, it is a family tradition." These responses indicate that the motivation to join is not always born out of personal conviction but could be the result of the influence of a priest, a friend, or a parent.

One major conclusion I draw from this exploratory research is that most people tend to join a CCR in search of either spiritual growth or a solution to a specific social problem. As mentioned earlier, some scholars have argued, that the renewal sought by the CCR is not only personal but also structural. One respondent writes that, "[f]or participants in the Charismatic renewal movements, the entire historic mission church needs the spirit of renewal. They are 'dry bones' that need the invasion of the Spirit of the Lord to experience new life."[20] Although there have been problems of collaboration here and there between some sections of the clergy and Charismatic leaders in the Catholic Church,[21] one striking discovery in my research is that the concern for structural renewal is a rather marginal one among CCR members in Africa. They are out not to change the Church from within but to seek solutions to their personal problems. This shift may, of course, be a result of the process of domestication which the CCR has undergone in the Catholic Church. Charismatic leadership has remained under the control of clerical and institutionalized power.

What Do People Get from CCR?

Based on my field research, I retain here the two main categories of social and spiritual to classify what people say they have gained from their membership in the CCR. Some are spiritual in nature, and others are social. Regarding spiritual benefits, the majority of respondents refer to joy, peace of heart, and a stronger personal commitment to Jesus. Other benefits include psychological and moral equilibrium; spiritual growth; comfort; liberation or spiritual healing; the ability to control anger; the power to forgive; detachment from material goods; and better knowledge of Scripture, etc. Some also refer to the reception of the gifts of the Holy Spirit, which include healing of the sick, illumination, and the power to face sorcerers and witches, etc. One respondent simply replied, "I talk to God," implying a deepened spiritual experience.

On the other hand, the social benefits mentioned include healing, marriage, success in school or in life, brotherly support, and social integration. A number of respondents feel that the CCR offers a more supportive environment in which people care about one another and are charitable. They refer to difficult situations in which they actually benefited from the spiritual and material support of group members.

Here again, the focus is on personal spiritual growth or transformation rather than on any structural change in the Church as an institution. This does not imply that there are no critics of the institutional Church in CCR circles, but it does not seem to me that they are any more critical of the Church than

20. Asamoah-Gyadu, "I Will Put My Breath," 201.
21. Lado, "Catholic," 35–7; Thomas, "Réveils," 403.

non-members of CCR. In many cases, the CCR provides some space in the Church where Christians who are spiritually unfulfilled or socially unsettled can experience spiritual growth and empowerment. The challenge here is to access spiritual power, to experience it, and to exercise it. But since this Charismatic empowerment can only be expressed in its tamed form in a hierarchical institution such as the Catholic Church, the portion of Charismatic group members who are seeking new spiritual experiences are likely to endure some form of frustration; they can hardly resist the seduction of new religious groups promising other kinds of revival or spiritual illumination.

The conclusion is that people do not join the CCR, or remain in it, for the same reasons. More importantly, the reasons for joining the CCR and the benefits drawn from membership are predominantly a spiritual call to change the widespread assumptions that CCR members are mainly interested in solving their worldly problems. There is at least one Charismatic prayer group in every major parish of Yaoundé, the city where I conducted this research, and in my view, one should not exaggerate the Charismatic movement's influence on African Catholicism today. After reaching its peak in the 1980s, the movement has now settled and is one movement among many others in the pastoral setting. In Cameroon, the CCR has been around for at least thirty-five years now.

Out of the 224 people targeted by my fieldwork, one hundred and twenty-nine had belonged to the CCR for up to five years; forty-one, up to ten years; thirty-eight, up to twenty years; and eight, up to thirty years. There were eight who did not specify. It appears that more than half of the sample had spent fewer than five years in the movement. The turnover is quite high, indicating that members of CCR are a very mobile population and that the movement could be described as a space of spiritual transit. It could be that, after ten years in the movement, most members feel some kind of saturation and go in search of new spiritual pastures. Another suggestive set of figures refers to the number of people active in CCR groups in parishes, ranging from fifteen to one hundred and fifty members in each local cell. Considering the number of Christians in each parish, this is another indication that one should not overrate the CCR's influence on African Catholicism today.

Many things can be said about membership in Charismatic circles. According to Allan Anderson, "The membership tends to consist of younger people who are less economically deprived and more formally educated."[22] From a historical point of view, the CCR's birth is closely linked to university campuses with young faculty and students. It appeared on the African scene in the early 1970s but only truly exploded in the 1980s. All social classes are

---

22. Anderson, *African Reformation*, 19.

represented: the rich as well as the poor, the learned as well as the illiterate. "As concerning the sex and age of participants, women are predominant. Then follow old people, adults, and then young people."[23] The social diversity of membership is consistent with the diversity of possibilities the movement offers for the fulfillment of personal goals and aspirations. Also, given the emphasis these movements put on healing and deliverance from the forces of evil—including witchcraft—it is not surprising that its clientele comes from various strata of the social spectrum. Some anthropologists have argued that the membership of ecstatic religion, including Christian mysticism, tends to be predominantly female, because it represents an outlet for the politically downtrodden, a disguised means of protest against the dominant order.[24] In the context of hierarchical structures such as the Catholic Church, where power is often monopolized by the male clergy, the theory of peripheral religion may indeed account for the predominance of women and youth in Charismatic groups where there is more space for the empowerment of the laity, male as well as female. But it is also the case that, in the context of Africa, women carry most of the burden of social crisis, which makes them more vulnerable.

Revisiting the Ecumenical Roots of Catholic Pentecostalism

A number of respected theologians and historians have argued authoritatively that, although the appearance of Pentecostal phenomena in the Catholic Church was sudden, a number of previous developments had somehow prepared the Church for this surprise. Drawing on earlier authors such as Edwards O'Connor, Francis Sullivan, Kilian McDonnell, Kevin and Dorothy Ranaghan, and others, Vinson Synan lists eight of these previous developments in his book mentioned earlier. I revisit them briefly here before looking at some factors specific to the African context:[25]

1. The rise of devotion to the Holy Spirit towards the end of the nineteenth century, which inspired the Pope Leo XIII to write an encyclical on the Holy Spirit and to proclaim an annual novena to the Holy Spirit in 1897;

---

23. Hebga, "Le Mouvement," 67–75.
24. Lewis, "Spirit Possession," 188–219.
25. Synan, *Holiness-Pentecostal Tradition*, 234–44.

2. The theology of charisma developed by some German theologians beginning in the 1820s, "which depicted the church as a Charismatic body constituted and enlivened by the Holy Spirit"[26];

3. The liturgical movement which started in the early nineteenth century to promote greater participation of the congregation in public worship;

4. The lay movement which, beginning in the early twentieth century, paved the way to a greater acknowledgment of the role and place of the laity in the Catholic Church;

5. The biblical movement, beginning in the mid-1940s, which epitomized the growth of biblical scholarship in the Catholic Church;

6. The Catholic openness to the ecumenical movement which was manifest in the establishment of the secretariat for Christian unity in the 1960s;

7. The Cursillo movement which originated in Spain in 1949, offering short courses to lay people for the deepening of their faith;

8. The vital role played by Vatican II, Pope John XXIII, and Cardinal Suenens in bringing to fruition the seeds of the previous movements for the renewal of the Catholic Church. It is worth recalling that Vatican II issued a revolutionary decree on ecumenism, "Unitatis Redintegratio," which spelled out Catholic principles of ecumenism and acknowledged the "separated brethren" as brethren.

Moreover, some (and even very many) of the significant elements and endowments which together build up and give life to the Church itself can exist outside the visible boundaries of the Catholic Church: the written word of God; the life of grace; faith, hope, and charity, with the other interior gifts of the Holy Spirit; and visible elements, too. All of these, which come from Christ and lead back to Christ, belong by right to the one church of Christ.[27]

It is also worth recalling that the Catholic Church had established contacts with classical Pentecostals before Vatican II, and following this, "the only classical Pentecostal leader present [at Vatican II] was David du Plessis, who came as an official 'observer.' Suenens and du Plessis were destined to play major roles in the Catholic Charismatic Renewal that unfolded shortly after the completion of the council."[28] According to Vinson Synan, "if the Charismatic renewal had begun in the Roman Catholic Church before

26. Synan, *Holiness-Pentecostal Tradition*, 238.
27. Vatican II, *Unitatis Redintegratio*, 3.
28. Synan, *Holiness-Pentecostal Tradition*, 244.

Vatican II, it would probably have been viewed as a 'Protestant' phenomenon and, therefore, forbidden to Catholics."[29]

Still, the now well-documented history of Catholic Pentecostalism tells us that Pentecostalism broke into the Catholic Church not from above, meaning from the hierarchy or theologians who determined the outcome of Vatican II, but from below, from the laity which had almost no public voice at the Council. It is out of their thirst for spiritual renewal that Catholic Pentecostalism was born. And the history of the Catholic Church shows that, by accommodating Pentecostal forms of spirituality, this was certainly not the first time that it was acknowledging the authenticity of a spiritual movement springing from the grassroots. But this was the first time since the Reformation that an experience borrowed by lay people from an offshoot of the Protestant tradition was knocking at the doors of the Catholic Church, seeking recognition and being accepted. Ralph Kiefer and Bill Storey, the lay pioneers of Catholic Pentecostalism at Duquesne University in 1967, and many others who followed them were baptized in the Spirit outside the Catholic Church. Indeed, most early Catholic Pentecostals sought help outside the Catholic Church to make sense of their experiences. Although the Catholic Church had been prepared theologically to welcome a new understanding and practice of the theology of the Holy Spirit and charismata, the Catholic clergy were not prepared to handle ecstatic experiences exhibited by Catholic Pentecostals under the influence of Protestant Pentecostals and their literature. Addressing participants at the International Conference on Catholic Charismatic Renewal in May 1975 in Rome, less than ten years after the beginning of the movement in the Catholic Church, Pope Paul VI described it as a "chance" for the spiritual renewal of the Church and the world. The CCR was being officially legitimated. However, I learned from my own research on the CCR in the context of Africa that this official acknowledgment was just the beginning of the long process of adjusting the movement's "Charismatic" dimension to the structural constraints of the Catholic Church as an institution and to local cultural contexts.

African Roots of the Charismatic Predicament

"African roots" refer here to what remotely prepared African Christians in general, and Catholics in particular, to make sense of the Charismatic predicament in the context of sub-Saharan Africa. I identify two main factors: (1) African precolonial beliefs in the invisible world of spirits and related experiences of spirit possession and (2) African beliefs in witchcraft and

---

29. Synan, *Holiness-Pentecostal Tradition*, 242.

related experiences of afflictions. How are these related to the Charismatic predicament?

It is worth recalling that Africans did not wait for Pentecostalism to discover ecstatic religion and learn the language of spirits. African religions had their own share of ecstatic experiences long before encountering Charismatic Christianity. Most precolonial African religions are based on human interactions with the world of spirits, nonhuman spiritual agents which have the ability to impact human lives positively or negatively. In some contexts, as a number of ethnographic studies have shown, these spirits have the ability to select a few humans whom they possess in order to serve them through possession cults. Possession cults include all those "cults of affliction" identified by anthropologists across the African continent.[30] This is the case, for example, with the water spirits (*jengu*, in the singular; *miengu*, in the plural), which were at the center of the ritual life of the coastal Sawa people of Cameroon before the arrival of missionaries. Some miengu rituals portray all the features usually linked with possession "cults of affliction" that anthropologists have studied in other parts of the world. Turner, who coined the term "cult of affliction," described these rituals as "[t]he interpretation of misfortune in terms of domination by a specific nonhuman agent and the attempt to come to terms with the misfortune by having the afflicted individual, under the guidance of a 'doctor' of that mode, join the cult association venerating that agent."[31] This applies to miengu possession cults among the coastal Bantu of Cameroon. What remains of miengu beliefs and rituals today in Cameroon exists in the postcolonial context, alongside Christianity and other ritual alternatives.

Obviously, miengu cults met with strong opposition from Christian missionaries when they started their work among the Sawa in the early 1840s.[32] Christian converts were not allowed to take part in traditional rituals; the intention was to suppress the existing cultic life altogether. But since the miengu were the owners and controllers of life and power, of fecundity and success, of well-being and prosperity, abandoning them altogether would have meant a complete reconfiguration of the Duala's worldview. The problem, of course, was whether Christianity could satisfactorily fill the resulting void. I contend that the Catholic Church in Africa is still struggling with these issues in Africa, especially those related to witchcraft.

---

30. Cf. Ardener, *Coastal Bantu*, 30–45; Turner, *Drums of Affliction*, 150–60; Lewis, "Spirit Possession," 188–219; Boddy, *Wombs and Alien Spirits*, 40–55; Lovell, *Cord of Blood*, 70–75.

31. Turner, *Drums of Affliction*, 15–16.

32. Bureau, *Ethno-Sociologie Religieuse*, 78.

The second reason for the Charismatic predicament's attraction in Africa is the resilience of witchcraft beliefs, still a major source of existential insecurity all over the continent. Concerning the particular issue of healing, which is a major demand in Charismatic circles, it has been shown that almost everywhere in Africa, early missionaries, collaborating with colonial establishments, sought to replace the African traditional systems of healing with Western ones. Their approach was predominantly ethnocentric.[33] Although much has been done to "indigenize" liturgical music in African Catholicism since the end of Vatican II in 1965, the Catholic Church has not changed its negative attitudes towards what remains of African traditional healing rituals. But neither Christianity nor Western medicine has been able to completely fill the void left by the displacement of local rituals.[34] Today in Africa, the Catholic clergy still face the challenge of containing complaints and accusations of witchcraft among the faithful. Among African Catholics, believers in witchcraft still outnumber unbelievers, as attempts by the unbelievers to translate disabling phenomena, traditionally explained in terms of witchcraft or spirit possession, into the language of psychopathology are still very marginal.

To face their existential insecurities, many Christian converts have developed ways of adapting to the new situation. They often distribute their loyalty among the three dominant religious systems of reference—traditional, Christian, and modern—to which they resort selectively, depending on the nature of the misfortunes confronting them. These different resources are seen as complementary, because what really matters for most people is the restoration of their health, whatever that means. In other words, although many Africans have happily embraced Christianity, a number of converts are not yet ready to completely give up their religious traditions. These multiple religious loyalties have been observed elsewhere by anthropologists among African Christians.[35] This selective recourse to tradition has gradually forced the Catholic clergy to question its methods of evangelization and to seek ways of initiating a "dialogue" between African traditions and Christian traditions. The theology of inculturation, which has dominated the theological debate in African Catholicism in recent decades, is supposed to carry out this task.

Colonizers and missionaries definitely believed that education, science, technology, and evangelization would progressively do away with

33. Messina and Slageren, *Histoire du Christianisme*, 146.

34. Bureau, *Peuple du Fleuve*, 40.

35. Hutchinson, *Nuer Dilemmas*, 325; James, *Listening Ebony*, 247; Bureau, *Peuple du Fleuve*, 44; Zeitlyn, *Sua in Somié*, 15.

witchcraft beliefs, seen as the prime expression of irrationality, but this has simply not happened. On the contrary, as a number of anthropological studies have shown, witchcraft beliefs have adapted to modernity and taken up new forms and contents.[36] Many African Christians do not find in mission churches the means to address the related fears and anxieties. Indeed, it is still a major pastoral problem in Catholic parishes in Africa, where the laity confront priests daily with witchcraft-related issues. Catholics who are disappointed by the clergy's inability to solve their problems turn to alternative solutions: traditional religions and diviners including other Christian churches, especially those that are Charismatic and Pentecostal. In fact, before the coming of the CCR, a number of African Christians turned to African Independent Churches to address witchcraft-related misfortunes. It is indeed worth also noting that, before Pentecostals and Charismatics appeared on the African scene, mission churches had already been challenged by the so-called African Independent Churches, many of which exhibited some Pentecostal features. There are indeed good reasons to extend the Pentecostal category to some of the well-known African Independent Churches that date from the colonial period, such as Kimbanguism (1921); the Aladura churches from Nigeria (1930s); Alice Lenshina's Lumpa Church in Zambia (1955); and others. The prophet-founders of these churches were undoubtedly charismatic figures, and almost all of them claimed to have been inspired by God or the Holy Spirit to carry out a very precise mission, particularly healing and leading a crusade against witchcraft and other traditional practices. Several of these indigenous churches of Pentecostal bent assign a revelatory function to dreams, or visions, and the prophetic use of trance in their gatherings is somewhat reminiscent of some local possession cults' ritual expressions. A number of African Christians who left mission churches to join these churches were looking for more appropriate responses to witchcraft-related problems.

Many Catholics, therefore, saw the rise of Catholic Pentecostalism as an opportunity to properly address problems of spirit possession or witchcraft within the Catholic Church. Indeed, as I show in my book, *African Pentecostalism and the Paradoxes of Africanization*, most of the misfortunes handled in the Catholic Charismatic movement which I was studying in Cameroon were closely or remotely related to suspicions of witchcraft attacks or spirit possession.[37] Therefore, it is no surprise that a number of Catholic priests are now borrowing extensively from Pentecostal and Charismatic religious habits and idioms to address the healing needs of their parishioners. Some

36. Geschiere, *Modernity of Witchcraft*, 100–125.
37. Lado, *Catholic Pentecostalism*, 170–90.

have done this in the framework of the CCR, others individually. In other words, with the coming of the CCR to Africa, the offer of healing ministries has grown to meet a rising demand. However, what is new is that, compared with Western missionaries, these African priests, like their parishioners, not only openly believe in the existence of witchcraft and local spirits but have sought to integrate these beliefs into the Christian system.

From Catholic Demonology to Local Demonology

Concerning how CCR spread to the Global South in general, Csordas is right when he writes: "Evidence suggests that the typical pattern for the movement's introduction in a third world region is as follows: a missionary priest visits the United States, is exposed to Baptism of the Holy Spirit, organizes a prayer group on his return . . . ."[38] This is true of Meinrad Hebga, a Jesuit priest who founded a Charismatic movement called Ephphata in Cameroon in 1976, after having been introduced to the Catholic Charismatic movement in the US in the early 1970s. He was a pioneer of the Catholic Charismatic movement in West and Central Africa and, subsequently, became a very prominent Catholic Charismatic figure in these regions and beyond.

As I have attempted to show in my previous work, the CCR in Africa is a locus of intercultural and interreligious experiments which exemplify processes of a global phenomenon's local appropriation. I focus here on the issue of the local appropriation of the biblical concept of "demon," or "devil," central in Charismatic terminology. Obviously, these localization processes are not specific to Africa. Thomas Csordas has shown how this has also happened in the United States.[39] Csordas treats Charismatic demonology as a form of "collective representation," with ethnopsychological and cosmological dimensions. The North American demonological landscape shows the personification—as devils—of negative emotions, behavior, and thought patterns constitutive of the local psychopathological repertoire.

In the context of Ephphata as a CCR movement, the "devil" takes on new faces, addressing local misfortunes. Local spirits and sources of misfortunes are repackaged as "devilish," and this explains why Pentecostals and Charismatics, including Catholic Charismatics, tend to demonize African Traditional Religions. Spirits related to these local religions are simply lumped together as "evil spirits" to be driven out of "possessed" patients. This raises a fundamental question about the place of interreligious dialogue in Pentecostal and Charismatic circles, including Catholic ones.

38. Csordas, *Sacred Self*, 28.
39. Csordas, *Sacred Self*, 181–88.

Interreligious dialogue does not seem to be among the priorities of the Pentecostal and Charismatic subculture in the Catholic Church, at least not in the African context. On the contrary, some of the most zealous Pentecostals and Charismatics have been not only vocal in discarding local religions as devilish but have even actively vandalized or destroyed local shrines identified as abodes of evil spirits.

Concerning the emerging local demonology in Ephphata, the CCR movement I studied in Cameroon, Fr. Hebga suggested, based on his patients' experiences, a rethinking of the Christian concept of "demon" to fit the needs of the local context. He distinguishes four categories of possession, with the nature of the possessing entity functioning as the discriminating factor: (1) spirits of the dead (*esprits des défunts*); (2) genii (*génies*); (3) living witches or sorcerers (*sorciers vivants*); and (4) demons (*démons*). Although Fr. Hebga acknowledges the ambivalence of some of these possessing entities, his working principle is that, apart from the Holy Spirit, nothing should be allowed to possess a human being. To illustrate what I mentioned earlier regarding the "demonization" of local spirits, I refer to the beliefs in *miengu*, water spirits among the Sawa, the coastal Bantu of Southern Cameroon. In the local religious cosmology, the miengu are the owners and controllers of life and power, of fecundity and success, of well-being and prosperity. They are not associated with evil and death but with life and prosperity, though they can possess human beings to serve them as healers.

Bishop Emmanuel Milingo was the very first high-ranking Catholic cleric in Africa to affiliate with the Charismatic movement. He claimed that he became involved with the CCR while searching for an appropriate pastoral response to his faithful followers' affliction by local spirits. Archbishop of Lusaka from 1969 to 1983, Bishop Milingo appeared on the Charismatic scene in 1973, claiming to have been empowered by the Holy Spirit to heal. This was the first time in the history of the Catholic Church in Africa that a bishop was claiming the Charismatic experience and was openly involving himself in public rituals of faith healing. He subsequently founded a Charismatic group (the Divine Providence Community) in the urban setting of Lusaka and established strong links with other Charismatic movements in the West. This is what he has to say about the discovery of his healing gifts: "I knew that the Lord was leading me to the healing of the disease of which many of my fellow Zambians are victims—*mashawe*. This disease cannot be treated in a hospital. During the whole of May, I thought out the different ways by which I could help my sick brothers and sisters."[40] Mashawe are ancestral "spirits" which are blamed for possessing mainly women and

---

40. Milingo, *World in Between*, 14–15.

are traditionally treated in the framework of cults of affliction. In terms of cultural translation, Bishop Milingo attempted to deal with mashawe by demonizing them, that is, by imposing on them a Christian category.

But his healing practices were to meet a fierce opposition from most of his fellow clerics, predominantly Irish missionaries, who felt that his healing ministry was not compatible with his duties as an archbishop and did not conform to the doctrine of the Church.[41] His attempts to adapt ritual healing to local needs, especially the deliverance from mashawe, were seen by his detractors as a breach of orthodoxy, as an accommodation of paganism in the Catholic Church. Denounced to Rome, he was subsequently banned from holding his public healing sessions. A decade of accusations coupled with Milingo's obstinacy culminated in his removal from office as archbishop of Lusaka in 1983 and his subsequent assignment in Rome. He was allowed to continue his healing practices and rapidly became popular among Charismatics in Italy and beyond. It must be said, however, that his recent flirtation with the Unification Church (Moonism) has not served the image of Charismatic renewal in Africa well. On September 25, 2006, Milingo was excommunicated from the Catholic Church for challenging the rule of priestly celibacy by consecrating married men as bishops without the permission of Vatican authorities. Milingo's saga shows already the tension between charisma and institutional power which is characteristic of the ongoing domestication of the Charismatic movement.

Conclusion

Based on empirical data collected in a dozen Catholic Charismatic groups in the city of Yaoundé, Cameroon, I have emphasized, first, that the CCR's influence within the Catholic Church may be on the decline and, secondly, that the renewal sought in Charismatic groups in the Catholic Church is more personal than institutional. However, it cannot be denied that the CCR in Africa, as elsewhere, has provided the laity with some space for spiritual empowerment, as the movement's leadership is predominantly lay, in spite of the clergy's desire to control and direct the lay leaders. I have also argued in this paper that, although the Catholic Church surprisingly opened its doors to accommodate some aspects of the Pentecostal movement in the 1960s, it has done so in a distinctively Catholic way through its own domestication processes. Indeed, the Catholic Church has managed to tame, in its midst, a movement like Pentecostalism which, by its very nature, resists structural control. The clergy ensures the movement's

---

41. Ter Haar and Ellis, "Spirit Possession," 189.

structural domestication and seeks to maintain an equilibrium between individual charisma and institutional mediation. This search for equilibrium has proven to be difficult and has often resulted in conflicts between the lay leadership of Charismatic movements and the traditional authority of the clergy. In this paper, I have also brought to the discussion some of the distinctively African features which have shaped Catholic Pentecostalism in the African context, indicating that it has also been an intercultural experiment. Still, the acceptance of an offshoot of the Pentecostal movement in the Catholic Church is a major ecumenical turning point in the history of global Christianity that indeed deserves to be revisited.

Bibliography

Anderson, Allan. *African Reformation: African Initiated Churches in the Twentieth Century*. Trenton, NJ: Africa World, 2001.

Ardener, Edwin. *Coastal Bantu of the Cameroons*. London: International African Institute, 1956.

Asamoah-Gyadu, Johnson Kwabena. "'I Will Put My Breath in You, and You Will Come to Life': Charismatic Renewal in Mainline Churches and Its Implications for African 'Diasporean' Christianity." In *Christianity in Africa and the African Diaspora*, edited by Afe Adogame, et al., 193–207. London: Continuum, 2008.

Boddy, Janice. *Wombs and Alien Spirits: Women, Men, and the Zar Cult in Northern Sudan*. Madison: University of Wisconsin Press, 1989.

Bureau, René. *Ethno-sociologie Religieuse des Duala et Apparentés*. Yaoundé: Institut de Recherches Scientifiques du Cameroun, 1962.

———. "Influence de la Christianisation sur les Institutions Traditionnelles des Ethnies Côtières du Cameroun." In *Christianity in Tropical Africa*, edited by Christian G. Baëta, 165–81. Oxford: Oxford University Press, 1968.

———. *Le Peuple du Fleuve. Sociologie de la Conversion chez les Douala*. Paris: Karthala, 1996.

Csordas, Thomas. *The Sacred Self: A Cultural Phenomenology of Charismatic Healing*. Berkeley: University of California Press, 1997.

de Rosny, Eric. "Renouveau Charismatique et Transe en Afrique." *Etudes* 370 (1989) 667–78.

Ela, Jean-Marc, and René Luneau. *Voici le Temps des Héritiers: Eglises d'Afrique et Voies Nouvelles*. Paris: Karthala, 2001.

Geschiere, Peter. *The Modernity of Witchcraft: Politics and the Occult in Postcolonial Africa*. Charlottesville: University of Virginia Press, 1997.

Gifford, Paul. *Ghana's New Christianity: Pentecostalism in a Globalizing African Economy*. London: Hurst, 2004.

Harris, Antipas. "Elements of African Religious Practices in African American Worship: Resounding Practical Theological Implications." In *Christianity in Africa and the African Diaspora*, edited by Afe Adogame, et al., 221–31. London: Continuum, 2008.

Hebga, Meinrad. "Le Mouvement Charismatique en Afrique." *Etudes* (July/August 1995) 67–75.

Hutchinson, Sharon. *Nuer Dilemmas: Coping with Money, War, and the State*. Berkeley: University of California Press, 1996.

James, Wendy. *The Listening Ebony: Moral Knowledge, Religion, and Power among the Uduk of Sudan*. Oxford: Clarendon, 1999.

Kasper, Walter. "Le Dialogue Ecuménique: Informations, Réflexions et Evaluations." *La Documentation Catholique* (March 2, 2008) 2397–98.

Kouassi, Jean. *Faut-il Croire au Renouveau Charismatique Catholique*. Abidjan: Paulines, 2011.

Lado, Ludovic. *Catholic Pentecostalism and the Paradoxes of Africanization*. Boston: Brill, 2009.

Lewis, Ivan Myrddin. *Ecstatic Religion: A Study of Shamanism and Spirit Possession*. London: Routledge, 1971.

———. "Spirit Possession in Northern Somaliland." In *Spirit Mediumship and Society in Africa*, edited by John Beattie and John Middleton, 188–219. London: Routledge and Kegan Paul, 1969.

Lovell, Nadia. *Cord of Blood: Possession and the Making of Voodoo*. London: Pluto, 2002.

Magesa, Laurenti. "Charismatic Movements as 'Communities of Affliction.'" In *Charismatic Renewal in Africa: A Challenge for African Christianity*, edited by Mika Vahakangas and Andrew Kyomo, 27–44. Nairobi: Acton, 2003.

Messina, Jean-Paul, and Jaap van Slageren. *Histoire du Christianisme au Cameroun: Des Origines à nos Jours*. Paris: Karthala, 2005.

Milingo, Emmanuel. *The World in Between: Christian Healing and the Struggle for Spiritual Survival*. London: Hurst, 1984.

Müller, Johannes, and Karl Gabriel, eds. *Evangelicals Pentecostals Churches Charismatics: New Religious Movements as a Challenge for the Catholic Church*. Quezon City: Claretian Communications Foundations, 2015.

Mwaura, Philomena. "The Role of Charismatic Christianity in Reshaping the Religious Scene in Africa: The Case of Kenya." In *Christianity in Africa and the African Diaspora*, edited by Afe Adogame, et al., 180–92. London: Continuum, 2008.

Ojo, Matthews. "Transnational Networks and Indigenous Pentecostal Missionaries Enterprises in the West African Costal Region." In *Christianity in Africa and the African Diaspora*, edited by Afe Adogame, et al., 169–79. London: Continuum, 2008.

Omenyo, Cephas N. "Charismatization of the Mainline Churches in Ghana." In *Charismatic Renewal in Africa: A Challenge for African Christianity*, edited by Mika Vahakangas and Andrew Kyomo, 5–26. Nairobi: Acton, 2003.

Synan, Vinson. *The Holiness-Pentecostal Tradition: Charismatic Movements in the Twentieth Century*. Grand Rapids: Eerdmans, 1997.

Ter Haar, Gerrie, and Stephen Ellis. "Spirit Possession and Healing in Modern Zambia: An Analysis of Letters to Archbishop Milingo." *African Affairs* 87 (1988) 185–206.

Thomas, Joseph. "Réveils Spirituels en France." *Etudes* 358 (1983) 401–14.

Turner, Victor. *The Drums of Affliction: A Study of Religious Processes among the Ndembu of Zambia*. Oxford: Clarendon, 1968.

Zeitlyn, David. *Sua in Somié: Aspects of Mambila Traditional Religion*. Sankt Augustin: Academia Verlag, 1994.

11

The Spirit in Africa

PAUL GIFFORD

In describing medieval Christianity of Europe around the year 1000, Dennis Nineham highlights points like the following: Europeans of that time had a very simple idea of the past; they had little idea of change. They had almost no interest in the natural world. Society was divided hierarchically: the religious, the aristocracy, and the peasants, with women virtually nowhere. Their life was almost literally "solitary, poor, nasty, brutish, and short," and with so little understanding of secondary causes, the evils that continually befell them were assumed to be punishments from God, with all the consequences that this had for their understanding of their own sin, guilt, and worthlessness; God must indeed be angry with his people, it was felt, if he visited so much suffering upon them. Since so little was known about the workings of nature, it was easy for what happened to be *experienced* as supernatural intervention. The supernatural was the "really real." Without technology to help them, the clergy were the only people believed capable of understanding what was going on and of producing, by their prayers and sacramental activities, the results which the age desperately needed but had not the knowledge to produce by secular means.[1]

Nineham's point is that all dimensions of life cohere; they form a unity, a *Totalität*, an *ensemble*—without demanding absolute tidiness; religion, for most, is lived more than it is theorized. It is, therefore, problematic to isolate one aspect of that *Totalität*, reify it, and assume identity with the purportedly same aspect in a radically different *Totalität*. Thus, to make normative the refusal to ordain women or a belief in a personal devil without taking into account the complete set of beliefs and values surrounding both areas,

1. Nineham, *Christianity Medieval and Modern*.

is very problematic. One might add others: to think that the stress on divine wrath has much relevance for a culture not built on honor or authority; to transpose an understanding of natural law from a culture with little knowledge of or interest in nature; to transpose the use of the Bible from a society with such a different understanding of the past.

I will not spend time discussing the details of his picture of medieval European Christianity—something I'm not qualified to judge anyway—but Nineham's main point is, I think, a good one: the coherence of all elements within a *Totalität*, and how problematic this makes trans-temporal comparison or transposing an element of one *Totalität*, isolating it from all the other components which gave that element its particular significance. It is rather rash to presume that such an element, in isolation, is directly identifiable with or comparable to what at first glance might seem exactly the same element in other complexes. I think this point has significance not just historically but geographically. In short, when we embark on what might seem a simple comparison between, say, Winners Chapel in Lagos and John Wimber's Vineyard Church in California, all sorts of issues arise. The contexts—economic, cultural, historical, political, and intellectual—are so very different that identifications with or comparisons between an element in one and that supposed element in the other, though obviously not impossible, are far more fraught than often realized.

In what follows, I want to make that point in reference to the notion of "spirit" in Africa and in the West. Right at the outset, let me be clear. Of course, "Africa" is as much a generalization as "the West." Of course, Botswana is not Niger, and Guinea Bissau is not Kenya. They have significant differences which, in particular contexts, may prove determinative. But one can make claims for Europe, quite aware of the differences between Ireland and Italy, Sweden and Sicily; one can talk of the United States, acutely aware of the real difference between California and Mississippi, and between both and Vermont, provided one makes the appropriate provisos and qualifications. I will talk of "Africa" while giving examples from Senegal, just because I have lived there for most of the last five years, without claiming that Senegal is normative or representative of Africa in any hard sense. Nevertheless, the particular allows me to make points of more general application.

Senegal's Religion

In Senegal, the pervasive religious imagination sees spiritual forces operative everywhere and understands causality primarily in spiritual terms, and worldly events as determined primarily in the spiritual realm. Let us call this the enchanted religious imagination. These spirit forces can be manipulated by individuals gifted with such powers and whose services are available to those who seek them. This gifted individual is, in West Africa, called a *marabout*, someone who claims power over the sacred and symbolic forces affecting our lives; *maraboutage* is the use of this power.

Manipulating the spiritual forces affecting us is aimed at ends like the following: to enjoy prosperity, status, and popularity; to control another (particularly in amatory matters, or for extracting money); to restrict another's physical movement; to cause division between others (from jealousy, or revenge, or material interest); to render oneself invisible (so one might, for example, pass through immigration and customs unobserved); to cause sickness or death at a distance; to avoid blows or attacks on one's person; to obtain general protection from malevolent others; to send another into exile or vagabondage, or, by contrast, to bring another back to the country; to find love; to make someone impotent on his marriage night; to drive someone to death or suicide. Obviously, some of these can be considered positive aims, but it is evident that, most frequently, the negative outweigh the positive, though some can be considered both. Manipulating spirits to ensure the health, harmony, and prosperity of one's family, on the face of it, seems something positive. However, there is often a downside; working to ensure promotion can entail the failure or firing of a competitor. To find love may mean eliminating rivals—especially in a polygamous society where this spiritual manipulation is often used to discredit, render infertile, or ensure dismissal of a co-wife.

Even if influencing spirits can be practiced anywhere, there are some places that have an aura or charge which makes them particularly suitable: places like trees, crossroads, beds, lintels, markets, morgues, wells, anthills. Some of these, of their nature, lend themselves to negative spiritual manipulation (morgues, cemeteries), some to positive (in Senegal, most notably the mosque). Some can lead in either direction: with fruit, sap, foliage, and roots, trees can possess a positive charge, but because they are considered the abode of spirits, also a negative one. Wells, with associations of life-giving water can lead in positive directions, but the hidden, cold, dark associations can also lead in negative directions.

In all cases, the marabout lays down specific and particular requirements for managing spirit forces: concoctions (requiring ingredients like powder, roots, salt, sugar, perfume to be mixed in various ways); objects (knives, nails, needles, rings, coins); bones or other parts of animals (even humans)—often made into talismans or what are called *gris-gris*. In all maraboutage, there is normally a certain objective or subjective resemblance between what is sought and what is used. A part can represent the whole, and to act on a part is considered to be acting on the whole, and to act on something representing the person is considered acting on the person himself. Substances can be used in various ways, as in baths, potions, and lotions. Sacrifices of all sorts (camels, cattle, sheep, chicken) are common, and offerings are essential, both to begin negotiations with the marabout and to ensure the success of the process. Failure to observe the most minute of these stipulations can cause the process to fail (constituting something of an escape: it is effectively impossible to falsify the process).

Spirits are manipulated for all aspects of life: love, business, travel, politics, not to mention relations between colleagues, neighbors, and husbands and wives. For men, the most common demands are for wealth, promotion, status, and power. For women, the most common are for love and domestic realities: a husband, children, and domestic security. Women seem particularly given to these spirit practices, probably because of their more vulnerable and marginalized place in society and the prevalence of polygamous marriages.

This is religion in Senegal: the detecting, identifying, and controlling of spirit forces thought to affect us.[2] It pervades all areas of life and all classes, the elite as well as the peasants, the educated as well as the illiterate. Yet, it is hardly studied (something to which I shall return). Ibrahima Sow notes that, on coming to do his pioneering research, he could find virtually no treatment of the phenomenon to build on.[3] Nor is the matter debated in serious fora. One cannot avoid observing it in the key fields of politics, football, and the national sport of *lutte*, but it is really only the middle-range and popular media, especially newspapers and radio talkback programs, that feature the phenomenon regularly, not to mention the often bizarre charges brought before the courts against false marabouts or charlatans. This enchanted imagination is not unchanging. Yet, it would be misleading to say that it is disappearing; in fact, most observers say that on the contrary, it is increasing.

Pervasive Spirits

Mysterious deaths (particularly around election time), disappearances, and kidnappings can all disclose this religious imagination—inevitably so, when corpses are discovered missing various limbs or organs. Often, this is expressed openly. The parents of a fourteen-month-old boy who had been

2. For a more extended treatment of religion in Senegal, see Gifford, "Religion in Contemporary Senegal," 255–67.

3. Sow, *Le Maraboutage au Sénégal*, 26.

kidnapped state: "All the marabouts we have consulted say that whoever took our baby wants to sacrifice him." In this case, the parents decide to fight fire with fire: "The grandparents of my son are from the Casamance. They say that they are only waiting for the green light to go into action. If he or she who has my son doesn't bring him back, he can expect the worst. He may even lose his life. We don't want this to happen. All that we wish is to recover our son. We give him twenty-four hours to bring him back; if not, we will be obliged to let them get involved."[4]

In Tambacounda, the major city of the East, in the space of about six weeks in the early months of 2014, ten intellectually handicapped loners were killed and had body parts removed (usually the penis; in one case, the Adam's apple also). Some other intended victims narrowly escaped. The missing body parts left few in doubt that these were ritual killings, and perhaps the work of a network of traffickers in body parts. Fear and insecurity gripped the region; people demonstrated to vent their frustration with the authorities. In explanation, many drew attention to the desperate conditions around Tambacounda, the steeply increasing price of living, the soaring population, and unemployment. The proximity to goldfields led others to speculate that prospectors saw this as a way to riches through *mystique*. Although the Interior Minister in Dakar denounced the killings, and the police and gendarmerie heightened their presence, there was a "troubling silence" on the part of local politicians. One commentator observed: "In this town, traditional religions, secret societies, and circles of initiates constitute a parallel world whose links with politicians are close, complex, and often mutually supporting."[5]

Finding gris-gris planted to harm others is frequently reported. Someone newly promoted to President Sall's government, on packing up his previous office at a bank, found gris-gris in the form of strange plants in a cushion and under the carpet. He linked this to his state of health: "Since coming to the bank, I have been ill and done the rounds of all the hospitals in Dakar."[6] The director general of a public body had his office refurbished only to find gris-gris hidden under the carpet. This led him to have the office thoroughly searched; finding what looked like new plasterwork, he had it removed and found more gris-gris. The removal of these became "the principal subject of conversation at the agency."[7] The president of the Legislative Assembly's accounts commission found gris-gris in the form of

---

4. *L'Observateur*, May 6, 2014, 3. All translations from the French are by the author.
5. Fall, "La Lute 'Sénégalaise,'" 5.
6. *L'Observateur*, August 20, 2013, 2.
7. *L'Observateur*, December 21, 2012, 2.

qur'anic texts hidden in a bag behind curtains; he accepted that, because his committee could discover irregularities in Assembly expenses, somebody was trying to bring him down.[8]

It seems widely accepted that show business is full of *maraboutage*. A singer (*griot*) explains her failures after a triumphant debut: "Mystical practices exist in music, and I was a victim of them. Only ten days after my album appeared, I fell sick. I was three years without singing. I received hospital treatment for four months. My father told me that this went beyond modern medicine and took me to Ourossogui where I was cared for, thank God, by traditional medicine."[9] Another child wonder—he had his first album at the age of eleven—descended into obscurity for thirteen years. On attempting a comeback and asked the reason for his long silence, he replied: "The world of showbiz is rotten. I can tell you that I was the victim of mystical attacks which fixed me. I consider that it is these mystical attacks which have held back my career."[10]

Senegal's national sport, *lutte avec frappe*, more popular than football, is as much a spiritual contest between the wrestlers' marabouts as a physical contest between the wrestlers themselves. At the bout itself, the wrestlers are bedecked with gris-gris containing protective bark and other substances, and they douse themselves with protective liquids. Take the much-touted contest between Tapha Tine and Balla Gaye II in June 2013, effectively for supremacy in Senegal. Two days before the bout, Tapha Tine's camp had sacrificed a bull at a crossroads, dividing the meat in sixty-four portions as an offering. On the day itself, he had had a black and white sheep sacrificed at his door; he had stepped over the blood, before sprinkling himself with blackish liquid. He took with him five calabashes decorated with qur'anic texts. For their part, the camp of Bala Gaye had some days before placed a camel's head near Tapha Tine's residence—which "*pour le destinataire de cet acte très mystique* means defeat or death."[11] In fact, on the day itself, Balla Gaye won the contest rather quickly. One of Tapha Tine's marabouts explained that, in a dream on the morning of the combat, "the *djinns* had informed him that Tapha was *atteint mystiquement*." The marabout possessed the *potion magique* to counter this attack, two small bottles *d'eau mystique*, one of which was for washing his arms and would restore their use; the other contained a liquid to sip four times before washing his face with what remained, which would enable him to see his adversary. But on arriving

8. *Le Populaire*, March 14, 2013, 2.
9. *Le Populaire*, October 26/27, 2013, 7.
10. *L'Observateur*, September 26, 2012, 8.
11. *Le Populaire*, May 23, 2013, 2.

at the ground, he and another marabout (there had been fifty marabouts present at a Tapha Tine midday conference) had been denied entry, so their remedy had not been applied—with the inevitable result.[12] The father of Balla Gaye admitted he had paid "at least" fifty million francs of the *communauté financière africaine* (US $100,000) to marabouts to ensure his son's success[13]—an insight into the economics of maraboutage, a topic in itself, but beyond our scope here.

In an equally hyped bout in April 2015, Balla Gaye II was defeated by Eumeu Sène. In speaking to the media afterwards, Eumeu Sène explained, in tears, that his aggression was due in large measure to his rage that the camp of Balla Gaye had profaned the tomb of his recently deceased mother to cripple him spiritually. (It was unclear whether the perpetrators, in planting gris-gris there, had actually disinterred the body.) Although Balla Gaye strenuously denied the accusation ("I am a Muslim, and for nothing in the world would I do such a thing"), this allegation dominated the media for days. If the alleged deed drew universal disapproval, it seemed equally agreed that such activities were part and parcel of the world of *lutte*—the theme of one newspaper's front-page headline and cover story: "La face horrible de la lutte: sacrifice humaines, profanations de tombes, morts suspects."[14]

Sow has suggested that the courts are one place where this enchanted religious imagination can be seen in all its variety. Many cases involve false marabouts or charlatans—thus, cases of fraud—but which nevertheless reveal the imagination we are examining. In a good many, the charlatan actually seeks out his victim, claims to be a powerful marabout (of a great religious family, even the marabout of the president or some other prominent figure), often telling the victim that she (it is most often a woman) may soon die, or suffer some serious loss, unless she submits to his prescriptions—for sacrifices, offerings, *bains mystiques*.[15] Sometimes, the convincing will be done

---

12. *L'Observateur*, February 21, 2014, 15.

13. *L'Observateur*, June 5, 2013, 16. The father had paid thirty million fcfa for a previous bout against the then-champion Yekini.

14. "The horrible face of 'the fight': human sacrifices, profanations of tombs, and suspicious deaths." *Walfadjri*, April 7, 2015, 7. This bout opened another window on the economics of maraboutage. One authority on the mystical side of lutte speculated shortly beforehand that each lutteur would have between eighty and ninety marabouts in his camp, each of whom would require *offrandes* of around eight million fcfa—so, in total, an outlay of at least six hundred and forty million fcfa or US $1,250,000 for each lutteur (*L'Observateur*, March 13, 2015, 16).

15. A charlatan is jailed for two years claiming to be the grandson of a famous marabout of a prominent religious figure and extorting seventy million fcfa for a promised return of three hundred million (*Le Quotidien*, October 25/26, 2014, 4). A wife sued her husband who claimed to be of the same religious family, and after *bains mystiques*,

with accomplices. For example, the fraudster will stop someone to ask directions, when an accomplice will "fortuitously" pass and greet the fraudster as a great marabout responsible for the accomplice's current good fortune. The offer is usually to make rich, but an astute charlatan can quickly establish a pressing need: success in study, travel overseas, fertility, or neutralizing a co-wife. Sometimes, the fraudster will demand whatever the victim has on her person—money, jewelry, cell phone, laptop—create some diversion, and simply abscond with what he has obtained. Other times, he will demand goods of the family or the family business. Sow accepts that the label of charlatan has wide application, but is equally clear that it would be a serious misunderstanding to reduce all marabouts to charlatans.[16]

Some cases coming before the courts deserve mention for their sheer effrontery. For example, a marabout stops young women in the street, foretells a dire and imminent catastrophe, to be averted only with gris-gris containing his semen; hence, the need to move somewhere discreet for fellatio.[17] A marabout received a year's imprisonment for defrauding a twenty-four-year-old student. He told her she had a spiritual husband who was blocking her progress; she paid seven million fcfa to be freed. The marabout then told her that her sister would fall ill unless a member of the family sacrificed her virginity; she sacrificed herself for her sister. The marabout went further: her father would die unless she slept with him again. She finally came to her senses and took the marabout to court.[18] One Senegalese woman in Italy found a marabout through the internet, who promptly told her that seven djinns threatened to kill her if she didn't take care. The marabout promised to ensure a complete cure at the cost of 500,000 fcfa (US $1,000), which eventually became 1.6 million fcfa (US $3,000). The woman came to her senses only when the marabout claimed her grandfather had revealed to him in a dream that she should marry the marabout.[19]

Often the motivation of enrichment drives the victim to seek out the marabout. Thus, a charlatan was jailed for two years for taking 1.5 million fcfa and promising in return to multiply banknotes to the value of ten billion fcfa. (His defense was that he was a genuine marabout and took only

---

was led to give him up to twenty million fcfa (*Le Populaire*, February 27, 2015, 10). A member of the Kounta religious family was sentenced to two years in jail for extorting forty million fcfa for a promised return of seven hundred million fcfa (*L'Observateur*, February 28–May 1, 2015, 4). Similarly, *Le Populaire*, December 19, 2014, 6).

16. Sow, *Le Maraboutage*, 239–64.

17. *L'Observateur*, May 23, 2014, 3; see also Sow, *Le Maraboutage*, 78, 257–8.

18. *L'Observateur*, October 17, 2014, 3; *L'Observateur* November 11, 2014, 5; *Le Populaire*, November 18, 2014, 12.

19. *Le Populaire*, December 24/25, 2012, 13.

45,000 fcfa for beer for the spirits, candles, and a goat for sacrifice.)[20] Some cases are hugely contrived. For example, a doctor had his Mercedes stolen. In a taxi, he lamented his loss, and the taxi driver proposed taking him to a "marabout féticheur." The marabout demanded the sacrifice of a sheep, a goat, and some chickens, and since the doctor followed his advice without question, the marabout upped his demands, promising to make him a millionaire through his *pouvoirs magiques*. The marabout performed tricks with banknotes of dollars and euros—and snakes. He had friends as djinns hidden behind a curtain to answer his questions before the mesmerized and bewitched (*éberlué* and *envoûté*) doctor. The marabout extorted seven million fcfa (US $14,000), but when he demanded a further three million (US $6,000) and that the doctor marry a djinn called Fatoumata Doumbia or risk dying along with two of his children, the doctor realized he was being defrauded.[21] It is often only the exorbitant sums demanded that break the spell and bring about the lawsuit.

These examples are taken from courts in the major cities, which suggests that they represent the mere tip of the iceberg. Nevertheless, the cases are frequent and surprise nobody. They are evidence of the widespread religious imagination on which charlatans can play. Any claimant to powers over the spirits is variously described as marabout, *charlatan, féticheur, maître coranique, faiseur de miracle*. In nearly all cases, the victim is initially convinced by the charlatan's claims and follows his demands completely: *bains mystiques*, prayers, blessed water, talismans, incense, candles, qur'anic verses, rings, sacrifices, and especially offerings. The victim submits himself to the marabout's will: *endormi, hypnotisé, envoûté, ensorcelé, marabouté*; overcome *pas d'armes conventionnelles*. The victims who fall under his power are *comme possédée, ne plus consciente, ne plus maîtresse de mes actes, devenue inconsciente, avant perdu mes esprits, sous l'emprise de cette magie, sous l'emprise de l'envoûtement, n'étant plus en possession de tous mes esprits, ne sachant plus ce que je faisais, ne pouvant pas dire non, victime d'un vraie mystification, avant perdu toute lucidité*.[22] Even if magistrates in most cases find the marabout-charlatans guilty, there seems little doubt that most

---

20. Author's translation. *Le Populaire*, January 24/25, 2015, 10. See also *L'Observateur*, January 24/25, 2015, 4; *Le Populaire*, February 25, 2015, 10; *L'Observateur*, February 25, 2015, 4.

21. *L'Observateur*, February 20, 2013, 4.

22. Author's translation: "as if possessed, no longer conscious, no longer in control of my actions, made unconscious, having lost my mind, under the control of this magic, under his spell, no longer in possession of my wits, not knowing what I was doing, no longer able to say no, victim of genuine mystification, having lost all perception."

observers in court and many of the journalists covering these cases accept that *pouvoirs mystiques* are in play, even if for evil ends.[23]

Let us return to the considerations with which we began, the idea of a *Totalität*. The connotations suggested when talking of "spirit" in the context of Senegal are very different from the connotations of "spirit" in the context of the West, where enchanted religion has ceased to have much traction. Thus, comparing the charismatic movement of, say, the Archdiocese of Dakar with a charismatic group at the University of Minnesota is not as easy as might be thought, because "spirit" in Senegal has such widely different connotations from the same term in Minnesota.

Islamization

If, then, this is Senegal's religion—the detecting, identifying, and controlling of the spirit forces that affect us—complications immediately arise, because nearly all Senegalese would claim to be Muslims. Virtually all marabouts are members of Muslim brotherhoods, and very often the requirements demanded involve recitation of qur'anic verses, or imbibing them. Certainly, one might argue that Islam has an affinity with some of these practices. For example, Mohammed himself cast out demons, which leaves the door open to detecting the influence of spirits and to diverse forms of exorcism. The fact that Mohammed was himself bewitched can even encourage the practice, based on the argument: "How much more vulnerable am I to exactly the same fate?"[24]

Examples of this blending of the traditional worldview with Islam are encountered everywhere, especially around Dakar in the case of the Lebou, closely identified with the Layenne brotherhood. In its origins, the Layenne is probably the least orthodox of the Muslim brotherhoods; the founder, Limamou Laye (1843–1909), claimed to be Mohammed reincarnated for the Black races, his son and successor Seydina Issa Rohou Laye (1876–1949), the reincarnation of Jesus. Over time, these claims have become less prominent, and the tendency has been towards Islamic orthodoxy. Although the Lebou declare themselves Muslim, sacrificial rituals like the annual *Tourou* sacrifice to the protecting spirit of Dakar are an integral part of Lebou identity.[25]

23. Thus, a carpenter immediately accedes to the exorbitant demands of two he meets for the first time in the street; the two *charlatans*, whom he didn't know "ni d'Eve ni d'Adam . . . avaient certainement usé de leurs pouvoirs mystiques." *Le Populaire*, October 8, 2014, 10.

24. Sow, *Le Maraboutage*, 103.

25. In 2011, Wade contributed one million CFA franc to this ceremony, a sum the priestess dismissed as derisory (*L'Observateur*, May 13, 2011, 6).

Many other Lebou ceremonies seem to be traditional with an admixture of Islam. The *Saraxu Ndakaaru* ceremony honors the founders of Dakar. It begins with the reading of the Qur'an twelve times, then the sacrificing of bulls on different sites, with parts of the animals deposited in the sea: "un rituel plein de mystères que l'esprit cartésien ne saurait comprendre."[26] This issue arose with particular clarity with the building of President Wade's controversial Monument of the African Renaissance—the statue of an African couple with child, higher than the Statue of Liberty—that Wade inaugurated on the Dakar skyline in early 2010. The local Lebou community understood traffic accidents in the locality as being caused by local tutelary spirits that were offended. Just days before the monument's inauguration, Wade had to spend two million fcfa (US $4,000) for a public procession and the sacrifice of a white bull and a brown goat at the foot of the statue, and a few days later, two more bulls in a more discreet ceremony.[27]

This fusing of the non-Islamic (even anti-Islamic) with the Islamic seems usually accepted, even unnoticed. We noted that maraboutage is obtrusive in lutte. There exists a manual for lutte, coauthored by a famous trainer and a marabout, well illustrating the fusing of the traditional with the Islamic. It spells out, in some detail, the spiritual arsenal available (blessed water, roots, barks, leaves, incense, and other powders) and their proper use (for drinking, bathing, anointing). Arranging gris-gris around the arena must be done while reciting qur'anic verses seven times and then writing the name Mohammed in the sand. A certain tree should be cut while reciting the sura "Fatiha," and other activity performed while reciting the sura "Bismillah." The *lutteur* himself should prepare by, among other things, sleeping on the ground rather than on a bed, not eating with a spoon, not shaking the hand of a woman, not wearing gris-gris in a cemetery, though wearing gris-gris to Islam's Friday prayers often increases their power. And so on.[28] Sometimes, the syncretism is so obtrusive it causes offense. In the bout we described above, that between Tapha Tine and Balla Gaye II in June 2013, the blatant fusion of qur'anic texts with *fétichisme* actually drew protests from several quarters. A khalife, and member of Senegal's most prominent religious family, denounced the "vulgar and extremely profanatory use of the Qur'an by certain lutteurs"; a Muslim NGO denounced the use of the

---

26. *Le Populaire*, September 21, 2012, 7.

27. *Le Populaire*, March 26, 2010, 7.

28. *L'Observateur*, February 26, 2015, 15. Even in many of the lawsuits mentioned above, the charlatans utilize the Qur'an; see *L'Observateur*, February 18, 2015, 4.

Qur'an for *fins mystique*; and a month later, a protest march to lutte's regulatory body demanded that they stop such abuse of the Qur'an.[29]

Thus, labeling this religion is complicated. What does one call it? Sow suggests that the basic worldview is traditional and often, in large measure, opposed to qur'anic orthodoxy or even to the spirit of Sufi mysticism. It seems hard to disagree with Sow: practices which have been impossible to abolish have been Islamicized.[30] Much engagement with spirits might more strictly be called analogical, participative, or symbolic magic.[31] In this matter, the distinction between religion and magic is hard to draw.[32]

In recent years, the tension has become more evident. There are outside pressures urging a more qur'anic Islam in Senegal, notably Iran and Saudi Arabia, for whom there is little sympathy with Sufism of any sort, much less of the brotherhoods as they operate in Senegal. Saudi- and Iranian-trained and sponsored imams are insistent in their calls for "pure Islam," which often are thinly-veiled criticisms of the form found in Senegal.

Christianity and the Enchanted Imagination

One might ask whether many of the observations just made in regard to Islam apply equally to African Christianity. In Senegal, the enchanted religious imagination seems to affect the Catholic sector as well as the Muslim; thus, a Catholic nun gave nearly thirty-seven million fcfa (US $74,000) to a marabout who had telephoned her out of the blue (given her number by spirits) promising to make her rich.[33] However, there is one obvious difference. If, as just noted, Islam has been largely prepared to accept a blending of Islamic and pre- or extra-Islamic, Christianity is more reluctant. All the mainline churches with their roots in the West and their massive involvement in development have traditionally been very wary of enchanted religion. More, official Catholicism is positively opposed. The Second Vatican Council is best seen in this light: whereas it is sometimes claimed that Vatican II was opening up to all cultures, in fact, Vatican II was bringing Catholicism into line with the modern, Western world. Comoro and Sivalon write: "The worldview and cosmology of pre-Vatican II Roman Catholicism were,

---

29. *Walfadjri*, June 5, 2013, 6; *Walfadjri*, June 11, 2013, 2; *Le Quotidien*, July 6/7, 2013, 2.

30. Sow, *Le Maraboutage*, 58, 347, 33, 40.

31. Sow, *Le Maraboutage*, 228.

32. Sow, *Le Maraboutage*, 36, 46, 58, 59. Riesebrodt similarly discounts any distinction between religion and magic in Riesebrodt, *Promise of Salvation*, 78.

33. *L'Observateur*, May 7, 2012, 4.

in fact, an inculturated understanding based on a culture and consciousness very similar to traditional African culture. Vatican II, while marking an opening up to the world, was in fact opening up to a world, worldview, and culture of modernity that are quite different from African culture. As the church accommodated itself to scientific and secularized culture, it moved dramatically away from the cultures of indigenous people around the world."[34] Catholicism's reluctance to indulge the enchanted imagination gave rise to the phenomenon of "dual allegiance" whereby one goes to Mass on Sundays but slips away on a weeknight to consult a healer-diviner. In my opinion, here lies the explanation for the exceptional success of Pentecostalism in Africa today—finally, a form of Christianity has become acceptable that gives full range to the enchanted imagination.

The Catholic Charismatic Movement (CCM) is sometimes said to do the same. In some countries, the CCM has become integrated into the official church, but in many other countries, it has not. In any event, it is most often a step on the way to fully-fledged enchanted Christianity outside Catholicism, rather than a means of integrating enchanted thinking within officially accepted Catholicism.[35]

This complicates any simple understanding of conversion. Such is the almost paradigmatic status of Paul's experience on the road to Damascus that the word "conversion" normally implies some drastic change in attitudes or worldview. Yet, it is obvious from this short study of Senegal that attitudes and worldview often persist in what might be considered a new religion. In 2012, countless Muslims—by far, outnumbering Christians—attended a crusade in Senegal conducted by the Ghanaian Pentecostal Dag Heward-Mills, not from any desire to turn from Islam to Christianity, but because Heward-Mills's publicity indicated he had more power over spiritual realities than local marabouts; Heward-Mills insists he has raised the dead.

Sharing what is, in essence, the one religious vision is quite compatible with fierce identification with either Islam or Christianity. These different allegiances can even serve as markers of identity in armed conflict, though only in a very loose sense could such conflict be called religious.

Sow notes the reluctance to analyze this enchanted religion. As remarked above, when he began, he could find no books to draw on. This reluctance to address the issue captures my reservations with inculturation theologians; it would seem this would be the first thing they might cover. I suspect I know

---

34. Comoro and Sivalon, "Tanzania," 170.

35. For the Catholic Charismatic Movement, see Gifford, *Christianity, Development and Modernity in Africa*, 118–21.

why they don't. African theologians, with their priority of asserting African culture, are determined not to draw attention to witches and spirits that the West dismisses as superstition. They are writing for the West, where the idea that spiritual forces cause events has ceased to have much force.[36]

Mary Douglas has written: "Doctrines about sin and evil are not minor, peripheral matters. On such a central issue the church in the industrial West is isolated. It does not believe in the devil. Should it, can it impose its historically unique view, peculiar to certain intellectual circles in the West, upon the rest of the Church? Trying to talk to African philosophers and theologians about the place of sorcery beliefs in Christianity, I received the strong impression that the subject was delicate. They are very aware of the disbelief of their fellow Christians from the West. They do not want to quarrel or expose themselves to ridicule, so their ways of dealing with the devil are driven underground. A frank discussion of sorcery and Satanism is only just beginning to emerge." She concludes: "My personal view is that the Third World theologians should take up these problems without regard to the contemporary bias of Western theology . . . The teaching on evil will come from Africa, and that is what Africanization will mean."[37]

Assessing Enchanted Religion

What can one say about enchanted religion? Much depends on what level one addresses it. I am an old-fashioned ethnographer. I try to study the phenomenon, establish the reality, and describe it. This is very different from addressing the issue on a theological level. A Catholic theologian has a different agenda. A theologian could hardly argue that the enchanted religious imagination is incompatible with Christianity. In fact, most forms of Christianity throughout history have surely been enchanted. Peter Brown has even claimed that, for early Christianity, the greatest single reason for its triumph was that it was superior to its rivals precisely in its claim to have conquered the spirits so threatening to inhabitants of the late Roman empire.[38] Such thinking was prominent in the West until relatively recent times. In his *Enchanted Europe: Superstition, Reason, and Religion 1250–1750*, Cameron has shown that nearly all the elements comprising enchanted religion were once common in Europe: the changeling, or human child replaced by a demonic one; ingesting a demon through food; sexual intercourse between spirits and humans; the "evil eye"; charms and spells;

---

36. A notable exception is Udelhoven, *Unseen Worlds*.
37. Douglas, "Devil Vanishes," 95–99.
38. Brown, *World of Late Antiquity*, 55.

hybrid practices in which rituals were combined with particular herbs; rituals to counter hostile sorcery; spirit possession and exorcisms; physical objects or fetishes considered specially empowered; divination through apparitions and dreams and through lots (like bones); omens; out-of-body flight with demonic forces; the demonic insertion of foreign matter into humans; pacts with demonic agents.[39] And unlike the Iranians and Saudis arguing that this imagination is un-qur'anic, a Christian theologian could not argue that it is unbiblical; one determined to do so can obviously find it in the Bible, as I have recently shown in the case of the prominent Nigerian Pentecostal Daniel Olukoya.[40]

But there is another level on which the enchanted imagination can be addressed—on the level of Development Studies, if one can so label a discipline. I would argue that the world has changed in the last couple of centuries, and one of the most remarkable features of that change is the superseding of the enchanted imagination by a functional rationality which seeks specific means to specific ends. The world now operates on principles different from those underpinning the enchanted religious imagination, principles which have led to penicillin, air travel, and computers (and, of course, nuclear arms, chemical warfare, and global warming). If Africa is to join that world, what place is there for the enchanted religious imagination? Sow can study the phenomenon with considerable empathy but claims this way of imagining reality belongs to another age, something which must change if Senegal is to join the modern world.[41] The enchanted world is not a world of established physical laws but one in which anything can be done, or undone, provided one finds the right marabout.[42] For Sow, what he calls a "recrudescence" of this imagination, far from developing the country, threatens to plunge Senegal into obscurantism.[43] A six-month jail sentence in 2007 for penis snatching—defended by the tribunal president on the grounds that "Africa has its own realities and mysteries"—Sow calls a "regression," both

---

39. Cameron, *Enchanted Europe*.

40. Gifford, "Contemporary Nigerian Reading," 38–56.

41. Sow, *Le Maraboutage*, 318, 322, 345, 378–79. Probably his biggest charge is that this enchanted imagination lessens human responsibility. Even a short time in the law courts reveals that a standard plea is that of diminished or even no responsibility. One accused of adultery attributed her lapses to the mystic powers of her partner. A woman is possessed by djinns to rob her boss. A man is bewitched to commit indecency on a minor. Another is marabouté-ed to commit bestiality and pedophilia. Another is possessed by Satan to kill his daughter. A woman accused of infanticide claims she was possessed by Satan. A bank cashier hands over twenty-five million fcfa (US $50,000) to a client who bewitched her with a piece of animal horn. And so on.

42. Sow, *Le Maraboutage*, 16, 130.

43. Sow, *Le Maraboutage*, 226, 347, 345, 347.

worrying and stupefying.⁴⁴ This brings us back to the debate on inculturation; while some insist that the only way forward is reinforcing traditional culture, others see the only way ahead as functional rationality. This latter is the view of one Senegalese observer: "The one and only way to ensure the economic and social development of a country is the quest for academic excellence in science and technology by the single route of education and training."⁴⁵ For him, countries advance not through invoking spiritual forces but through scientific and technological education. Is it too much to say: theologically speaking, there is obviously no contradiction in an enchanted Catholicism, but for one who wants Africa to take its rightful place in today's world, enchanted Christianity raises considerable problems.

Conclusion

In these pages, I have sought to argue that elements of a culture form a *Totalität*, and isolating one element of a culture and making it stand alone without reference to the other elements which give it meaning can be rather distorting. "Spirit" is one such element. In much of Africa, spirits are embedded in a worldview very different from that prevalent in the West. Spirits are lived and experienced. They are not abstractions but ineluctable realities, encountered in every aspect of daily life, to be feared and used. The contrast with the West is stark. To compare the one reality from such different contexts is far from easy.

Bibliography

Brown, Peter. *The World of Late Antiquity*. London: Thames and Hudson, 1971.
Cameron, Euan. *Enchanted Europe: Superstition, Reason, and Religion 1250–1750*. New York: Oxford University Press, 2010.
Comoro, Christopher, and John Sivalon. "Tanzania: Marian Faith Healing Ministry." In *Popular Catholicism in a World Church: Seven Case Studies in Inculturation*, edited by Thomas Bamat and F. Wiest, 157–82. Maryknoll, NY: Orbis, 1998.
Douglas, Mary. "The Devil Vanishes." In *Mary Douglas: A Very Personal Method: Anthropological Writings drawn from Life*, edited by Richard Fardon, 95–99. London: Sage, 2013.
Fall, Abdoulaye. "La lute 'sénégalaise' a fait reculer la société sénégalaise," *Le Quotidien*, February 26, 2013.
Gifford, Paul. *Christianity, Development, and Modernity in Africa*. London: Oxford University Press, 2016.

44. Sow, *Le Maraboutage*, 117.
45. Fall, "La lute 'sénégalaise'," 5.

———. "A Contemporary Nigerian Reading of the Bible." *Journal of Theology for Southern Africa* 152 (2015) 38–56.

———. "Religion in Contemporary Senegal." *Journal of Contemporary Religion* 31 (2016) 255–67.

Nineham, Dennis. *Christianity Medieval and Modern*. London: SCM, 1993.

Riesebrodt, Martin. *The Promise of Salvation: A Theory of Religion*. Chicago: University of Chicago Press, 2012.

Sow, Ibrahima. *Le Maraboutage au Sénégal*. Dakar: IFAN/CAD, 2013.

Udelhoven, Bernhard. *Unseen Worlds: Dealing with Spirits, Witchcraft, and Satanism*. Lusaka: FENZA, 2015.

PART FOUR

Prosperity and Poverty

12

Poverty and Prosperity: Comparing Pentecostal Protestant and Charismatic Catholic Groups' Values and Attitudes in Brazil

Cecília L. Mariz

Introduction

There is a considerable literature discussing the relationship between the Pentecostal-Charismatic movement and economic prosperity and poverty in contemporary scholarship. These studies address two main questions. Some authors discuss the special appeal that this movement has to poor people, mainly the inhabitants of countries of the global South.[1] Another group of researchers also investigate the consequences in people's lives of the teachings and promises of prosperity preached by several Pentecostal and Charismatic groups and churches.[2] Part of this literature turns to the theology of prosperity (or, the "health and wealth" gospel), which asserts a strong link between individuals' material success and their proximity to God.

In contemporary societies, individual economic success is highly valued, and the desire for material prosperity is legitimate and supported by almost everyone. However, religious discourse in society, especially within the more established Christian groups, has historically taken the stance of relativizing material wealth's value. So, in this sense, religions offer alternative values that contrast with those of the secular world. Indeed, religions are sometimes accused of alienating people and discouraging them from

---

1. For example, see Chesnut, *Born Again in Brazil*; Corten, *Os Pobres*.
2. For example, see Heffner and Berger, *Global Pentecostalism*.

earning money or fighting for better lives.[3] The theology of prosperity seems to go in the opposite direction. Pentecostal and Charismatic churches and groups that are oriented toward this theology place a high value on prosperity in this world, and spiritual relativization would be weaker, or even nonexistent, in these communities. In this chapter, I call attention to the fact that, despite the many Pentecostal Charismatic groups that value individual economic prosperity, there are some that emphasize the complete opposite. Instead of valuing individual prosperity in this world, they make a vow of poverty. Although this group is a minority, it deserves to be analyzed in comparison with the prevailing discourse of prosperity. This comparison may help in understanding what is at the core of Pentecostal Charismatic spirituality and how that relates to valuing prosperity.

Some of the ideas I present here were inspired by observations made during research I carried out with colleagues in Rio de Janeiro between 2003 and 2006. At that time, our attention was drawn to two religious groups with Pentecostal and Charismatic inclinations who were engaging in social work with street dwellers: Toca de Assis, a Catholic community aiming to mobilize young people from the Catholic Charismatic Renewal (CCR) and a group from a Brazilian church known as the Universal Church of the Kingdom of God (UCKG). These groups differ radically in many respects, but the most striking divergence was in their attitudes toward individual poverty and economic prosperity. While the consecrated members of the Catholic group (Toca) make vows of poverty, the UCKG is well-known for preaching an "outlandish type of prosperity theology,"[4] especially in Brazil and Africa.[5] In Brazil, their televised sermons were often interwoven with "testimonies" of people who said they once were very poor and plagued by various evils but that, after joining the UCKG, their lives changed, and they prospered.

This comparison attempts to contribute to understanding the very marked, visible diversity within Pentecostal Charismatic spirituality; everyone who has studied this religious movement has noticed it.[6] Such wide variety reflects the different socioeconomic, cultural, historical, and ecclesial contexts in which each group or church has flourished. Although diverse,

---

3. In chapter 7 of D'Epinay, *Haven of the Masses*, one of the first books about this subject, Pentecostalism is described as a hindrance to social and economic individual improvement.

4. Mesquita, "Em Busca da Prosperidade"; Mafra, *Na Posse da Palavra*.

5. About UCKG's theology of prosperity teachings in Africa, see Van de Kamp, "Violent Conversion"; and Van Wyk, "All Answers."

6. For example, see the following works: Bergunder, "Cultural Turn"; Attanasi and Yong, *Pentecostalism and Prosperity*; Maxwell, "Social Mobility and Politics."

Pentecostal Charismatic spirituality has a central core of beliefs, which make it possible for this movement to expand globally. In this chapter, I highlight some of these beliefs.

Comparing the two aforementioned social work experiences is, therefore, merely a starting point in the search for differences and similarities between the UCKG and Toca de Assis. The distinctions between them illustrate that the Pentecostal Charismatic spirituality can give rise to a multiplicity of social practices and beliefs. Because these groups are so different from each other in so many ways, a comparison between them may seem rather strange and unproductive. However, through this comparison, I intend to show that they share some cognitive presumptions, which stem from their Pentecostal Charismatic background, about the relationship between the individual and God.

In search of a better grasp of the diversity within Pentecostal and Charismatic Protestant spirituality, scholars and intellectual Protestant leaders created distinct categories; those used in Brazil, for example, are *neo-Pentecostal* and *igreja renovada* (renewed church). Because this spirituality is very dynamic, with new trends and churches constantly emerging, these categorizations must be constantly revised. There is also great variety within the Catholic Charismatic Renewal, and this is illustrated in Brazil, at least, by the plurality of lay and clerical leaders who have founded prayer groups and "new communities."[7] Each of them claims to have received special "charismas" and, thus, distinct missions and callings. This diversity certainly exists, however, within the limits imposed by the unity of the Catholic Church and obedience to the pope. The two groups I am comparing are both special types within the Pentecostal Protestant and Charismatic Catholic field; the UCKG is considered a neo-Pentecostal church, while Toca de Assis is a church renewal project. I will first describe each group and its social work and then, highlight their similarities.

The UCKG and Its Social Work

Founded in 1977 in Rio de Janeiro, the UCKG has since spread to various parts of the world. In Brazil, it is probably the most studied church and has been the subject of much academic research, including a large number of doctoral dissertations and masters' theses. The UCKG's presence in the media and in politics, as well the proliferation of its churches, which are sometimes luxurious, draws attention and raises many questions. Its history, its

---

7. Carranza et al., *Novas Comunidades Católicas*.

founder's profile, and its pastors and members in Brazil, as well as in several other countries, have been widely discussed in various publications.[8]

As mentioned earlier, the UCKG strongly emphasizes prosperity theology. Its bishops and pastors teach that the believer can achieve prosperity by having faith and attending church, tithing, and giving offerings. Moreover, they preach that rituals of "liberation," or "deliverance," enhance prosperity, because they drive out demons and "poverty-causing" evil spirits. In Brazil, evil spirits are generally identified as spirits of the Afro-Brazilian religions (orishas and others). By expelling these spirits, UCKG leaders integrate dominion theology and prosperity theology. They assert that people's ancestral non-Christian religious traditions are responsible for some kind of curse that leads the individual to experience several types of suffering, including poverty. Because of such pronouncements, the UCKG leaders have received heavy criticism from various sectors of society. There are criticisms of the UCKG's intolerance toward other religious groups and traditions, as well as criticisms of its emphasis on ritual and on exchanging money for miracles. Critics say that, by adopting these practices, the UCKG is moving away from Christianity and other ethical and salvation religions. Moreover, according to these critics, the UCKG's strong emphasis on economic success and the great value it places on consumerism and money go against the Christianity that it claims to preach.

In 1997, the UCKG created the Associação Beneficente Cristã (ABC; in English, the Christian Beneficent Association)[9] to develop social projects motivating church members to join them as volunteers and give more money.[10] Between 2003 and 2005, while my colleagues and I were researching Toca de Assis and its social work with the homeless in Rio de Janeiro, we found an ABC project for the homeless that was announced in the UCKG's newspaper, *Folha Universal*. The ABC's activities with the homeless were developed as a "joint effort" (they called it *mutirão*) with UCKG members. The association occasionally gathered a large group of volunteers on certain days to meet with the homeless in the streets, giving them food and new clothes. In addition, they could bathe, get a haircut and shave, and have their nails trimmed. They could also receive medicine or bandages if needed. While treating the street dweller's bodies, the volunteers also cared for their souls by praying for deliverance and other graces from God, by singing or praising God with hymns, and by preaching the Word.

8. For example, see Oro et al., *Igreja Universal*; Mafra, *Na Posse da Palavra*; Van de Kamp, "Violent Conversion."

9. The ABC became defunct in Brazil around 2008 but still exists in Africa.

10. For more information on these social projects, see Machado, "Igreja Universal"; Rosas, "As Ações Sociais."

The presumption about this kind of social action was that, after such an emotional spiritual experience, which could last a day or two, several of the homeless people assisted could be free of the evil spirits that caused their illnesses, their addiction to alcohol and/or drugs, or other problems. It was assumed that, by getting rid of these spirits that caused them to lose their jobs and families, the street dwellers could be reintegrated into society. The kind of work that the ABC established with the homeless seemed to assume the possibility of immediately rescuing them from total deprivation and transforming them into Christians, church members, workers, and citizens. The organizers of this social work apparently believed that, through the experience of "liberation," contact with the Word, and changing their physical appearance, the homeless could overcome their problems. UCKG pastors and bishops preach of the possibility that one's life can totally change after a special moment or experience. In UCKG churches and media, one often hears people testifying to the radical and rapid resolution of various problems after an extraordinary experience of liberation. They say that, after a single, powerful religious event, they were cured of a disease or that they recovered from dependence on alcohol and other drugs. Following this event, people would need only to tithe, continue praying, and going to deliverance (or liberation) services in order to keep at bay those evil spirits or demons that controlled them in the past.

The ABC's work with the homeless seems to assume that they can only overcome the problems that put them on the street if they are made to accept Jesus and delivered from their evil spirits. Though the UCKG leaders have not explained why this particular project ended, we can deduce why it was discontinued and replaced by projects of a very different nature. Currently, the main UCKG social project in Rio de Janeiro is called "Social Cement." Directly connected to Bishop Crivella,[11] a senator from the State of Rio de Janeiro and a 2014 candidate for governor there (he reached the second round), Social Cement helps residents of disadvantaged areas to build homes. Along the lines of government projects, this project helps low-income workers and, obviously, has more political benefits than the homeless project. Researchers who study the UCKG's social projects, including the ABC, unanimously connect them to the political aspirations of this church.[12] The ABC itself can be understood as a response to the various criticisms that the UCKG received from the media and other sectors of society. The joint events (*mutirões*) to help the homeless were seen as ways to

---

11. Nephew of the UCKG founder (Macedo), Crivella worked for years in UCKG in Africa.

12. For instance, Machado, "Igreja Universal"; and Mariano, *Neopentecostais*.

improve the UCKG's public image, providing it with positive visibility and legitimacy as a socially useful institution. However, in practical terms of the number of actual individuals who left their homeless street life, this type of project would probably not bring many benefits.

As previously mentioned, the UCKG has now developed other types of projects very different from those with the homeless. Nina Rosas describes another project that is similar to Social Cement called "A Gente da Comunidade" (People of the Community), which supports small business initiatives.[13] According to our field research, both tend to help mainly members who are often in the churches and are closer to the pastors.

Toca de Assis and Its *Pastoral da Rua* (Street Ministry)

The origins and history of the Toca de Assis are quite different from those of the UCKG. It is a Catholic group established in 1994 by Fr. Roberto Lettieri who claimed to have a special calling from God to take care of the homeless. In Campinas, São Paulo, Fr. Roberto invited eight young men who also felt this same calling to live in community, following in the steps of St. Francis of Assisi and dedicating themselves to the poorest of the poor. Since its beginning, Toca has been concerned with the homeless and their problems. Known for his sermons on the importance of the Blessed Sacrament, Mary, and the archangels, Fr. Roberto also used to emphasize the need to pray for those Catholic priests who did not respect the sacrament of Holy Orders they had received and who did not recognize the value of the Blessed Sacrament. His sermons were published on Toca's website and often mentioned the presence of the devil and sin in contemporary society, while also calling attention to the importance of sacrifices and prayers. For unannounced reasons, in 2009, Fr. Roberto was removed from the leadership of the group, which initiated a crisis that resulted in Toca losing a large number of its members and closing several of its houses. The community survived the crisis, however, and kept working with the homeless. Though less numerous, new members continue to join Toca, making vows (including a vow of poverty), and being "consecrated."[14]

Toca de Assis is the group's nickname, but officially, it refers to itself as the *Instituto de Vida Consagrada Filhos e Filhas da Pobreza e do Santíssimo Sacramento* (Institute of Consecrated Life: Sons and Daughters of Poverty

13. For more information about this project, see Rosas, "As Ações Sociais."
14. For more about the survival of Toca de Assis after the removal of Fr. Roberto, see the following works: Medeiros, *Juventude e Religião*; Medeiros and Mariz, "Toca de Assis em Crise"; Fernandes and Souza, "As Moças e os Pobres."

and the Blessed Sacrament). This official name expresses the purpose as well as the "charisma" of the community. Its members explained that they were following the canonical paths to become a new Catholic order whose callings were the perpetual adoration of the Blessed Sacrament and caring for the homeless. When the founder was still the group's administrator, members were supposed to kneel for two hours a day in front of the Blessed Sacrament. They did so by taking turns in a twenty-four-hour relay in order to keep perpetual adoration. Such charisma involved physical suffering for the members; they mentioned experiencing fatigue and pain in their knees. Thus, this group ran counter to various contemporary spiritualities. Its practices more closely resembled those of medieval Catholic groups, or Catholic groups in rural Brazil such as *Ave de Jesus* ("Hail, Jesus") in Juazeiro do Norte Ceará, a group described by Roberta Campos.[15]

Since the departure (or removal) of its founder, Toca has undergone several transformations. Nowadays, the sacrifices demanded of members are much less strict. While they still go to the chapel daily to worship the Blessed Sacrament, they no longer need to kneel for two hours. Under Fr. Roberto, much more sacrifice was asked of them in order to perform Toca's second "charisma," that of caring for the homeless. Despite the value they place on sacrifice and pain,[16] they told researchers that they were very happy and that their lives were full of joy. For them, pain and sacrifice did not necessarily involve sadness. On the contrary, being able to withstand these experiences of suffering can generate a sense of personal strength and unity with others and with God that can elicit euphoria.

In contrast to most Pentecostal and Charismatic groups, Fr. Roberto and Toca follow a kind of Christianity that is closer to the Weberian ideal type of "otherworldly" religion oriented toward the transcendent realm. This otherworldliness is quite evident in Toca's first charisma, the adoration of the Blessed Sacrament, but it is also noticeable in the second charisma as Toca's members recounted in their experience of helping the homeless. In Fr. Roberto's time, the interviewed members said that the aim of this work was also to try to be closer to Jesus, who was not only in the Blessed Sacrament but also in the worst suffering among the neediest.[17] Evaluating their social work, they give more emphasis on the spiritual value of the

---

15. Campos, *Quando a Tristeza é Bela*.

16. For more details on their value on pain, see Pinto, "A Loucura da Cruz"; Portella, "Em Busca do Dossel Sagrado."

17. Medeiros, *Juventude e Religião*, 89–91.

hardship they had faced during their work than the positive results for those who they tried to help.[18]

Unlike the ABC's occasional joint efforts, Toca carried out its work with the homeless in small groups twice a week or even more frequently. This work also differed from that of the ABC (or the UCKG) in that it was not focused on getting the homeless off the streets. In interviews, Toca members commented that these street dwellers generally grappled with drug problems and/or mental illness. They mentioned that some of them were able to leave the streets but only for a while. Nevertheless, Toca's people did not see their work as a failure, because they assigned it a spiritual meaning following the example of Jesus Christ.

Also unlike the ABC, which no longer exists in Rio de Janeiro, the Toca community still exists and continues to focus on homeless assistance. Nevertheless, the way they carry out work has changed in several respects, most notably after the departure of its founder. Some male Toca members recalled spending nights sleeping on the streets with the homeless.[19] At the time, these experiences of suffering were highly esteemed in their speeches. In addition, they used to believe that they did not need training for this kind of work, even when providing health care; they believed that they just needed to be inspired by God. As Portella[20] observes, some reported that they could make bandages for the homeless to treat wounds with nothing but the inspiration of the Holy Spirit. Because they had no prior nursing training, some even treated the wounds without wearing gloves, so that the homeless would not interpret the gloves as some sign of disgust or rejection of them. The homeless complained that nurses at public hospitals loathed them. Medeiros also points out that one Toca member commented that she had been alerted to the importance of using gloves and that its purpose is to protect the patient.[21]

At that time, Toca members would also bring the homeless to sleep on their beds in Toca's *Casas de Acolhida* ("Hospitality Houses"), or shelters, while they would sleep on the floor.[22] After Fr. Roberto was removed, these kinds of practices were suspended. They stopped not only because Toca's new leaders (supervised by the Catholic hierarchy) reevaluated some aspects of their radical lifestyle but also because of state requirements for social work.

18. Mariz and Lopes, "O Reavivamento Católico," 94, 96–97.
19. Medeiros and Mariz, "Toca de Assis em Crise," 148.
20. Portella, "Em Busca do Dossel Sagrado," 145–46.
21. Medeiros, *Juventude e Religião*, 181–82.
22. For example, see Medeiros, *Juventude e Religião*; Mariz and Lopes, "O Reavivamento Católico."

Government agencies have more effectively controlled social work activities and closed most of Toca's homeless shelters for not meeting the required standards.[23] Nevertheless, Toca continues its daytime and nighttime street work. The latter is only possible, as Igor Accioly observed in his study in Niteroi (Rio de Janeiro State), thanks to unconsecrated Catholic lay people who volunteer alongside two Toca girls.[24] Nowadays, the group goes to the streets to distribute soup or other food and to talk and pray with the homeless, but no one stays to sleep on the street with them or brings them home. On Saturday mornings, the Catholic lay volunteers and the Toca group offer the homeless a place in a parish where they can take a shower.

As mentioned, several of Toca's shelters were closed for not meeting the standards of the Organic Law of Social Assistance (*Lei Orgânica de Assistência Socia,* or *LOAS*) issued by the federal government, which, in recent years, has been increasingly concerned about regulating social work. Toca's social work also faced problems, because the community became smaller; after the founder's departure, membership dropped sharply. Furthermore, after all the changes Toca experienced, its members seemed to perceive different aims for the social work with the homeless and to give it a different meaning. In the research they carried out after the founder's departure, Fernandes and Souza[25] commented on female Toca members' reports about the homeless, mentioning how some did recover and how they managed to get them back in touch with their families. The researchers did not mention hearing any references to the importance of suffering, as they had previously.

In recent decades, several of the "new communities" that have emerged from CCR in Brazil ask their consecrated members to take a vow of poverty, but most of these communities do not intend to be religious orders. They have different discourses and lifestyles. Most of them do not necessarily have these pre-Vatican II elements of Catholicism. In their words, they have "different charismas."

Although Toca de Assis's proposal is a specific one, in Rio de Janeiro there is another community that is similar called *Preciosa Vida* (Precious Life). Like Toca, it was also created by a CCR priest, Fr. Geovane Ferreira da Silva, and intends to become a Catholic order. Fr. Geovane is attracting mostly young people from his parish in a *favela* (slum) located in an area of Rio de Janeiro known as Complexo da Maré. There in Preciosa Vida's main house, the consecrated members live together in small houses (as with Toca,

23. Medeiros, *Juventude e Religião*; Medeiros and Mariz, "Toca de Assis em Crise," 150–51; Accioly, *Os Caminhos da Santíssima Pobreza.*
24. For more information, see Accioly, *Os Caminhos da Santíssima Pobreza.*
25. Fernandes and Souza, "As Moças e os Pobres."

there are separate homes for men and women); wear habits (like nuns and monks do); take vows of poverty, obedience, and chastity; and adopt new names. Before creating the Preciosa Vida community, Fr. Geovane even sent youths from his parish to join Toca de Assis, as one Precious Life member recalls in his testimony, which is available on the group's website. Also available there is the community's history and the recollections of Fr. Geovane, which note that he created this community in 2006. By 2015, there were twenty-six consecrated members in seven houses (fourteen males and twelve females). The community also had thirty-two members—*Oblatos* (Oblates)—who did not live together. The same Toca spirituality that emphasizes suffering can be seen in the new names adopted by those consecrated.[26] And Preciosa Vida's main "charisma" is also to work with the marginalized of all kinds, including drug addicts and the homeless. Currently, as its website states, it also carries out other tasks, including running a nursery.

An analysis of the speeches by Pentecostal and Charismatic leaders (both Protestant and Catholic) on social service performed by their churches and religious groups revealed that the majority of social assistance programs they develop involve caring for those addicted to alcohol and drugs, including the homeless. They believe that these people (primarily alcohol and drug addicts) need much more than material goods; they need God.[27]

Similarities between the UCKG and Toca de Assis: Sharing Cognitive Presumptions

Despite their enormous differences, the UCKG and Toca have their roots in a Pentecostal-Charismatic kind of Christianity, in which God shares his love and power with human beings by distributing the Holy Spirit's gifts. Through healing and prophesying, among other gifts, people would be able to know God's will. Both the UCKG and Toca would agree that, in receiving God's gifts (or charismas), human beings can be so close to God that their aspirations and desires are identical to God's will and plan for them.

In their view, God surely wants joy and happiness for everyone. However, joy and happiness are not the opposite of pain and suffering; the Charismatic-Pentecostals would argue that individuals experience happiness and joy while struggling to reach God's aims because they are sure of the fulfillment of God's will, which is also the fulfillment of their own dreams.

---

26. These include names such as Sister Maria Pia das Graças do Sofrimento de Jesus Crucificado and Brother Tarcísio Matias de Maria Imaculada e da Paixão do Senhor. Both names refer to Jesus' death and sufferings.

27. Mariz, "Ação Social de Pentecostais," 8 and 11.

Both UCKG and Toca members say that waging this struggle brings them happiness. The expression "victory in God" is commonly used in this sense by Brazilian Pentecostals in general, as well as the UCKG.

For Charismatic-Pentecostals, therefore, a person who is faithful to God is one who not only affirms God's existence but takes action relying on God's power. Thus, those who have faith should risk everything, perhaps every day, to be able to fulfill God's will; they cannot have fears or doubts about the actualization of their dreams. Researchers point out that, according to UCKG leaders, believers must accept challenges (*desafios*). In more than one service, I heard pastors propose that those present should not hesitate to pass the UCKG a bad check, because if they had faith, they could be sure that God would put funds in their bank account before the check was cashed. Moreover, members of Toca would take risks for their faith. When they slept on the street, they risked acquiring a disease or suffering violence, such as being submitted to hazing. They also counted on God's "providence" for their survival. They used to say they "knew" that all their needs would be met; they recounted times when, once or twice, the food in their house had just run out, and they received a new, unexpected donation.

For those who adhere to a Charismatic Pentecostal spirituality, God's plans are not necessarily mysterious and unknown. On the contrary, everyone can come to know those plans, and by praying, receive "revelations" (*revelações*) of them. When Fr. Roberto headed the Toca community, he discouraged theological studies, and similarly, the UCKG used to preach "liberation from theology." The UCKG does not have, and never had, a Sunday school, though it is common in other Pentecostal and Protestant churches in general. Access to the knowledge of God's will and design for the world or for each person is possible through praying and experiencing the Holy Spirit's gifts; thus, there is no need to study canonical teachings offered by the hierarchy. The experience with the sacred, therefore, tends to foster a certain individual autonomy but not necessarily one that results in isolated, individual religious practice. This belief—that anyone can know God's plans—also allows for the emergence of leaders, or persons who, by their special virtues, are considered to have more access to the sacred and to God than others. Thus, Charismatic and Pentecostal spirituality stimulates the emergence of individuals perceived as possessing special gifts and who may become leaders that inspire great respect and even passion from their followers.

In Brazil's CCR community, several leaders have appeared, including some priests, as in the case of Toca founder, Fr. Roberto. Toca members, who are mostly young,[28] would speak of him with a fervent veneration.

---

28. Almost all whom we met were younger than twenty-five years old when Fr. Roberto was the head of Toca. Mariz and Lopes, "O Reavivamento Católico," 97–98.

While he was still in charge of Toca, there were pictures of him all over Toca's houses, along with pictures of the saints (including Fr. Pio). Fr. Roberto's pictures and words were also amply available at Toca's website, but with his removal in 2009, this, too, changed. Among Brazil's emerging CCR leaders, there are also lay people, men and women, who are described as spiritually gifted people. Some are supported by the hierarchy; others are not. The same happened with priests; there are some who are not supported by the institutional Church. Among them are some who supposedly have had visions of Our Lady, and several studies have shown a relationship between the CCR and new apparitions of Our Lady in Brazil.[29] Evidently, some of these leaders, though not all, face problems related to the Catholic Church. There is a great diversity of leaders' profiles and proposals, and as Steil points out, CCR may be a "revolving door for the Catholic Church,"[30] because through it, people enter (or re-enter) and leave.

Due to its dynamism, Pentecostal Charismatic spirituality is constantly fostering new leadership. However, because there are so many leaders, they cannot all attract large followings. Even those who do attract many followers do not necessarily keep all of them for a long time. Reinforcing the individual's direct relation to God, this spirituality is consequently very dynamic and, above all, fosters the autonomy and power of the individual to question some aspects of the status quo.

Bishop Macedo, who founded the UCKG, has passionate followers; nevertheless, his church sees high turnover—many come and many leave. Moreover, some bishops and pastors of this church broke with him, as was the case with Valdomiro Santiago, founder of a new church, the Igreja Mundial do Poder de Deus (World Church of the Power of God), which is similar to and competing with the UCKG. Santiago, in turn, has inspired such veneration that people seek out the handkerchiefs he uses to wipe away his sweat while preaching; they pay for them, believing they are full of grace.

This spirituality, therefore, may foster ruptures, because it gives its adherents the strength and courage to go against the majority and the status quo, not only of the church but also of society. For Clara Mafra,[31] the UCKG speeches (as well of speeches of other Pentecostals in general) express the value of their marginal position in a hegemonic society. Likewise, Toca members recall with some pride that their parents, relatives, and friends were shocked by their decision to join the group and wondered if they had gone crazy. They believe that their closeness to God causes this rejection

29. For example, see Steil et al., *Maria Entre os Vivos*, 32, 180, 235–36.
30. Steil, "Renovação Carismática Católica," 182.
31. Mafra, *Na Posse da Palavra*, 54–58.

and marginalization, and they quote the Bible on the importance of being a bit mad. They believe they are, in a sense, outcasts, but they are proud of being outcasts for having chosen their particular path.

For both groups, and for those who share Pentecostal Charismatic spirituality in general, God relates to human beings in a way that allows each individual to have the strength to break with the status quo and traditional, institutional authorities. They are able to break with the old discourses, which could be based on old traditions, but conversely, they are able to break with the new values of contemporary society. In their similar social assistance programs, Toca de Assis and Preciosa Vida break with some values of modern society and also break with Church practices introduced after Vatican II. In addition to changing names and wearing habits, Toca men also wear a traditional monk's tonsure. Portella[32] noted that, despite their traditional aesthetic, the behavior of young Toca members—their anti-consumerism and their rebellion against broader society—reminded him of the counterculture youth of the 1960s and 1970s.

In contrast to Toca, UCKG tends to value contemporary society's consumerism and economic success. But this church stimulates other types of rupture. In Brazil, UCKG fosters breaks with some traditional Pentecostal values and behaviors but focuses mainly on the break with the Afro-Brazilian religions. Nowadays, the UCKG messages found online on *Folha Universal* are very similar to those of self-help literature, teaching people to change themselves by overcoming past psychological problems with God's help. By promoting individuals' criticisms and autonomy, the various expressions of Pentecostal Charismatic spirituality encourage individuals to embrace new values and a new way of life. This spirituality tends to stimulate rupture, either with traditional values (as in the case of UCKG) or with modern values (as in the case of Toca). By encouraging individuals' autonomy and efforts to adopt new lifestyles, this spirituality has easily spread throughout areas that are undergoing intense socioeconomic and cultural transformations. Even though (or perhaps because) they share the same cognitive assumptions about how God relates to the individual, Pentecostal Charismatic groups can be very diverse and can sometimes defend opposing values.

A Short Conclusion

The purpose of this chapter was to understand the Pentecostal Charismatic relationship to prosperity and poverty by analyzing the attitudes and values of two very different groups, each of which emerged from this spirituality

32. Portella, "Em Busca do Dossel Sagrado," 154–57, 159, 177.

in very distinct contexts. The discussion's starting point was a comparison of the social work programs the groups carried out with the homeless in the city of Rio de Janeiro. Besides illustrating the diversity among Pentecostal-Charismatics, the comparative analysis of these different groups found that they shared important similarities, notably in the way they encourage individuals to change their lives.

This chapter's main argument is that Pentecostal Charismatic spirituality understands that human beings can individually relate to God, and that through this relationship, they can be free of all social, natural, and supernatural forces that have dominated them before knowing God and before accepting Jesus and the Holy Spirit's gifts. This individualist interpretation of human subjectivity has an elective affinity with the modern capitalist worldview; therefore, as many authors have argued, it can help people better adjust to this society and its values. For that reason, most Pentecostal Charismatic groups can grow and integrate themselves (as well as help to integrate individuals) in this society, reinforcing the value it places on individual economic social prosperity and aspirations for upward social mobility, but these values originated from the social contexts out of which most of those groups grew. In other contexts, such as some Catholic and clerical ones (for example, the case of Toca), opposite values, such as the vow of poverty discussed here, may develop among those inspired by the Holy Spirit.

Bibliography

Accioly, Igor. *Os Caminhos da Santíssima Pobreza: Um Estudo sobre a Pastoral de Rua da Toca de Assis*. Master's thesis, Universidade do Estado do Rio de Janeiro (UERJ), 2015.
Attanasi, Katherine, and Amos Yong, eds. *Pentecostalism and Prosperity: The Social Economics of the Global Charismatic Movement*. New York: Palgrave Macmillan, 2012.
Bergunder, Michael. "The Cultural Turn." In *Studying Global Pentecostalism: Theories and Methods*, edited by Allan Anderson, et al., 51–73. Berkeley: University of California Press, 2010.
Campos, Roberta Bivar C. *Quando a Tristeza é Bela: O Sofrimento e a Constituição do Social e da Verdade entre os Ave de Jesus*. Juazeiro do Norte-CE, Recife: Editora Universitária UFPE, 2013.
Carranza, Brenda, et al., eds. *Novas Comunidades Católicas*. São Paulo: Ideias e Letras, 2009.
Chesnut, R. Andrew. *Born Again in Brazil: The Pentecostal Boom and the Pathogen of Poverty*. New Brunswick, NJ: Rutgers University Press, 1997.
Corten, Andre. *Os Pobres e o Espírito Santo: O Pentecostalismo no Brasil*. Petrópolis: Vozes, 1996.

D'Epinay, Christian L. *Haven of the Masses: A Study of the Pentecostal Movement in Chile*. London: Lutterworth, 1969.

Fernandes, Sílvia R. A., and Elizabeth S. de Souza. "As Moças e os Pobres: Considerações Sobre a Comunidade Feminina 'Toca de Assis.'" *Religião e Sociedade* 34 (2014) 86–113.

Heffner, Robert, and Peter Berger, eds. *Global Pentecostalism in the Twenty-First Century*. Bloomington: Indiana University Press, 2013.

Lindhardt, Martin, ed. *Pentecostalism in Africa: Presence and Impact of Pneumatic Christianity in Postcolonial Societies*. Leiden: Brill, 2015.

Machado, Maria das Dores C. "Igreja Universal: Uma Organização Providência." In *Igreja Universal do Reino de Deus: Os Novos Conquistadores da Fé*, edited by Ari Pedro Oro, et al., 303–20. São Paulo: Paulinas, 2003.

Mafra, Clara C. J. *Na Posse da Palavra: Religião, Conversão, e Liberdade—Pessoal em Dois Contextos Nacionais*. Lisbon: Imprensa de Ciências Sociais do Instituto de Ciências Sociais da Universidade de Lisboa, 2002.

Mariano, Ricardo. *Neopentecostais: Sociologia do Novo Pentecostalismo no Brasil*. São Paulo: Loyola, 1999.

Mariz, Cecilia L. "Ação Social de Pentecostais e da RCC no Brasil: O Discurso de seus Líderes." *Revista Brasileira de Ciências Sociais* 31 (October 2016) 1–16. http://www.redalyc.org/articulo.oa?id=10747709004.

Mariz, Cecília L., and Maria das Dores C. Machado. "Religião Trabalho Voluntario e Gênero." *Revista Interseções* 9 (2007) 309–25.

Mariz, Cecilia L., and Paulo V. Lopes. "O Reavivamento Católico no Brasil e o Caso da Toca de Assis." In *Catolicismo Plural: Dinâmicas Contemporâneas*, edited by Faustino Teixeira and Renata Menezes, 75–108. Petrópolis: Vozes, 2009.

Maxwell, David. "Social Mobility and Politics in African Pentecostal Modernity." In *Global Pentecostalism in the Twenty-First Century*, edited by Robert Heffner and Peter Berger, 91–114. Bloomington: Indiana University Press, 2013.

Medeiros, Katia. *Juventude e Religião: Significado da Adesão e Vivência Religiosa na Comunidade Católica Toca de Assis no Rio de Janeiro*. PhD diss., Universidade Federal do Rio de Janeiro, 2012.

Medeiros, Katia, and Cecília Mariz. "Toca de Assis em Crise: Uma Análise dos Discursos dos que Permaneceram na Comunidade." *Religião e Sociedade* 33 (2013) 141–73.

Mesquita, Wânia. "Em Busca da Prosperidade: Trabalho e Empreendedorismo entre Neopentecostais." PhD diss., Instituto Universitário de Pesquisas do Rio de Janeiro, 2003.

Oro, Ari, et al., eds. *Igreja Universal do Reino de Deus: Os Novos Conquistadores da Fé*. São Paulo: Paulinas, 2003.

Oro, Ari Pedro, and Pablo Semán. "Pentecostalism in the Southern Cone Countries: Overview and Perspectives." *International Sociology* 15 (2000) 605–27.

Pinto, Flávia Slompo. "A Loucura da Cruz: Sobre Corpos e Palavra na Toca de Assis." Master's thesis, Universidade Estadual de Campinas SP, 2012.

Portella, Rodrigo. "Em Busca do Dossel Sagrado: A Toca de Assis e as Novas Sensibilidades Religiosas." PhD diss., Universidade Federal de Juiz de Fora-Minas Gerais, 2009.

Rosas, Nina. "As Ações Sociais da Igreja Universal: Recrutamento e Empreendedorismo no 'A Gente da Comunidade' de Belo Horizonte." *Ciencias Sociales y Religión/ Ciências Sociais e Religião* 14 (2012) 27–51.

Scheliga, Eva L. "Educando Sentidos, Orientando uma Prática: Etnografia das Práticas Assistenciais de Evangélicos Brasileiros." PhD diss., Universidade de São Paulo, 2010.

Simmel, Georg. "The Poor." *Social Problems* 13 (Autumn 1965) 118–40.

Steil, Carlos A. "Renovação Carismática Católica: Porta de Entrada ou de Saída do Catolicismo? Uma Etnografia do Grupo São José em Porto Alegre (RS)." *Religião e Sociedade* 24 (2004) 182–90.

Steil, Carlos A., et al., eds. *Maria Entre os Vivos*. Porto Alegre: Universidade Federal do Rio Grande do Su, 2003.

Van de Kamp, Linda. "Violent Conversion: Brazilian Pentecostalism and the Urban Pioneering of Women in Mozambique." PhD diss., Vrije Universiteit Amsterdam, 2011.

Van Wyk, Ilana. "'All Answers': On the Phenomenal Success of a Brazilian Pentecostal Charismatic Church in South Africa." In *Pentecostalism in Africa: Presence and Impact of Pneumatic Christianity in Postcolonial Societies*, edited by Martin Lindhardt, 136–62. Leiden: Brill, 2015.

Wiegele, Katharina. "The Prosperity Gospel Among Filipino Catholic Charismatics." In *Pentecostalism and Prosperity: The Social Economics of the Global Charismatic Movement*, edited by Katherine Attanasi and Amos Yong, 171–88. New York: Palgrave Macmillan, 2012.

13

The Prosperity Theology of Africa's Neo-Pentecostals: Socioeconomically Transforming or in Need of Transformation?

BEN-WILLIE KWAKU GOLO

Introduction: Locating Africa's Neo-Pentecostals

Constituting one of the fastest growing strands of Christianity in Africa during the 1980s and the 90s[1] and still reconfiguring into diverse forms, Africa's neo-Pentecostals are a brand of Pentecostals in Africa, distinguished from the classical Pentecostals in terms of history and theology. Omenyo[2] and Anderson[3] refer to this brand of Pentecostalism within African Christianity as "African Pentecostalism." The emergence of neo-Pentecostal churches heralded a new wave of evangelicalism in contemporary Africa, which ushered into African Christianity doctrinal and practical pneumatological emphases and certain dimensions of spiritual revivalism reminiscent of the fire from heaven in the book of Acts of the Apostles. Therefore, as I indicated elsewhere, neo-Pentecostals can be defined as "a category of churches that have radically redefined the gospel message and the task and mission of evangelism as a core part of their activities, in response to the Great Commission (Matt 28:19–20)."[4] Scholars are unanimous in dating the emergence of these churches to the aftermath of the evangelical and charismatic renewal

---

1. Ojo, "Transnational Religious Networks," 167–79.
2. Omenyo, "Spirit-Filled Goes to School," 44.
3. Anderson, "African Independent Churches," 22.
4. Golo, "Groaning Earth," 201.

movements that swept over Africa during the late 1960s and 1970s,[5] especially within the historic mission-established churches,[6] usually championed by college and university students in West Africa.[7] It is particularly important to keep in mind the roots of these neo-Pentecostal churches, especially the charismatic churches within earlier evangelical witness movements laid by international Christian student organizations.[8]

These neo-Pentecostals—unlike the broader category "Pentecostals" or "Pentecostalism," which is defined generally in relation to the active "workings of the Spirit in the church"[9] and manifesting in diverse pneumatic phenomena such as prophecy and speaking in tongues—seem to have defied any definite typology. This is because, though generally identified initially as Charismatics,[10] their central defining assumptions and phenomena become rather eclectic as their configurations continue to unfold. Today, the popular forms of these neo-Pentecostal churches manifest themselves as Charismatic churches and neo-prophetic churches and in this study, I use the term neo-Pentecostal in reference to these brands of African Christianity. However, it is important to underscore that neo-Pentecostal identity and confessions extend beyond neo-Pentecostalism into Western mission-established and classical Pentecostal churches, thereby rendering the category "neo-Pentecostal" very heterogeneous, if not entirely confusing. Consequently, there exists a hybridity of theologies and Christian identities in African Christianity today, although largely tilting towards neo-Pentecostal beliefs and claims, and a corresponding mixture of hybrid believers with a consumerist religious orientation.

The above clarification is crucial at this point, because concerns of socioeconomic challenges in Africa and the responses offered initially by Charismatic churches to engage and transform the situation now find a home in almost all shades of Christianity in Africa. It is for this reason that some scholars claim that neo-Pentecostalism is defining the agenda and trajectory of Christianity in Africa. Asamoah-Gyadu's claim with reference to Ghana is an example: "Pentecostalism at the moment represents the most cogent, powerful, and visible evidence of religious renewal and influence in Ghana . . . even the new lease of life being experienced by

---

5. See, for instance, Omenyo, *Pentecost Outside Pentecostalism*, 96; Ojo, "Growth of Charismatic Movements," 90; and Anim, "Prosperity Gospel in Ghana," 31.

6. Omenyo, *Pentecost Outside Pentecostalism*, 95–98.

7. Ojo, "Growth of Charismatic Movements," 92.

8. See the case of Nigeria in Ojo, "Growth of Charismatic Movements," 92.

9. Anderson, "African Independent Churches," 22.

10. Omenyo, *Pentecost Outside Pentecostalism*, 96.

some of the older churches in Ghana is explicable in terms of their, albeit recent, tolerant and open attitude towards Pentecostal phenomena and renewal movements in their midst."[11]

Methodologically, I come to this discussion as an insider who has worshiped with three popular neo-Pentecostal churches over the past nine years, stretching from East London in the UK to Accra in Ghana. These have been periods of deep reflection on the topic under discussion. These reflections have been augmented by conversations and discussions with some neo-Pentecostal believers and a few non-Pentecostals. My focus and examples are drawn from West Africa, the terrain with which I am most familiar.

Socioeconomic Deprivation in Africa and the Promise of Neo-Pentecostalism: Prosperity "Gospeling"

The emergence of neo-Pentecostal churches coincided with a period of social deprivation and economic difficulties in sub-Saharan Africa, especially in the late 1970s and 80s, and this has, to a large extent, influenced their message.[12] It is noteworthy that, in Ghana[13] and Nigeria,[14] when confronted with social and economic challenges and squalor, neo-Pentecostals found it difficult to understand why children of God would be poor in the midst of the abundance promised by God that they read about in Scripture, and have received through salvation through Jesus Christ. What these neo-Pentecostal prosperity preachers grapple with, according to Folarin, are vital issues of how an all-loving, all-holy, all-just, and all-powerful God can "coexist, as he does in the world, with evil."[15] Consequently, neo-Pentecostal prosperity preachers sought to demystify certain teachings of the mainline churches against wealth, for they believe "their salvation entails redemption from poverty and mediocrity."[16]

Listening to and observing neo-Pentecostals closely, at least three forms of poverty to which they responded can be distinguished: structural poverty, self-imposed poverty, and spiritually-imposed poverty. Structural poverty is what neo-Pentecostals acknowledge as socioeconomic poverty caused by mismanagement of the state economic structure, thereby creating problems

11. Asamoah-Gyadu, *African Charismatics*, 14.
12. Larbi, *Pentecostalism*, 50.
13. Omenyo, *Pentecost Outside Pentecostalism*, 96; Larbi, *Pentecostalism*, 49–50, 401; see also Gifford, *Ghana's New Christianity*, 3–19.
14. Ojo, "Pentecostalism, Public Accountability, and Governance," 115.
15. Folarin, "Prosperity Gospel in Nigeria."
16. Golo, "Africa's Poverty," 370.

such as unemployment, accessibility to and affordability of good medical care, a good education, and security. This undoubtedly is one basic reason for the emergence of the prosperity gospels (and not the neo-Pentecostal churches per se) in the first place—they were a response to structural poverty in sub-Saharan Africa.[17] Neo-Pentecostals also acknowledge poverty that is self-imposed due to lack of education and requisite skills, certain socioeconomically destructive attitudes and behaviors such as drinking, smoking, spending beyond your means, extramarital affairs, and indiscipline. Also included in self-imposed poverty is the claim that people are poor because of some sinful act or because they have opted not to pay tithes or give generously to the church or the "man of God" and are being too stingy to God. Poverty can also be spiritually imposed, caused by witches, ancestral curses, demonic spells, and the occult, or any other spiritual entity. Irrespective of the cause and type, neo-Pentecostals believe that any of these can be and are usually induced by Satan as noted by Oyedepo, one of the ardent preachers of the prosperity gospel: "[p]overty mentality is satanic slavery."[18] Thus, Africa's neo-Pentecostal's definition of poverty, encompassing all of the above forms, is based on "interpreting and naming the structures and realities that induce poverty as disguised principalities and powers."[19]

Consequently, one sees that prosperity messages were responses to the difficult socioeconomic situation in sub-Saharan Africa within which neo-Pentecostal churches emerged.[20] Bishop David Oyedepo writes: "The end time church is a prosperous church. So, it is important for you to understand how to prosper in the kingdom, how to enjoy true prosperity. It is not 'God, just give me something to eat and to drink.' No! He wants to make you a blessing, and all the people of the earth shall see it."[21] This has become popularly known as the prosperity gospel or the "health and wealth gospel," which "advocate[s] the importance of wealth as a by-product of Christian salvation."[22] This gospel has accounted for the mass movement of people from historic mainline and earlier African Initiated Churches (AICs) into neo-Pentecostal churches.[23] It is evident that neo-Pentecostalism appeals to droves of believers because of its promise to lift believers from the doldrums of poverty, sickness, and demonic bondage.

17. Larbi, *Pentecostalism*, 50–51.
18. Oyedepo, *Understanding Financial Prosperity*, 14.
19. Golo, "Africa's Poverty," 372.
20. Larbi, *Pentecostalism*, 50.
21. Oyedepo, *Understanding Financial Prosperity*, 6.
22. Asamoah-Gyadu, *African Charismatics*, 205.
23. For instance, see Folarin, "Prosperity Gospel in Nigeria."

It is noteworthy that there is no single monolithic canon to which the prosperity gospels can be reduced.[24] Wariboko,[25] for instance, identified about five paradigms of economic prosperity in Africa: covenant, spiritual, leadership, nationalist, and developmental. Daniels[26] broadly divides the prosperity gospel groups into what he calls the classical prosperity gospel and the pragmatist prosperity gospel. Wariboko places prosperity theology as just one variant of the covenant paradigm (the other being the excellence model). He also admits that other paradigms with their diverse practices and rituals are motivated by the need to fight poverty and usher in economic transformation in Africa; this is because "they consider poverty as the primary economic problem."[27] This demonstrates that the preoccupation of these groups are often concerns about poverty and socioeconomic dependency. Indeed, the diverse and complex yet pervasive nature of prosperity preaching among neo-Pentecostals and other Pentecostal and Charismatic groups in Africa makes any categorization rather tentative, if not impossible.

As a baseline, these neo-Pentecostal prosperity churches preach that, courtesy of the redemptive work of Christ (salvation) and the presence of the Holy Spirit in the world, believers are freed from and have power over situations of sickness, poverty, mediocrity, and bondages to demonic powers, which are capable of inducing the first three conditions. According to Gifford, prosperity preachers teach that "God has met all the needs of human beings in the suffering and death of Christ, and every Christian should now share the victory of Christ over sin, sickness, and poverty. A believer has the rights to the blessings of health and wealth won by Christ . . . ."[28] Going beyond the muteness on spiritual growth in most definitions, Folarin defines the prosperity gospel as "the teaching that the solutions to people's problems of sin, sickness, poverty, and demon oppression are in Jesus Christ."[29] However, its emphasis on health and especially wealth mutes its concern for spiritual growth, thus giving it the rather derogatory name, "health and wealth gospel."

With the core teaching based on the interpretation of 3 John 2,[30] Pastor Mensah Otabil, the general overseer of the International Central Gospel

---

24. Heuser, "Religious-Scapes," 16.
25. Wariboko, "Pentecostal Paradigms," 37–53.
26. Daniels, "Prosperity Gospel," 266–69.
27. Wariboko, "Pentecostal Paradigms," 37.
28. Gifford, *African Christianity*, 39.
29. Folarin, "Prosperity Gospel in Nigeria."
30. "Beloved, I pray that you may prosper in all things and be in health, just as your soul prospers" (NKJV).

Church (ICGC) in Ghana, interpreted this line from Scripture to mean "financial prosperity, material prosperity, and spiritual prosperity"[31] for the believer. This interpretation of 3 John 2 is unanimous among neo-Pentecostals in Africa (and the world as a whole), although the exact meaning and extent of these prosperities remain relative. While some (if not the majority) of prosperity preachers exhibit extravagant and materialistic lifestyles, accumulating financial and material wealth and property, some preach modest prosperity by more generally emphasizing the blessings and possibilities available to believers, courtesy of their salvation in Christ.[32] Therefore, although the extravagant, affluent, and materialistic lifestyles of prosperity gospelers and their ministries betray their emphasis on material and financial prosperity—as plainly seen in the claims of Eastwood Anaba that believers "cannot be paupers in a world created by our heavenly Father"[33]—the prosperity gospels are not limited to material prosperity alone. The prosperity gospels, as is clear in their definitions, also include prosperity in health and in spirit, which is the quest for spiritual growth and the salvation from sin.[34] Prosperity in spirit, which is total salvation from sin and the resolve not to return to sin, is particularly crucial for neo-Pentecostals because it is the fundamental principle required to be in covenant with God before receiving any favor from him.

Prosperity Gospel and Socioeconomic Transformation

What are the prospects of the prosperity gospels for lifting believers out of poverty and leading them into socioeconomic transformation in sub-Saharan Africa? The economic growth potential of the Pentecostal movement has been the subject of debate among scholars and researchers. Some, utilizing Weber's Protestant ethic, express positive sentiments about the socioeconomic prospects of the prosperity gospel,[35] while others question such connections and its potential to have positive socioeconomic effects, especially in Africa.[36] Still others conclude: "we do not yet know if the

---

31. Asamoah-Gyadu, *African Charismatics*, 205.
32. Asamoah-Gyadu, *African Charismatics*, 206.
33. Asamoah-Gyadu, *African Charismatics*, 206.
34. See Folarin, "Prosperity Gospel in Nigeria"; Golo, "Africa's Poverty," 375.
35. See two works published by the Centre for Development and Enterprise (CDE): Bernstein, *Under the Radar,* and Schlemmer, *Dormant Capital*. See also Berger, "Max Weber is Alive and Well," 3–9.
36. Gifford and Nogueira-Godsey, "Protestant Ethic and African Pentecostalism," 5–21.

Pentecostal movement as a whole will bring economic growth,"[37] so the discussion continues on the potential of the movement in general and the prosperity gospel in particular.

At this point, it is important to clarify my understanding and use of the term "socioeconomic transformation." The idea here is not to use this term as a synonym for "development," or even narrowly for what is regarded as economic growth, although my use of the term is related to each. Rather, I am interested in the development discourse that has become integral to any genuine and holistic development and hems into the discourse on the social and life's spiritual dimension of development: human development.[38] The emphasis on human development, which is "a broad category focusing on societal stability, security, and relative prosperity with political, economic, social, moral, and psychological dimensions"[39] is of importance to me, because the majority of believers who attend these neo-Pentecostal churches do not regularly raise questions about theoretical economic growth debates and dimensions of development. Rather, they are concerned about the (micro) socioeconomic context and how it conditions their social lives and aspirations, either constraining or enhancing them. Therefore, using the huge macroeconomic growth picture as a primary point of reference, although necessary, may be unhelpful in appreciating certain basic, fundamental aspects of the lived realities of believers and societies where neo-Pentecostal churches claim their relevance. In other words, as individuals or groups, neo-Pentecostals seem to have a different vision and goal of socioeconomic transformation and/or development. This must not be substituted for the vision and goal of the state, which has as its sole aim to work out a holistic development framework and agenda at both macro and micro levels of society in order to transform the social and economic lives of the citizenry.

Thus, within the context of this work, I understand socioeconomic transformation as those processes and conditions that enhance people and societies, enabling them to participate and benefit fully and equally in society's resources. This includes improving the affordability of the basic life necessities such as health care, education, democratic participation, a clean non-polluted environment, etc., while ensuring the psychological, spiritual, and financial dimensions of people's lives. This definition of socioeconomic transformation also avoids asking too much of neo-Pentecostals. I opted for this approach because, though neo-Pentecostals' goals and aims are not conventionally defined as moving toward the pursuit of national economic

37. Drønen, "Now I Dress Well," 262.
38. Haynes, *Religion and Development*, 3.
39. Haynes, *Religion and Development*, 4.

development, they may still have a functionally augmenting and performance role to play in today's African society. This becomes clearer when one keeps in mind that religious ideals, aspirations, and goals are not entirely different from the modern Western idea of development but are rather a religious (if not even spiritual) expression of and contribution to it,[40] although they unfold along different, at times even conflicting, paths: the secular and the religious. In other words, I understand the modern idea of development and socioeconomic transformation as a secular interpretation of the Christian belief of the possibility of a world that is just and liberating and that engenders a flourishing life—prosperity. Humans must work toward this. It is from this perspective that I assess the socioeconomic transformative potential of neo-Pentecostal theology and dynamics of prosperity.

Assessing the Prosperity Gospel's Socioeconomic Transformative Potential

One would dare say "yes" and "unlikely" if asked whether Africa's neo-Pentecostals, with their prosperity gospel, have potential for socioeconomic transformation both at the micro and macro levels. Considering that most religious people in Africa "have a religious outlook on the world"[41] and also that religious beliefs equip many believers with the "will to improve their lives,"[42] it has been generally suggested that Pentecostal theology has the tendency to enforce attitudes and work ethics that are relevant for socioeconomic development. For instance, Köhrsen suggests that Pentecostal churches emphasize teachings that lead the believer to break with the past and cultivate new moral patterns and behavioral codes, and that these changes are helpful to the convert in the modern labor market.[43] Wasteful behaviors and attitudes which are detrimental to one's socioeconomic standing—such as extramarital affairs, drunkenness, and gambling—have been demonized by neo-Pentecostals, and believers are encouraged to break away from them. Furthermore, some prosperity preachers, such as Otabil, emphasize excellence, diligence, hard work, and investments irrespective of how much one earns.

Because neo-Pentecostals demonize socioeconomically destructive habits such as drinking, smoking, spending beyond one's means, and

---

40. Ter Harr and Ellis, "Role of Religion in Development," 354–55. See also Haynes, *Religion and Development*, 4–5.

41. Ter Haar and Ellis, "Role of Religion in Development," 353.

42. Ter Haar and Ellis, "Role of Religion in Development," 353.

43. Köhrsen, "Pentecostal Improvement Strategies," 58.

extramarital affairs, it has been further suggested that the neo-Pentecostal prosperity teaching has enforced economically transforming lifestyle changes among its believers. It encourages believers to fight against the spirit of poverty and substitute it with an entrepreneurial spirit, such as investing and building entrepreneurial skills, thus spurring them on to engage in business.[44] Yong rightly notes that

> prosperity theology may also have a galvanizing effect, motivating the transformation of economic habits and practices that gradually result in upward socioeconomic mobility. This is particularly in cases involving the informal economy, where many of the urban poor in the 'global South' reside and among whom the global renewal movement has made significant inroads.[45]

Evidently, as is common in Ghana, neo-Pentecostal churches are active in the economic sector where they run businesses and establish structures of socioeconomic relevance. For instance, neo-Pentecostal churches are now visible in Ghana's media landscape, running radio and television stations that not only provide employment opportunities but also advertise local businesses' goods and services. Clearly, the interlocking nature of businesses means that neo-Pentecostal businesses, to a large extent, keep other ones in business. Furthermore, neo-Pentecostal church establishments employ large numbers of people, including their own members, and the many schools and colleges of neo-Pentecostal churches (such as Central University College, owned by the International Central Gospel Church (ICGC)) run courses that both target the market and also provide many jobs for Ghanaians. Some prosperity-preaching neo-Pentecostals in Ghana also engage in social action such as free medical outreach into local communities and rehabilitation centers; regular blood donations; distribution of clothes to the poor; and the building of facilities to support the social lives of communities. For example, the ICGC had water boreholes constructed in nineteen communities of the Ga-West Municipality, and it also provides educational aid called CentralAid that is open to any Ghanaian.

While worrying, the fact that Africa's neo-Pentecostalism resorts to the pneumatic in order to explain the socioeconomic realities of a deplorable economic system can be crucial for the psychosocial stability of its members and other citizens when seen in light of their beliefs. To a large extent, these pneumatic explanations help believers develop values such as hope, patience, and resilience, turning their energies to the anticipation

---

44. Köhrsen, "Pentecostal Improvement Strategies," 58.
45. Yong, "Typology of Prosperity Theology," 28.

that God will carve out a way through their economic uncertainty. This psychosocial role of neo-Pentecostalism, although not limited to Pentecostalism alone, has long-term socioeconomic benefits. Furthermore, the inspiration from prosperity messages and the emphasis on hard work, positive thinking, and resilience are undoubtedly transformative in a socioeconomic sense. Thus, in circumstances where believers and citizens would rather have chosen other courses of action detrimental to socioeconomic development, the "prosperity message will engender hope and perhaps motivate a certain course of action that anticipates the gradual, if not more efficient, overcoming of poverty."[46]

Just as any other faith, the Christian faith is full of mystery and recourse to the supernatural, dimensions of faith unavailable to rational scrutiny and/or falsifiability. In these realms are manifest the benevolence and will of the Almighty God who graciously blesses believers who faithfully and diligently seek God. Consequently, I have no qualms about neo-Pentecostals' seeking God through prayers, giving, and the "sowing of seeds" through tithing in order to touch the heart of God to bless believers in return. However, after a deeper reflection on some aspects of African neo-Pentecostalism's prosperity theology, such as seed sowing, one becomes curious whether these prosperity theologies and churches are able to engender any sustainable socioeconomic transformation in sub-Saharan Africa. This is due to some weaknesses within neo-Pentecostal prosperity theology, three of which I discuss below.

Neo-Pentecostal Wealth-Accumulating Individualism and Wealth Distribution

The extreme, individuated emphasis on material wealth as prosperity comes across as a distortion of what socioeconomic wealth entails. If prosperity, even socioeconomic wealth, were defined as individual wealth accumulation, then that itself creates disharmony between the self and community, thereby creating another problem for socioeconomic transformation in the wider society—in this case, Africa. A phenomenon similar to what Duchrow describes as "property-accumulating individualism" or "money-accumulating individualism,"[47] the individuated material wealth accumulation of the prosperity gospel neo-Pentecostals is not a good recipe for socioeconomic transformation. Instead, it feeds into the individualism that is itself a canker on our contemporary society, where the "Big Man" syndrome festers with a few

---

46. Yong, "Typology of Prosperity Theology," 19.
47. Duchrow, *Alternatives to Global Capitalism*, 51.

elites taking charge of states and building up "enormous wealth at the expense of the ordinary people they purport to serve."[48] This situation, as we shall see, is prevalent in Africa's neo-Pentecostalism. The tendency to define wealth and prosperity through the grids of economic growth markers, measurable in terms of property and material objects, betrays the liberal Western orientation of Africa's neo-Pentecostals and, consequently, their individualist focus. Such orientations end up commoditizing neo-Pentecostalism as a market appropriate for consumption as typified by the hybridity of the neo-Pentecostal identity in Africa today. Indeed, the idea of prosperity as property-accumulating individualism—widespread among prosperity preachers and their followers—reduces a human to a being of wants who is always desirous of affluent materialism and financial security. These desires must be satisfied through following certain covenant principles, which the neo-Pentecostals provide. This view of the person ignores the fact that there are believers who want to live a life of modesty and feel more comfortable with less.

Furthermore, the individualist focus of working out one's prosperity, very characteristic of prosperity gospeling, distorts the relationship and distinction that exists between social and economic well-being which, although related, are not necessarily the same. One is necessary for the realization of the other, and both are crucial for socioeconomic transformation in general. From the African communitarian perspective, wealth cannot be limited to the individual's egoistic accumulation of property and sheer materialism, but to the extent that these are put to use to advance recognizably communal goals and welfare. This is because, for African communities, living according to communitarian norms—rather than self-seeking individualism—is a cornerstone for a healthy society.[49] Similarly, it must be emphasized that Africans seek and value wealth because of the contribution the wealthy person can make to the welfare of the whole community[50] and what wealth can "do for the individual, the members of the family, and the state as a whole."[51] According to African communitarian values and principles, a socioeconomically viable community is one in which wealth easily transcends the individual and is distributed among and shared by other individuals in community, even if just members of the church. It is, thus, unlikely that the accumulation of individual wealth and prosperity, which is definitive of one's social status in today's society,

---

48. Gifford, "Prosperity Theology of Oyedepo," 99.
49. Gyekye, "Person and Community," 102.
50. Gyekye, *African Cultural Values*, 99.
51. Gyekye, *African Cultural Values*, 100.

would be defined as transforming, except in an exploitative manner, creating a society of patrons and clients.

Replicating Africa's Debilitating Economic Structures

Considering the inability of Africa's prosperity preachers to challenge and/or work towards transforming the very structures that induce socioeconomic strife and retardation in Africa, it remains quite debatable whether Africa's neo-Pentecostals are able to engender any genuine socioeconomic transformation. The majority of these preachers crave social and economic power themselves, which they seek to realize through a kind of spiritual capitalism. Consequently, theirs is an engagement in a spiritual capitalism driven by the logic of empire and realized through a theologically shallow but alluring doctrine of commitment to church and leader. Usually, this is achieved through giving, tithing, and seed sowing, whereby wealthy church benefactors are encouraged to give more than they receive financially, and poorer members give what they can materially to church and leader.[52]

It is suggested that these neo-Pentecostals commitments have both positive and negative payoff structures. The positive payoff is reflected in terms of social services: these prosperity preachers and their churches are likely to establish schools and colleges and health facilities. The negative payoff can be seen in exploitative relationships whereby "a Pentecostal form of big man rule can exacerbate the exploitation of common citizens in patron-client relationships, at least in financial terms."[53] I contend that, while exploitation of both unsuspecting wealthy and poor believers has become common among prosperity-preaching churches, even claims of a positive payoff structure (though, to some extent, evidently true as mentioned earlier) are just part of the story. With financial prowess, largely garnered through the preaching of this doctrine, some of these preachers have established socioeconomic structures that unfortunately simply regurgitate the debilitating state systems and structures that induce socioeconomic depravity. Usually, neo-Pentecostal social services are registered as private investments or businesses and can be rather expensive, typically making them affordable only to the wealthy. They may not be accessible to the poor, even within their own church membership.

Based on the above, it becomes clear that the quest for power and status among neo-Pentecostal leaders in Africa—what McCauley refers to

---

52. McCauley, "Africa's New Big Man Rule," 13–14.
53. McCauley, "Africa's New Big Man Rule," 14.

as the "Pentecostal form of big-man rule"[54]—cannot be discounted. This is typified by the structural Pentecostal institutionalization of the wider socioeconomic and political context, where issues of leadership and succession come to the fore. While leadership in most of these neo-Pentecostal churches is usually of the one-man dictatorial hegemonic type, successors are usually a biological or spiritual child of the leader, with the "big man" predecessor still tending to control from the background. Thus, instead of challenging national political leaders for their poor leadership, which clearly is at the root of socioeconomic problems of Africa,[55] neo-Pentecostal leaders instead establish alternate socioeconomic systems over which they superintend and exalt themselves as entrepreneurs and successful people. Ironically, the majority of the systems they establish do not function any differently from those of the state, providing one of the reasons they have no moral grounds to challenge the leaders of the nation state in its failures. One understands, therefore, why Africa's neo-Pentecostal leaders are not able to openly challenge the poor leadership in Africa that has induced socioeconomic despondency in their countries but choose instead to establish alternative economies of a Pentecostal nature. Gifford avers that, amidst a dysfunctional sociopolitical system, Bishop Oyedepo of Nigeria "does little to challenge Nigeria's totally dysfunctional 'Big Man' sociopolitical system."[56] He continues that "it is clear that Oyedepo perpetuates and personifies these dysfunctional structures, as it were institutionalizing them of the religious plane."[57] This affirms the assertion by Wariboko that prosperity preachers are not oriented to social change, as they emphasize self-development and personal wealth accumulation and either replicate the status quo or ignore it entirely.[58]

Furthermore, the lopsided wealth and materialist orientation of the majority of prosperity preachers and their churches complicates their ability to engender any sustained socioeconomic transformation. The preponderance of spiritual empowerment seminars, conferences, and summits, and deliverance and breakthrough sessions organized by neo-Pentecostal churches (including on weekends and national holidays) can be bewildering. Even if one took the productive hours spent on these activities for granted (and there is no reason for doing so), the majority of these "breakthrough" and "empowerment" gatherings are financially draining on church members, as

54. McCauley, "Africa's New Big Man Rule," 11–13.
55. Mills, "Why is Africa Poor?" 2–4.
56. Gifford, "Prosperity Theology," 99.
57. Gifford, "Prosperity Theology," 99.
58. Wariboko, "Pentecostal Paradigms," 36.

excessive demands of money are made on them, in the words of Gifford, to "provoke divine blessings."[59] At times, the financial commitments required of participants raise suspicions as to whether these church arrangements are truly purposed for believers or, instead, for the preachers and their cohorts to make financial gains. Yet, given churches' investments in alluring advertisement strategies, many people regularly attend because they either do not have enough or do not have at all and are desirous of breakthroughs.

Clearly, the structures established by these prosperity preachers themselves are modeled along the principles and "values of an un-checked capitalist economy which is based on unjust power relations and which thrives on the suffering of many."[60] It seems highly improbable that these structures can engender any genuine and lasting socioeconomic transformation, especially for the benefit of the majority poor. Evidently, this runs counter to what the prosperity neo-Pentecostal churches preach, except for the prosperity preachers themselves who become testimonials of what they preach, though the means they used is another subject worth investigating. Commenting on the prosperity model, Wariboko rightly observes that, although with good intentions aimed at providing answers to existential questions posed by people in dire socioeconomic situations, this approach is the least likely to contribute to national development, particularly when "pastor entrepreneurs have hijacked it for filthy lucre."[61]

Tensioning Transforming Faith (Theology) and Rationalized Belief

The idealist nature of the prosperity gospel, in general, can be theologically superficial, biblically misleading, and delusional to the majority of people as well as, in the long term, detrimental to socioeconomic transformation. It is unrealistic to think that all people can come into the level of wealth preached, promised, and displayed by these prosperity preachers. Would God have desired that all believers become prosperous, the way the neo-Pentecostals define it, whether it is in terms of finances or health? Asamoah-Gyadu notes that, while "blessings," "prosperity," "success," "breakthrough," "victories," and "achievements" are recurring themes in neo-Pentecostal preaching and theology, themes such as "suffering, pain, the high cost of discipleship, and the inevitability of death are conspicuously absent."[62]

---

59. Gifford, "Prosperity Theology," 99.
60. Kahl, "Jesus Became Poor," 114.
61. Wariboko, "Pentecostal Paradigms," 40.
62. Asamoah-Gyadu, *African Charismatics*, 206.

Reducing poverty to a spiritual problem, whereby people remain poor because they have not responded positively to the covenant principles of God and/or did not sow into the ministry of the church or pastor (identified as the "good soil"), creates another theological problem. Here, we confront an obvious weakness of prosperity preaching, for it "stands in direct contradiction to the Gospel of the predilection of God for the poor, the weak, and outcasts in society."[63] Neo-Pentecostal preachers teach that one is justified to receive from God through his or her effort and work of committing financial and time resources to the church. This is antithetical to the fundamental Christian claim that justification is by grace through faith in Jesus Christ. Thus, neo-Pentecostals seem to place faith in God's transforming grace in tension with justification by works (rationalized belief). The question here is: what happens when people have done all that they have been taught to do—such as giving, tithing, and seed sowing—yet they still are not able to come into the prosperity they so much desire? Would that be an indictment against God, as it stands contrary to the prosperity-preaching neo-Pentecostals' claims of about God?

Therefore, we encounter a huge theological problem here, as neo-Pentecostals tend to reject or not come to terms with certain negative ontological realities of human existence, which are categories to which poverty and ill health belong. Clearly, it is the inability of human beings to make sense of these realities and/or subject their existence to rationalization that allows God to be God in his sovereignty. However, neo-Pentecostal claims and efforts, through both human agency (secular) and spiritual means, to overturn and reverse these ontological phenomena deny God's sovereignty. This posture is similar to that of a modernist liberal believer who disbelieves the mysteries of the Christian God, which in itself is unbelief (unfaith) and not Christian. It is on this point that prosperity-preaching neo-Pentecostals would be cast in the shadows of theological liberalism. What is becoming apparent is that neo-Pentecostals—just as all human beings who are aware of their vulnerability to the ontological realities of life—have sought to accumulate material possessions as a mechanism and system to safeguard human security.[64] It is not surprising that the covenant prosperity preacher Oyedepo's prosperity theology has been defined as having "more in common with liberal Protestantism, although with Jesus as an exemplar rather than a teacher."[65] Clearly, one of the debated, if not controversial, theological

---

63. Kahl, "Jesus Became Poor," 114–15.
64. Golo, "Engaging the Violence," 326.
65. Gifford, "Prosperity Theology," 98.

developments in contemporary (African) Christianity is the question of the prosperity gospel's orthodoxy and its authenticity. Kahl notes:

> The hermeneutics of the prosperity preachers is marked by a conflationist and isolationist reading of the Bible combined with at times, metaphorical, at times typological exegesis where a literal sense does not support the reading expectation . . . By means of these approaches, any text can assume any kind of desired meaning. Counter-indicative voices of the Bible are silenced. This means that the Bible—in contradiction to inverse claims of a literal understanding by prosperity preachers—is not taken seriously. It is rather (mis)used to fulfill functions within a prosperity discourse.[66]

Kahl thus concludes that "the prosperity messages serve first and foremost the function of having the preachers' material need and greed be fulfilled by spiritually misleading their congregants: Prosperity Gospel, works best for prosperity preachers,"[67] as they become "prime examples of successful believers. As a matter of fact, these preachers tend to demonstrate the 'favor they have before God' by displaying flashy lifestyles—in the midst of general poverty."[68]

One then understands why the hermeneutics of these neo-Pentecostal preachers is a personalized experiential one, evolving around the preachers' prosperity as practical manifestations of the possibilities of God's children becoming wealthy. However, because these preachers, especially those espousing covenant prosperity, teach that people come into the massive blessings of God through prayer and giving their time and money to the church, it is not uncommon for believers to spend productive hours—including official working hours which could have been channeled into socioeconomically transforming activities—at church or in church activities. Naturally, the socioeconomically transforming capabilities of these theologies come under scrutiny. Scrutiny becomes more necessary when it is not evident that wealth and prosperity, even if measured through material things as prosperity preachers would want us to believe, have inundated even very committed neo-Pentecostals and have correspondingly eluded members of non-prosperity preaching churches. With reference to Nigeria, Folarin notes:

---

66. Kahl, "Jesus Became Poor," 113.
67. Kahl, "Jesus Became Poor," 114.
68. Kahl, "Jesus Became Poor," 112.

> A major problem with the prosperity gospel as presently practiced in Nigeria is that it is not fully delivering on its promises. There are still many sincere Christians who are financially poor, sick, and/or demon-oppressed. For Christians who believe in the truth of Scripture, the fault cannot be with God and his promises. It must be the interpretations that prosperity gospel preachers use to justify the theology that are wrong. Some Christians tend to believe that in the attempt to provide answers to the existence of evil on earth despite belief in an all-powerful and all-good God, preachers of prosperity have sometimes ended up creating a truncated gospel of salvation."[69]

The above cannot be said of Nigeria alone; there is a similar trend in my own country of Ghana, and I believe the story is no different in many other contexts in Africa. It is undeniably the case that there remain droves of people attending these churches who are still financially poor, unhealthy, and oppressed by demonic powers. That the theology of prosperity is not transforming believers' socioeconomic situation is not surprising, because it is the result of a faulty interpretation of the Bible from the perspective of a human expectation of God that does not allow God to speak through the Scriptures or the Scriptures to emphasize God's sovereignty. It is instead a purposive hermeneutic approach through which human beings proclaim what they expect God to do.

Poverty and social deprivation constrain the human person and society in many ways. If a land flowing with "milk and honey" was a promise of God first offered in Exod 3:8 and reaffirmed to the children of Israel several times in the Scriptures, then one would reasonably conclude that God wills abundant and flourishing life to those who diligently seek him. It must be emphasized that, while Christians must positively and prayerfully emphasize and work through the liberative paradigms of the ministry and death of Jesus Christ as a model for overcoming the structural impediments (even the demonic ones) that do not ensure a flourishing life, neo-Pentecostals need to understand that God still remains sovereign over his creation and that sin and evil do not occur on his blind side. Not all of humankind's aspirations are necessarily the will of the sovereign God, and neither is everything in the power of humankind to will and have.

---

69. Folarin, "Prosperity Gospel in Nigeria."

Conclusion

Although the intentions of Africa's neo-Pentecostals are undoubtedly good, their theologies of intervention are not clear-cut enough to engender socioeconomic transformation. With the current theology, Africa's neo-Pentecostals face a clear danger of being distracted from pure commitments to God and becoming engrossed in the dynamics of the secular system—the economic system—with its emphasis on human agency. These complex secular socioeconomic systems have exposed Africa's neo-Pentecostals to certain criticisms and weaknesses, both in terms of their ability to engender any genuine and sustainable socioeconomic transformation as well as a holistic salvation message that is not entrapped by the negative ontologies of the here and now. This is because poverty is largely an economic issue that requires primarily, though not entirely, structural economic interventions, especially at the macroeconomic level. Therefore, the approach of neo-Pentecostals to poverty and socioeconomic challenges in a secular postmodern society through an entirely spiritualized and covenant Pentecostal economic model with which they operate is very inadequate. This is not to suggest that the creator God is powerless and clueless in the face of economic poverty. Rather, being created in his image and empowered by the Spirit, humans must work to improve their condition while holding on to the faith and hope they have in the God of Christ to seed them with his enabling power that bestows success and breakthrough—this the neo-Pentecostals also believe.

Therefore, when one considers the context within which the neo-Pentecostals emerged, the task that they have set for themselves, to lift believers out of socioeconomic deprivation, was not misguided. Although their interpretation of the socioeconomic situation and responses may be inadequate, their reactions to the situation "underline that religious responses to economic globalization increasingly include a stress on social interests that go way beyond the confines of what might be called conventional religious concerns."[70] Conservatively, Africa's neo-Pentecostals perceive a demonic or evil hand operating behind Africa's socioeconomic depravity, especially that of poverty. It is in this light that one would define the neo-Pentecostal engagement of poverty towards socioeconomic transformation as a renewal of the "fire from heaven" that set on course a new wave of Christian theological orientation in order to purge and transform the socioeconomic depravity that has become the yoke of God's children. Unfortunately, this theological orientation is capable of doing what is required of it, and if neo-Pentecostals

---

70. Haynes, *Religion and Development*, 3.

are to engender any socioeconomic transformation, prosperity theology is clearly in need of transformation towards a much more pragmatic theology that is just and liberating.

Africa's neo-Pentecostals are undoubtedly positioned institutionally to contribute meaningfully to the socioeconomic transformation of African societies and economies. What is required of them is to transform and repackage their theological responses to socioeconomic deprivation—not through an entirely spiritualized grid but through pragmatic, institutionalized means such as faith-based organizations. This they could do by complementing other faith-based organizations, and even secular state institutions, rather than the alternative systems they currently seem to be operating. It has become clear that, for now, the kind of neo-Pentecostal economy inspired by spiritual capitalism has become delusional to many who strenuously strive to live the covenant principles but to no avail. This has the tendency of putting out the "fire from heaven," which the Pentecostals have seemingly reignited and required to engage and transform debilitating those structures and systems of postmodern society which do not ensure a liberating and flourishing life. Clearly, with the prosperity gospel's current trend of implausibility, unreliability, and impracticability, the future rather looks bleak and uncertain. Indeed, the evidence so far indicates that theologies of prosperity are in need of transformation themselves if they are to engender socioeconomic transformation.

Bibliography

Anderson, Allan. "African Independent Churches and Pentecostalism: Historical Connections and Common Identities." *Ogbomoso Journal of Theology* 13 (2008) 22–42.

Anim, Emmanuel. "The Prosperity Gospel in Ghana and the Primal Imagination." *Trinity Journal of Church and Theology* 16 (2009) 31–53.

Asamoah-Gyadu, Johnson Kwabena. *African Charismatics: Current Developments Within Independent Indigenous Pentecostalism in Ghana*. Leiden: Brill, 2005.

Berger, Peter L. "Max Weber is Alive and Well and Living in Guatemala: The Protestant Ethic Today." *The Review of Faith and International Affairs* 8 (2010) 3–9.

Bernstein, Ann, ed. *Under the Radar: Pentecostalism in South Africa and Its Potential Social and Economic Role*. Johannesburg: Centre for Development and Enterprise, 2008.

Daniels, David D. "Prosperity Gospel of Entrepreneurship in Africa and Black America." In *Pastures of Plenty: Tracing Religio-Scapes of Prosperity Gospel in Africa and Beyond*, edited by Andreas Heuser, 265–77. Frankfurt am Main: Peter Lang, 2015.

Drønen, Tomas Sundnes. "'Now I Dress Well. Now I Work Hard'—Pentecostalism, Prosperity, and Economic Development in Cameroon." In *Pastures of Plenty:*

Tracing Religio-Scapes of Prosperity Gospel in Africa and Beyond, edited by Andreas Heuser, 249–64. Frankfurt am Main: Peter Lang, 2015.

Duchrow, Ulrich. *Alternatives to Global Capitalism: Drawn from Biblical History, Designed for Political Action*. Utrecht: International, 1998.

Folarin, George O. "The Prosperity Gospel in Nigeria." *CyberJournal for Pentecostal-Charismatic Research* 16 (January 2007). http://www.pctii.org/cyberj/cyberj16/folarin.html.

Gifford, Paul. *African Christianity: Its Public Role*. Bloomington: Indiana University Press, 1998.

———. *Ghana's New Christianity: Pentecostalism in a Globalizing African Economy*. London: Hurst, 2004.

———. "The Prosperity Theology of David Oyedepo, Founder of Winners' Chapel." In *Pastures of Plenty: Tracing Religio-Scapes of Prosperity Gospel in Africa and Beyond*, edited by Andreas Heuser, 83–100. Frankfurt am Main: Peter Lang, 2015.

Gifford, Paul, and Trad Nogueira-Godsey. "The Protestant Ethic and African Pentecostalism: A Case Study." *Journal for the Study of Religion* 24 (2011) 5–21.

Golo, Ben-Willie Kwaku. "Africa's Poverty and Its Neo-Pentecostal Liberators." *Pneuma* 35 (2013) 366–84.

———. "Engaging the Violence of Individuated Greed in Contemporary Africa: Towards a Christian-Muslim Subversive Theological Ethic." In *Our Burning Issues: A Pan African Response*, edited by Edison M. Kalengyo, et al., 317–34. Nairobi: All Africa Conference of Churches, 2013.

———. "The Groaning Earth and the Greening of Neo-Pentecostalism in Twenty-First Century Ghana." *PentecoStudies: An Interdisciplinary Journal for Research on the Pentecostal and Charismatic Movements* 13 (2014) 197–216.

Gyekye, Kwame. *African Cultural Values: An Introduction*. Accra: Sankofa, 2002.

———. "Person and Community in African Thought." In *Person and Community: Ghanaian Philosophical Studies 1*, edited by Kwasi Wiredu and Kwame Gyekye, 101–22. Washington, DC: Council for Research in Values and Philosophy, 1992.

Haynes, Jeffrey. *Religion and Development: Conflict or Cooperation*. Basingstoke: Palgrave Macmillan, 2007.

Heuser, Andrea. "Religious-Scapes of Prosperity Gospel: An Introduction." In *Pastures of Plenty: Tracing Religio-Scapes of Prosperity Gospel in Africa and Beyond*, edited by Andreas Heuser, 15–30. Frankfurt am Main: Peter Lang, 2015.

Kahl, Werner. "Jesus Became Poor So That We Might Become Rich." In *Pastures of Plenty: Tracing Religio-Scapes of Prosperity Gospel in Africa and Beyond*, edited by Andreas Heuser, 101–16. Frankfurt am Main: Peter Lang, 2015.

Köhrsen, Jens. "Pentecostal Improvement Strategies: A Comparative Reading on African and South American Pentecostalism." In *Pastures of Plenty: Tracing Religio-Scapes of Prosperity Gospel in Africa and Beyond*, edited by Andreas Heuser, 49–64. Frankfurt am Main: Peter Lang, 2015.

Larbi, Emmanuel Kingsley. *Pentecostalism: The Eddies of Ghanaian Christianity*. Accra: CPCS, 2001.

McCauley, John F. "Africa's New Big Man Rule: Pentecostalism and Patronage in Ghana." *African Affairs* 112:446 (2012) 1–21.

Mills, Gregg. "Why is Africa Poor?" *Development Policy Briefing Paper 6* (December 6, 2010). Washington, DC: Cato Institute's Centre for Global Liberty and Prosperity.

Ojo, Matthews A. "The Growth of Charismatic Movements in Northern Nigeria." *Ogbomoso Journal of Theology* 13 (2008) 83–117.

———. "Pentecostalism, Public Accountability, and Governance in Nigeria." *Ogbomoso Journal of Theology* 13 (2008) 110–33.

———. "Transnational Religious Networks and Indigenous Pentecostal Missionary Enterprises in the West African Coastal Region." In *Christianity in Africa and the African Diaspora: The Appropriation of a Scattered Heritage,* edited by Afe Adogame et al., 167–79. London: Continuum, 2008.

Omenyo, Cephas N. *Pentecost Outside Pentecostalism: A Study of the Development of Charismatic Renewal in the Mainline Churches in Ghana.* Zoetermeer: Boekencentrum, 2006.

———. "'The Spirit-Filled Goes to School': Theological Education in African Pentecostalism." *Ogbomoso Journal of Theology* 13 (2008) 41–57.

Oyedepo, David O. *Understanding Financial Prosperity.* Lagos: Dominion, 2005.

Schlemmer, Lawrence, ed. *Dormant Capital: Pentecostalism in South Africa and Its Potential Social and Economic Role.* Johannesburg: Centre for Development and Enterprise, 2008.

Ter Harr, Gerrie, and Stephen Ellis. "The Role of Religion in Development: Towards a New Relationship Between European Union and Africa." *The European Journal of Development Research,* 18 (September 2006) 351–67.

Wariboko, Nimi. "Pentecostal Paradigms of National Economic Prosperity in Africa." In *Pentecostalism and Prosperity: The Socio-Economics of the Global Charismatic Movement,* edited by Katherine Attanasi and Amos Yong, 35–59. New York: Palgrave Macmillan, 2012.

Yong, Amos. "A Typology of Prosperity Theology." In *Pentecostalism and Prosperity: The Socio-Economics of the Global Charismatic Movement,* edited by Katherine Attanasi and Amos Yong, 15–34. New York: Palgrave Macmillan, 2012.

PART FIVE

Politics and Modernity

14

The Brazilian Catholic Charismatic Renewal: A Spiritual Style Between Tradition and Modernity

MARCELO AYRES CAMURÇA

Introduction

The theme of this conference evokes the famous book by theologian Harvey Cox, *Fire from Heaven: The Rise of Pentecostal Spirituality and the Reshaping of Religion in the Twenty-First Century*,[1] which introduces the phenomenon of a large religious revival in the modern world. It is interesting to note that, as Cox points out in his introduction, three decades earlier this same theologian wrote *The Secular City* in the context of the so-called secularization paradigm. However, in this second book, Cox rejects the mistaken prediction that religion, particularly the Pentecostal and Catholic Charismatic denominations, would lose its role within Western societies. Contrary to those of *The Secular City*, his findings showed that Pentecostal Christianity, which emphasizes the immediate experience of God through speaking in tongues, trance, and ecstatic bodily motion, is not a backward-looking movement but rather a strong force that speaks to the spiritual emptiness of our time by tapping into the core of human religiousness.

Following the perspective of Harvey Cox's book, I would like to focus this chapter on the Catholic Charismatic Renewal (CCR) in Brazil: its influence within the Catholic Church and religious environments by establishing a new way of being Catholic without renouncing the millennial heritage of this institution. I make the claim that the "recreation of

---

1. Cox, *Fire from Heaven*, xv–xviii.

tradition" undergone by CCR praxis leads to an innovative openness to modern and postmodern worlds.

Tradition via Modernity

The first point I would like to introduce is the concept of religious tradition as understood by charismatic Catholics in my country of Brazil. *Tradition*, in their view, is less a theoretical concept than a set of practices such as the following: the veneration of images of the Virgin Mary at home, in churches, and at sites of her claimed apparition; giving rites of blessing with the Blessed Sacrament (in homes, for objects, and for people); anointing of the sick; praying the rosary; praying novenas on First Fridays; and so on. Everything that appeared obsolete after the "internal secularization" undergone by the Second Vatican Council was reintroduced en masse by the CCR in Brazil.[2] This appraisal of tradition, however, comprises all kinds of charismatic elements, including gifts of the Holy Spirit, speaking in tongues (glossolalia), prophecy, and "baptism" and resting in the Spirit.

In my view, we miss the point if we interpret this phenomenon as simply a liturgical setback or a sort of "irrational regression" to the past. Based on what I have observed, it is more than that: it is a re-creation of tradition, so to speak, driven by the need to adapt old rituals to modernity. In this sense, the re-creation of tradition is close to Eric Hobsbawm's notion of "the invention of tradition"[3] in a modern fashion. It is tradition renewed by subjective experience and the personal choice of the faithful, tradition lived as an *atavistic, binding* force, yet experienced as a free option.

Despite the fact that the CCR in Brazil presents itself as a movement of the Spirit and not as an organization, it must operate in the bosom of the Roman Catholic Church. I would like to highlight some examples of this modern return to tradition brought about by the CCR. It is evident in the enthronement of the Blessed Sacrament by Charismatic priests during Masses and liturgies as a ritual to be experienced by the faithful, no longer with the Tridentine model's reverence, solemnity, and discretion but rather with intimacy, affection, and informality. We see it in the permissible practice of placing photos, work identification cards, and clothes on or near the Blessed Sacrament[4] . . . in the charismatic woman I once saw reciting the Byzantine rosary in a bathing suit as she strolled along the seafront of Ipanema Beach in Rio de Janeiro . . . and even the "Jesus aerobics" done in gyms

2. Oro, *Avanço Pentecostal e Reação Católica*, 97.
3. Hobsbawm and Ranger, *A Invenção das Tradições*, 9–14.
4. Silveira, *Corpo, Emoção e Rito*, 170.

using Christian songs[5] as well as other practices like the unceremonious "Mass show" of "pop star priest" Marcelo Rossi.[6] Individual membership in the Church does not necessarily occur via the imposition of catechesis but via mystical experiences such as glossolalia, healing, and prophecy, to which all the baptized have access.

Modern, with a Traditional Twist

The CCR claims to offer a unique spiritual experience to individuals and to promise a dramatic renewal of Church life based on the spirituality of a personal relationship with Jesus and direct access to power and inspiration through a series of spiritual gifts or charisms. Charismatics in Brazil are more likely to say that religious experience allows them to discover their "real self" rather than claim that they have been given a "new self." Identity is expressed as a sense of coming to know "who I am in Christ." This kind of CCR identity combines a modern lifestyle with traditional religious practices. However, the sinful aspect of profane modern life passes through a kind of purification process, or spiritual exorcism, so that incorporation into the Charismatic ethos is possible.

What we can observe in the dynamics of the Charismatic Renewal in Brazil is a modern lifestyle coated with and marked by sacred and traditional practices, where the expressions of secular life are exorcised of their sinful content and incorporated into the Holy Mother Church's sacred space. The examples below illustrate how this blend of traditional and (post)modern elements unfolds during Charismatic events in my hometown of Juiz de Fora in southeastern Brazil:

- "Happy Day" party—An All Saints' Day party for Charismatic youth is called a "Happy Day," as opposed to "Halloween," party. Young people wear costumes of their favorite saints (Cecilia, Lucy, Anthony, Benedict, Francis, etc.) and dance to techno, rock, and samba in the parish hall under the vigilant eyes of adult chaperones from the local CCR group. The ambiguity that often occurs at parties, such as overt sensuality, tends to erupt as a risk of sinning. But it is controlled by performances in which "evil spirits" (drugs, sex, and violence) are choreographically exorcised in a dance where everyone stands up and lays on hands with the refrain: "Demon, get out!"[7]

---

5. Prandi, *Um sopro do Espírito*, 68–95.
6. Carranza, *Catolicismo Midiático*, 58–60.
7. Silveira, "O Pop no Espírito," 148–50.

- The "Mass show"—Held in large venues like the Aerodrome of São Paulo, this hybrid religious celebration-show brings together church authorities and famous singers. The Charismatic priest, Marcelo Rossi, performs with his "Jesus, yeah, yeah, yeah" and "Jesus aerobics," followed by a crowd of the faithful.[8]
- "Canção Nova"—The CCR's internet portal, "Canção Nova" contains links to a detailed history of the lives of the saints, real-time virtual pilgrimages, testimonies, online Stations of the Cross, recited or sung virtual psalms, and virtual candles. As part of these internet devotions for Catholic saints, it's even possible to create virtual altars where the faithful can "visit" the saint, light a candle, request graces, and express thanks—right there on the site.[9] Such sites also use the virtual language and youthful vocabulary as forms of Charismatic evangelization. For example, Canção Nova has a virtual chat room where conversation is punctuated by expressions such as "Jesus is cool," "Jesus rules," and user nicknames like "Belongs to Jesus Only," "Praying for You," "Web angel," "Loved by God," etc.[10] In short, it is an entirely technological and modern format mixed with conservative content that opposes the ideologies of free sex for all, use of condoms, and the practice of homosexuality. The rejection of sin, combined with the subjective logic of Alcoholics Anonymous in its "just for today" formula, adapted to "just for today I will not sin," appears in Charismatic Renewal TV programs and on network sites.

These examples are all combined with the mystical-charismatic experience of baptism and resting in the Holy Spirit. It is a phenomenon of the masses, a mystical boom that is no longer restricted to a few elect like St. John of the Cross or St. Teresa of Avila. Anyone can be touched by the gift of praying in tongues, healing, and prophesying by the mouth of God and Jesus. Simultaneously, all of this is publicized on Catholic websites and cable TV stations.

Notice that all these multimodal, self, and mass media communication tools are at the service of a deeply conservative agenda which combines old, preconciliar rituals with charismatic experiences and the moral condemnation of contraceptives and homosexuality with expressions of postmodern mysticism. Thanks to this blend, anyone today can receive the gifts of praying in heavenly tongues, healing the sick, and prophesying through the power of Jesus.

8. Souza, *Igreja in Concert*, 49–77.
9. Camurça, "As Muitas Faces," 264–65.
10. Silveira, "Terços, 'Santinhos' e Versículos," 60–62.

Subjectivism and Tradition

It is through the Church's great tradition of the Pentecost mystery that members of the Charismatic Renewal seek to establish continuity between the original Church and the Church of today. Divinely and charismatically founded, the Catholic Church has always remained in essence the *societas perfecta*, but it is also in need of revitalization and reconversion so that the faithful can recognize this perfect condition through their personal experiences.

The CCR not only socializes the faithful as a visible organization with its heritage of dogmas, images, rituals, and sacraments but also through an "inner personal encounter" with Jesus. This successful arrangement promotes the traditional Catholic idea of salvation by the Church, opposing the Protestants' modern notion of salvation by faith. It is an ingenious formula, as we are indeed saved by faith, but only in and through the Church.

In a "cenacle," a CCR meeting held in soccer stadiums with more than one hundred thousand people, including the Church's upper hierarchy but under the direction of lay people, priests, and leaders of the CCR, the bishop says during his homily: "The blood of Jesus is being poured upon us in this moment of God's forgiveness that is coming onto us." An acolyte takes the floor and says, "If you felt touched by this grace, thank God, God who took away the burden of sin. The blood of Jesus fell upon us; marriages are being restored . . . show your wedding ring to the Lord; take it off your finger and show it to the Lord." Many women follow, doing just that.[11]

What appears to take place in these charismatic experiences is postmodern, with modern processes of individualization and subjectivity characterized less by intellect and more by emotional trials. Becoming a member does not occur by complying with the obligations of catechesis and catechism but through the mystical experience of baptism in the Spirit and the gifts of glossolalia, healing, and prophecy, to which everyone has access.

"Sacred Self" and Healing

Similar to its counterpart in North America, the CCR in Brazil is a movement that incorporates Pentecostal practices into Catholicism. In the nearly three decades since its inception, the movement has developed a system that includes several genres of language used in its ritual settings. *Prophecy* is a first-person pronouncement in which the "I" is God who speaks through someone, revealing his mind and will. *Teaching* is a ritual that clarifies spiritual truth and helps the faithful to live a better life. *Prayer* includes worship,

---

11. Prandi, *Um Sopro do Espírito*, 74–75.

petition, and intercession on behalf of another for a special purpose such as physical or emotional healing, or deliverance from evil spirits. Finally, *sharing* is a kind of ordinary conversation, except that its content must have some spiritual value: experiences, events, problems, or thoughts that have some significance for the religious understanding of daily life.

Thomas Csordas describes the faith healer's performances and therapeutic rituals using the language of the "phenomenology of self and self-transformation."[12] Blending ethnographic description and detailed case studies within these various charismatic healing genres, Csordas works out a theory of self and therapeutic efficacy grounded in the notions of "embodiment and orientation" developed by Merleau-Ponty in his phenomenology of the body. With this theory, Csordas examines the experience of sensory imagery and performative utterance, and explicates the sense of the sacred that is cultivated by participation in a coherent ritual system. The system, in turn, is embedded in the charismatic world of meaning within which the *sacred self* comes into being: to be healed is to dwell in the charismatic world as a *sacred self*. Csordas calls this approach cultural phenomenology, because it is concerned with synthesizing the immediacy of embodied existence with the multiplicity of cultural meaning in which we are immersed.

In my view, the kind of sacred self engendered by Catholic Charismatics in Brazil also comprises a successful combination of traditionalism and postmodernity in the way they socialize themselves into the local Church. The traditional way is by affiliating with a visible organization, the Roman Catholic Church, with its millennial heritage of dogmas, images, rituals, and sacraments. The postmodern way, widely followed by CCR members, happens mostly through an *inner, personal encounter with Jesus*, which defines us by what is beyond our limits.

That is precisely the kind of collective phenomenon that we can observe on a large scale during the massive CCR meetings held in Brazilian football stadiums. With the Catholic Church's upper hierarchy present, Charismatic priests and lay people run the show, determining which participant will be allowed to prophesy or share. Rituals of self-affirmation, like healing and deliverance, address modern psychological problems such as low self-esteem, depression, and anxiety. Charismatic leaders perform these rituals in prayer groups, seminars, and healing and deliverance Masses. In these rituals, painful memories of the past are activated and trauma is revealed, experienced, and healed with the help of varied holy intercessions. At the core of CCR rituals of self-affirmation—for example, prayer meetings, initiation ceremonies, and healing services—lies a belief in oral and

---

12. Csordas, *Sacred Self*, 269–75.

mental performative actions. It is through the power of *the word, memory,* and the *staging of dramas* that transformation occurs.

Healing Rituals as a "Wild Psychology" and a Dramatic Enactment

The Charismatic rituals of healing and deliverance aim to eliminate and harmonize personal crises and psychological symptoms such as stress, sadness, and anxiety.[13] They are performed by priests and lay members of CCR prayer groups and are held in specific places such as Masses and seminars of healing and deliverance.[14] During these rituals, we observe the role that memory plays in the healing process. By activating past painful memories, trauma is revealed, experienced, and extinguished through the intercession of sacred Catholic images in what Thomas Csordas calls ritual psychotherapy.[15]

The following is one such example. A middle-aged man and two CCR healers stand in a small chapel, with a tabernacle and a table with images of the Virgin Mary and St. Michael, who is commonly associated with deliverance. When asked by the healers the reason for his visit, the man answers, "To cure my depression." They begin the healing prayer. Laying hands on the man's head, the first healer says, "Lord Jesus, we invoke your blood, wash him, oh Lord . . ." The second healer initiates a prayer in tongues: "Shumalá, rianlá, doch in giving, builiiia . . ." The first healer continues, "Jesus, touch his brain, every area of his pituitary gland, the seat of feelings. Heal the memories that motivated the lack of serotonin, especially the one of the day that his daughter said she was ashamed of her father." The man begins to cry. Toward the end of the ritual, the first healer stands in front of the man; the second healer asks him to embrace the first, imagining that he is his daughter and that between them is Jesus, taking his hand and his daughter's and placing them on his bleeding heart.[16]

Healing rituals usually begin with the identification of the patient's symptoms (depression, low self-esteem, self-rejection).[17] Then, the healers search the biographical memory of the patient, looking for the original memory that caused the trauma. Because of accumulated experience, healers have experience with a wide range of situations: a pregnant mother who,

13. Silveira, *Corpo, Emoção e Rito*, 168.
14. Silveira, *Corpo, Emoção e Rito*, 168.
15. Csordas, *Sacred Self*, 25–29.
16. Silveira, "Tecnologia e Ética de Si," 172–73.
17. Silveira, "Tecnologia e Ética de Si," 172–73.

insecure about having the baby, sent negative feelings to the fetus; children who witnessed their father beating their mother; sexual abuse suffered as a child; an abortion performed under conditions of distress; etc. With the mediation of sacred images, the healer prays: "Touch, Lord Jesus, this abortion that was committed," or "Jesus, heal the child's memories of his father hitting his mother." At this point, the person receiving the healing often falls into tears. The symbolic method of introducing a Catholic image—"the blood of Jesus that washes and heals"; "the mantle of Mary that covers and protects"; "the wounded palm of Jesus' hand enters the heart and plucks out the hurts and resentments"; "the fire of the Spirit that baptizes"—all of these serve as explanatory modes for interpreting and healing of trauma, extinguishing it through the forgiveness of those who caused the suffering through the introduction of a negative force.[18]

Conclusion

The value that the Catholic Charismatic Renewal places on the symbolic imagery and heritage of the Catholic tradition in a modern context, turning the Pentecost's mystery into a personal, subjective, and emotional experience, enabled the success and growth of this movement within the Catholic Church in Brazil. Although encouraging a neoconservative message that opposes the advances of moral behavior in Western societies regarding issues such as gender, sexuality, assisted reproduction, stem cell research, and abortion, the CCR has the strong support of the Brazilian middle class and youth. It emphasizes the individual's emotional experience to treat anxiety, suffering, and crises of the modern world, and it is all combined with the effective use of mass media, communications, and religious marketing.

Charismatic healing in Brazil is not only the relief of illness or distress but also an instrument for both healers and patients to use to build the *sacred self*. The Charismatic *sacred self* is an authentic expression of a postmodern subjectivity driven by religious, emotional experiences. The very *locus* of the healing's efficacy is not symptoms, psychiatric disorders, symbolic meaning, or even social relationships but *the self* that encompasses all of these. The aspect of the sacred self fully accepts the symbolic heritage of Catholic tradition, albeit dressed in a modern fashion, and turns the Pentecostal experience into amazing individual experiences. The Charismatic Renewal has made the Catholic Church, as a religious agency, competitive in the religious market, fighting against Evangelical-Pentecostal competition in an effort to maintain Catholicism as the religion of most Brazilians.

18. Silveira, "Tecnologia e Ética de Si," 101.

Bibliography

Camurça, Marcelo A. "As Muitas Faces das Devoções: Das Romarias e Dos Santuários ai Turismo, ao Marketing Religioso e Aos Altares Virtuais." *Fragmentos de Cultura* 16 (2006) 257–70.
Camurça, Marcelo A., and Mabel Salgado Pereira, eds. *Festa e Religião: Imaginário e Sociedade em Minas Gerais*. Juiz de Fora, Brazil: Templo, 2003.
Carranza, Brenda. *Catolicismo Midiático*. Aparecida: Idéias e Letras, 2011.
Cox, Harvey Gallagher. *Fire from Heaven: The Rise of Pentecostal Spirituality and the Reshaping of Religion in the Twenty-First Century*. Reading, MA: Addison-Wesley, 1995.
Csordas, Thomas J. *The Sacred Self: A Cultural Phenomenology of Charismatic Healing*. Berkeley: University of California Press, 1997.
Hobsbawn, Eric, and Terence Ranger. *A Invenção das Tradições*. Rio de Janeiro: Paz e Terra, 1997.
Oro, Ari Pedro. *Avanço Pentecostal e Reação Católica*. Petrópolis: Vozes, 1996.
Prandi, Reginaldo. *Um Sopro do Espírito: A Renovação Conservadora do Catolicismo Carismático*. São Paulo: EDUSP/FAPESP, 1997.
Silveira, Emerson J. Sena. *Corpo, Emoção e Rito: Antropologia Dos Carismáticos Católicos*. Porto Alegre, Brazil: Armazém Digital, 2008.
———. "O Pop no Espírito: Festa, Consumo e Artifício no Movimento Carismático/Pentecostal." In *Festa e Religião: Imaginário e Sociedade em Minas Gerais*, edited by Mabel Salgado Pereira and Marcelo Ayres Camurça, 137–58. Juiz de Fora, Brazil: Templo, 2003.
———. "Tecnologia e Ética de Si: Subjetividade e Performance na Cura Interior Católico-Carismática a Partir da Figura do Curador." PhD diss., PPCIR/Universidade Federal de Juiz de Fora, 2006.
———. "Terços, Santinhos e Versículos: A Relação entre Católicos Carismáticos e a Política". *Rever—Revista de Estudos da Religião* 8 (2008) 54–74.
Souza, André Ricardo. *Igreja in Concert: Padres Cantores, Mídia, e Marketing*. São Paulo: Annablume/FAPESP, 2005.

15

Fear and Trembling in Haiti: A Charismatic Catholic Prophecy of the 2010 Earthquake

TERRY REY

> "If anyone on the verge of action should judge himself according to the outcome, he would never begin."
>
> —KIERKEGAARD, *FEAR AND TREMBLING*

Introduction

Though founded there in 1973,[1] the Catholic Charismatic Renewal got off to a relatively slow start in Haiti, with only six hundred members to show for its efforts by the end of that decade.[2] Because of this, there were few signs that it would soon change the face of the Haitian Catholic Church. Linguistic domination and classism had much to do with the Renewal's inauspicious start, as in its early years the movement held its healing services and revivals in French, a language spoken by only 10 percent of the national population, thereby shutting out the poor almost entirely. Poor Catholics

---

1. Corten, *Misère*, 98, n.24. Thomas Csordas suggests instead that the Renewal's Haitian cradle was the northern city of Cape Haitian, where it was founded "by Carmelite nuns." He attributes this information to newsletters from the International Communications Office (ICO). Csordas, "Catholic Pentecostalism." The ICO was founded in Ann Arbor, Michigan, in 1972, and moved to Brussels four years later, in 1976, and then to Rome in 1981, when it was renamed the International Catholic Charismatic Renewal Office (ICCRO). Four years later, the ICCRO relocated to the Vatican proper, where in 1993–1994, its name changed slightly to International Catholic Charismatic Renewal Services (ICCRS 1999).

2. Csordas, "Catholic Pentecostalism," 145.

in Haiti were instead being captivated then by liberation theology, which spawned a base church movement in the Caribbean nation that was called *Tilegliz* (Haitian Creole: "Little Church"). *Tilegliz* priests generally did not rail against the "idolatry" of Vodou from the pulpit, instead denouncing political injustice and the structural causes of the perpetually abject poverty of the nation's masses. In fact, Father Jean-Bertrand Aristide, *Tilegliz's* leading prophet, had Vodouist symbols embroidered onto his cassock and was widely believed to actively participate in Vodou rituals himself, like most Haitians. Aristide was also a leading force behind *Tilegliz's* contribution to the fall of the dynastic Duvalier regime, which had ruled Haiti with an iron fist from 1957 to 1986.

In a stunning sociopolitical development four years later, in 1990, Aristide was elected president of Haiti by the greatest electoral margin of victory in Latin American history. For the first time ever, the Haitian masses had a president who understood them and cared about them; hope, thus, abounded among the subaltern. The economic elite and the army were none too pleased to see the leftist, firebrand prelate in power, however, and soon they burst the elation of the poor by orchestrating a coup d'état, driving Aristide into exile, and placing General Raoul Cédras in charge of the junta. The Cédras regime orchestrated a systematic campaign to terrorize, torture, and eliminate Aristide supporters, thereby sounding the death knell of *Tilegliz*, which echoed loudly throughout the land and cast the poor Catholic and Vodouist masses adrift once again.

At around the time that this macabre political drama was unfolding, the Catholic Charismatic Renewal began speaking Haitian Creole, and the results have been astonishing. By the mid-1990s, the Renewal's annual congress had become the second largest public gathering in the country, after carnival, routinely drawing between fifty thousand and one hundred thousand Charismatic Catholics during its three days of prayer and revival. By the turn of the century, there were roughly 782,400 Pentecostal Catholics in Haiti. If the movement's present trajectory holds, then there will be 1,771,123 Charismatic Catholics in Haiti by 2025.[3] Out of a projected total national population of 12,004,000,[4] this means that, within ten years, nearly one in every seven persons in Haiti will be part of the Catholic Charismatic Renewal. Furthermore, if the percentage of Catholics remains the slight

---

3. ICCRS, "*Then Peter Stood Up,*" 120.
4. UN Department of Economic and Social Affairs, "World Population Prospects."

majority that it was in 2007—roughly 55 percent[5]—then by 2025, at least one in every three Haitian Catholics will be Pentecostal.[6]

I have argued elsewhere that the impressive expansion of the Renewal among Haitian Catholics is largely understandable in terms of the centrality of the healing quest in Haitian religious culture and the movement's enabling people to distance themselves from the sometimes taxing and dangerous demands of Vodou spirits while also remaining Catholic, which is a fairly new phenomenon in Haiti.[7] And, while I still hold this to be true, there is also something fundamentally important to the Renewal that has less to do with healing or the quest for miracles but more to do with the simple joy of lively, ecstatic, communal worship. To be amidst brothers and sisters of like faith in Charismatic Catholic revival is to be swept up into the elated time and place that Émile Durkheim calls "collective effervescence": "And because his companions feel transformed in the same way at the same moment, and express this feeling by their shouts, movements, and bearing, it is as if he was in reality transported into a special world entirely different from the one in which he ordinarily lives, a special world inhabited by exceptionally intense forces that invade and transform him."[8] Three key questions for charting the Renewal's future course in Haiti are: How does the 2010 earthquake change things in that special world? What new forms of invasion and transformation by such exceptionally intense forces are manifesting in the wake of the greatest tragedy in modern Latin American history? How do such forces prime the faithful to believe and to act? Before exploring these questions specifically and analyzing Father Jules Campion's prophecy of the catastrophe during Lent of the previous year, let us take a look at two of the largest earlier earthquakes in Haitian history (1770 and 1842), in a quest for similar prophesies of doom and destruction.

---

5. U.S. Department of State, "International Religious Freedom Report 2007."

6. This trajectory should be tempered, however, by the rise of Protestant sects in the country, many of which are Pentecostal.

7. Rey, "Catholic Pentecostalism in Haiti." Alfred Métraux observed in Haiti, nearly half a century ago, that Catholics who wished to sever their ties with Vodou spirits needed also to leave the Catholic Church and become Protestant. Métraux, *Voodoo in Haiti*, 351–52. Looking at the Catholic Charismatic Renewal more broadly in the region, Csordas alludes to a shift in popular religion in which Catholicism can now serve the same function of refuge from obligations to African spirits and the dead that previously only Protestantism could; equally appealing is the recent emergence of faith healing in Catholicism, and taken together, these amount to a formidable "potential for re-Catholicization of nominal adherents." Csordas, "Catholic Pentecostalism," 159.

8. Durkheim, *Elementary Forms*, 220.

1770

On June 20, 1770, a French planter named des Rouaudières wrote an arresting letter to his sister in France describing the cataclysmic earthquake that had rocked the plantation colony of Saint-Domingue nineteen days earlier. It was sent from Les Fonds, a small town in the northwest that was, fortunately for its author, distant from ground zero, which was near Léogâne. I translate here from the first of the letter's two long paragraphs:

> We have just gone through one of the most horrible events through which divine rage can terrify the human being. The day of Pentecost ... we endured several brisk quakes of the earth ... In an instant were in ruins three of the colony's cities: Port-au-Prince, Léogâne, and Petit-Goave.... [A] number of slaves and free coloreds were also crushed under the ruins of their houses. If the houses here were of more than one story, the scene would have been even more horrible than Lisbon.... Meanwhile, the bell still rings in the plantation tower, and we have seen a loaded wagon roll by unhitched to any horses, moved by the simple trembling of the earth.

Striking at about seven o'clock in the evening on June 2, the quake's climax took the form of two massive shocks that together lasted four minutes, causing the soil in, under, and around Port-au-Prince and the Cul-de-Sac to liquefy, such that "(d)uring the entire night, the earth was floating."[9] A massive tsunami followed, which extended and "inundated 7.2 km inland" and left the base of La Saline Mountain submerged.[10] Though "only" an estimated two hundred people were killed in the quake itself, upwards of fifteen thousand more died in the ensuing famine, while a similar number succumbed to "intestinal anthrax, apparently caused by eating uncooked *tasajo* (jerked beef) sold to them by the Spanish."[11] One observer described the immediate aftermath in language that could be straight out of the Book of Revelation or Dante's *Inferno*:

> The dust which obscured the air and made it hard to breathe, the groans, the cries of wailing, the sad mourning of the wounded and dying, the fear of being swallowed up or drowned, all inspired fright and horror. The pale light of the moon shining upon the ruins and devastated buildings added further to the dismay ... The sun at last rose to shine on the destruction and

---

9. Durkheim, *Elementary Forms*, 36.
10. UNESCO, "Intra-America Sea Tsunami," 32.
11. Sublette, *Cuba and its Music*, 108.

presented the most frightful spectacle. The earth was open in a thousand places.[12]

In light of this disaster and of the horrible brutality of slavery, it is not surprising that a prophetic movement emerged in the wake of the quake. Many Africans in the colony had heard prophetic messages and partaken in revitalization movements in Africa prior to their enslavement and forced migration.[13] Thus, when a French Jesuit began preaching about the divine plan behind the earthquake, and that the end—for some, at least—was near, he found a receptive audience and nearly caused not only a riot but a slave rebellion. It is in this light that we should read the second paragraph of des Rouaudières's remarkable letter:

> That is not all, dear sister; an imposter attempted to profit the occasion by adding furies of fanaticism to the chaos of the elements. This man, dressed in the habit of a Spanish Dominican, went about exhorting the people to repent for their sins by giving abundant sums of charity, which in fact he never failed to pocket himself. The slaves and the free blacks gave everything to him. To repay them, he prophesied that the island "was to be destroyed but that only the whites would perish." These gullible, superstitious, and mischievous people thereby amass themselves in a kind of abandon that could well bring this prophecy to truth.[14]

Though the Jesuit prophet of doom was arrested along with some of his followers, the movement that he inspired amid the destruction of the 1770 earthquake was an intriguing precursor to those Catholic priests who collaborated with revolutionary slaves when the Haitian Revolution broke out in 1791.[15] It also portended Campion's 2009 explanation that natural disasters are punishment for human sins—not slavery, of course, but other kinds of sins that have long since brought curses upon Haiti.

---

12. Cited in Scherer, "Great Earthquakes," 175.

13. For an excellent discussion of one such movement in Central Africa in which thousands of slaves in Saint-Domingue had surely partaken, see Thornton, *Kongolese Saint Anthony*.

14. Lettre de Rouaudières, June 20, 1770, in Debien, *Lettres de colons*, 24–26. Rouadières, for his part, owned an indigo plantation that he transformed into a coffee plantation, which required more slaves, such that by 1757, he owned "one hundred beautiful blacks." Debien, *Lettres de colons*, 11.

15. On Catholic clerics collaborating with slave insurgents in Saint-Domingue in 1791, see Hurbon, "Le clergé catholique"; Peabody, "'A Dangerous Zeal'"; and Rey, *Priest and the Prophetess*.

1842

Of the devastating earthquake of 1842, J. Scherer writes that "it is at Cap Haitien that destruction came with the most frightful shock":

> Of all the earthquakes felt until then in the Antilles, that of May 7, 1842, was the most terrible... It was accompanied by tremors so violent that most of the solid masonry work fell. In less than a minute, the tows, Cap Haitien, Santiago de los Caballeros, Port de Paix, Môle St. Nicolas, Fort Liberté, were reduced to heaps of ruins and several thousand people were buried under the debris of their houses.[16]

Though Cape Haitian seems to have been spared the worst of the ensuing tsunami, "Port-de-Paix had even more to suffer; it was thrown down by the shock and overwhelmed by a wave. The sea drew back two hundred feet from the shore and then threw itself upon the city, covering it with fifteen feet of water." The water eventually receded to reveal that the entire town had been leveled. "Nothing remained standing, not even the church."[17]

Démesvar Delorme recalled that he, then an eleven-year-old boy, was playing marbles with his brother not far from the Cathedral when the quake struck: "The bell tower of the cathedral before me started to sway all over the place, its bells chiming without rhythm a sinister, horrible death knell. Next the bell tower tumbled... Then the entire church collapsed."[18] Once the earth settled, Delorme took off his shoes because he believed it to be the "end of the world" and at such an apocalyptic moment as this "it is necessary to appear barefoot before the Eternal."[19] Before long, Monsignor Torribio, the Spanish curate of the parish, with a crucifix in his hand, approached the boys and implored them with words that Delorme would never forget: "My children, my children, run for the hills, as fast as you can, run for the hills." Delorme eventually made it to refuge on higher ground in Grande Rivière with relatives, who took him immediately to "Abbé Cazalta, a Corsican priest, curate of the town, to implore him to come with us to the church to praise God for having saved me."[20]

As would occur on a grander scale following the dreadful catastrophe of 2010 in Port-au-Prince, once the 1842 quake relented, people in Cape Haitian gathered in the streets to worship: "A considerable degree of alarm

---

16. Scherer, "Great Earthquakes," 165.
17. Scherer, "Great Earthquakes," 165.
18. Delorme, *1842 au Cap*, 2.
19. Delorme, *1842 au Cap*, 3.
20. Delorme, *1842 au Cap*, 10.

prevailed among the population. Religious processions were seen going through the streets at different intervals through the night, as well as the day, with the object of invoking the Divine mercy."[21] Mercy was slow, however, for Cape Haitian, where fire ensued for days, consuming many who had initially survived but were trapped beneath the rubble, "poor creatures" who "met a shockingly painful death."[22] Widespread looting soon erupted, a detail over which the foreign press obsessed: "[T]o complete the scene of misery, thousands of savages, from the plains and mountains, are now pillaging the ruins, in organized and armed bodies, plundering the unfortunate survivors and murdering the wounded they find among the ruins." The "banditti" were reportedly so lost in their "enthusiasm for plunder," that none of them accepted Theogene Dupuy's generous offer of "one thousand dollars to anyone to dig a grave for his wife."[23]

The 1842 earthquake was so epochal that it simply became referred to as "the event" (*l'événement*), and people oriented their personal histories in reference thereto: "I was born so many years before the événement"; "I took my first communion before the événement, etc."[24] But *l'événement* did have at least one positive impact on Haitian religious history and culture: the 1842 earthquake also created one of the most beautiful places and one of the most moving forms of human religious expression in the world. A mountaintop split and a waterfall appeared, right where the Virgin Mary was believed to have appeared the year prior. The place is called Sodo (Saut d'Eau—Water Fall), near the town of Ville Bonheur (Happiness Town). Every year in the middle of July, tens of thousands of pilgrims flock to Sodo to sing songs to the Virgin Mary and to the ancestral spirits of Africa beneath the cool waters of the falls, reinvigorating their faith that "God is good," that *"Bondye bon,"* as is often said in Haiti, even in the wake of unspeakable misfortune.

---

21. "Further Particulars of the Great Earthquake."

22. "Earthquake at Hayti." Delorme reports that some who were trapped under the rubble drowned during the ensuing tsunami, while others were killed two days after the quake by looters "without fear of ultimate redress." He estimates that one thousand people met such a fate. Delorme, *1842 au Cap*, 5, 13, 14.

23. "Earthquake at Hayti," 510. According to the Consumer Price Index, one thousand US dollars was then worth $27,200 dollars.

24. Scherer, "Great Earthquakes," 167.

2010

Of course, persistent belief in the goodness of God makes the question *why* all the more daunting. *Why? Why Haiti? Why this?* In 2009, four hurricanes occurred in three weeks. Last decade, a civil rebellion ousted a president. The decade before that, a military junta slaughtered thousands of innocent Haitian citizens and systematically raped hundreds of Haitian women and girls.[25] The century before that, another earthquake killed thousands, and the century before that included one hundred years of human bondage. *Why Haiti?* To some observers, the answer to this question is that Haiti is cursed by or indebted to Satan. Here is one version of this interpretation of events by American evangelist Pat Robertson:

> Something happened a long time ago in Haiti, and people might not want to talk about. They were under the heel of the French, you know, Napoleon III and whatever. And they got together and swore a pact to the devil. They said, "We will serve you if you will get us free from the prince." True story. And so, the devil said, "OK, it's a deal." And they kicked the French out. The Haitians revolted and got something themselves free. But ever since, they have been cursed by one thing after another.[26]

Robertson's comments caused quite an uproar and were widely and deservedly criticized, but one important fact was seldom alluded to in the ensuing media rancor. Many *Haitians*, especially evangelical Protestants, believed precisely the same thing—that Haiti's now legendary woes were the result of its founders having sold the nation's soul to the devil.[27]

Furthermore, as a result of this theory's currency in post-quake Haiti, Vodou practitioners are now sometimes forced to defend themselves against violent crowds of angry Christians. Thus, there is good reason for concern that a new wave of religious persecution is rising out of the rubble of the earthquake. With this sad reality in mind, Mario Joseph, a leading Haitian human rights attorney, has recently asked the Inter-American Commission for Human Rights to investigate attacks on Vodouists in the weeks following

25. On the campaign of sexual violence orchestrated by the Cédras junta against Haitian women and girls, see Rey, "Junta, Rape, and Religion."
26. Whane the Whip, "Pat Robertson Haiti Comments."
27. Wade Davis, for one, in an interview with *National Geographic*, called Robertson's comments, "Cruel, ignorant, unforgivable, the ravings of a lunatic. He doesn't even know what he's talking about," never mentioning anywhere that this has been a widespread belief in Haitian evangelical Christianity for several decades. Davis, "Haiti Earthquake and Voodoo." For an astute analysis of the origins and trajectory of this belief, see McAlister, "From Slave Revolt to Blood Pact with Satan."

the quake, as especially in "Verrettes in the Artibonite, literal witch hunts have been launched against priests and practitioners of this religion."[28] Meanwhile, the most influential Vodou priest in the country, the recently deceased Max Beauvoir, vowed that the response to "war" waged by Christians on Vodouists would be "war."[29] Another Vodou priest, meanwhile, has suggested just the inverse of Robertson's theory, that the 2010 earthquake was the fault of Christianity, or at least of the Catholic Church and other supposedly corrupt institutions in Haiti. Shortly after the earthquake, Richard Morse wondered what it meant that the Catholic cathedral and presidential palace were leveled in the earthquake, while on the Champs de Mars, the *Neg Mawòn* statue—one strongly evocative of Vodou and the legendary events at Bois Caiman—remained standing:

> If all of a sudden, in fifteen seconds, twenty seconds, all the physical representations of corruption are destroyed, it gives you pause for thought. The Justice Ministry: down. The National Palace: down. The United Nations headquarters: down... When there is all this corruption going on, whose role is it in society to speak out? Isn't the church supposed to say something?[30]

The Church would have much to say, of course, in the wake of the tragedy, and none of its religious specialists would say more and with more influence than Father Jules Campion. He had prophesied the earthquake, after all, so who better than he to explain its divine meaning? And just what was the content of his remarkable prophecy of April 2009? We will answer that question in a moment, but first, let us take a glimpse at his ministry leading up to that stunning event.

The Rise of Father Jules Campion as Haiti's Pentecostal "Pope"

Over the years, I have had numerous conversations with Haitian Catholic priests about the Charismatic Renewal. Generally speaking, those whose seminary training occurred during or after the demise of *Tilegliz* tend to embrace it, while older priests who had been active in the *Tilegliz* movement regret what they perceive as the Renewal's depoliticization of popular Catholicism in Haiti. For example, the founder of Haiti's first *Tilegliz* group in

28. Charles and Daniel, "As Unity Unravels."
29. As quoted in "Tensions Mount in Haiti."
30. "Earthquake Tests Haitians Faith." It should be noted that Morse was raised in the United States by his American father and Haitian mother and that he was educated at Princeton, hence it is possible that his interpretation is not typical of other Vodou priests in Haiti.

1974 and a one-time rector of the nation's Catholic seminary, Father Gabriel Charles, had this to say when I asked him about the Renewal: "For me, it's tremendously painful."[31] Another of the most influential priests in the *Tilegiz* movement, Father Gérard Jean-Juste, once derisively referred to Father Campion as "the pope" of the Haitian Catholic Renewal.[32] Obviously, the recent transition in the Haitian Catholic Church from street protest to baptism in the Holy Spirit has thus been both divisive and painful for many.[33]

Unlike the courageous denunciations of social injustice that characterized *Tilegliz* homiletics, strong denunciations of Vodou are often cast from the pulpits of Charismatic Catholic priests in Haiti. Having studied in Jerusalem and Rome and being a successful fundraiser and mesmerizing preacher, Father Jules Campion is clearly the most influential Haitian priest in the movement, if not its "pope." Charismatic in both the sociological and theological senses of the word, Campion often rails against, among other things, the sometimes taxing fear that Vodou's ancestor cult can engender, especially in poor Haitians, a widespread assumption that misfortune in life is more often than not caused by discontented ancestors. But the dead and the *lwa* (Vodou spirits) are, in Campion's theology, no match for the Holy Spirit and the Communion of Saints, especially Our Lady of Fatima, who is the de facto patron saint of the Haitian Charismatic Renewal, and Saint Michael the Archangel, the conqueror of demons. Thomas Csordas notes that, worldwide, in the movement, "Michael the Archangel is invoked as a protector against evil spirits."[34] This is certainly true in Haiti, as expressed in the larger-than-life sized statue of Michael that stands in one of the Renewal's most important churches in Port-au-Prince, Sacred Heart, an icon that Campion himself had installed there.

Saint Michael the Archangel is prominent among the dozens of icons which inhabit Sacred Heart Catholic Church in the Turgeau neighborhood of Port-au-Prince. Soon after Campion assumed its pastorate in 2000, he transformed the storied urban church into the *axis mundi* of the Charismatic Renewal, with large revivals hosted in the sanctuary nearly every day. I quote here just part of a long description of one such service that I attended and tape recorded, one that, for obvious reasons, I shall never forget:

> Right before ten o'clock, Campion enters the rear of the church
> and lights several candles and places them here and there. Next,

---

31. Charles, interview with Terry Rey, Trou-du-Nord, Haiti, July 27, 2001.
32. Jean-Juste, interview with Terry Rey, Port-au-Prince, Haiti, October 3, 2002.
33. For more on this tension in Haitian Catholicism, see Rey and Stepick, *Crossing the Water*, 96–100.
34. Csordas, *Language, Charisma, and Creativity*, 65.

he drops to his knees behind the altar, facing the crucifix and the tabernacle with his arms outstretched in silent prayer. He stays like this for several minutes. By now there are well over one thousand people in the church, roughly 90 percent of them women. It is a standing room only crowd. A few minutes pass, then Campion approaches the pulpit to call the faithful to prayer: *"Dix-Heures-Sept; À genoux!"* ("Ten o'seven; to your knees!"). And in a single heartbeat, the faithful fall collectively to their knees. It is a striking moment. Campion next proceeds to lead a series of formulaic prayers. This continues over the next hour or so . . . with frequent chanting of "Jesus, Hallelujah."

Next, Campion begins preaching in Haitian Creole and denounces the "spies" that infiltrate Sacred Heart Church in stealthy efforts to undermine him. He explains that he knows that there are spies in the church today who have tape recorders and cameras and that these malefactors would awaken tomorrow to find boils all over their bodies, having provoked the wrath of God. A woman behind me notices my tape recorder and points it out to several people around her, at one point calling me a spy and screaming as much out loud, *"Min li! Min Espyon a! Se blan sa li e!"* ("There he is! There is the spy! It's this white guy!"). For a moment, I, the only white person in the church, am gripped by an image of one thousand entranced, enraged women tearing me apart limb by limb for my sacrilegious transgression. I demurely turn off the tape and slip the recorder into my backpack and am relieved when the denunciations end and the ecstatic chanting begins anew, the collective effervescence quelling the rage against the spy. I would be even more relieved to awake the next morning to discover no boils on my skin (Jesus Hallelujah, indeed!).[35]

Father Campion's Prophecy of the 2010 Earthquake

It was no surprise to anyone familiar with his ministry that Campion would launch into yet another diatribe against Vodou at the Charismatic Renewal's annual congress in April of 2009. What many of the thousands of faithful gathered there might not have expected, though, was the priest's explanation that God's plan for Haiti is to make it first among all nations, and that Vodou, along with two other grave sins (namely abortion and homosexuality), were impeding this divine plan from being realized. Furthermore, he

---

35. Rey, "Catholic Pentecostalism in Haiti," 92–93.

said, these sins so anger God that his wrath could well soon be provoked in the most biblical of proportions. Before an audience of over fifty thousand people at the campus of the Our Lady of Fatima Biblical Center in Tabarre, on the outskirts of Port-au-Prince, Campion thunderously issued a warning that God had been revealing to the priest in his heart: Should they not convert, repent, abandon Vodou, abortion, and homosexuality, the wrath of the Lord would crush their capital city. Pointing at the mountains in the distance, he prophesied that there "would be an earthquake, and people will be crushed in their houses for miles around." Standing attentively upon a stage and draped in a white soutane, Campion wore, as usual, a rosary around his wrist that day, something called by Charismatics in Haiti a "weapon," and his backdrop was a large icon of Our Lady of Perpetual Help, Haiti's patron saint, and an altar on which stood a monstrance. He calmly began his sermon from behind a lectern, strolling closer to the crowd as his enthusiasm swelled. Some phrases of his historic sermon are difficult to discern, but I have transcribed most of it, translated here into English:

> My brothers and sisters, in just a few minutes we are going to celebrate the evening of Pentecost and the effusion of the Holy Spirit. This will be preceded by a teaching that I am going to share on the subject of the Holy Spirit, a sermon . . .
>
> This could be the last chance that you have for me to deliver to you this message . . . I'm bringing this message to you because, over the last few months, God has been placing it in my heart. It's a message to deliver before we receive the sacrament at 3:30 because Jesus is telling me to give you this message . . . You shouldn't panic . . . when God gives you messages, it is to invite us to prayer and to conversion.
>
> Thus, the message; pay very careful attention, because this is the last time. Yes, we have our land. Haiti is the first among nations. Of this, there is no doubt. Haiti is the first among nations. The sun rises over Haiti so that it may be good, in every sense of the word: spiritually, politically, economically. And there is not a single human being who will do this—it is Jesus who will do it. I don't know when he is going to do it, or how he is going to do it, but Jesus is going to do it. Jesus is going to do it through Our Lady of Perpetual Help, Queen and Patroness of Haiti, so that he honors the country of Haiti.
>
> But God, in order to do this, has conditions. God had promised Israel that he was going to lead them to the land of Canaan, but there were conditions. Israel reached and entered Canaan under similar conditions. But all generations that are expected to enter into the Promised Land do not enter because they do

not meet these conditions. Thus, if we want Haiti to become the light of nations, it is necessary that we meet the expectations that God has given us . . .

Look at this big mountain that surrounds Port-au-Prince . . . Early this morning, there is a mountain that surrounds the city of Port-au-Prince. This mountain is called Morne de l'Hôpital. According to many studies conducted by scientists that have been published, and you can find them on the internet—it's science—they see that, beneath that mountain, there is something that they call a geological fault, that is to say a cliff under that mountain. And according to scientific calculations—because there are people who do not believe in the word of God but in science, people of Satan—according to what science tells us, at some point in time there will be an earthquake . . . people will be crushed in their houses for miles around . . . . And even the earthquake can cause something of a tsunami . . . these are scientific warnings. The facts are there.

Now, who is it that can save Port-au-Prince from such a cataclysm? Not a single person. Only Jesus of Nazareth. Jesus calmed the stormy sea. Jesus is God . . . Jesus can stop hurricanes. Jesus can stop floods. Jesus can stop earthquakes, which have already twice destroyed Port-au-Prince and which threaten us now, in every hill . . . Jesus can do it. Jesus can shut down that fault beneath that mountain.

But of course, there are conditions. And there are two conditions that I will say for the protection of Port-au-Prince. Where we have houses, where we live, where we have family, where our children are—*for the protection of Port-au-Prince*!!!—to save this city, I say to you today in the name of Jesus, fall to your knees in prayer. *Prayer! Prayer! Prayer!* Prayer has an extraordinary power. I ask you to pray. And I would like to invite my brother priests, because our Mother is our greatest prayer. It's Number One. It is only us, fathers, who can celebrate Mass. I supplicate you in the name of Jesus, say Mass, say Mass! My brothers, priests, say Mass for the protection of Port-au-Prince in particular against the earthquake, for the protection of the island of Haiti in general. Say Mass. And for the rest of you, you are going to participate in the Mass and the charism . . . it's the presence of Jesus that descends upon Haiti, the presence of Jesus that descends upon the city of Gonaives to protect it from floods and hurricanes. Mass! Mass! Mass!

But, at three o'clock in the afternoon, the hour of mercy, fall to your knees, with a rosary in your hand, and ask of God grace and mercy for Haiti, grace and mercy for Port-au-Prince.

Pray the rosary to Our Lady of the Rosary; say Mass. Perform the Adoration of the Sacrament. Regardless of whatever science predicts, God can stop it, through his intermediary Our Lady of Perpetual Help, who has intervened to save Haiti numerous times . . . She can do it, and she will do it again. But it is necessary to pray.

Second condition: Jesus has a plan for Haiti, and the plan can be realized through the intercession of Perpetual Help. We have our place in this, and above all we must be converted. And we must try to avoid sinning, particularly . . . there are certain sins that really anger God, and you can open the Bible to see. One such sin that makes God angry with us is idolatry. It's the Vodou spirits, and most Haitians are devoted to them. Even those who go to church regularly, and they are hypocrites . . . They turn to Vodou priestesses and priests and perform services for the spirits, play music for the spirits, turn people into zombies, employ sorcery to kill people . . . They are half in the Church and half in the Vodou temple, and this compromises the Church . . . We must avoid the sin of idolatry; if not, God will know . . . Jesus lives in the sacrament, and if our people do not turn away from Vodou, Jesus will cause something to happen beneath those mountains.

To throw away a child. Another sin that angers God is abortion. Abortion. To throw away a child. It's something grave, extremely grave.

And the third thing—and if you are doing any of these things you must beg forgiveness, be repentant—the third thing that makes God angry with this country, something that made God destroy the cities of Sodom and Gomorrah . . . which today are found beneath the hills of Israel, the third sin that provokes the wrath of God and a deluge of destruction . . . This vice . . . that so angers God, and so many people, we cannot understand, are involved with this. Boy with boy, girl with girl . . . . You yourselves do not respect God's plan. Look at nature. We never see a male dog lying with another male dog. You never see a female dog lying with a female dog. Even rarer, you never see a male pig lying with a male pig. That which a dog doesn't do, which a pig doesn't do, the children or Mary are doing, and it outrages God. I say unto you.

I conclude with this: I leave you with one final message in the name of Jesus. If you do not cease with this evil behavior, as we have the living Jesus in the Sacrament, there will be no Port-au-Prince anymore. The plan of Jesus will be realized, and it will be another generation. In Truth! In Truth! Either we convert, or we will all die. Even little babies will die, and we will be cast into the flames of hell, a double death . . . Amen.[36]

And, nine months later Port-au-Prince was indeed crushed in the earthquake and many, many people died, including little babies.

Denunciation, Death, and Dialogue

Among those killed in the 2010 earthquake was Monsignor Serge Joseph Miot, archbishop of Port-au-Prince, the spiritual father of the Haitian Catholic Church. He died in the rubble of his office, a place where I had had the good fortune to interview him a few years before. Just across the street, Haiti's largest church, the Cathedral of Our Lady of the Assumption, collapsed, as did the very church that Father Campion had himself pastored and transformed into the Mecca of the Charismatic Renewal in Haiti: Sacred Heart, the oldest church edifice in Port-au-Prince. One wonders how Campion might interpret these particular losses in light of his discourse on the wrath of God and the sins of the Haitian people. Quite likely, Miot's perspective would have been very different from Campion's, marked by tolerance and dialogue rather than intolerance and sanctimony, but sadly, one can only speculate about that today.

Meanwhile, one can move beyond speculation to assess the social ramifications of the earthquake and of Campion's prophecy and broader influential ministry on interreligious relations in Haiti. Some historical context is needed here. Generally speaking, since the colonial era and through the second half of the twentieth century, religious intolerance in Haiti has reared its ugly head in myriad and destructive ways. For instance, in 1795 and through the end of the Haitian Revolution, the leaders of Haiti's independence struggle—namely Toussaint Louverture and Jean-Jacques Dessalines—embarked on military campaigns to eliminate any religious leaders who were deemed too superstitious or mired in the practice of sorcery.[37] In the interim, most Catholic priests in Haiti have perceived "Voodoo as the work of the devil—a demonic manifestation against which they must fight with every means at the Church's disposal."[38]

Turning to additional "means" by securing state sanction, the Church created the "League against Voodoo" in 1896, embarking on a war against

---

36. Campion's sermon can be viewed on YouTube: https://www.youtube.com/watch?v=rqKNui3xCEc. At the time of writing, it had been viewed more than forty-six thousand times.

37. Ramsey, *Spirits and the Law*, 45–51.

38. Métraux, *Voodoo in Haiti*, 336.

"fetishism" and denying the sacraments to anyone known to attend Vodou ceremonies. This was followed by a pastoral denunciation against "the monstrous mixture" in 1913, which was to little avail, with most Catholics in Haiti still practicing Vodou without any qualms of the heart or conscience. So, the Church ramped up the offensive in the form of the 1939–1941 "Anti-Superstition Campaign," whose objective was nothing less than the total defeat of Vodou. Now, all Catholics were forced to take an oath "never to sink to superstitious practice . . . And I promise that with God's help I shall abide by this Oath until death," while the devout Catholic president, Elie Lescot, enlisted the Haitian army to aid the Church in the physical destruction of Vodou temples and ritual paraphernalia. The Campaign, in effect, orchestrated widespread human rights abuses against Vodouists and the destruction of generations of Vodouist art. Alfred Métraux recalls the "veritable *auto-da-fès*" throughout Haiti, "seeing in the back-yards of presbyteries vast pyramids of drums, painted bowls, necklaces, talismans—all waiting for the day fixed for the joyous blaze which was to symbolize the victory of the Church over Satan."[39]

Thankfully, Vodou survived the blaze and would enjoy increasing openness with the suspension of the Anti-Superstition Campaign and with the emergence of the Pan-Africanist, Black Pride *Négritude* movement among Haitian artists and intellectuals. Meanwhile, anthropologists, ethnomusicologists, historians, poets, performers, and scholars of dance began helping to slowly bring the religion's sophisticated worldview and remarkable artistic culture to favorable international light. Haiti's 1987 constitution formally abrogated the last remaining anti-superstition law and guaranteed freedom of religion to all. Furthermore, in 2003, President Aristide signed an ordinance that recognized Vodou as an official religion in Haiti and an "essential constitutive element of national identity," which by extension recognizes baptisms, marriages, and funerals performed by Vodou priests and priestesses as legally binding.[40] More recently, in 2007, Monsignor Miot had been tendering invitations to Vodouists to interreligious dialogue, traveling outside of the capital to Léogâne to meet with leading Vodou priests and priestesses and to implore them "to remind their flock that they were 'still Catholics.'" In doing so, as Karen Richman points out, Miot "effectively profaned the divide between Vodou and Catholicism—the very separation that the church had tried to protect for the previous two centuries."[41]

39. Métreaux, *Voodoo in Haiti*, 343.
40. Rébublique d'Haiti, "Arrêté relatif à la reconnaissance."
41. Richman, "Vodou State and the Protestant Nation," 283–84. Richman explains that one motivation behind Miot's effort was to stop the flow of Catholics converting to Protestant sects, a daunting challenge in a once largely Catholic (and Vodouist) nation that is clearly on the path to becoming one of a Protestant majority.

Archbishop Miot's remarkable effort to launch something of a pro-superstitious campaign seems to have died with him, sadly, in the 2010 earthquake,[42] and thus, the separation between Catholicism and Vodou is now being sanctified again and by no one more so than Father Jules Campion. The charismatic priest passes up no occasion to preach about these things, prophesying recently that "if you do not convert, you will perish." More precisely: "If Haitians do not convert, do not abandon idolatry, there will be another 2010 . . . . At that time, many people will lose their lives, and only a small minority will survive."[43]

Conclusion

All of this leads me to wonder what a conversation about the earthquake between Reverend Pat Robertson and Father Jules Campion would be like. Robertson surely knows little about Haiti and had few details to offer when he blamed the 2010 earthquake on Haiti's putative Faustian pact with the devil. Campion did also mention Satan in his prophecy, and he has since posted lectures on YouTube, explaining how the faithful may combat the devil and thereby turn Haiti's woeful tides. Thus, Robertson and Campion were essentially saying the same thing, that Haiti was punished by God with the earthquake, because its people give in to Satan and commit grave sins. Although Robertson was widely lambasted for his outrageous claim, Campion continues to preach uncontested in Haiti and the Haitian diaspora, his stature as a prophet flourishing, the "likes" on his Facebook page accumulating. They each preach what is essentially the same narrative about Haiti's deserving its plights because of sin, the end result being sanctimonious hatred for Vodouists and gay people and a step back into the religious intolerance that has not just metaphorically, but in fact, cursed the nation—more so than any Faustian pact—since the colonial era.

And thus does Campion's Charismatic crusade continue, now accentuated by a warning that "a second January 12" will befall the Haitian people should they not convert.[44] Many people are listening and believe his proclamation that Haiti is the new Israel and that for God's plan for the nation to be realized, there has to be "a cleansing" [his frightening words]. Among the sins to be cleansed, Campion highlights Vodou, abortion, and

---

42. Richman, "Religion at the Epicenter," 162.

43. Campion made these comments while preaching at a Charismatic revival in St. Marc at the Our Lady of Fatima Biblical Center in February of 2014. As cited in Mercéus, "Un premier congrès charismatique réussi."

44. Mercéus, "Un premier congrès charismatique réussi."

homosexuality, and cleansing the nation of these things seems to be his understanding of the *raison d'être* of the Catholic Charismatic Renewal. Though I have not done the requisite fieldwork to know this for sure, I suspect that the recent rise in homophobic demonstrations and attacks on gay people in Haiti are not unrelated to Campion's rise in popularity. The International Gay and Lesbian Human Rights Commission reported an increase of attacks on homosexuals following the earthquake, while a new ecumenical interfaith organization, the Haitian Coalition of Religious and Moral Organizations, has orchestrated large anti-gay demonstrations in Port-au-Prince, one of which, in 2013, featured the beating to death of two men presumed to be gay. "Gay people will curse our country," as one protester put it. "And we already have curses."[45] One can only fearfully wonder if human hatred also angers God into causing earthquakes. At any rate, the shift in the Haitian Catholic Church from liberation theology to Pentecostal revival has not been without deleterious social effect. Prophecy kills, and one can only hope that Pope Francis's *Amoris Laetitia* be translated quickly into Haitian Creole and read to the faithful throughout the land.

Bibliography

Charles, Jacqueline, and Trent Daniel. "As Unity Unravels, a Battle for Souls in Haiti is Stirring." *Miami Herald*, April 12, 2010.

Corten, André. *Misère, Religion, et Politique en Haïti: Diabolisation et Mal Politique.* Paris: Karthala, 2001.

Csordas, Thomas J. "Catholic Pentecostalism: A New Word in a New World." In *Perspectives on Pentecostalism: Case Studies from the Caribbean and Latin America*, edited by Stephen D. Glazier, 143–76. Washington, DC: University Press of America, 1980.

———. *Language, Charisma, and Creativity: Ritual Life in the Catholic Charismatic Renewal.* New York: Palgrave, 2001.

Davis, Wade. "Haiti Earthquake and Voodoo: Myths, Ritual, and Robertson." *National Geographic Daily News*, January 25, 2010. http://news.nationalgeographic.com/news/2010/01/100125-haiti-earthquake-voodoo-pat-robertson-pact-devil-wade-davis/.

Debien, Gabriel, ed. *Lettres de colons.* Laval: Publications de la Section d'Histoire, 1965.

Delorme, Démesvar. *1842 au Cap: Tremblement de terre.* Cape Haitian: Imprimerie du Progrès, 1942.

Durkheim, Emile. *The Elementary Forms of Religious Life.* Translated by Karen E. Fields. New York: Free Press, 1995.

"Earthquake at Hayti." *Westminster Review* 38 (1842).

"Earthquake Tests Haitians Faith." *The Washington Times*, January 19, 2010. http://www.washingtontimes.com/news/2010/jan/19/quake-tests-haitians-faith/.

---

45. As cited in Littaur, "Two Men Beaten to Death."

"Further Particulars of the great Earthquake." *The Liberator,* June 17, 1842.

Hurbon, Laënnec. "Le clergé catholique et l'insurrection de Saint-Domingue." In *L'Insurrection des esclaves de Saint-Domingue,* edited by Laënnec Hurbon, 29–39. Paris: Karthala, 2000.

International Catholic Charismatic Renewal Services. *"Then Peter Stood Up": Collection of Popes' Addresses to the Catholic Charismatic Renewal from its Origin to the Year 2000.* Vatican City: ICCRS, 2000.

Littaur, Dan. "Two Men Beaten to Death during Haiti Anti-Gay Demonstration." *LGBT Nation.* January 20, 2013.

McAlister, Elizabeth. "From Slave Revolt to Blood Pact with Satan: The Evangelical Rewriting of Haitian History." *Studies in Religion/Sciences Religieuses* 41 (2012) 187–215.

Mercéus, Bertrand. "Un premier congrès charismatique réussi." *Le Nouvelliste,* February 12, 2014. https://lenouvelliste.com/article/127402/un-premier-congres-charismatique-reussi-pour-le-cbndf.

Métraux, Alfred. *Voodoo in Haiti.* Translated by Hugo Charteris. New York: Schocken, 1972 (1959).

Peabody, Sue. "'A Dangerous Zeal': Catholic Missions to Slaves in the French Antilles, 1635–1800." *French Historical Studies* 25 (2002) 53–90.

Ramsey, Kate. *The Spirits and the Law: Vodou and Power in Haiti.* Chicago: University of Chicago Press, 2011.

Rébublique d'Haïti. "Arrêté relatif à la reconnaissance par l'État haïtien du vodou comme religion à part entière sur toute l'étendue du territoire national, donné au Palais National, à Port-au-Prince, le 4 avril 2003." http://haiti-reference.com/pages/plan/religions/vodou-haitien/vodou-arrete-2003/.

Rey, Terry. "Catholic Pentecostalism in Haiti: Spirit, Politics, and Gender." *Pneuma* 32 (2000) 80–106.

———. "Junta, Rape, and Religion in Haiti, 1993–1994." *Journal of Feminist Studies in Religion* 15 (1999) 73–100.

———. *The Priest and the Prophetess: Abbé Ouvière, Romaine Rivière, and the Revolutionary Atlantic World.* New York: Oxford University Press, 2017.

Rey, Terry, and Alex Stepick. *Crossing the Water and Keeping the Faith: Haitian Religion in Miami.* New York: New York University Press, 2013.

Richman, Karen. "Religion at the Epicenter: Agency and Affiliation in Léogâne after the Earthquake." *Studies in Religion: Sciences Religieuses* 41 (2012) 148–65.

———. "The Vodou State and the Protestant Nation: Haiti in the Long Twentieth Century." In *Obeah and Other Powers: The Politics of Caribbean Religion and Healing,* edited by Diana Patton and Maarit Forde, 267–87. Durham: Duke University Press, 2012.

Scherer, J. "Great Earthquakes in the Island of Haiti." *Bulletin of the Seismological Society of America* 2 (1912) 174–79.

Sublette, Ned. *Cuba and its Music: From the First Drums to the Mambo.* Vol. 1. Chicago: Chicago Review, 2004.

"Tensions Mount in Haiti after Voodoo Ceremony Attack." *Agence France-Presse.* February 25, 2010.

Thornton, John K. *The Kongolese Saint Anthony: Dona Beatriz Kimpa Vita and the Antonian Movement, 1684–1706.* New York: Cambridge University Press, 1997.

United Nations (UN) Department of Economic and Social Affairs, Population Division. "World Population Prospects: The 2015 Revision." http://www.un.org/en/development/desa/publications/world-population-prospects-2015-revision.html.

UNESCO Intergovernmental Oceanographic Commission. "An Intra-Americas Sea Tsunami Warning System Proposal." In *Caribbean Tsunami Hazard*, edited by Aurelio Mercado-Irizarry and Philip Liu, 7–40. Singapore: World Scientific, 2006.

U.S. Department of State, Bureau of Democracy, Human Rights, and Labor. "International Religious Freedom Report 2007." http://www.state.gov/j/drl/rls/irf/2007/90257.htm.

Whane the Whip. "Pat Robertson Haiti Comments on the Devil, a Curse, and the Earthquake." YouTube video. January 14, 2010. https://www.youtube.com/watch?v=MOQrcg9y1iA.

Index

"Big Man" syndrome, 256–59

Accioly, Igor, 239
Ad Gentes (Vatican II document), 163
Adogame, Afe, 101–2
Adorno, Theodor, 104
Africa
    Central, 8, 66n49, 206
    Christianity, 55–70
    East, 7, 66n49, 83
    sub-Saharan, 193, 202, 249–50, 252, 256
    West, 206, 213, 248–49
African Independent Churches. *See* African Initiated Churches
African Initiated Churches (AICs)
    generally, 8, 60, 83, 85, 102, 176–90, 205, 250
    Zionist, 92, 92n32
African Initiatives in Christianity. *See* African Initiated Churches
African Instituted Churches. *See* African Initiated Churches
African Traditional Religion
    African worldview and, 59, 60–61, 65, 66n49, 67, 70, 85, 90
    AICS and, 102, 177–88
    Catholicism and, 56, 204–5, 223–26
    Christianity and, 61, 203–4
    Haiti and, 286
    JIAM and, 92
    neo-Pentecostalism and, 89, 94

Pentecostal and Charismatic movements in Africa, and, 9, 57, 93, 100–1, 111, 206, 243
    Senegal and, 212–13, 216, 220–22
    UCKG and, 234, 243
AG. *See* Assemblies of God
AICs. *See* African Initiated Churches
Akatsa, Prophetess Mary Sinaida, 183
alabanza, 34
Aladura Church, 124, 205
Albania, 142
Alberoni, Francesco, 47
Algeria, 107
Alpha Course, 148
Álvarez, Carmelo, 138
Amadankhawa, Daniel, 61
American Baptist Convention, 158n19
Amoris Laetitia (Francis, Pope), 297
Anabaptists, 154
anamnesis, 17
ancestors, 8, 67–68, 87–88, 90, 93–94, 96, 179–83, 187, 207–8, 234, 250, 286, 289
Anderson, Allan, 59–61, 193–94, 199, 247
Anglicans, 64, 126–27, 148, 154, 157–58
Anointing of the Sick, Catholic sacrament (Extreme Unction), 117–18
anomia, 109
anthropology, 177, 187, 200, 203–5, 295
Apollonaris, 21
Apostolic Faith Church, 103

Argentina, 35, 145
Aristide, Father Jean-Bertrand, 281, 295
Arius, 20
Asamoah-Gyadu, Kwabena, 63, 86, 90, 248, 260
Asia, 8, 25, 63, 81, 85, 115, 123, 127–28, 132, 137–45, 147–50, 171
Asia Pentecostal Society (APS), 143, 143n27
Asian Movement for Christian Unity (AMCU), 142–43, 143n27
Assemblies of God (AG)
    Division of Foreign Missions, 159–60
    Evangel Temple, 160
    generally, 83, 141–42, 144, 146–47, 149, 154–57, 155n10, 157n15, 158n18, 159–60, 163, 169–70
    Philippines, 169
    Theological Seminary, 163
Associação Beneficente Cristã (ABC; Christian Beneficent Association), 234–35, 234n9, 238
Association of Christian Therapists, 119
Asuza Revival, 103
Audo, Eminence Anton, 142
Augustine, Saint, 18–19
Ave Maria Press, 118

Baal, prophets of, 87
bains mystiques, 217, 217n15, 219
Balla, Gaye II, 216–17, 221
Balokole Movement, 83–84
baptism
    Catholic sacrament, 6, 36–37, 39, 48
    Spirit, 31, 36–41, 48, 81, 157–58, 166–67
Baptists, 154
Barratt, Thomas Ball, 138
Barrett, David, 62
Bartley Patrick, 63
Basic Ecclesial Communities. *See* Ecclesial Base Communities
Baudrillard, Jean, 100
Bauman, Zygmunt, 4
Bea, Cardinal Augustin, 155–56
Beane, Wendell C., 91

Beauvoir, Max, 288
Belgium, 159, 165
Bethel Mission, 84
Biblijsko Teološki Institut, 161
Birmingham, University of, 164
Blessed Virgin Mary
    generally, 18, 242, 277, 286, 293
    Marian devotion, 2, 47, 146, 159–60, 236, 272
    Our Lady of Fatima, 289
    Our Lady of Perpetual Help, 291, 293
    Our Lady of the Rosary, 293
    Virgin of Guadalupe, 33
Bolivia, 35, 118, 120–22, 155n9
Bond, Alan, 104
Bordoni, Carlo, 5n1
Botswana, 66n49, 105
Brazil
    Aparecida, 50, 51n53, 52
    country, 2, 5, 9–11, 35, 49n49, 125, 168n44, 231–34, 234n9, 237, 239, 241–43, 271–73, 275–78
    Juazeiro do Norte Ceará, 237
    Juiz de Fora, 273
    Rio de Janeiro, 232–33, 235, 238–39, 244, 272
    São Paulo, 236, 274
Bridges-Johns, Cheryl, 138, 141–42
Brown, Peter, 224
Brown, Raymond, 18
Buddhism, 25
Bundy, David, 138

Calvin, John, 170n54
Cameron, Euan, 224
Cameroon
    country, 8, 196, 199, 203, 206–8
    Yaoundé, 196, 199, 208
Campion, Father Jules, 19, 282, 284, 288–91, 294, 294n36, 296–97, 296n43
Campos, Roberta, 237
Canada, 83, 120, 153n2
Canção Nova, 274
capitalism, 99–100, 102–5, 108–9, 111–12, 244, 256, 258, 260, 265
Cappadocian Fathers, 22

INDEX 303

catequista, 44
Cathedral of Our Lady of the Assumption (Port-au-Prince), 294
Catholic Action, 50
Catholic Charismatic Encounter. See Encuentro Carismático Católico Latinoamericano
Catholic Charismatic Movement (CCM), 223, 223n35
Catholic Charismatic Renewal (CCR)
    Africa and, 192–93, 195–99, 201–3, 205–9
    Asia and, 138, 145, 148
    Brazil and, 10, 232–33, 239, 241–42, 271–78
    Francis MacNutt and, 7, 115–22
    Haiti and, 280–82, 282n7, 288–90, 297
    ICCRS and, 58
    Latin America and, 6, 31–52
    worldwide, 2, 5, 9, 11, 169
Cazalta, Abbé, 285
CCR. See Catholic Charismatic Renewal
Cédras, General Raoul, 281, 287n25
Central University College (Ghana), 255
CentralAid (Ghana), 255
Centre for Development and Enterprise (CDE), 252n35
Chafwatandumea, Boniface, 58
Chalcedon, Council of, 22–23, 26
Chaldean Catholic Bishopric of Aleppo, 142
Charismatic Encounter
    Catholicism, 6, 31–52
    Christianity, 6, 46
    Evangelization, New, 6
Charismatic Leaders Fellowship (Charismatic Concerns Committee), 118
charismatic renewal, 1–2, 8, 26–28. See also CCR
charlatan, 107, 214, 217–19, 220n23, 221n28
Charles, Father Gabriel, 289
Chawanangwa, Robert, 59
Chege, Bibiana, 88
Chesnut, Andrew, 51, 120

Chigona, Gerald, 66–67, 69–70
Chile, 35, 120
Chimbetu, Simon, 104
China, 107, 118
Chingwenembe, Joachim, 61
Christ-event, 29
Christian Base Communities. See Ecclesial Base Communities
Christian Healing Ministries, 116
Christian mission, 2, 3
Christology, 5, 6, 17–18, 20–23, 26, 29, 188
christomonism, 29
Church of God, 155n10
Church of Pentecost, 169
Church of the Lord, 84
Clatterbuck, Mark, 122
Cleary, Edward L., OP, 33, 52, 120–21, 169–70, 170n51
clericalism, 4
co-wife, 213, 218
Cole, David, 153n2, 161n26, 169
Colombia
    Africa and, 61–62, 105, 107, 194
    AICs and, 179, 205
    Bogotáj, 41, 121
    colonialism
    country, 33, 35, 37, 120, 122, 126
    Haiti and, 283–84, 294, 296
    institutions, 103, 204
    Medellín, 44
    neocolonial, 112
    postcolonial, 7, 109, 112
    precolonial, 202–3
Comunidades Eclesiales de Base (CEBs). See Ecclesial Base Communities
Communion of Convergence Churches, 147
Communion of Evangelical Episcopal Churches, 147
Comoro, Christopher, 222–23
confirmation (Catholic sacrament), 36–37, 39, 48
Constantinople, Council of, 21–22, 186
Costa Rica, 120–21
Cox, Harvey, 63, 271
creedal developments, 19–20
Creemers, Jelle, 165

Crivella, Bishop Marcelo, 235, 235n11
Croatia, 160
Csordas, Thomas, 206, 276–77, 280n1, 282n7, 289
cultural imaging, 17, 23, 25–26, 29
cultural infusion, 23–26
Cursillo movement, 26, 201

Daniels, David, 251
danza, 34
Davis, Wade, 287n27
Deliverance Churches of Kenya, 83–84
Delorme, Démesvar, 285, 286n22
Demetrios, Metropolitan Youhanon Mar, 142n25
demonic possession
  African Christianity and, 183, 189, 202–7
  African Traditional Religion and, 225, 225n41
  exorcism and, 125–126
  India and, 127
  neo-Pentecostalism and, 89–90, 93, 96
  Pentecostalism and, 90, 93
  Senegal and, 213
demons
  Africa and, 109, 123, 125
  African Christianity and, 88, 263
  Catholicism and, 189, 206–7
  CCR and, 41–42, 206–7, 273
  Europe and, 224–25
  existence, 126–32
  Haiti and, 289, 294
  Islam and, 220
  JIAM and, 88–90, 92
  neo-Pentecostals and, 90, 94–95, 251, 264
  Pentecostals and, 88, 99, 106–7, 111–12
  poverty and, 250–51
  scriptural, 86–87, 89
  symbolic, 11
  UCKG and, 234–35
  See also devil, the; Satan
Dessalines, Jean-Jacques, 294
devil, the
  Africa and, 88, 181, 224

  AJIM and, 92
  CCR and, 41–42, 197, 206–7
  Europe and, 211
  Haiti and, 287, 294, 296
  neo-Pentecostals and, 94
  Pentecostals and, 107
  Toca de Assis and, 236
  See also demons; Satan
Diop, Birago, 180
Divine Providence Community, 207
djinn. See *jinn*
doctrine
  AICs and, 179, 189
  Catholic, 31, 186, 208
  Catholic-Pentecostal dialogue and, 8, 224
  CCR, 32, 36, 39
  missionaries and, 187, 189
  neo-Pentecostal, 137, 247, 258
  Pentecostal, 137
  scripture and, 131
  Trinitarian, 19–20, 24
dogma, 21, 23, 32, 36, 275–76
Dominican Republic, 120–21, 168
Dominicans, 115–18, 120–23, 168, 284
Donaldson, Clement, 68
Douglas, Marcellino, 60
Douglas, Mary, 224
Dow, James, 93–94
Duala, 203
Duchrow, Ulrich, 256
Duprey, Bishop Pierre, 156
Dupuy, Theogene, 286
Duquesne University, 32, 117, 202
Durkheim, Émile, 95–96, 109, 282
Duvalier, François and Jean-Claude, 281

East African Revival Movement, 83
Easthope, 96
Eastwood, Anaba, 252
Ecclesia in Asia (John Paul II), 144
Ecclesial Base Communities, 34, 44, 121–22, 138
ecclesial structures, parallel, 32, 44–49
ecclesiology, 3, 4, 5, 6, 31–33, 36, 43–49, 51–52
Economic Structural Adjustment Program (ESAP), 103

Ecuador, 35, 120
ecumenism
  AG and, 160
  Catholicism and, 3, 161, 209
  Catholics and Pentecostals, 9, 68, 138–39, 141–42, 144–46, 162
  CCR and, 47, 120, 192, 200–2
  Cecil Robeck and, 161n24
  councils, 20, 22, 25, 29, 61n29
  David du Plessis and, 155n10
  Francis MacNutt and, 118, 122
  generally, 8, 297
  Pentecostals and, 153–54, 157
  Protestants and, 144n29
Edwards, David L., 186
Egypt, 59, 185
El Salvador, 155
El Shaddai, 138, 146–47
Ela, Jean Marc, 196
Elijah, 87
Elim Pentecostal Church of Great Britain and Ireland, 169
Encuentro Carismático Católico Latinoamericano (ECCLA), 121
Enlightenment, the, 128, 187
Ephphata (CCR movement), 206–7
epiclesis, 17, 19
epistemology, Western, 5
Ervin, Howard M., 158n19, 161
Espinosa, Gastón, 51
ethnography, 8–9, 13, 32, 37, 193, 203, 224, 276
Eucharist (Communion, Blessed Sacrament)
  adoration, 2, 293
  CCR and, 47
  liturgy, 17, 19, 28, 39, 150, 186
  theology, 17, 28, 236–37, 272
Europe
  Africa and, 66n49, 177, 187
  Catholicism, 52
  charismatic movements, 47, 60, 102, 132
  Christianity, 126, 131, 188, 211–12
  Enlightenment and, the, 128
  missionaries, 85, 123–24, 127, 177, 179, 187
  religion, 129, 224
  saints, 181
  studies, 160n23
Evangelicals, 10, 46, 47n45
Evangelii Gaudium (Francis, Pope), 188
Evangelii Nuntiandi (Paul VI), 50
Evangelische Theologische Faculteit, 165
Evangelization, New (Catholic), 6, 32, 46, 49–52, 148
evil spirits
  African Christianity and, 185–87
  Catholicism and, 117, 124–26
  CCR and, 39–41, 115, 197, 200, 206–8, 273, 276
  existence of, 130–32
  Haiti and, 289
  JIAM and, 88–89
  native religion and, 129, 182
  neo-Pentecostalism and, 90, 94–96, 264
  Pentecostalism and, 99, 178
  UCKG and, 234–35
Exercises of Saint Ignatius, 171
exorcism
  African Pentecostal, 7, 81, 93, 99–103, 106–113
  AICs 181–84
  Catholic, 125–26, 131
  CCR and, 40–41, 48, 273
  Islam, 220, 225
  neo-Pentecostal, 92, 95
  scriptural, 57

Faith Evangelistic Ministries (FEM), 81, 83, 90, 97
Fanon, Franz, 107–8
Farrell, Bishop Brian, 168–69
Federation of Asian Bishops Conference (FABC), 140, 142, 144
Fernandes, Sílvia, 239
Finland, 169
Finnish Pentecostal Movement, 161–62
Folarin, George, 249, 262–63
Foucault, Michel, 208
France, 107
Francis, Pope, 11, 12, 145, 188, 297
Francis of Assisi, Saint 10, 236
Freud, Sigmund, 107
Friends African Mission (Quakers), 83

Fuller Theological Seminary, 160n23, 161, 161n24

Gabriel (angel), 18
Gee, Donald, 138
General Conferences of the Latin American Bishops (CELAM), 50
genii. See *jinn*
Germany, 201
Ghana
    Accra, 249
    country, 5, 10, 169, 183, 194–95, 223, 248–49, 252, 255, 263
    Ga-West, 255
Gifford, Paul, 9, 99, 194–95, 211, 251, 259–60
Gikuyu, 83
Global Christian Forum (GCF), 139, 141–42, 149
global North, 60, 63
global South, 2, 60, 63, 65, 81, 131–32, 140–42, 149, 206, 255
glossolalia, 26, 31, 36, 39, 184, 272–73, 275. *See also* tongues, speaking in
Gomez, Monsignor Juan Usma, 162–63, 169
Gongora, María E. de, 47
Gooren, Henri, 37
Gordon-Conwell Theological Seminary, 160n23
Graham, Billy, 84, 190
Gramsci, Antonio, 5n1
grassroots, 8, 13, 68, 70, 120, 137–38, 145, 147, 150, 193, 202
gris-gris, 213, 215–18, 221
Guatemala
    Bishops Conference, Catholic, 43, 46
    country, 6, 32, 34–35, 39, 49, 49n49, 120
    Guatemala City, 37–38, 45, 48n47, 49
    Huehuetenango, 49

Hagin, Kenneth, 147
Haiti
    Anti-Superstition Campaign, 295
    Bois Caiman, 288
    Cape Haitian, 280n1, 285–86
    country, 10–11, 280–97
    creole, 281, 290, 297
    earthquakes, 10, 280, 282–88, 290–92, 294, 296–97
    Fort Liberté, 285
    Gonaives, 292
    League against Voodoo, 294–95
    Léogâne, 283, 295
    Môle Saint Nicolas, 285
    Petit-Goave, 283
    Port-au-Prince, 283, 285, 289, 291–94, 297
    Port de Paix, 285
    Revolution, 284, 294
    Saint-Domingue, 283, 284n13, 284n15
    Santiago de los Caballeros, 285
    Sodo, 286
    Ville Bonheur, 286
Haitian Coalition of Religious and Moral Organizations, 297
healing. *See* spiritual healing
Hebdige, Dirk, 100, 110
Hebga, Father Meinrad, 195–96, 206–7
Heelas, Paul, 100, 112
hermeneutics, 3, 4, 47, 262–63
Heward-Mills, Dag, 223
Hillsong, 148
Hinduism, 61, 143
Hobsbawm, Eric, 272
Hocken, Peter, 145
Hollenweger, Walter, 59, 164
Holy Orders (sacrament of), 236
homoousia, 20, 22
Horkheimer, Max, 104
hypostasis, 21–23

ICCRS. *See* International Catholic Charismatic Renewal Service
idolatry, 33, 155n9, 281, 293, 296
Igreja Mundial do Poder de Deus (World Church of the Power of God), 242
Imago Dei, 25
incarnation, 18, 22–23
inculturation, 9–10, 100, 204, 223–24, 226

INDEX 307

India
    Conference of Catholic Bishops, 140–41, 144
    country, 123, 127, 144n30
individualism, 43, 256–57
Inter-American Commission for Human Rights, 287
International Catholic Charismatic Renewal Service (ICCRS)
    Doctrinal Commission, 39
    generally, 47, 58–59, 116, 169n49, 280n1
International Central Gospel Church (ICGC), 251–52, 255
International Church of the Foursquare Gospel, 169
International Communications Office (ICO), 280n1
International Communion of the Charismatic Episcopal Church (ICCEC), 147
International Conference on Charismatic Renewal, 118, 202
International Gay and Lesbian Human Rights Commission, 297
International Roman Catholic-Pentecostal Dialogues, 8, 138–45, 153–72, 158n18, 168n42
Iran, 222, 225
Islam, 9, 61, 106, 106n22, 177, 213, 216–17, 219–23
Italy 164, 208, 218
    Rome, 47, 61n29, 132, 138, 144–45, 169, 202, 208, 280n1, 289
    Catholic Church and, 47, 61n29, 138, 144–45, 202, 208
    empire, 224
    generally, 132, 280n1, 289
    Pentecostals and, 169

Japan, 127–28, 144, 144n30
Japanese New Religions, 127
Jean-Juste, Father Gérard, 289
Jenkins, Gerald, 65
Jerusalem Church of Christ, 183
Jerusalem Council, 171
Jesuits, 120, 192, 206, 284

Jesus is Alive Ministries (JIAM), 81, 83, 88–90, 92, 95, 97
JIAM. *See* Jesus is Alive Ministries
jinn, 94–95, 207, 216, 218–19, 225n41
John of the Cross, Saint, 43, 274
John Paul I, Pope, 159
John Paul II, Saint Pope, 1, 56, 58, 159, 168
John XXIII, Pope, 1, 61n29, 201
Johnson, T.M., 62
Joseph, Mario, 287

Kahl, Werner, 262
Kalu, Ogbu U., 82–83, 85, 87–88, 102, 124
Kansas City Charismatic Conference (1977), 118
Kariuki, Bishop Mark, 83
Kärkkäinen, Veli-Matti, 161–62, 165
Kasper, Cardinal Walter, 153n1, 169, 195
Kayo, Joe, 84
Kenya
    Catholicism, 82
    country, 7, 11, 81–97, 183
    Kaimosi, 83
    Kawangware, 183
    Limuru, 141
    Nairobi, 81, 85, 183–84
    Students Christian Fellowship, 84
Kiefer, Ralph, 202
Kierkegaard, Søren, 280
Kiernan, J.P., 92
Kimani, David, 84
Kimbanguism, 205
Kimberly, George, 63
Kiswahili, 96
Kleinman, Arthur, 92
Klinken, Adriaan van, 101, 110
Köhrsen, Jens, 254
Koinōnia, 65n48, 160–62
Koka, Kgalushi, 69
Korean
    Americans, 26–29
    Catholicism, 5–6, 24–29
    Charismatic renewal, 26–28
    prayer, 24–26

Kraft, Charles H., 87
Kuzmic, Peter, 160, 160n23

laity
    Balokole Movement and, 84
    Catholic, 1–2, 4, 25, 31, 46, 122, 125, 200–202, 205
    CCR and, 31–34, 38–40, 44, 49, 51, 196, 208
    ECCLA and, 121
    Protestant, 118
    See also lay preaching
Land, Steven J., 138
Latin America, 119, 127, 132, 138, 149, 155n9, 168–70, 281–82
lay preaching, 34, 44–45, 48–49. *See also* laity
Laye, Limamou, 220
Laye, Seydina Issa Rohou, 220
Lebou people, 220–21
Lee, Father Paul D., 161–62
Legio Mariae, 26, 183
Lei Orgânica de Assistência Socia (LOAS, Organic Law of Social Assistance), 239
Lenshina, Alice, 205
Leo XIII, Pope, 200
Lescot, Elie, 295
Lettieri, Father Roberto, 236–38, 236n14, 241–42, 241n28
Leuven, University of, 159
Lewis, Raphael, 64
liberation theology, 32, 34, 42, 50, 121, 281, 297
Life in the Spirit Seminar (LISS), 148
Lisbon (Portugal), 283
Louverture, Toussaint, 294
Luganda, 83
Lugo, Gameliel, 138
Lumpa Church, 205
Lutherans, 146, 154
lutte, 214, 216–17, 217n14, 221–22

Ma, Wonsuk, 141–42
Macedo, Bishop Edir, 235n11, 242
MacNutt, Francis, 7, 115–32
MacNutt, Judith (née Sewell), 116
Mafra, Clara, 242

Magesa, Laurenti, 59, 66, 66n49, 89, 194, 196
magic, 88–89, 107, 219, 219n22, 222
Magudumu, Lawrence, 66–67
Makandiwa, Emmanuel, 107
Malaysia
    Catholic Bishops' Conference, 143
    Christian Federation of Malaysia (CFM), 143
    Council of Churches, 143
    country, 143, 149
    National Evangelical Christian Fellowship, 143
mapepo, 94–96
marabout, maraboutage, 213–26, 225n41
Marshall, Ruth, 83
Marx, Karl, 108n25
mashawe, 207–8
Maximum Miracles Centers, 83
Maxwell, David, 60
Mbigi, Lovemore, 67
Mbiti, John, 59
McCauley, John, 258–59
McClung, Grant, 63
McDonnell, Father Kilian, 18–19, 153n1, 156, 158n17–18, 159, 162, 164, 200
McGee, Gary B., 163
McVeigh, Malcolm, 63
Medeiros, Katia, 238
Meeking, Bishop Basil, 156
Merleau-Ponty, Maurice, 276
Methodists, 120, 146, 154
Métraux, Alfred, 282n7, 295
Mexico, 33, 35, 120–21, 153n2
Meyer, Brigit, 88
Michael, Saint, 277, 289
migrants (immigrants), 12, 28
Milingo, Emmanuel, 9, 177–78, 207–8
Minuto de Dios, 41
Miot, Monsignor Serge Joseph, 294–96
miracles
    AICs and, 190
    Catholics and, 170
    CCR and, 197, 282
    neo-Pentecostals and, 83
    Pentecostals and, 57, 81

Senegal and, 219
UCKG and, 234
Missiological Institute, 163
modernity
  Catholicism and, 2, 10, 117, 148, 170, 222–23, 278
  CCR and, 271–76
  challenges for Christianity, 9, 61n29, 67–68, 194, 204, 225, 243–44, 254, 261
  liberation theology, 42
  liquid, 4–5, 5n1
  medicine and, 216
  Pentecostalism and, 5, 82, 100, 108, 194
  witchcraft and, 205
Mohammed, 220–21
Morse, Richard, 288, 288n30
Moses, 87
Mozambique, 103, 105
Mphikitso, Geoffrey Ronald, 56
Mugabe, Robert, 103–6
Mugambi, Jesse N.K., 85
Muiru, Bishop Pius, 83
Müller, Father Karl, 163–64
Mumderanji, George, 64
Murphy, Karen Jorgenson, 165
Muslim brotherhood
  generally, 220, 222
  Layenne, 220
Musopole, Augustine, 66
Mvume, Alfred Nyontho, 65
Mwaura, Philomena, 7, 81, 193
Myanmar, 143
mysticism, 89, 91–92, 200, 216–17, 217n14, 222, 225n41, 273–75

Nadar, Sarojin, 101, 110
National Service Committee, 118
Native Americans, 122–23
Ndebele, 103
Ndembu, 91
Neno Evangelism Ministries, 83, 95, 97
neo-Pentecostalism
  Africa, 10
  beliefs, 41–42, 87
  Catholicism and, 140–41
  CCR and, 47–48

churches (NPCs), 81, 88–97, 92n32, 233
Guatemala, 45, 49n49
Kenya, 7, 81–83, 81n1, 85
prosperity theology, 247–65
New Testament, 19–20, 31, 62, 131, 161, 177, 185
Ng'ang'a, James, 83
Nicaea, First Council of, 20–22, 186
Nicene-Constantinopolitan Creed, 186
Nigeria
  country, 10, 83, 85, 123–24, 205, 225, 248n8, 249–52, 259, 262–63, 264
  Lagos, 212
Nineham, Dennis, 211–12
Nostra Aetate (Vatican II document), 61
Notre Dame, University of, 118
novena, 33, 46, 189, 200, 272

O'Connor, Edwards, 200
Oestmann, Bishop Eduardo Aguirre, 49n49
Ojo, Matthews A., 85, 101, 193–94, 249
Old Testament, 177, 181, 184–85
Olembuntine, Emmanuel, 61
Olukoya, Daniel, 225
Omenyo, Cephas, 194, 196, 247
Onuh, Cornelius, 61
Onyinah, Opoky, 182–83
Open Bible Church, 169
Oral Roberts University, 116, 158n19, 160–61
Orthodox Church, 142, 142n25, 149, 149n43, 154, 157–58
Osborne, T.L. 84
Ositelu, Gabriel II, 188
Ospina, María, 37, 41–43, 46
Otabil, Pastor Mensah, 251–52, 254
Otwang, Samuel, 60–61
ousia, 21–23
Oyedepo, Bishop David, 250, 257, 259, 261

Parsons, Talcott, 93
patristics, 166
Paul VI, Pope, 50, 60, 159, 202

Paul, Saint, 18, 62, 85, 88, 171, 185, 189–90, 223
payoff structures, 258
Peel, Robert, 57
Pentecost, 1, 2, 18, 58, 275, 278, 283, 291
Pentecostal and Charismatic Churches of North America (PCCNA)
    Christian Unity Commission, 153n2
    generally, 153n2
Pentecostal movement in Finland, 169
Pentecostal World Fellowship (PWF), 139, 139n10
Peru, 35, 120–21
Pethrus, Lewi, 138
Pew Forum on Religion and Public Life, 35, 82
Pfeiffer, Charles, 56
phenomenology, cultural, 276
Philippines, 5, 138, 145–47, 149, 169
Phulamtenga, Dickson, 59
Pio of Pietrelcina, Saint, 242
Pius XII, Pope, 56
Plessis, David du, 138, 155–58, 155n10, 159–60, 201
Plessis, Justus du, 158n18, 159, 162, 164
pneumatology
    ecclesial, 32, 43, 50–51, 161–62
    imaging, 28
    lived, 6, 31, 36
    Orthodox, 149n43
    Trinitarian, 5, 17, 19–20, 23, 141, 247
pneumatomachians, 21
Pobee, John S., 188–89
polygamy, 179, 213–14
Pontifical University of Saint Thomas Aquinas, 161, 163
Portella, Rodrigo, 238, 243
postmodernism, constructive, 7, 108–9, 108n25, 110–13
postmodernity, 5, 7, 99–100, 108, 110–13, 264–65, 272, 274–76, 278
Preciosa Vida, 239–40, 243
priesthood, universal, 37, 43–45, 51
Prior, John Manfred, 139
prophecy
    Africa and, 62, 100, 183, 205
    Baal, 87
    CCR and, 275–76
    charistamata as, 34, 36, 118, 169, 171, 188, 272–73, 275
    dialogue as, 139
    Haiti, 10, 280–82, 284, 288, 290, 294, 296–97
    healing, as, 60
    neo-Pentecostal, 92, 94–95, 248
    Paul VI and, 60
    Pentecostal, 101, 106–9
    preaching as, 170n54
    scriptural, 31, 184–86
proselytism, 47, 137–38, 140, 142n25, 143, 145, 147, 162–65
prosperity gospel
    Africa and, 10, 63, 106–7, 203, 207, 213, 247–65
    CCR and, 43
    El Shaddai and, 146–47
    JIAM and, 92
    neo-Pentecostals and, 83
    Pentecostals and, 9, 231–32, 243–44
    scriptural, 251n30
    UCKG and, 232–233, 232n5, 234
Protestantism
    Catholicism and, 115–121, 124, 138, 140–41, 143–44, 144n29, 146–47, 150
    CCR and, 47, 192
    Evangelical, 25–26, 46, 50, 287
    generally, 32, 48, 64, 144n29, 170, 177, 202, 252, 261, 275
    Pentecostal, 7, 8, 31, 82, 157–58, 195, 231, 233, 240–41, 282n7, 295n41
psychology
    ailments, 39, 182, 243, 276–77
    psychotherapy, 115, 277
    research, 7,
    treatment, 94, 107, 119, 123, 131,
    well-being, 198, 206, 253,
Puerto Rico, 121

Qur'an, 216, 219–22, 221n28, 225

Radano, Monsignor John A., 162
Ranaghan, Dorothy and Kevin, 200

Ranger, Terrence, 99
Reformation, 58–59, 154, 170, 177, 193–94, 199, 202
Reformed Church, 154, 172
Regent University, 160
reincarnation, 180–181, 220
resting in the Spirit. *See* Spirit, resting in the
Richman, Karen, 295, 295n41
Riesebrodt, Martin, 222n32
Rite of Christian Initiation of Adults (RCIA), 166
Rivera, Juan Carlos, 48n47
Robeck, Cecil M., Jr., 8, 64, 138–40, 153–55, 157–65, 158n18, 162, 164, 167–69, 171
Roberts, Oral, 147, 150
Robertson, Pat, 147, 287–88, 296
Rogawski, Ralph, 118
Rosas, Nina, 236
Rosny, Eric de, 196
Rossi, Father Marcelo, 273–74
Rouaudières, des, 283–84, 284n14
Rwanda, 83

sacraments (Catholic)
    CCR and, 36–37, 39–40, 47–49, 51, 275–76
    Haiti and, 291, 293, 295
    Pentecostals and, 147, 159, 161
    Trinity and, the, 20
    See also individual sacraments
Sacred Heart Catholic Church (Port-au-Prince), 289–90, 294
Sall, Macky, 215
salvation by conversion, 81
sanctification, instantaneous, 81
Sandidge, Jerry, 156, 158n18, 159–62, 164
sangoma, 102
Santiago, Valdomiro, 242
Satan
    evil power, as, 11, 42, 90, 94–96, 130–32, 225n41, 250
    Haiti and, 287, 292, 295–96
    Satanism, 125, 224
    scripture, in, 86–87
    See also devil, the; demons

Saudi Arabia, 222, 225
Sawa, 203, 207
Scherer, J., 285
Schreiter, Robert, 188
science, 12, 62, 101, 126–28, 130, 204, 223, 226, 292–93
self, sacred, 276, 278
Second Vatican Council
    generally, 61n29, 155–156, 163
    outcomes, 1–2, 44, 52, 61, 117, 161, 201–2, 204, 222–23, 243, 272
    pre-, 239
Sène, Eumeu, 217
Senegal
    Casamance, 215
    country, 9, 180, 212–14, 214n2, 216, 218, 220–23, 225–26
    Dakar, 215, 220–21
    Ourossogui, 216
    Tambacounda, 215
Seymour, William, 138
shamanism, 24–26, 128, 132
Shona, 103
Silva, Father Geovane Ferreira da, 239
Simatei, Peter Shadreck, 65
Singapore
    Alpha Singapore, 146
    country, 144, 149
    Ecumenical Charismatic Healing Service, 146
    Interreligious Organization, 144
    National Council of Churches of Singapore (NCCS), 144, 146
    Presidential Council for Religious Harmony, 144
    Singapore Archdiocesan Catholic Council for Ecumenical Dialogue, 146
Sivalon, John, 222–23
Smith, Ian, 103
Social Cement, 235–36
Society for Pentecostal Studies, 160
socioeconomic transformation, 10, 247–65
socioreligious values, 55, 57, 61, 66, 69–70
Somalia, 106
sorcery, 88–90, 94, 224–25, 293–94

South Africa
  Apostolic Faith Mission of, 155n10
  country, 66n49, 101n11, 105, 155n10
Souza, Elizabeth de, 239
Soviet Union, 103
Sow, Ibrahima, 214, 217–18, 222–23, 225–26
Spain, 201, 282, 285
Spirit, resting in the, 5, 27, 34, 37–39, 63, 272, 274
spiritual deliverance
  AICs and, 181–83
  CCR and, 115–17, 119, 121, 123–32
  Emmanuel Milingo, 208
  neo-Pentecostalism, 81–85, 87–93, 96, 259
  Pentecostalism, 58, 70
  pneumatic element as, 7, 63, 193, 200, 234–35, 276, 277
  scriptural, 57
spiritual healing (prayer for healing, healing prayer)
  Africa and, 66n49, 204–5
  African Pentecostalism and, 81–97, 99–103, 105–113
  AICs and, 179, 181–83, 188–90
  Catholicism and, 61, 146
  Catholicism and Pentecostalism and, 159, 169, 171
  CCR and, 39–41, 44–45, 48, 115–32, 197–98, 200, 206, 273–78
  Emmanuel Milingo and, 178, 207–8
  Haiti and, 280, 282, 282n7
  Mass, 27
  neo-Pentecostalism, and, 81–97
  pneumatic element, as, 6–7, 12, 26, 31, 34, 36–38, 57–58, 63, 193, 196
  prophet, 60
  UCKG and, 240
spiritual warfare
  Africa and, 99–100
  CCR and, 42
  neo-Pentecostalism and, 81–82, 85–89, 93, 96
  pneumatic element, as, 6–7, 115, 129–31

Spittler, Russell P., 157n16
Steil, Carlos, 242
Storey, Bill, 202
Structural Adjustment Program (SAP), 104
Suenens, Cardinal Leo, 59, 201
Sufism, 222
Sullivan, Francis, 200
Summi Pontificatus (Pius XII), 56
Synan, Vinson, 157n16, 159, 192, 200–201
syncretism, 155n9
Syriac Orthodox Church of Antioch, 49n49

Tanzania, 66n49, 83
Taoism, 25
Teresa of Avila, Saint, 274
Thendolafewa, Luke, 64
Theweralatha, Robert, 64
Third Wave evangelical charismatics, 148
Tilegliz, 10, 281, 288–89
Tine, Tapha, 216–17, 221
Toca de Assis, 2, 9, 232–34, 236–44, 236n14
tongues, speaking in
  AIC and, 184
  CCR and, 27, 34, 38, 41, 118–19, 146, 148, 197, 272, 274, 277
  Holy Spirit and, 190
  neo-Pentecostals and, 93, 248
  Pentecostals and, 63, 81, 83, 271
  scripture and, 185, 188
  See also glossolalia
Torribio, Monsignor, 285
Totalität, 211–12, 220, 226
Touraine, Alain, 104
Trinity
  economic, 19, 23–24, 29
  generally, 5–6, 17–25, 28–29, 36, 40, 90, 95, 158n18, 186
  immanent, 22, 23–24, 29
Trinity Theological College (TTC), 144n29
Turner, Victor, 91, 203
Tyson, Bishop James, 138

INDEX 313

Ubuntu, 6, 55–57, 66–70, 66n49
UCKG. *See* Universal Church of the Kingdom of God
Udelhoven, Father Bernhard, 182, 189
Uganda, 66n49, 83
Umoya, 92
Umunthu. *See Ubuntu*
Unification Church (Moonism), 208
Unitatis Redintegratio (Vatican II document), 161, 201
United Christian Forum of Human Rights in India, 143
United Church of Christ in the Philippines (UCCP), 149
United Kingdom, 127, 148, 164, 169, 249
Universal Church of the Kingdom of God (UCKG), 9, 232–44, 232n5, 235n11
University of Helsinki, 162, 165
United States
    country, 6, 83, 105, 119, 122, 126, 160, 169, 206, 212
    Catholicism, 28, 32, 52, 120
    Central Intelligence Agency, 168
Ustorf, Werner, 95

Vatican
    Congregation for the Doctrine of Faith, 168
    Culture, Asian Convention of the Pontifical Council for (2006), 139
    generally, 116, 144–45, 167–68, 169n49, 178, 208, 280n1
    Laity, Pontifical Council of, 116
    Promoting Christian Unity, Pontifical Council of, 153n1, 155–56, 158, 162–63, 168–69, 195, 201
Vatican II. *See* Second Vatican Council
Velarde, Brother Mike, 147
Venezuela, 35, 121, 128
Verenigde Pinkster Evangeliegemeenten, 169
Vian, Monseñor Julio, 45
Vineyard Church, 148, 212
Vodou. *See* voodoo

Volf, Miroslav, 160, 160n23
Voodoo, 10, 281–82, 287–91, 293–97, 295n41

Wade, Abdoulaye, 220n25, 221
Wagner, Peter, 130
Wairimu, Teresia, 83
Wako, Amos, 82
Waliggo, John Mary, 59
Wangari, Bishop Margaret, 84
Wanjiru, Bishop Margaret, 83
Wariboko, Nimi, 251, 259–60
water spirits (*jengu, miengu*), 203, 207
Weber, Max, 109, 237, 252
Weigel, George, 50
Whitaker, Godfrey, 57
Willebrands, Cardinal Johannes, 156
Wimber, John, 212
Winners Chapel, 212
Winters, Mark, 83
witch (wizard)
    bewitchment, 219–20, 225n41
    Catholic Church and, 189, 203–206
    doctors, 123–24, 127–29, 132
    generally, 11, 60
    grouped with other evils, 88–80, 88–90, 92, 94–95, 197–98, 200, 202, 207, 224, 250
    healing and, 183, 205
    hunts, 183, 288
    witchcraft, 41–42, 178, 182
World Alliance of Reformed Churches–Pentecostal Dialogue, 172
World Church, 3, 4, 11
World Council of Churches (WCC)
    Christian Conference of Asia (CCA), 140, 142
    Commission on Faith and Order, 161
    generally, 140–41, 154, 161
World of Faith (movement), 83
World War II, 112

Yale Divinity School, 160n23
yeondo, 6, 24–26
Yong, Amos, 255
Yugoslavia, 160

Zakka I Iwas, Patriarch Ignatius, 49n49
Zambia
    country, 9, 105, 177, 182, 189, 205, 207
    Kabwe, 189
    Lusaka, 9, 207–8
Zhakata, Leonard, 104
Zimbabwe
    country, 7, 66n49, 99, 102–8, 112
    Farmers Union, 103
    Movement for Democratic Change (MDC), 105
Zimmerling, Peter, 40
Zuesse, Evan, 91
Zulu, Raphael Dingaka, 62
Zwide, Peter Mhlambani, 60

www.ingramcontent.com/pod-product-compliance
Lightning Source LLC
Chambersburg PA
CBHW021344300426
44114CB00012B/1076